Collins

Cambridge International AS & A Level Literature in English

STUDENT'S BOOK

Series editor: Noel Cassidy
Authors: Maria Cairney, Mike Gould,
Ian Kirby and Richard Vardy

William Collins' dream of knowledge for all began with the publication of his first book in 1819.

A self-educated mill worker, he not only enriched millions of lives, but also founded a flourishing publishing house. Today, staying true to this spirit, Collins books are packed with inspiration, innovation and practical expertise. They place you at the centre of a world of possibility and give you exactly what you need to explore it.

Collins. Freedom to teach.

Published by Collins
An imprint of HarperCollins*Publishers*
The News Building
1 London Bridge Street
London
SE1 9GF

Browse the complete Collins catalogue at
www.collins.co.uk

© HarperCollins*Publishers* Limited 2019

10 9 8 7 6 5 4 3 2 1

978-0-00-828761-0

British Library Cataloguing-in-Publication Data

A catalogue record for this publication is available from the British Library.

Authors: Maria Cairney, Mike Gould, Ian Kirby and Richard Vardy
Series editor: Noel Cassidy
Development editor: Sonya Newland
Commissioning editor: Catherine Martin
In-house project lead: Caroline Green
Copyeditor: Hugh Hillyard-Parker
Permissions researcher: Rachel Thorne
Picture researchers: Holly Woolnough and Caroline Green
Proofreader: Catherine Dakin
Cover designers: Kevin Robbins and Gordon MacGilp
Cover illustrator: Maria Herbert-Liew
Typesetter: Ken Vail Graphic Design
Production controller: Sarah Burke

Printed and bound by: Grafica Veneta SpA in Italy

The publishers wish to thank the following teachers for reviewing materials:

Woody River, Head of English at the British School of Lomé, Togo; Kate Kelly, The British School of Barcelona, Spain; Rachel Evans, Principal, Novaschool Sunland International, Málaga, Spain; Naghma Shaikh, JBCN International, Mumbai, India; Emma Page, Sir John Roan School, London, UK; Lucy Toop, The Norwood School, London, UK.

The publishers gratefully acknowledge the permission granted to reproduce the copyright material in this book. Every effort has been made to trace copyright holders and to obtain their permission for the use of copyright material. The publishers will gladly receive any information enabling them to rectify any error or omission at the first opportunity.

MIX
Paper from
responsible sources
FSC www.fsc.org FSC® C007454

This book is produced from independently certified FSC paper to ensure responsible forest management.

For more information visit:
www.harpercollins.co.uk/green

Contents

Contents

Introduction

The *Collins Cambridge International AS and A Level Student's Book* offers a skills-building approach to the syllabus. It is designed to help you develop the knowledge and give you the tools you need to explore your set texts in depth and to prepare for examinations with confidence.

In every chapter, you will read an exciting range of texts from different eras and cultures, chosen to expand your experience of and enjoyment of literature in English. Our aim is to encourage and support you in developing a dynamic, personal relationship with poetry, prose and drama which will promote a lifelong interest in literature.

Chapter 1 introduces the concepts, terminology and skills that underpin the AS and A Level course. This chapter could be used to support your transition from IGCSE™ or upper secondary study or as an introduction for those who are new to studying literature.

Chapters 2, 3 and 4 provide starting points from which you might explore each of the major forms in the AS and A Level course. The key concepts and skills from Chapter 1 are revisited and developed in the context of prose, poetry and drama. This will help you appreciate what is unique about each form and understand the different methods and techniques that poets, novelists, short-story writers and dramatists employ.

Chapter 5 focuses in detail on techniques to help you respond with confidence to unseen texts. You will be guided through an effective process for engaging with an unseen text, and planning and structuring your response.

Analysis and writing skills are developed throughout the book. Units end with a substantial independent **final task** and successful writing is modelled throughout the units.

Thinking more deeply sections ask you to explore a concept in greater depth or to develop a skill or way of writing with more sophistication, to extend your learning.

At the end of **Chapters 2 to 5**, you are given the opportunity to apply your learning to a range of exam-style tasks. Sample responses are provided to help you assess and improve your work. The tasks, responses and commentaries have been written by our team of experienced authors, not by the examination board.

Finally, a set of resources is included at the end of the book to support you across the course. The **key terms** defined throughout the book have been collated into a **glossary of literary terms** to provide an easy reference for you as you study and revise.

A brief **introduction to literary critical theory** is designed to extend your own sophisticated interpretations of literary texts and prepare you for further study, and a **timeline of literary history** will help you to contextualise the texts you are studying.

A free resource for your teachers is provided on the Collins website www.collins.co.uk/cambridge-international-downloads. This includes additional texts which are referenced where relevant in the Student's Book.

We hope that your use of this book will not only help you with preparing for your examinations, but will give you confidence in exploring ideas in texts, inspire you to read more carefully and widely, and help you to develop a lifelong love of reading.

Noel Cassidy, series editor

HOW TO USE THIS BOOK

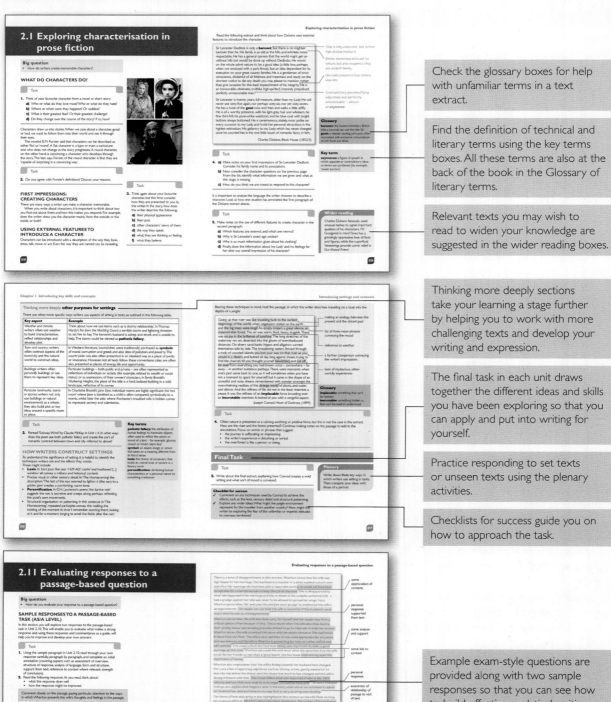

Check the glossary boxes for help with unfamiliar terms in a text extract.

Find the definition of technical and literary terms using the key terms boxes. All these terms are also at the back of the book in the Glossary of literary terms.

Relevant texts you may wish to read to widen your knowledge are suggested in the wider reading boxes.

Thinking more deeply sections take your learning a stage further by helping you to work with more challenging texts and develop your writing and expression.

The final task in each unit draws together the different ideas and skills you have been exploring so that you can apply and put into writing for yourself.

Practice responding to set texts or unseen texts using the plenary activities.

Checklists for success guide you on how to approach the task.

Example exam-style questions are provided along with two sample responses so that you can see how to build effective analytical writing.

Chapter 1 Introducing key skills and concepts

This chapter introduces the key concepts for studying literature in English at an advanced level, giving you a toolkit of terms to use throughout your course. Chapter 1 also introduces some of the skills you will need to develop in your own writing about literary texts, from close analysis to interpretation and structuring a critical response.

You will revisit the key concepts in the later chapters on prose, poetry and drama, deepening your understanding and extending your writing skills as you do so.

Big question

- How can you make an informed personal response to the texts you read?

WHAT IS TEXT APPRECIATION?

When you 'appreciate' something, you recognise its value. You give credit to the skills that have gone into producing it – for example, admiring the brushstrokes or vibrant colours of a piece of art. Equally, you can be intrigued by a painting even if you can't work out its meaning straightaway or engage with it on an emotional level. It is the same with texts.

Read this short, untitled poem.

In the desert
I saw a creature, naked, bestial,
Who, squatting upon the ground,
Held his heart in his hands,
And ate of it.
I said, 'Is it good, friend?'
'It is bitter—bitter,' he answered;
'But I like it
Because it is bitter,
And because it is my heart.'
Stephen Crane (1895)

[handwritten annotations]: heart – happiness goodness free-will given by God

Task

1. Consider these questions about the poem:

a) What story – if any – does it tell? Is there anything surprising or unusual about the story? Do you fully understand what is happening?

b) What do you notice about the **form** or **structure?** How long or short is it? How is it divided up?

c) How are sound and rhythm used? Does the poem have a regular rhythm? Does it use rhyme?

d) What do you notice about the language? Do any particular words or phrases stand out or make an impression on you?

Key terms

form: the way a text is ordered, presented or shaped on the page
structure: the organisation or sequence of ideas, events or language in a text

[handwritten annotations]: Free Verse   Tercet   Poverty

The process you have just gone through is at the start of appreciation. You have dissected the poem and considered how it has been constructed. However, this alone does not equal 'appreciation'. It is almost impossible to carry out the dissection without referring to feeling or effect; if something 'stands out', then it must have created an impact of some sort on you. If you don't understand something, then this, too, creates effects. It could be frustration or irritation – though that will not get you very far. Or it could be curiosity, or a sense of enquiry and reflection.

Task

2. Imagine Stephen Crane is sitting in front of you now. What would you like to ask him?

Through the spirit of enquiry, you can move towards understanding – not in the sense of decoding the poem as if it were a riddle, but being able to express how it works on the reader.

Task

3. Below are three comments about the poem from different students. Which of these:
   - responds on an emotional level without engaging with the ideas?
   - analyses the poem without any sort of engagement with its effects?
   - offers an appreciation of the poem and the effects it creates?

Student A

> The poem is made up of one **stanza**, so is short and concise: there are just ten lines in total. In the poem, the speaker meets a 'creature' in a desert and has a brief conversation with him. The word 'bitter' is repeated, which means it is important. It is told in the past tense and there is no rhyme.

Student B

> I find the poem difficult and infuriating. It is like a riddle, and it irritates me that I cannot work it out. I don't see the point of writing something you can't understand at all. Why would anyone eat their own heart? It's not in the least realistic! Stephen Crane should focus on things we all know about.

Student C

> The poet creates a strange but very striking encounter between the speaker and a creature in the desert. The poem is full of **ambiguity** – the creature finds its own heart 'bitter' but likes it; the speaker calls the creature 'friend', as if sympathetic.

Key terms

stanza: group of lines in a poem, similar in meaning to 'verse'
ambiguity: the quality of being open to more than one meaning or interpretation

DEVELOPING A PERSONAL RESPONSE

It is fair to say that Student B has responded personally and to that extent engaged with the poem on one level. However, by reducing the poem to something that has to make sense, this student closes off other potential responses. You need to give a text a chance, even when it seems alien, at least on the surface, to your way of life or what you know of the world.

There are a number of ways you can do this, and this book will help you develop many of them, but, in brief, you can try the approaches in the following table.

Approaches	What this means	Example
Read and reread	Don't always settle on your first response. Rereading texts or parts of texts several times helps you reveal the different layers.	Read the poem for a third or fourth time – what new things that you didn't focus on originally begin to be revealed as you progress?
Explore **connotations** and **allusions**	Allow words, phrases and images to spark connections in your mind or link with other stories or texts you know.	What other ideas come to mind when you visualise the 'heart'? How might the idea of the naked figure in the desert link to myth or religion?
Look for **universality**	Seek out thematic or symbolic links with your own emotions or actions, or those of people in general (even when what is described is beyond your experience).	How might a lover feel both 'bitter' and yet still 'like' someone else? Have you ever felt bitter about something that should have been enjoyable?
Ask questions to which there may be more than one answer	Consider a range of interpretations rather than settle on a fixed meaning that you pursue despite evidence to the contrary.	Why does the poet ask whether eating the heart is 'good'? What might this suggest about the poet's own feelings?

Task

4. Work through each of the questions in the third column, and see how you are slowly drawn into the poem's spell.

Of course, you will be engaging with a wide range of forms and types of text from poetry, prose and drama, but the basic approach holds true for all of them.
- Be open to the possibilities of the text.
- Do not be afraid of ambiguity or complexity.
- Use a range of techniques to engage with the text – and don't always expect to make meaningful connections on first reading.

Key terms

connotation: an idea or feeling that a word brings to mind in addition to its primary meaning (for example, 'dove' may connote 'peace')

allusion: a word or phrase that makes reference to another place, person, story or event, thereby bringing to mind other, related ideas

universality: a quality that allows a text's meaning to speak to all people at any time

Final Task

Read this second poem by Stephen Crane from the same series.

The ocean said to me once

The ocean said to me once,
'Look!
Yonder on the shore
Is a woman weeping.
I have watched her.
Go you and tell her this, –
Her lover I have laid
In cool green hall.
There is wealth of golden sand
And pillars, coral-red;
Two white fish stand guard at his **bier**.'

'Tell her this
And more, –
That the king of the seas
Weeps too, old, helpless man.
The bustling **fates**
Heap his hands with corpses
Until he stands like a child,
With surplus of toys.'

Stephen Crane (1895)

Task

5. Begin by making some quick notes about the poem's form, structure and choice of language. Then, use a similar sequence to the one in the table to work through the poem. You may not be able to do all four things, but simply having a go will help you engage with the poem.
6. Write a short personal response to the poem of 75–100 words. Aim for a balance between analysis (referring to the specific things the poet does) and engagement (how it makes you feel and what effects it has).

Glossary

bier: table or support for a coffin
fates: the Fates, three European mythological gods often depicted as weavers whose tapestry showed the future for particular people

Plenary

What techniques would you use to help you engage with particularly difficult or challenging texts?

Wider reading

The desert or wilderness is often used as a **trope** in literature in the Western tradition to represent a place where individuals are tested morally or spiritually. Shelley's famous poem 'Ozymandias' tells the story of a traveller who finds the broken statue of an ancient king lying in the sand, suggesting human ambition overreaching itself.

Key term

trope: a recurrent literary device in which something has symbolic or metaphorical significance

1.2 Introducing literary style

Big question

- What is literary style and why is it important to understand it?

WHAT IS LITERARY STYLE?

'**Style**' is a word with which we are all familiar. In everyday speech, it is used in relation to appearance – what someone wears, their haircut and so on; in sport it refers to the manner in which a team or individual plays; in social situations it describes someone's way of interacting with others ('confronting people is not his style'). In all of these, what is really being described is the *particular, distinctive approach or effect* that gives that person, group, form or object its unique identity.

It is the same when you are thinking about literary style. What elements create that 'style' and how can you describe the unique identity of a poem, play, story or novel?

Read these two short extracts from texts describing trees and plants.

> Green is the plane-tree in the square.
>   The other trees are brown;
> They droop and pine for country air;
>   The plane-tree loves the town.
>
> Amy Levy, 'A London Plane-Tree' (1889)

> Even the pale yellow lemons, that hung in such profusion from the mouldering trellis and along the dim arcades, seemed to have caught a richer colour from the wonderful sunlight, and the magnolia trees opened their great globe-like blossoms of folded ivory, and filled the air with a sweet heavy perfume.
>
> Oscar Wilde, 'The Birthday of the Infanta' (1891)

Key term

style: the particular, distinctive approach or effect of a writer's use of language

Task

1. What can you say about the different styles of these two extracts? Write a sentence about each.
2. What things did you look at in order to decide what their style was?
3. How did you describe 'style'? What words or phrases did you use?

EXPLORING STYLE MORE CLOSELY

Now read this poem – you will recognise the first verse.

A London Plane-Tree

Green is the plane-tree in the square.
  The other trees are brown;
They droop and pine for country air;
  The plane-tree loves the town.

Here from my garret-pane, I mark
  The plane-tree bud and blow,
Shed her **recuperative** bark,
  And spread her shade below.

Among her branches, in and out,
  The city breezes play;
The dun fog wraps her round about;
  Above, the smoke curls gray.

Others the country take for choice,
  And hold the town in scorn;
But she has listened to the voice
  On city breezes borne.

Amy Levy (1889)

When deciding on the style of the opening two extracts, you probably explored at least one of the following – the text's form, language or structure – and possibly a combination of all of them. For example, it is quite difficult to separate Wilde's rich vocabulary from the long, drawn-out sentence, which itself seems to mirror the hanging plants stretched across the trellis.

Glossary

recuperative: able to grow and refresh itself

Key term

rhyme scheme: the way a poet chooses to rhyme lines – for example, the nursery rhyme 'Baa Baa black sheep have you any wool? / Yes sir, yes sir, three bags full' is an *aa* rhyme scheme – as 'wool' and 'full' are almost perfect rhymes at the end of the first two lines.

Task

4. Now, focusing on Levy's poem, make notes on each of these aspects by copying and completing this grid and answering the questions shown. An example answer to the first question has been given.

What is distinctive about the *form* of the text?	How is it set out on the page? *In a series of four stanzas of four lines.* How short/long are the lines? Are they consistent in length? Is there a **rhyme scheme**?
What is distinctive about the *structure*?	How does the 'story' of the poem unfold (What are you told about first? How are new ideas introduced as the poem progresses?) What patterns of sound or repetition do you notice?
What is distinctive about the *language*?	How is the plane-tree described? (In what way, for example, is personification used?) How is the city described? (What aspects of the city does the poet refer to?) How is the voice of the poet conveyed? (Is the poet 'present' in the poem? If so, what do they say or make comments about?)

This is just the beginning of how you might approach style. It can also help to think of how other writers might have described the same scene – would Oscar Wilde have described it in the same way?

You will need some concise words or expressions to help you define a writer's style.

Task

5. Read through the adjectives in the word bank below.
   - Choose which adjectives best describe the style of the poem. (There may be several.) You may need to check the meaning of some of these terms.
   - Why have you chosen these particular adjectives?
   - What can you point to in the poem to support your ideas?

multi-layered	simple	regular	abstract	unconventional	detached	rich
personal	impersonal	direct	concise	impressionistic	lyrical	complex
complex	informal	reflective	focused	observational	chatty	compact

Part of your skill as a critical writer will be to expand on these ideas, and equally to track how style develops or changes. In novels, for example, writers might employ a range of styles to represent different character voices or locations.

Here, a student has written about the style of 'A London Plane-Tree':

Levy's style is straightforward and observational. [1] She describes simple aspects of the tree as she sees it: it is 'green'; it 'sheds its recuperative bark' [2] suggesting a truthful and considered impression. [3]

But the simplicity of the form and language does not mean the message is trite or empty. [3] Levy seems to be acknowledging the dirt and grime of the city – its 'dun fog' and 'smoke', but the plane-tree actively thrives, as if the rest of nature is out of step.

This is an effective comment on style because:
[1] it sums it up efficiently with well-chosen adjectives
[2] it provides evidence for the idea expressed
[3] it considers the effect of the style, not limiting comment to one aspect but raising new questions.

Thinking more deeply: **reflecting on style and meaning**

It is important not to make broad assumptions about style without reflecting carefully: a simple mode of expression does not necessarily convey a simple meaning. For example, is this just a poem about how plane-trees do well in cities? In much Romantic or late Victorian literature, the 'city' was seen as a place of sin, corruption and disease.

Task

6. **a)** What is surprising about the poem in this context?
   b) What does Levy seem to be saying by placing herself in this scene, rather than outside it – for example, as a country girl?

Wider reading

William Blake's poem 'London' is superficially also very straightforward in style and form. However, his message in the poem is anything but simple. (The text of Blake's poem is included in Unit 3.9, on p. 195.)

Final Task

Read this prose passage, which also comes from the short story by Oscar Wilde called 'The Birthday of the Infanta' (the Spanish King's daughter). Here he describes the princess and her friends.

> There was a stately grace about these slim Spanish children as they glided about, the boys with their large-plumed hats and short fluttering cloaks, the girls holding up the trains of their long brocaded gowns, and shielding the sun from their eyes with huge fans of black and silver. But the Infanta was the most graceful of all, and the most tastefully attired, after the somewhat **cumbrous** fashion of the day. Her robe was of grey satin, the skirt and the wide puffed sleeves heavily embroidered with silver, and the stiff corset studded with rows of fine pearls. Two tiny slippers with big pink rosettes peeped out beneath her dress as she walked. Pink and pearl was her great gauze fan, and in her hair, which like an **aureole** of faded gold stood out stiffly round her pale little face, she had a beautiful white rose.
>
> Oscar Wilde, 'The Birthday of the Infanta'

Glossary

cumbrous: heavy
aureole: a circle of light or brightness

Task

7. Make notes on Wilde's style (here and in the earlier extract). Consider:
   - the vocabulary he uses to describe the appearance of objects or people
   - any patterning devices, such as repetition of particular words or phrases or any ways in which the grammatical structures mirror or repeat across the extract
   - the overall **tone** of the extracts (compared with Levy's plainer, more direct approach).

   Now write up your ideas in a paragraph.

Key term

tone: the mood or feeling created in a text

Plenary

How would you explain literary style to someone else in one minute? Try to do so, drawing on what you have learned in this unit.

1.3 Understanding characterisation

Big question
- How do writers construct character?

WHAT IS CHARACTER?

When you are reading a novel or watching a play, it is easy to think of the people in the story or on the stage as 'real'. You can become very attached to them, laugh with them or feel their fear or pain. There is nothing wrong with this – in fact it is part of understanding the effect characters have. However, it is important to remember that characters are constructed by writers. How they are constructed is a central part of your study.

At a basic level, a character is simply a person in a story, poem or play. The character might be a king or a carpenter, a child or an elderly person on the point of death – and perhaps several things at the same time.

Task

1. Think about a short story or novel you are studying or know well. Write a brief cast list for up to ten of its characters. Keep it simple – for example:
   Great Expectations by Charles Dickens
   Pip: *an orphan, mysteriously inherits a fortune*
2. How easy was it to do this? Was it more difficult to define main characters rather than less important ones? Why?

In these simple definitions of characters, it is likely you mentioned one or more of the following:
- age or family relationship (brother of…)
- job or role in life (queen, soldier)
- status (rich, poor)
- location (the places where they go, work, live)
- their actions in the text (a queen battling to secure her country and her lover).

UNDERSTANDING CHARACTERISATION

All of these pieces of information are valid in terms of defining or summing up a character, but they are only part of the picture.
Characterisation – the various methods whereby a writer constructs character – is the real key to understanding the impact character makes. Characterisation exists on two levels:
- At the **macro-level**, characterisation is about how a character acts and changes or develops across the whole text. Pip is a child for the early part of *Great Expectations*, but he is a grown man by the end.
- At the **micro-level**, it is about how a writer depicts a character in individual moments – on their own, when they first appear or finally leave, in their interactions with others, in their private thoughts at a particular time. For example, you could analyse Pip's final conversation with Estella at the end of the novel.

Key terms

characterisation: the ways in which a writer creates or constructs a fictional character
macro-level: across a large scale
micro-level: at an individual or detailed level

It is like looking through two lenses of a camera at the same time: one close up on the here and now; one a wide-angle shot taking in everything the character has done or said over the course of the text.

"TELL US YOUR NAME!" SAID THE MAN. "QUICK!"

Task

3. In what ways does the following student comment on both aspects of characterisation?

> Pip's character is explicitly linked to 'expectations' across the novel. It begins with him believing that he has been specially selected to be educated and made into a 'gentleman' by a rich old lady, but he is shocked to discover it is actually the murderer and convict Magwitch who has helped him and who claims to be like a father to him. As Magwitch says in Chapter 39, 'Look'ee here, Pip. I'm your second father. You're my son – more to me nor any son.' These words and events serve to fundamentally alter Pip's view of himself and his past life.

Writers therefore construct character in a range of ways:

Context	The place and/or time in which they live: these may reflect or be linked to character, for example through a setting or family's social background
Appearance	What they look like: their physical form, face, clothes, gestures
Speech	What they say and how they say it: the language they use, their particular voice and tone
Interactions	How they interact with others: physically, in speech, and through what we are told directly about their relationships
Observations	What they see and observe: their viewpoint and perspective on people, places, actions, ideas

Read these three short extracts. Each writer has constructed character in a slightly different way.

Extract A

I stared at him, taking in every detail. Then, I stared again, harder, and more details came into focus: the Tissot watch with the metal strap, the ball-point pen attached to the shirt pocket. The face with the hair swept away from it, the flattened cheekbones, the cleft in the chin, the eyebrows black and heavy, the teeth uneven, crowding each other here, parted from each other there, and the glint of a filling.

Anita Desai, 'The Man Who Saw Himself Drown' (2000)

Extract B

My prime of youth is but a frost of cares,
My feast of joy is but a dish of pain,
My crop of corn is but a field of tears,
And all my good is but vain hope of gain.
The day is past, and yet I saw no sun,
And now I live, and now my life is done.

Chidiock Tichborne (on his forthcoming execution in 1586)

Extract C

Messenger [*speaking about Mark Antony, Cleopatra's lover*]: Madam, he's married to Octavia.

Cleopatra: The most infectious pestilence upon thee!

Strikes him down.

Messenger: Good madam, patience.

Cleopatra: What say you?

Strikes him.

        Hence,

Horrible villain, or I'll spurn thine eyes

Like balls before me! I'll unhair thy head!

*She **hales** him up and down.*

Thou shalt be whipped with wire, and stewed in brine,

Smarting in ling'ring pickle!

              William Shakespeare, *Antony and Cleopatra*
                        (Act 2 Scene 5) (1606)

WRITING ABOUT THE CONSTRUCTION OF CHARACTER

It is vital you develop a language for explaining how writers construct character. These terms and techniques can be useful in your writing:

- 'character' references and terms: characteristics, nature, personality, status, sympathy, empathy, traits, feature, aspect, function, evolution, development, self-knowledge, contrast
- overview statements: that sum up or encapsulate the overall presentation of a character in a scene or across a text – for example, 'Cleopatra's fiery and passionate nature is exemplified in her treatment of the servant'
- carefully selected character adjectives ('dominant', 'fiery', 'passionate') or paraphrasing of someone actions or feelings ('she aims a tirade of insults and threats at the cowering servant').

In the following extract, a student has begun to write about the poem on page 17, using some of this language:

Tichborne presents himself through a series of contrasts, all of which serve to construct a picture of him in a desperate situation. [1] He is still young and in the 'prime of youth' [2] yet this fact is contradicted by the self-knowledge represented by the deadening 'frost of cares' [2] – a metaphor implying his youth is frozen in time. [3]

Task

4. What do we learn out about the following characters?
   - the man with the 'eyebrows black and heavy'
   - the speaker in the poem
   - Cleopatra
5. What evidence did you find in each text to arrive at your answer? Think about the five aspects from the grid on page 17 (not all of them apply).

Glossary

hales: drags by the hair

Task

6. Link the highlighted sections of the extract at the bottom of page 18 to the annotations below:

   a) thoughtful **analogy** of why 'frost' has been used and its effect

   b) quotations chosen to illustrate the point

   c) overview explaining writer's core method.

Key term

analogy: using your own imagery or comparison to explain characterisation

Notice how the student has explained the way the poet has constructed the image of himself, and has then carefully commented on it and its effect, using apt examples.

Task

7. Write a further 2–3 sentences explaining how the same use of contrast is used elsewhere in the verse. You need only comment on one or two further contrasts. You could begin:

Tichborne goes on to present his emotions as a series of further contrasts. Firstly, he uses the analogy of food, stating that…

Final Task

Task

8. Write 100–125 words (total) about how Cleopatra is characterised in the passage.

Checklist for success

✓ Begin with an overview statement about Cleopatra's presentation in the extract.

✓ Use appropriate character terminology, adjectives and/or paraphrasing to describe the characterisation.

✓ If you can, create your own analogy for Cleopatra (what does her behaviour remind you of?).

Plenary

Choose any one character (or narrative voice/speaker, if a poem) at a particular point in a text you are studying (for example, a speech from a play, the opening to a chapter). Note down 3–4 ways in which the writer has constructed the character at this point and what these tell you about the character.

Big question

- How do writers use texts to explore particular issues or ideas?

WHAT ARE ISSUES AND CONCERNS?

At the most fundamental level, poems, plays, short stories and novels provide some sort of narrative, and usually a controlling voice or perspective. Describing William Wordsworth's poem 'I wandered lonely as a cloud' you might say: 'The poem describes how a man on a walk sees some beautiful daffodils by a lake.'

But this does not give the whole picture. It is natural for us to ask 'why?'. What was so important about these daffodils that Wordsworth wanted to write about them? Perhaps he was worried about the destruction of the countryside or perhaps daffodils reflected his joy at spring coming. Or was his interest more intimate and personal – how nature's beauty can help us when we feel low? Or perhaps it was something else altogether – or even lots of different things at the same time!

These 'things of interest' to a writer are issues and concerns. They might be stated obviously and directly, or, as is often the case, they arise through a combination of what is said and how it is said.

Read this poem by Claude McKay, an African-American writer born in the Caribbean.

Subway Wind

Far down, down through the city's great gaunt gut
    The gray train rushing bears the weary wind;
In the packed **cars** the fans the crowd's breath cut,
    Leaving the sick and heavy air behind.
And pale-cheeked children seek the upper door
    To give their summer jackets to the breeze;
Their laugh is swallowed in the deafening roar
    Of captive wind that moans for fields and seas;
Seas cooling warm where native **schooners** drift
    Through sleepy waters, while gulls wheel and sweep,
Waiting for windy waves the keels to lift
    Lightly among the islands of the deep;
Islands of lofty palm trees blooming white
    That lend their perfume to the tropic sea
Where fields lie idle in the dew-drenched night,
    And the **Trades** float above them fresh and free.

Claude McKay (1922)

Wider reading

'I wandered lonely as a cloud' by William Wordsworth (1770–1850) is one of the best-known poems in the English Romantic tradition. It is easily found online. What do you think it is about?

Glossary

cars: train carriages
schooners: sailing boats
Trades: short for 'trade winds' – winds that help boats sail between countries to sell goods

Task

1. At the simplest level of 'story', what is the poem describing?
   - What is being described in lines 1–8 of the poem? (What form of transport? Where?)
   - What is being described in lines 9–16 of the poem? (What different scene and place?)
2. Now think about the different ways each location is described. What words or phrases are used to describe the following?
   - the city (in the first line)
   - the wind and air, in and around the subway train
   - the seas and waters in the second location
   - the palm trees
   - the Trade winds
3. Based on these notes, what do you think the poet was interested in exploring?
4. Read this conversation between three students discussing the poem. What do you think? Is there any evidence to support Scott's views or your own?

Jake

> I think this text is about how cities are places of dirt and grime – you can never feel 'free' in them...

Sumitra

> Yet the children 'laugh' as they try to get the cool wind. So, surely this isn't about them. It's the poet. He might not mention himself, but he's thinking about his home – Caribbean islands…

Scott

> Yes, this isn't just about how much more pleasant tropical islands are. He might be exploring memory.

Key terms

interpretation: evaluation and explanation of the different ideas within a text

context: the relationship between a text and its historical, social and cultural backgrounds

alluding: making a subtle reference or link

Task

5. What evidence is there of the poet expressing:
   - alienation from his city surroundings?
   - a sense of home representing liberation?

CONTEXT AND CONCERNS

When considering the issues and concerns in the texts you study, you need to make sure what you say is a reasonable **interpretation**. Do not make complete guesses or assertions that are unsupported by the text. For example, it would be wrong to say: 'The speaker is trying to persuade readers that the subway trains need to have proper air-conditioning.'

Equally important is how you make use of the **context** or background to the text or the writer. For example, Claude McKay was an African-American writer who, in many of his poems, commented forcefully on civil rights and the status of African-Americans in the United States. This is not the case here, but it could be argued he is **alluding** to his own sense of belonging as an African-American.

Wider reading

'The White House' by Claude McKay tackles issues of race head on. It describes a black man passing a house on a street that is closed to black people. Why do you think McKay chose the title? You can read the poem in Unit 1.6.

WRITING ABOUT ISSUES AND CONCERNS

It is important to develop a usable vocabulary to describe the issues and concerns of a writer. From your previous study of literature, you may be used to talking about key themes expressed in general ways, such as 'conflict', 'marriage' or 'desire'. For your study now, it is important to unpick these general terms and express ideas in more detail. This can be done in several ways:

- by being *precise*: 'the play explores the conflict that arises when women confront patriarchal forces… (this explores what sort of conflict it is)
- by tracing how an author's concerns develop *across a text*: 'whilst the writer initially explores how one woman seeks to break free from family ties, by Act 2 it has become a play about a particular society and how it suppresses women's independence…'
- by expressing the possibility of *different interpretations* (how texts might be 'about' numerous things, some of which might seem to contradict each other): 'the writer not only explores patriarchal forces but equally could be said to explore male suffering…'

Task

6. Choose one of the shorter poems you are studying – or one at random from a poetry collection – and write three sentences about it. The first should be a precise statement ('The poem describes how…'), the second a structural one ('At the start, the poem… while at the end…'), and the third an interpretative one ('On the one hand, the poet could be said to be exploring… However…').

Read the extract opposite, taken from Jane Austen's *Pride and Prejudice*. Here, the heroine Elizabeth Bennet, who is relatively poor, is visited by a rich older woman Lady Catherine, who has come to find out whether her nephew is really in love with Elizabeth and intending to marry her. Lady Catherine expects her own daughter, rather than Elizabeth, to be his bride.

Task

7. What issues do you think Austen is exploring in this scene? Make notes about:
- why Lady Catherine believes her daughter is best suited to marry her rich nephew
- what Lady Catherine has to say about Elizabeth's family
- how Elizabeth responds to Lady Catherine's statements.

8. Here are a number of possible interpretations of the issues arising from the extract. What evidence can you find for each one? Which, if any, is best supported by the text?
- **a)** Austen is exploring the way in which older people automatically assume they have authority over younger ones.
- **b)** Austen is exploring how love can conquer anything, even lack of money or social status.
- **c)** The main issue Austen is exploring is the importance of standing up for your rights and demanding respect for them.
- **d)** The text concerns snobbery: Lady Catherine assumes Elizabeth should give way because her family is of a lower social status.

'I will not be interrupted. Hear me in silence. My daughter and my nephew are formed for each other. They are descended, on the maternal side, from the same noble line; and, on the father's, from respectable, honourable, and ancient – though untitled – families. Their fortune on both sides is splendid. They are destined for each other by the voice of every member of their respective houses; and what is to divide them? The upstart pretensions of a young woman without family, connections, or fortune. Is this to be endured! But it must not, shall not be. If you were sensible of your own good, you would not wish to quit the sphere in which you have been brought up.'

'In marrying your nephew, I should not consider myself as quitting that sphere. He is a gentleman; I am a gentleman's daughter; so far we are equal.'

'True. You *are* a gentleman's daughter. But who was your mother? Who are your uncles and aunts? Do not imagine me ignorant of their condition.'

'Whatever my connections may be,' said Elizabeth, 'if your nephew does not object to them, they can be nothing to *you*.'

'Tell me once for all, are you engaged to him?'

Though Elizabeth would not, for the mere purpose of obliging Lady Catherine, have answered this question, she could not but say, after a moment's deliberation:

'I am not.'

Lady Catherine seemed pleased.

'And will you promise me, never to enter into such an engagement?'

'I will make no promise of the kind.'

Jane Austen, *Pride and Prejudice* (1813)

Her ladyship, with great condescension, arose to receive them.

Final Task

Task

9. Choose either 'Subway Wind' or the extract above. Write 150–200 words on the issues or concerns raised in the text.

Checklist for success
✓ Remember that texts can be about more than one idea or issue.
✓ Do not assert your ideas without being able to support your point of view with textual evidence.
✓ Try to move beyond simply saying a text is about 'love' or 'pride' – be as specific as the text allows.

Plenary

Think again about any of the texts you have studied so far, or are currently studying. For each one, write 3–4 sentences like the ones in Task 8, concisely summing up what you believe are the core issues or concerns in it.

1.5 Introducing settings and contexts

Big question
- How do writers use settings and contexts to create meaning and impact?

WHAT ARE SETTINGS?

Setting is a very broad term that can encompass everything from a time (yesterday, the end of the 19th century, childhood) to a place (a bedroom, New York, the bottom of the ocean). How specific a writer is about setting will depend largely on their purpose. In many texts, setting is fundamental. The setting can:
- reflect key ideas, issues or concerns – for example, the valley of ash in *The Great Gatsby* as a reflection of moral corruption or deceit
- tell the reader about the social or historical contexts or times – for example, a cotton plantation forming the setting for a story about a slave's fight for survival in Solomon Northrup's *Twelve Years a Slave*
- mirror a character's development – for example, Elizabeth's move from an '**entailed**' middle-class home to Darcy's wealthy estate in *Pride and Prejudice*.

Equally important, a setting can add colour and detail, creating tone, mood, and atmosphere.

Read these short extracts. As you read, think about how the setting is being used in each case.

Extract A

A fine spring morning on the river Meuse, between Lorraine and Champagne, in the year 1429 AD, in the castle of Vaucouleurs.

Captain Robert de Baudricourt, a military squire, handsome and physically energetic, but with no will of his own, is disguising that defect in his usual fashion by storming terribly at his steward, a trodden worm, scanty of flesh, scanty of hair, who might be any age from 18 to 55, being the sort of man whom age cannot wither because he has never bloomed.

The two are in a sunny stone chamber on the first floor of the castle. At a plain strong oak table, seated in chair to match, the captain presents his left profile. The steward stands facing him at the other side of the table, if so deprecatory a stance as his can be called standing. The mullioned 13th-century window is open behind him. Near it in the corner is a turret with a narrow arched doorway leading to a winding stair, which descends to the courtyard. There is a stout four-legged stool under the table, and a wooden chest under the window.

George Bernard Shaw, the opening stage directions to *Saint Joan* (1923)

Extract B

The last of the rays seemed to lighten it to a golden glow. I am sure this would make a beautiful colour picture: the two of us walking behind each other in the narrow path with my luggage on our heads, silhouetted against the setting sun. One December I saw a large picture like that, only it was of a giraffe. I remember standing there, looking at it and for a moment longing to smell the fields after the rain. But I was in Swakopmund with my *miesies* and her family as she needed a rest. It was holiday time, family time, but I was without my own family, just as I was for the rest of the year and for most of my adult life.

Now all that has changed. I am on my way home.

Milly Jafta, 'The Homecoming' (1999)

Extract C

By the river
In the black wet night as the furtive rain slinks down,
Dropping and starting from sleep
Alone on a seat
A woman crouches.

I must go back to her.

I want to give her
Some money.

D.H. Lawrence, 'Embankment at Night,
Before the War' (1916)

Glossary

miesies: mistress, the woman she worked for

Task

1. For each extract, what sort of setting is being described?
   - Is it a specific place and/or time?
   - Is more than one place described?
   - Is the setting described in a way that creates effects for the reader: optimism or negativity, hope or despair – or some other sort of emotional response?

   For each of these, provide examples to support your views.
2. What is the purpose of the setting (or settings) in each case? For example, can it be linked to:
   - issues, ideas or concerns (family relationships, the realities of war)?
   - social or historical contexts (during a rebellion or trial)?
   - character change or development?

Thinking more deeply: **other purposes for settings**

There are other, more specific ways writers use aspects of setting in texts, as outlined in the following table.

Key aspect	Example
Weather and climate: writers often use weather to build characterisation, reflect relationships and develop plot.	Think about how we use terms such as 'a stormy relationship'. In Thomas Hardy's *Far from the Madding Crowd*, a terrible storm and lightning threaten to set fire to hay. The heroine's husband is asleep and drunk and is unable to help. The storm could be viewed as **pathetic fallacy**.
Town and country: writers often contrast aspects of the town/city and the natural world to construct ideas.	In Western literature, towns/cities were traditionally portrayed as **symbols** of moral corruption and greed, and also sites of pollution and poverty. The countryside was also often presented in an idealised way as a place of purity or innocence. However, not all texts follow these conventions; cities are often also presented as places of energy, life and opportunity.
Buildings: writers often personify buildings or use them to represent key ideas.	Particular buildings – both public and private – are often represented as reflections of individuals or society (for example, related to wealth or social status) or as expressions of their owners' characters. In Emily Brontë's *Wuthering Heights*, the place of the title is a hard, isolated building in a wild landscape, reflective of its owner.
Particular landmarks, rooms or spaces: writers not only use buildings or natural environments as a whole, they also build plot or key ideas around a specific room or place.	In Charlotte Brontë's *Jane Eyre*, individual rooms are highly significant: the 'red room' where Jane is banished as a child is often compared, symbolically, to a womb, whilst later the attic where Rochester's troubled wife is hidden comes to represent secrecy and submission.

Task

3. Reread 'Subway Wind' by Claude McKay in Unit 1.4. In what ways does the poet use both pathetic fallacy and create the sort of romantic contrast between town and city referred to above?

HOW WRITERS CONSTRUCT SETTINGS

To understand the significance of setting, it is helpful to identify the techniques writers use and the effects they create.

These might include:

- **Lexis**. In *Saint Joan*, 'the year 1429 AD', 'castle' and 'mullioned [...] window' all convey a military and historical context.
- Precise visual or other sensory detail. In 'The Homecoming' the description 'The last of the *rays* seemed to *lighten it* (the sun) to a *golden glow*' creates a comforting, warm tone.
- **Personification**. In D.H. Lawrence's poem, 'the furtive rain' suggests the rain is secretive and creeps along, perhaps reflecting the poet's own movements.
- Structural organisation or patterning. In this sentence in 'The Homecoming', repeated participles convey the waiting, the holding of the moment in time: 'I remember *standing* there, *looking* at it and for a moment longing to smell the fields after the rain.'

Key terms

pathetic fallacy: the attribution of human feelings to inanimate objects, often used to reflect the action or mood of a text – for example, 'gloomy clouds' or 'clock's stern face'

symbol: an object, image or action that takes on a meaning different from its literal sense

lexis: the choice of vocabulary that builds an overall tone or picture in a literary work

personification: attributing human characteristics or a personal nature to something nonhuman

Bearing these techniques in mind, read this passage, in which the writer describes travelling on a boat into the depths of a jungle:

Going up that river was like travelling back to the earliest beginnings of the world, when vegetation rioted on the earth and the big trees were kings. An empty stream, a great silence, an impenetrable forest. The air was warm, thick, heavy, sluggish. There was no joy in the brilliance of sunshine. The long stretches of the waterway ran on, deserted, into the gloom of overshadowed distances. On silvery sand-banks hippos and alligators sunned themselves side by side. The broadening waters flowed through a mob of wooded islands; you lost your way on that river as you would in a desert, and butted all day long against shoals, trying to find the channel, till you thought yourself bewitched, and cut off for ever from everything you had known once – somewhere – far away – in another existence perhaps. There were moments when one's past came back to one, as it will sometimes when you have not a moment to spare for yourself; but it came in the shape of an unrestful and noisy dream, remembered with wonder amongst the overwhelming realities of this strange world of plants, and water, and silence. And this stillness of life did not in the least resemble a peace. It was the stillness of an **implacable** force brooding over an **inscrutable** intention. It looked at you with a vengeful aspect.

Joseph Conrad, *Heart of Darkness* (1899)

- making an analogy between the present and the distant past
- list of three noun phrases conveying the mood
- reference to weather
- a further comparison conveying the writer's impressions
- lexis of mysterious, other-worldly experiences

Glossary

implacable: something that can't be resisted

inscrutable: something hidden or that can't be read or understood

Task

4. Often nature is presented as a calming, soothing or positive force, but this is not the case in this extract. How are the river and the forest presented? Continue making notes on the passage to add to the annotations. Focus on words or phrases that suggest:
   - the journey is suffocating or imprisoning
   - the writer's experience is disturbing or unreal
   - the river/forest is like a person or being.

Final Task

Task

5. Write about the final extract, explaining how Conrad creates a vivid setting and what sort of mood is conveyed.

Plenary

Write down three key ways in which writers use setting in texts. Then compare your ideas with those of a partner.

Checklist for success

✓ Comment on any techniques used by Conrad to achieve the effects, such as the lexis, sensory detail and structural patterning.

✓ Explore any wider ideas. What might the jungle environment represent for this traveller from another country? How might the writer be exploring the fear of the unfamiliar or imperial attitudes to overseas territories?

1.6 Writing about language

Big question

- What particular aspects of language should you look for in your study?

WHAT IS LANGUAGE?

Language refers primarily to the vocabulary a writer chooses and their use of literary devices. It can also refer to the way words, phrases and/or lines combine to create effects, such as through sound patterning or rhythm, or to the way particular types of sentence are used to create an impact on the reader or audience.

Task

1. Look at this bank of language techniques. Which of these terms are you already familiar with? Can you think of examples to demonstrate their use? Which do you need to find out more about? (You will learn more about all these techniques during your studies.)

simile	metaphor	imagery	lexis	syntax
alliteration	assonance	onomatopoeia	analogy	rhythm
personification	rhyme	dialogue	allusion	juxtaposition

Read the following speech from William Shakespeare's play, *Antony and Cleopatra*, and look at the annotations to remind yourself of some of the techniques used. In this speech, Enobarbus describes Cleopatra's arrival.

I will tell you.
The barge she sat in, like a burnished throne,
Burned on the water. The **poop** was beaten gold,
Purple the sails, and so perfumèd that
The winds were lovesick with them. The oars were silver,
Which to the tune of flutes kept stroke, and made
The water which they beat to follow faster,
As amorous of their strokes. For her own person,
It **beggared** all description: she did lie
In her pavilion – cloth-of-gold, of tissue –
O'erpicturing that **Venus** where we see
The fancy outwork nature. On each side her
Stood pretty dimpled boys, like smiling **Cupids**,
With **divers**-colored fans, whose wind did seem
To glow the delicate cheeks which they did cool,
And what they undid did.

simile

personification (a form of metaphor, here)

assonance

alliteration

analogy

rhythm

Glossary

poop: raised platform or deck at the stern of a ship
beggared: made other description seem poor (weak)
Venus: Roman god of love
Cupid: son of Venus and the God of desire and attraction
divers: varied

Task

2. What other examples of the following can you identify in the speech?
- Personification. How is the water described in relation to the strokes of the oar?
- **Simile**. What are the 'pretty-dimpled boys' compared with?

3. **Imagery** is a general term we use to describe powerful language that draws vividly on the senses. It also includes techniques such as simile and **metaphor**. Which images from the speech do you find especially vivid?

4. Lexis refers to the writer's overall choice of vocabulary and is a helpful term if you are trying to identify whether patterns of words or phrases appear in a text. This is a speech about a queen arriving by boat. What words or phrases in the speech refer specifically to boats or how they operate?

5. At first glance, the verse does not rhyme, but if you look more closely, you will see there are a number of repeated words and **internal rhymes**. Can you identify any? Why do you think Shakespeare chose to have so many repeated words in a speech about a moving boat?

Key terms

simile: a figure of speech comparing one thing with another thing of a different kind (for example, 'cunning as a fox'); usually indicated by a word such as 'like' or 'as'

imagery: a general term used to describe powerful language that draws vividly on the senses; it includes techniques such as simile and metaphor

metaphor: a figure of speech that directly refers to one thing by mentioning another for effect (for example, 'a cold white blanket covered the earth' referring to snow)

internal rhyme: rhyming of words within the text, not at the end of the lines

LANGUAGE EFFECTS

Identifying these language features is useful, but you will need to go further in your study. You will need not only to explore the effects of individual words or phrases, or particular literary devices, but also to comment on the overall mood or impact.

A student, commenting on one aspect of the text, has written:

> The alliterative opening lines with the emphasis falling on the 'b' of 'barge', 'burnished' and 'burned' create a vivid and immediate impact on the listener, so that we feel as if the image of Cleopatra's boat has been 'burned' into our minds too. The image of the 'gold' poop develops this idea of the dazzling impact of her arrival.

Task

6. In what way is this an effective exploration of the language? Identify the following:
- two language features the student has commented on
- the effect the student feels these language features have
- how the student has linked the two features to suggest a larger effect
- how the selected 'evidence' has been included in the paragraph.

7. The student's paragraph has begun to draw ideas together about the way Cleopatra's arrival is described. Now read the speech again.
- What other colours are referred to? What do they have in common?
- How is Cleopatra herself described? Which of her features does Enobarbus mention?

Task

8. Write your own paragraph about language effects in the passage, beginning with reference to the other colours mentioned or to how Cleopatra is described. You could start:

The reference to 'purple' sails adds a lavish, rich tone to the gold.

Thinking more deeply: **looking for supporting evidence**

Task

9. Which of these overall interpretations of the text do you think is most convincing? You should make sure none of these is an **assertion** unsupported by the language of the text.

a) 'Cleopatra's beauty is emphasised throughout the text, so that we have no doubt she is the most desirable woman in the world.'

b) 'Cleopatra's allure is presented as god-like and unattainable, beyond earthly description.'

c) 'Cleopatra is entirely absent from the description, which suggests she is a puppet of the forces of love and war.'

> **Key term**
>
> **assertion:** a statement of belief that is not founded on facts or evidence

EXPLORING THE LANGUAGE OF TEXTS FOR THE FIRST TIME

Having seen how the language of one text has been constructed, and had the chance to comment on one aspect of it, you now need to develop techniques for tackling texts independently.

Read this poem. It is by Claude McKay, whose poem 'Subway Wind' you looked at in Unit 1.4.

The White House

Your door is shut against my tightened face,
And I am sharp as steel with discontent;
But I possess the courage and the grace
To bear my anger proudly and unbent.
The pavement slabs burn loose beneath my feet,
A **chafing** savage, down the decent street;
A passion rends my vitals as I pass,
Where boldly shines your shuttered door of glass.
Oh, I must search for wisdom every hour,
Deep in my wrathful bosom sore and raw,
And find in it the superhuman power
To hold me to the letter of your law!
Oh, I must keep my heart inviolate
Against the potent poison of your hate.

Claude McKay (1922)

> **Glossary**
>
> **chafing:** soreness caused by friction

Task

10. Read through the poem, noting down language features you recognise from your earlier work in this unit.

Checklist for success
✓ START – by identifying particular language features or literary devices.
✓ DEVELOP – by noting any effect they have (for example, do they create a particular mood or paint a particular picture). Don't hold back – for now, just jot down whatever comes to mind.
✓ LINK – by looking for connections or patterns in the language (for example, similar sounds, rhymes, echoes of ideas or images) and what *overall effect* these create.

Final Task

Task

11. Choose either the extract from *Antony and Cleopatra* or 'The White House' and write about how either Shakespeare or McKay has used language to create character or explore issues and concerns.
You could:
* work through each text, line by line, or section by section (for example, each couple of lines at a time), beginning: *The poem/play opens with…*
OR
* work through particular language features one at a time, beginning: *The use of imagery is particularly striking in…*
OR
* start with particular ideas or effects, and then explain how the language has created these ideas, beginning: *Enobarbus creates a striking picture of Cleopatra as…* OR *McKay's bitter reflections about racist attitudes are reflected in…*

Checklist for success
✓ Identify relevant techniques.
✓ Comment on the effects they create.
✓ Try to link effects to suggest overall concerns or characterisation.

Plenary

What language techniques or literary devices that you have learned about in this unit will you look out for in the current prose texts you are studying? Taking one of these texts, select a section of about 175–200 words to comment on.

1.7 Introducing form

Big question

- How does the form of a text influence the way we read it?

WHAT IS FORM?

Form usually refers to the distinctive shape and layout of a text or a particular text type. So, whilst novels, poetry and plays all represent different general forms of writing, within each one there are distinct subforms too: for example, sonnets and ballads in poetry; one-act plays and verse plays in drama; **epistolary** narratives or fictional diaries in novels.

Task

1. What do you know about the general forms of novel, play and poem? Look at the terms in the word bank below and decide which form they relate to. Some might be relevant to more than one form.

chapter	**verse**	stanza	line	**couplet**
title	**epilogue**	**prologue**		paragraph
act	stage direction	exit	sentence	line break
direct speech	dialogue	**soliloquy**	scene	**monologue**

It is vital to get your terminology right when referring to particular forms of text because they can have different effects. For example, a poet's ability to break a sentence by forcing a line to end at a particular point ('line break') is fundamental to its effect.

Now read these two short texts.

Version A

November Night

Listen.
With faint dry sound,
Like steps of passing ghosts,
The leaves, frost-crisp'd, break from the trees
And fall.

Version B

Listen. With faint dry sound like steps of passing ghosts, the leaves, frost-crisp'd, break from the trees and fall.

The first is the original – a **cinquain** by the inventor of the form, Adelaide Crapsey (1878–1914).

Task

2. What is different about the two forms? Think about:
   - how they are set out on the page
   - how lines and sentences are used.

Key terms

form: conventions of literary forms of prose, poetry and drama

epistolary: narratives told through letters

verse: a group of lines that form a unit in a poem or song; a stanza

couplet: a pair of lines of verse, typically rhyming and of the same length

epilogue: a concluding section or speech at the end of a literary work, often serving as a comment on what has happened

prologue: a separate, introductory section at the start of a literary or dramatic work

soliloquy: a speech given by a character speaking their thoughts aloud, either alone or oblivious of any possible hearers

monologue: a long speech given by a single character

cinquain: a poem of five lines with the number of syllables rising from 2 to 4 to 6 and then 8 before returning to 2 for the final line

Task

3. **a)** How does the arrangement of the text draw your attention to individual words? Which words, if any, are your eyes drawn to in Version A. Why might these have been foregrounded?

    b) What words or phrases, if any, stand out in Version B?

    c) Why do you think the final line of the form always has just two words? How does that add to the effect of the cinquain form?

4. What topics or subjects do you think are best suited to the cinquain form? (Could you tell a story with multiple plot lines in a cinquain?)

Here is another of Adelaide Crapsey's poems called 'Niagara', written in prose. Read it, and then complete Task 5 opposite.

> How frail. Above the bulk of crashing water hangs, autumnal, evanescent, wan, the moon.

DRAMATIC FORM

The form of plays is usually very different from that of poems and is used for different effects. For example, how would Crapsey's 'November Night' or 'Niagara' have worked as a play script? Try converting either of them into dramatic form – is it possible? What do you find challenging?

Now read this opening to a play by Oscar Wilde. What do you notice about the form (how it is set out)?

SCENE

*The Market Place of Padua at noon; in the background is the great Cathedral of Padua; the architecture is Romanesque, and wrought in black and white marbles; a flight of marble steps leads up to the Cathedral door; at the foot of the steps are two large stone lions; the houses on each aide of the stage have coloured awnings from their windows, and are flanked by stone arcades; on the right of the stage is the public fountain, with a **triton** in green bronze blowing from a conch; around the fountain is a stone seat; the bell of the Cathedral is ringing, and the citizens, men, women and children, are passing into the Cathedral.*

[Enter GUIDO FERRANTI and ASCANIO CRISTOFANO.]

ASCANIO: Now by my life, Guido, I will go no farther; for if I walk another step I will have no life left to swear by; this **wild-goose errand** of yours!

(Sits down on the step of the fountain.)

GUIDO: I think it must be here. *[Goes up to passer-by and **doffs** his cap.]* Pray, sir, is this the market place, and that the church of Santa Croce? *[Citizen bows.]* I thank you, sir.

ASCANIO: Well?

GUIDO: Ay! it is here.

Oscar Wilde, *The Duchess of Padua* (1891)

Task

5. Consider how it would work better as a cinquain.
    *   First, reconstruct it in cinquain form.
    *   Then, make brief notes explaining what the effect is of placing the final two words on the final line. What does it make the reader do – or feel? What is the effect of isolating or drawing attention to those final words?

Glossary

triton: a Greek god of the sea, usually half man, half fish in form

wild-goose errand: a confused or lengthy search which seems unlikely to succeed

doff: remove or raise one's hat as a mark of respect

Task

6. Reread the script, and identify:
   - details of the set/staging
   - the main characters
   - information about gesture or movement
   - any other information or detail provided (other characters, for example).
7. What does the reader (or audience) learn from this opening? Think about:
   - the location/setting
   - the plot (what is happening)
   - the relationship between the two men.

As you can see, the stage or set is not very different from a description in a novel, except that in scripts such a setting is conventionally indicated at the start of a play, act or scene. However, the key difference is that plot and characterisation are largely driven by dialogue. If the dramatist wants us to know how a character feels, then it must be conveyed through the written speech and action on the page, as well as through an actor's performance.

Task

8. How would Ascanio's first line and the stage direction 'Sits down' have been written in a prose text written in the first person? What thoughts could you add that aren't shown in the extract? Begin:

   I was exhausted. It was all Guido's fault…

The following takes place a little bit later in *The Duchess of Padua*. Guido is supposed to meet someone who knows about his real father, but the person hasn't come.

Glossary
broidered: embroidered or woven
lineament: features

ASCANIO:	[…] By the great gods of eating, Guido, I am as hungry as a widow is for a husband, as tired as a young maid is of good advice, and as dry as a monk's sermon. Come, Guido, you stand there looking at nothing, like the fool who tried to look into his own mind; your man will not come.
GUIDO:	Well, I suppose you are right. Ah! *[Just as he is leaving the stage with ASCANIO, enter LORD MORANZONE in a violet cloak, with a silver falcon **broidered** on the shoulder; he passes across to the Cathedral, and just as he is going in GUIDO runs up and touches him.]*
MORANZONE:	Guido Ferranti, thou hast come in time.
GUIDO:	What! Does my father live?
MORANZONE:	Ay! lives in thee. Thou art the same in mould and **lineament**, Carriage and form, and outward semblances; I trust thou art in noble mind the same.
GUIDO:	Oh, tell me of my father; I have lived But for this moment.
MORANZONE:	We must be alone.

Oscar Wilde, *The Duchess of Padua* (1891)

Final Task

Task

9. How does the dramatic form contribute to the effect of this extract? Begin by making notes on the following questions.
   - How does the action switch from the light-hearted to the dramatic? Think about how Ascanio's comic comparisons are broken by a dramatic stage direction.
   - How is the relationship between the two men conveyed in Ascanio's opening speech? Think about the tone. How might an actor speak these words? Angrily? Ruefully? Happily?
   - How does what is said by Moranzone and Guido create suspense and mystery in the audience? Think about whether we are told their inner thoughts at this point.

10. Now, write up your ideas in 100–125 words about why this extract is dramatically effective.
    You could use these prompts to help you:

    The writer engages our interest in a range of ways. First, we enjoy seeing the way Wilde presents the two friends and their relationship. On the one hand, Ascanio is…

    There is also a sudden change in the dramatic pace of the scene. It begins with…

    However, when Moranzone appears…

    Finally, the dramatic form creates mystery in what isn't revealed. As an audience we want to know…

Plenary

The form of prose texts often allows the reader to see the inner workings or motives of a particular character. Select a passage from a prose text you are studying that contains dialogue between two characters.
- How close is the passage to a drama text?
- How easily could it be converted to dramatic form?
- Are there references to a character's inner thoughts that would need to be turned into speech or action? How could this be done?

1.8 Introducing structure

Big question

- How do writers use structure to create an impact?

WHAT IS STRUCTURE?

Structure refers to the different ways in which writers organise their material.

At whole-text level, structure can mean the overarching sequence or shaping of events in a novel or a play, as well as aspects of narration (such as whether the story is told via multiple perspectives). It might also relate to an element of the whole structure, such as the use of time, or the function and impact of beginnings or endings (for example, the use of **circularity**).

At a passage-based level, structure might relate to how particular techniques are used, such as how tenses change or how the order of lines, sentences or paragraph affects meaning. It might also touch on a writer's use of sounds, patterns, repetitions, and in this sense link to the form of the text (see Unit 1.7).

Read the following plot outline of a short story by Anita Desai called 'The Man Who Saw Himself Drown'.

Key terms

structure: the organisation or sequence of ideas, events or language in a text, including its shape and development

circularity: the way in which the ending of a text reflects or revisits its opening

- A middle-aged businessman takes a walk at night while staying at a hotel on a trip.
- He reaches a river and playfully considers jumping onto a boat and escaping on it out to sea, but doesn't.
- Then he sees some local people pulling a body out of the water.
- He approaches and sees the body is his own. In a state of shock, he does not follow the body to the morgue but returns to the hotel.
- Two to three days later, he sees his death reported in the newspaper.
- He leaves the hotel without his luggage and 'blunders around' for days.
- Then he gets a train back to his home town and visits his house.
- He watches from a distance as his widowed wife and children leave the house to go and stay with his in-laws. Should he intervene? Speak to them? He decides not to and feels a sense of relief as if his 'load' has been lightened.
- He wanders around his home city and finds himself at the edge of a narrower, muddy 'trickle' of a river.

Task

1. How do you think the story might end? Think of three possible alternatives.

Most writers aim for their endings to be 'satisfying'. This does not mean the ending has to be happy or unhappy – simply that it should in some way fit with what has come before.

STORY STRUCTURE

Stories are sometimes structured around an arc that shows action developing towards a dramatic climax. This is just one of many narrative structures.

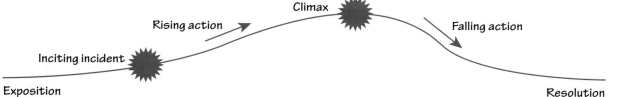

- Exposition: The initial setting or background to the story, which might introduce a main character or group of people. Sometimes the story begins *in media res*.
- Inciting incident: An event, **reversal of fortune** or complication that jolts the story into action.
- Rising action: The tension builds; the story develops.
- Climax: The moment of highest drama; often the turning point for the main character.
- Falling action: Things begin to be resolved; tension begins to drop.
- Resolution: The story comes full circle; events may be 'tied up' for good or bad, or the reader left with further mysteries or questions.

Task

2. Based on this structure, try to fit the details of the plot from Anita Desai's story under each bullet heading (minus the resolution).

STRUCTURE AND GENRE

Structure is also closely linked to form and **genre**. For example, classical tragedies follow these conventions:
- A heroic or noble figure is introduced.
- The hero makes an error of judgement which is usually linked to a character flaw (such as greed or pride).
- Fate conspires to make the error fatal or damaging in some other way.
- The noble hero fights against it but ultimately fails and is destroyed.
- Order – or a form of it – is restored.

In Anita Desai's story, we are not told directly about the main character having a flaw or fault, although we *are* told that he is away on a business trip and is tired of business meetings; we are also told that the family house he lived in was, in fact, owned by the company he worked for.

Task

3. In what way could Desai's story be said to be a 'tragedy'? Think about:
- the main character
- what happens to him
- how he feels towards the end of the part you have read about.

Key terms

in media res: Latin term meaning 'in the middle of things', used here to define stories that begin with the character already in the heart of the action (for example, 'She slammed the door and walked out…')

reversal of fortune: an obstacle or sudden problem a main character has to overcome; in longer texts, there may be several such reversals before the main character reaches the end of their journey, whether emotional or real

genre: the characteristics of different text types (for example, tragedy, comedy and satire)

BEGINNINGS AND ENDINGS

What is the function of a 'beginning' to a text? It can serve many purposes – for example, to introduce the context of a story or experience, to engage our curiosity or to present the main character or voice of the text. But often the beginning only comes to have meaning when the ending resolves or sheds new light on what has gone before.

Read the following poem, and consider how the structure appears to follow one course before shifting to another.

The Washer-Woman

A great **swart** cheek and the gleam of tears,
The flutter of hopes and the shadow of fears,
And all day long the rub and scrub
With only a breath betwixt tub and tub.
Fool! Thou hast toiled for fifty years
And what hast thou now but thy dusty tears?
In silence she rubbed… But her face I had seen,
Where the light of her soul fell shining and clean.

Theodore Henry Shackelford (1888–1923)

Rhyming couplet establishes a sad picture.

The short word 'Fool!' signals a turning point.

The final couplet rewrites the meaning with a different idea of cleanliness.

Task

4. How does the structure of the poem shape how it is read? Think about:
- the picture of the washer-woman painted at the start
- how the poet or society might be seen to criticise her in line 5
- how the poet actually 'saw' her (what he has to say about her 'soul').

5. What broader picture of poor, black people's lives does the poet seem to be building through the use of structural features? Write a paragraph explaining your views. You could use these prompts:

Shackelford's poem begins by presenting the reader with…

However, by line 5, the perspective appears to change when…

By the end, though, his words make it clear that…

You could draw a comparison with 'The Man Who Saw Himself Drown'. That story begins in an understated way: a man on a business trip goes for a walk from his hotel room. The story begins to develop when the 'inciting incident' occurs – when he sees his own body pulled out of the river. From this point, as readers, we want to know answers to some questions:
- How is it possible he sees himself drown?
- What will he do with this knowledge?
- How is the writer going to make it all make sense – if she does?
Endings are designed to offer satisfactory conclusions, but this does not always mean everything is tied up neatly.

Glossary

washer-woman: someone who washes other people's clothes for a living
swart: black, dark

Wider reading

Theodore Henry Shackelford was a young African-American writer who was part of the 'Harlem Renaissance' from 1910 to the 1930s, in which a New York neighbourhood became a cultural centre for black writers, artists and musicians. Claude McKay, whose work you looked at in earlier units, was another poet of the same movement.

Task

6. Read the ending of Desai's story. It begins with the narrator standing by the side of the muddy 'trickle' of river trying to work out what his 'death' means.

a) What sort of ending is it? Does it resolve things neatly?

b) In what way is its structure unusual? (Does it stay fixed on one perspective or change to someone else's?)

> [...] could that death have meant that my double had died on my behalf, that his life was finished, freeing me, my new self, my second self, to go on with another life, a new life?
>
> I searched in myself for an instinct, an urge that would provide the answer. Was it to be death, or life? I remembered how I had once stood on a river bank – in how different a state! – and considered leaping onto a boat and letting it carry me down the river and out to sea, but now I felt no impulse at all, not even one that needed to be confronted and stifled.
>
> It seemed to me that by dying my double had not gifted me with possibility, only robbed me of all desire for one: by arriving at death, life had been closed to me. At his cremation, that was also reduced to ash.
>
> Then I was filled with such despair that I sank onto my knees into the mud.
>
> At daybreak the child with the pot returned to the river for water. What he saw made him stop and stare, first from the slope of the bank, then from closer up, the stones in the shallows. When he made out it was a man's body that lay in that trickle, face down, he dropped the pot on the stones in fright. Its clattering rang out so loud and clear, a flock of crows settling on the sands in curiosity took off in noisy flight.
>
> Anita Desai, 'The Man Who Saw Himself Drown' (2012)

Final Task

Task

7. Write about the structure of the story as a whole (based on the information you have been given) and in particular the ending. You could comment on the following:
- The overall structure of the story. Does it follow the six-step arc you learned about? Does Desai's plot/action draw the reader in? If so, in what ways?
- What sort of story it seems to be. Does it have a specific mood or tone? Is it saying something about the nature of life? If so, what?
- How satisfying (or not) you found the ending. In what way, if at all, is it circular? Did it answer any of the questions you might have had? Does it matter one way or the other?

Plenary

Write down four key reasons why structure so important in texts based on these areas:
- how beginnings serve certain purposes
- how certain types or genres of text share similar structures
- how texts can have turning points
- the function and 'satisfaction' of endings.

1.9 Developing close textual analysis

Big question

- What are the key techniques you should use when analysing an extract or a short text?

WHAT IS ANALYSIS?

When you analyse a text, you look at specific elements of it in great detail. You are trying to understand how it works, much as you would do if you were taking apart an engine or looking at a butterfly under a microscope. However, analysis alone will only take you so far – you will also need to draw conclusions, and explore how the writer:

- develops the reader's understanding about a character or relationship
- presents ideas and attitudes
- expresses a tone or mood
- creates effects or makes a specific impact.

EXPLORING TEXTS CLOSELY

Close textual analysis involves selecting specific details from a text and then analysing them. These might be specific sounds, combinations of letters, single words or phrases, or a particular line or sentence that you break down into parts.

Take this first line from a poem by Stella P. Chipasula, 'I'm My Own Mother, Now'. Imagine you have been asked to explore the speaker's relationship with her mother.

> Mother, I am mothering you now;

You could consider:

- the individual vocabulary – 'Mother', 'mothering'
- the grammar – 'I am…', 'mothering', 'now', 'you'
- the sound/rhythm – where the stresses in the line fall.

Task

1. As you can see, there is a lot you could analyse. For example, what are the connotations of the verb 'mothering'? Add your own ideas to a spider diagram like the one shown here.
2. Now, look at the grammar and think about these questions:

> Mother, I am <u>mothering</u> [1] you <u>now</u>; [2]

a) Is this a current, ongoing situation or something from the past?

b) What does 'now' suggest about the speaker's act of mothering? Was it always the case?

c) What can you say about the sound of the line? Think about any effects created when you speak the words out loud.

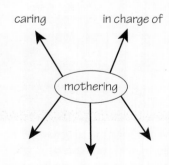

caring   in charge of

mothering

[1] present participle ('-ing')
[2] adverb

Task

3. After calling to the mother, the line continues with an emphatic 'I' and ends with a strong 'now'. What is the point being emphasised? Who is 'now' doing the mothering?
4. What have you learned about the relationship from this analysis? Write a sentence or two summing up your ideas.

RELATING THE DETAIL TO THE WHOLE TEXT

Although you can draw a great deal from this sort of close analysis, you need to look at the whole text to bring together your individual points.

Now look at the whole poem by Stella P. Chipasula in relation to this task.

Discuss the effects of the following poem in detail, commenting in particular on ways in which Chipasula presents the speaker's relationship with her mother.

I'm My Own Mother, Now

Mother, I am mothering you now; → repetition of 'mother'
Alone, I bear the burden of continuity.
Inside me, you are coiled → simile
like a hard question without an answer.
On the far bank of the river → nature imagery – which may be symbolic
you sit silently, your mouth shut,
watching me struggle with this bundle
that grows like a giant seed, in me.
In your closed fist you hide
the riddles of the fruit or clay child
you told before you turned your back
and walked, fading, into the mist.
But, mother, I am mothering you now;
new generations pass through my blood,
and I bear you proudly on my back
where you are no longer a question.

Stella P. Chipasula (c.1995)

The key aspects of the analysis to address are a) the techniques used by the poet to present the relationship between speaker and mother, and b) the effects created.

STAGE 1: IDENTIFYING THE TECHNIQUES

Some of the techniques used by the poet have already been identified in the annotations, and you have already explored the opening line.

Task

5. What other techniques can you identify? (Some may be the same as the ones already highlighted.) You could consider:
   - further examples of simile or metaphor
   - any imagery that might be considered symbolic
   - the structural shape of the poem – how it begins and ends
   - sound or rhythm patterns.

STAGE 2: ANALYSING THE TECHNIQUES AND THEIR EFFECTS

Task

6. You have already explored in some detail the word 'mothering'. Now do the same for the words 'burden' and 'riddle', using spider diagrams. Again, consider the connotations – any words, phrases or ideas that come to mind.

WRITING ANALYTICAL PARAGRAPHS

In close analysis, you must not lose sight of the focus – in this case the relationship between the speaker and her mother.

A student has written the following analytical paragraph about the words 'mother' and 'mothering'.

In the opening line of the poem, the speaker uses the words 'mother' and 'mothering' to indicate closely related but different perspectives. First, the noun is used to address her own 'Mother' directly, and then the verb describes the ongoing process of 'mothering'. This suggests a continual process of caring, of looking after a child, but the effect is surprising, as we don't expect the child to 'mother' the parent. This line does not entirely reveal the relationship between speaker and mother, but the use of the word 'now' at least tells the reader that something has changed.

addresses the two ways in which the root word is used.

useful phrase for explaining or exploring meaning

interprets the effect of the techniques identified

Task

7. Write your own analytical paragraph about one of the following details from the poem:
   - the metaphor of the 'burden of continuity'
   - the similes 'coiled / like a hard question without an answer' or 'like a giant seed'

- the image of the mother who 'turned' her back and 'walked, fading, into the mist'
- the final lines of the poem – 'I bear you proudly on my back / where you are no longer a question'.

Follow these three steps:

Step 1: Begin your paragraph by explaining the technique the poet has used.	In the […] line, the speaker…
Step 2: Continue by exploring the possible connotations, explanations or meanings.	This suggests / conveys the idea that / seems to represent…
Step 3: Finish by saying something about what it tells us about the speaker, mother or their relationship.	From this, we get a sense of…

Thinking more deeply: **looking beyond the literal**

This is a difficult poem because the language appears in some cases to describe literal things: the mother is described as watching from the 'far bank', yet is also 'inside' the poet and on her 'back', which suggests the mother is both real and unreal. Rivers are also sometimes used symbolically to represent the barrier between life and death that must be crossed.

Task

8. What might be the 'burden' the speaker carries? Why might the burden have disappeared or lessened?

ANALYSING PROSE OR DRAMA TEXTS

When you analyse a prose or drama extract, you need to take the same approach: aim to identify techniques in relation to a particular focus and then explore the effects created.

Read the following task in relation to the text that follows.

> Comment closely on the following passage, paying particular attention to ways in which Jafta presents the narrator's thoughts in this passage.

Task

9. Begin by making notes identifying the particular techniques you wish to comment on, for example:

   a) choice of vocabulary, literary devices (imagery, symbolism), sound (alliteration, assonance) or verbal patterns (repetition).

   b) use of short or long sentences for effect, or structural shifts in focus through paragraphing (change, time, action followed by reflection).

In this extract, a mother has returned to her home village after many years away.

Maria bent down and kissed me on the lips – a dry and unemotive gesture. She smiled, picked up the larger of the two suitcases and placed it on her head. Then she started walking ahead of me. I picked up the other case, placed it on my head and put both my hands in the small of my back to steady myself. Then I followed her. I looked at Maria's straight back, the proud way she held her head and the determination with which she walked. I tried desperately to think of something to say, but could not find the words. Thoughts were spinning in my head, but my mouth remained closed and empty. So we continued in silence, this stranger – my daughter – and I.

So this was it. My homecoming. What did I expect? The village to come out in celebration of a long-lost daughter who had come home. How long had it been? Forty years? It must have been about forty years. How I have lost track of time. How could I be expected to keep track of the time, when I could only measure it against myself in a foreign land? When I planted seeds but never had the chance to see them grow, bore children but never watched them grow… when I had to make myself understood in a foreign tongue… had to learn how an electric kettle works, how and when to put the stove off, that doors are not opened to strangers, and that you do not greet everyone you meet with a handshake.

Milly Jafta, 'The Homecoming'

Wider reading

Milly Jafta was born in South Africa in the 1950s. This was her first published story. It is set in Namibia, which, like South Africa had been colonised by European countries, before gaining independence in 1990. Like South Africa, **apartheid** was part of Namibian life until recent times.

Glossary

apartheid: institutionalised racial segregation and discrimination

Final Task

Task

10. Write two paragraphs analysing the passage in response to the set task. Comment on at least two techniques or ways in which the writer presents the narrator's thoughts.

Checklist for success

✓ Explain what the effect is of the features you identified in the note-taking stage.

✓ Draw some conclusions about what they tell us about the narrator's feelings, perhaps commenting on how this reflects not just on her personal experience but on wider social or racial issues.

Plenary

Explain the process you would use to analyse a short text to a partner. Try to recall the three main steps you would use to make sure you made fruitful comments on the material.

1.10 Developing an interpretation

Big question
- How can texts be read in different ways?

WHAT IS INTERPRETATION?
When readers respond to texts, they do so in different ways. Part of the response will be emotional ('Am I moved by what happens?'), but readers also want to make sense of what they think the text is 'about'. This could relate to what the writer's concerns are, but a reader may see things in the text that the writer didn't intend or that reflect their own concerns and ideas. These multiple ways of reading a text are **interpretations**.

Key term
interpretation: evaluation and explanation of the different ideas within a text

WAYS OF SEEING
Here is a summary of a short story from 1922 by Katherine Mansfield, called 'The Garden Party'.

A full version of 'The Garden Party' is provided in the Teacher Resource.

A rich family is about to hold a glamorous garden party. Workmen and servants work hard to prepare. However, just as it is about to start the family finds out that a poor neighbour, a labourer with a family of five, has been killed in an accident, leaving his family penniless. Laura, the central character and younger daughter of the rich family, feels that it is wrong for the party to go ahead, but it does. Her older sister and her mother persuade her she is being 'silly'. She decides to 'forget' thinking about the death until after the party is over. When it is finished, her mother sends her to the dead man's cottage with some leftover food from the party. Laura is frightened but on seeing the body finds it beautiful. Meeting her brother on the way out, she is unable to express what she feels.

Task

1. Based on this plot outline alone, what ideas or issues do you think Mansfield might be exploring? You could think about:
   - the fact that the main character is a girl on the cusp of adulthood
   - the status of the two families
   - the way Laura, her mother and sister interact.
2. Responding at a personal level is also important. What are your own immediate responses to the story?
   a) Which characters would you most empathise with?
   b) In what ways does the story remind you of any situations you have experienced or read about?
   c) What aspects of the story do you find most interesting?

EXPLORING ONE INTERPRETATION

Task

3. Now read this extended extract from towards the end of the story. Does this passage support one or more of the interpretations you considered? Do you respond to it personally in the way you expected?

'It was a horrible affair all the same,' said Mr Sheridan. 'The chap was married too. Lived just below in the lane, and leaves a wife and half a dozen kiddies, so they say.'

An awkward little silence fell. Mrs Sheridan fidgeted with her cup. Really, it was very tactless of father…

> Mother feels father will upset the children by dwelling on the facts.

Suddenly she looked up. There on the table were all those sandwiches, cakes, puffs, all uneaten, all going to be wasted. She had one of her brilliant ideas.

'I know,' she said. 'Let's make up a basket. Let's send that poor creature some of this perfectly good food. At any rate, it will be the greatest treat for the children. Don't you agree? And she's sure to have neighbours calling in and so on. What a point to have it all ready prepared. Laura!' She jumped up. 'Get me the big basket out of the stairs cupboard.'

> Phrase depersonalises the widow.

> Mrs Sheridan suggests the leftovers will be a big 'treat' for the dead man's children.

'But, mother, do you really think it's a good idea?' said Laura.

Again, how curious, she seemed to be different from them all. To take scraps from their party. Would the poor woman really like that?

> Laura questions the decision.

'Of course! What's the matter with you to-day? An hour or two ago you were insisting on us being sympathetic, and now –'

Oh well! Laura ran for the basket. It was filled, it was heaped by her mother.

'Take it yourself, darling,' said she. 'Run down just as you are. No, wait, take the arum lilies too. People of that class are so impressed by arum lilies.'

> Gives mother's viewpoint on 'that class'.

'The stems will ruin her lace frock,' said practical Jose.

So they would. Just in time. 'Only the basket, then. And, Laura!' – her mother followed her out of the marquee – 'don't on any account –'

> Incomplete sentence suggests a warning – of what?

'What mother?'

No, better not put such ideas into the child's head! 'Nothing! Run along.'

It was just growing dusky as Laura shut their garden gates. A big dog ran by like a shadow. The road gleamed white, and down below in the hollow the little cottages were in deep shade. How quiet it seemed after the afternoon. Here she was going down the hill to somewhere where a man lay dead, and she couldn't realise it. Why couldn't she? She stopped a minute. And it seemed to her that kisses, voices, tinkling spoons, laughter, the smell of crushed grass were somehow inside her. She had no room for anything else. How strange! She looked up at the pale sky, and all she thought was, 'Yes, it was the most successful party.'

Now the broad road was crossed. The lane began, smoky and dark. Women in shawls and men's tweed caps hurried by. Men hung over the palings; the children played in the doorways. A low hum came from the mean little cottages. In some of them there was a flicker of light, and a shadow, crab-like, moved across the window. Laura bent her head and hurried on. She wished now she had put on a coat. How her frock shone! And the big hat with the velvet streamer – if only it was another hat! Were the people looking at her? They must be. It was a mistake to have come; she knew all along it was a mistake. Should she go back even now?

No, too late. This was the house. It must be. A dark knot of people stood outside. Beside the gate an old, old woman with a crutch sat in a chair, watching. She had her feet on a newspaper. The voices stopped as Laura drew near. The group parted. It was as though she was expected, as though they had known she was coming here.

Katherine Mansfield, 'The Garden Party' (1922)

Task

4. The issue of class is central to the text, but what is Mansfield's perspective?

   One interpretation could be that Mansfield is critical of the attitude of the upper classes to the poor. Is this supported by the text? Consider these questions:

   a) How is Laura's mother presented? (What does she say and how does she respond to the situation?)

   b) How is Laura presented? (In what way is her perspective presented as different from that of the family as a whole?)

5. Although you are looking at the text through a class perspective, what Mansfield has to say is still open to debate.

   a) Whose is the dominant voice in the text? (Whose perspective is the story told from?)

   b) What voice, if any, is given to the poor?

   c) In what way are the poor seen as 'alien' or dangerous?

   d) In what way are the poor '**commodified**'? (How might you see the sending of the basket of leftovers?)

6. Bearing these approaches in mind, consider the following questions:

   a) Where, on balance, do you think Mansfield's sympathies lie?

   b) How do you feel about the way the classes are represented?

   Explain your ideas using interpretative phrases.

   I think/it seems/it could be argued

   It is worth considering…

   One way of looking at… is

   Perhaps/maybe/conceivably

MULTIPLE INTERPRETATIONS

There are also other lenses through which a text can be viewed. For example:

- Gender issues. How significant is it in the story that Laura is a girl?
- Social/historical contexts. How significant is it that Mansfield is writing about the world she knew growing up as a girl in early-20th-century New Zealand?
- Narrative or psychological theories. To what extent does the story depend on a reader's understanding of other stories, myths or the power of particular symbols?

This third interpretation, relating to the **intertextuality** of stories, is worth exploring.

Many countries' myths and legends feature stories in which a small child, often a girl, is sent out on a quest into a forbidden or unwelcoming place, such as a forest, where she encounters creatures or adults who threaten her. Most famous is the fairy tale of 'Little Red Riding Hood'. Such stories are often associated with a metaphorical journey of 'growing up'.

Key terms

commodified: turned into a commodity – something to be bought or sold

intertextuality: the way in which a text relates or alludes to other texts

Task

7. Read from 'Oh well. Laura ran for the basket' to the end. In what way does this part of the passage support this interpretation? Think about:

a) The ways in which the story could link to 'Little Red Riding Hood'. In the original fairy tale, where is Red Riding Hood going? What is she carrying?

b) How Laura's journey to the dead man's house is described. Think about her anxious feelings, the time of day and the references to light/dark. What might they suggest about the journey?

c) How the people in the area she sees are described. Think about the woman by the gate.

8. Having read the extract, and the plot outline, develop your own interpretation of the story. Make notes, jotting down evidence from the text to support your view.

a) How do you respond to the text personally? (Do you have particular sympathy with any characters, or have a view about the way people or ideas are presented?)

b) What interpretations from this unit seem most convincing?

Wider reading

There are many stories that could be classed as 'coming of age' tales – that is, ones in which a young person moves from innocence to experience. In 'The Darkness Out There' by Penelope Lively, a girl of similar age is told a gruesome tale about how a German pilot was left to die in some local woods. You might see some similarities with 'The Garden Party'.

Final Task

Task

9. Write 150 words offering your own interpretation of what you think the passage is about.

I think the story explores the idea that…

Checklist for success

✓ Use 'interpretative' language such as: *I think/it seems/it could be argued.*

✓ Include reference to the text or quotations as supporting evidence.

Plenary

Think about one other text you are studying. Note down any ways in which the interpretations you explored in this unit might be applied to it.

1.11 Structuring an essay

Big question

- How do you structure your essays effectively?

WHAT IS ESSAY STRUCTURE?

Structure relates to the way in which you organise and present your ideas in response to a task. This might be as simple as what you choose to include in each paragraph, but it could also relate to the priority you give to certain ideas, how you develop an argument, or how you begin and end a response.

STRUCTURING IDEAS

The key to an effective response will be to present your ideas – or those of the writer – in a clear and fluent way. This means that:

- the structure of your response must be easy to follow
- there should be a logical progression in ideas
- ideas should be effectively linked.

How would this work in practice? For a start, you need to decide quickly what the core focus of your response will be, and the order of ideas you will include.

Look at this task:

> Discuss the ways in which the writers of two stories you have studied explore how characters deal with the transition from childhood to adulthood.

This tells you to explore the ideas widely – you are not arguing for or against a particular view.

You need to comment on what the writer in each case does.

This is the focus.

For this task, you would need to read the whole of 'The Garden Party' (available online) and one other story about childhood. Another story by Katherine Mansfield, 'Her First Ball', also deals with growing up and can be found online.

All tasks require you to write about various ways, methods or effects – not just one. Even if you decide that there is one overall approach to how the authors present the transition to adulthood, you will still need to give different examples from the two texts.

For the task above, a student has noted the following about 'The Garden Party', and has begun to think about 'Her First Ball':

She presents the transition in 'The Garden Party' as:

– difficult

– shocking

– frightening

– beautiful

– mysterious

– sad

Some of these are also true of 'Her First Ball'.

Not all of these ideas will necessarily find their way into a response, but they could help you to decide on the overarching structure.

> **Paragraph 1:**
>
> Introduction – a clear statement about how the two stories address the transition. This needs to say something meaningful – perhaps an overview outlining the differences and similarities between the two texts. For example:
>
> > Both 'The Garden Party' and 'Her First Ball' present the glamour of adult celebration, as well as the difficult emotional journeys of their protagonists, but they end with different perspectives.
>
> **Paragraph 2:**
>
> Entering the adult world is difficult – not knowing what to say (for example, how to challenge authority) or the 'right way to act'. Laura lacks the confidence to challenge her mother; Leila doesn't know how to conduct herself during the ball.
>
> **Paragraph 3:**
>
> Lack of experience means that both Laura and Leila are shocked by the realities of life (the impact of Laura seeing the dead body; Leila's dancing with an older man whose words cast a shadow over her enjoyment).

Alternatively, a question focusing specifically on a character's development would allow you to work through the text or texts stage by stage:

> At the start of 'The Garden Party', Laura is presented as excited by the responsibility of organising the garden party.
>
> As the story progresses, Laura's interactions with the workers and her mother make her question her perspectives; shows her realising that growing up is 'difficult' and 'mysterious'.
>
> Towards the end, Laura has to face the realities of life, the outside world, ideas about mortality – 'shocking' but also 'beautiful'.

EFFECTIVE CRITICAL LANGUAGE

Whatever order you decide to follow for your essay, when you express or discuss ideas, there are a number of techniques you can use to ensure your work sounds engaged and scholarly at the same time. The box below explains some of these techniques, giving examples from 'The Garden Party'.

Skill or technique	Meaning	Example (based on 'The Garden Party')
1. Use literary or linguistic terminology appropriately and purposefully.	Technical terms can help a reader understand what you are commenting on, but make sure there is a clear reason for using the term.	Lilies are *symbolically* associated with funerals, so it is *ironic* that they are not sent to the widow's house in 'The Garden Party' for fear of staining Laura's dress.
2. Vary the way in which you explain the author's choices.	Sometimes for impact you can assert ideas strongly. At other times, a more tentative, interpretative tone is needed. But you will always need to refer to the writer and what they do.	Mansfield *draws our attention to* the motif of the lilies, but their meaning is uncertain. The notion of them staining Laura's dress *might suggest* that she too could be 'stained' by the experience of death.
3. Use discourse markers and tenses to express different times or episodes in a text.	If you are asking your reader to make leaps between different sections of a text, make the process as clear as possible.	*When* Laura stands in front of the dead body *at the end of the story*, we can't help thinking of the tall workman whom she had observed *earlier* smelling the lavender, a moment that had a profound effect on her.
4. Use discourse markers to develop, contrast, explain ideas.	As you explore possible ideas, your language should direct your reader around the possibilities.	*While* Laura's mother seems unaffected by the reality of the death, Laura, *in contrast*, feels it deeply. *Yet* she gets no support from her older sister.

The following is an extract from one student's essay discussing how Mansfield explores the social conditions in her stories.

> We see the differences between the social classes when the story mentions the 'men' who have come to 'put up the marquee'. This means the family can afford a marquee and that they have people to put it up for them. Laura speaks to the men and tries to copy her mother's voice but thinks it sounds 'fearfully affected'. Speech is a marker of social status. Laura recognises this. Speech lets Laura down when she has to see the dead body. All she can say is 'Forgive my hat'. She is embarrassed by its showiness. Words are inadequate.

Task

1. Identify:
   a) places where the writer's name should be used
   b) sentences that could be usefully joined by discourse markers (perhaps conjunctions such as 'and' or 'so', adverbs or adverbials such as 'In this way', or relative pronouns such as 'which' or 'that')
   c) places where verbs or phrases could be added (or replace current ones) to express a more tentative interpretation ('suggest', 'might mean').

2. Now rewrite the whole paragraph.

QUOTATION AND REFERENCE

Another important part of critical writing is how you reference evidence. There are various ways you can do this, but it is worth considering the following.

Method	Example	Why this method is useful
Quoting a longer sentence or line which is important in its own right	Towards the end of the story, Laura wonders about the dead man: '*What did garden-parties and baskets and lace frocks matter to him?*' The question seems to sum up the core concerns of the text all in one go: the fripperies of a privileged life against mortality as well as the brutal reality of life, which the child is seeing for the first time.	This is useful if you want to explore a larger idea, perhaps as a prelude for discussing elements of the quotation, or to sum up an approach that has already been discussed.
Quoting individual words or phrases, and embedding them in your explanation.	Laura sees the fripperies of her privileged life as fragile against the assault of reality. She wonders what '*lace frocks*' matter to the dead man. The item is well chosen, expressing the superficial beauty that can be measured against the '*beauty*' of death Laura observes.	This is an effective way of exploring the impact of a particular word or phrase, or to identify and analyse it as part of a pattern (for example, 'lace frocks', 'lilies' and the hat she wears).
Paraphrasing or restating ideas in your own words without quoting.	Laura finds the experience of seeing the worker's corpse overwhelming and transformative; it raises questions in her mind about her child-like attachment to mortal things and ideas.	You may wish to refer concisely to an episode (a shorter section of a given scene or passage) in a text without exploring it word by word; equally, restating or rewording an event or description can indicate your understanding of what has happened.

Knowing what to include when you quote from a text and how to introduce the quotation are especially important.

DOs

Only quote what is absolutely necessary. This is important because:
- you need to focus the examiner's attention on the right detail
- you don't want to waste valuable time copying out a long sentence or paragraph.

Adjust the grammar of your sentence and crop the quotation if needed. This is important because:
- you need to guide the reader fluently through what you say
- it will also help you in selecting only what is absolutely necessary.

Example:
You wish to make a point about Mrs Sheridan's lack of understanding about the death of the local man.

Possible evidence:
'Let's send that poor creature some of this perfectly good food. At any rate, it will be the greatest treat for the children.'

How to do it:

Select the words and phrases from the quotation which can fit into your point from your view (as you can't write from Mrs Sheridan's first-person perspective). Paraphrase any parts which you do not wish to comment on (e.g. 'poor creature'). If it is a section of a sentence that you are embedding, then you simply need to include the quotation marks and insert the quoted words.

Comment on, or analyse the language choice – particular words, phrases or formal elements, such as punctuation.

For example:

Mrs Sheridan shows her lack of real empathy for the grieving family by suggesting sending food 'will be the greatest treat for the children'. The phrase 'greatest treat' implies that the unique experience of eating leftovers from a party conducted by their social superiors will in some way compensate for their loss.

Task

3. Here is a quotation from the extract you read from 'The Garden Party':
   'People of that class are so impressed by arum lilies.' (Laura's mother)
   Imagine you want to make a further point about the mother's character, or about social class, or any further point of your own. How would you use this quotation? Would you:
   - quote it in full, and offer an explanation?
   - select a specific word or phrase and explore it in detail?
   - paraphrase the quotation – and the section of the text it comes from?

4. Now, using the quotation or parts of it, write a sentence or two in the style of one of the examples above from the grid or from the example about the leftovers, above. Try to embed the quotation, or parts of it, in the explanatory sentence, so that you do not break the grammatical flow of your writing.
   Try using one of these sentence starters if you wish.

   Laura's mother shows herself to be…

   Mansfield sheds light on the different social classes through…

   After the party, Laura's mother agrees to send flowers…

Final Task

Read these two paragraphs from a response dealing with 'The Garden Party' and 'Her First Ball'. This addresses the question about the way in which Mansfield explores 'coming-of-age' in young people.

A full version of both stories is provided in the Teacher Resource.

At the start of the 'The Garden Party', the division between the adult and child world is exemplified by Laura's mother's decision to 'leave everything' to the children in terms of organising the party. She also states, 'Forget I am your mother,' a phrase which takes on ironic significance later in the story, when Laura begins to question, perhaps for the first time, the wisdom and judgement of her parents and siblings. In 'Her First Ball', the division seems to be blurred by Leila's inability to know 'Exactly when the Ball began' as if the Ball itself represents a shifting moment in time between childhood and adulthood.

In 'The Garden Party', Mansfield further develops our understanding of the troublesome journey from child to adult in the episode when Laura is sent to instruct the workmen where to position the marquee. She tries to copy her mother's voice but 'that sounded so fearfully affected that she was ashamed, and stammered like a little girl'. Laura is aware that adopting her mother's language is 'affected', suggesting either a criticism of the elevated tones of the upper classes or her own lack of readiness to step into the adult world. It is revealing that she slips back into child-like language and speaks 'like a little girl'. However, the simile, 'like a little girl' implies that she is no longer a child. She is caught between two worlds, much as Leila is in 'Her First Ball' as she negotiates her first dances on the dance-floor.

Task

5. Now identify:
   - the two episodes from 'The Garden Party' selected for comment
   - the key point being made about the child/adult world in each paragraph
   - how the use of quotations differs (i.e. where a longer quotation is used; where specific words are analysed)
   - where particular language choices or literacy devices or features are referred to
   - a sentence that sums up the student's interpretation of Laura's situation and links it to Leila's.

Plenary

Create your own question for any one of the texts you are studying, using one of these formulations.

Discuss the ways in which [name of writer] explores [idea, issue or concern] in [name of text or texts].

OR

Discuss [name of writer]'s presentation of [name of character] considering [his/her] significance to the [play/novel].

Now, decide how you would approach the question, planning the order in which you would present your various points.

DEVELOPING YOUR WRITING

When you write about literature, you need to consider a number of different features of your writing.

Everything starts with knowing your texts well, so you will need to read them several times to make sure you are confident in your knowledge. However, it's not only what happens in a text or *what* a text is concerned with that is important, but also how it is communicated. This gives you a literary understanding of the text.

In essays, you show that literary understanding by looking closely at the choices the writer has made – the language, imagery and structure of the text. When you look closely at features of the writing and discuss them in class, you will find that different people will respond in slightly different ways, showing that everyone has a personal response. Sometimes you might modify your own views because of what someone else has said, which may have highlighted an aspect of the text you had not considered. When you write an essay, you need to put all these aspects together in an organised way that can be read and understood easily.

These are all the different elements on which you will be assessed. Each is listed separately in the chart below, but the paragraph above demonstrates that these aren't really separate strands; they interweave and support each other constantly.

Knowledge and understanding	You need to show knowledge of your text by using specific references and quotations. You also need to show a literary understanding of its form – prose, poetry or drama – and how the form is used to communicate the text's concerns. Some knowledge of context is also important, which might be historical, political, literary or philosophical. The type of context does not matter, but it's really important that it's directly relevant to the text and what you have to say.
Analysis	When you quote from the text, you should try to say something about the writer's choices of words, images or structure, considering the effect they have. Make wider comments on narrative, poetic or dramatic structure using references. Always aim to write about ways in which the writer presents ideas, rather than just the ideas themselves.
Personal response	Show how you respond to and interpret the text. Consider how the writer's expression of ideas helps you understand the concerns, characters and plot events.
Communicating effectively	Clear communication of your ideas is important. Structuring your ideas well is key: aim for a clear opening to your essay that shows that you understand the question; write using connected paragraphs to develop ideas; and work towards a conclusion that returns to the question.
Literary criticism (A Level only)	This is particularly relevant to A Level, but you can of course include it in AS Level responses if you wish. The aim is to show that you are aware that works of literature can be read in different ways; their meaning and people's responses to them are not fixed. There are different ways of doing this: you could make reference to a critical theory; you could cite what a particular critic has said; or you can offer alternative readings – all these are fine and a combination is great.

Remember: in an examination it may not be possible to present your points as clearly and accurately as you would like, but as long as the meaning is clear and the point is valid, you would still gain credit.

Chapter 2

Studying prose fiction

This chapter explores in detail the essential concepts and skills required when studying prose fiction as part of Literature in English at an advanced level. You will learn how to approach prose texts by engaging with examples of prose fiction from different time periods and from a variety of genres and forms. You will develop your skills and confidence in analysing the language of prose fiction and also in writing effectively about character, narration, narrative structure, contexts, and wider issues and concerns. You will also develop your own personal responses to texts and learn how to engage meaningfully with alternative readings and interpretations.

In addition, you will develop and extend your own writing skills, building towards full exam-style responses at the end of the chapter, and you will have the chance to evaluate your progress against a range of sample responses.

2.1 Exploring characterisation in prose fiction

Big question

- How do writers create memorable characters?

WHAT DO CHARACTERS DO?

> ### Task
>
> 1. Think of your favourite character from a novel or short story.
>   - **a)** Who or what do they love most? Who or what do they hate?
>   - **b)** Where or when were they happiest? Or saddest?
>   - **c)** What is their greatest fear? Or their greatest challenge?
>   - **d)** Do they change over the course of the story? If so, how?

Characters draw us into stories. When we care about a character, good or bad, we want to follow them into their world and see it through their eyes.

The novelist E.M. Forster said that characters can be described as either 'flat' or 'round'. A flat character is a type or even a caricature: one who does not change as the story progresses. A round character, on the other hand, is convincing: a character who develops through the story. The test, says Forster, of the round character is that they are 'capable of surprising in a convincing way'.

> ### Task
>
> 2. Do you agree with Forster's definitions? Discuss your reasons.

FIRST IMPRESSIONS: CREATING CHARACTERS

There are many ways a writer can make a character memorable.

When you write about characters, it is important to think about *how* you find out about them and how this makes you respond. For example, does the writer show you the character mainly from the outside or the inside, or both?

USING EXTERNAL FEATURES TO INTRODUCE A CHARACTER

Characters can be introduced with a description of the way they look, dress, talk, move or act. Even the way they are named can be revealing.

> ### Task
>
> 3. Think again about your favourite character, but this time consider how they are presented to you by the writer. In the story, how does the writer describe the following:
>   - **a)** their physical appearance
>   - **b)** their past
>   - **c)** other characters' views of them
>   - **d)** the way they speak
>   - **e)** what they are thinking or feeling
>   - **f)** what they believe.

Read the following extract and think about how Dickens uses external features to introduce this character.

> Sir Leicester Dedlock is only a **baronet**, but there is no mightier baronet than he. His family is as old as the hills, and infinitely more respectable. He has a general opinion that the world might get on without hills but would be done up without Dedlocks. He would on the whole admit nature to be a good idea (a little low, perhaps, when not enclosed with a park-fence), but an idea dependent for its execution on your great county families. He is a gentleman of strict conscience, disdainful of all littleness and meanness and ready on the shortest notice to die any death you may please to mention rather than give occasion for the least impeachment of his integrity. He is an honourable, obstinate, truthful, high-spirited, intensely prejudiced, perfectly unreasonable man.
>
> Sir Leicester is twenty years, full measure, older than my Lady. He will never see sixty-five again, nor perhaps sixty-six, nor yet sixty-seven. He has a twist of the **gout** now and then and walks a little stiffly. He is of a worthy presence, with his light-grey hair and whiskers, his fine shirt-frill, his pure-white waistcoat, and his blue coat with bright buttons always buttoned. He is ceremonious, stately, most polite on every occasion to my Lady, and holds her personal attractions in the highest estimation. His gallantry to my Lady, which has never changed since he courted her, is the one little touch of romantic fancy in him.
>
> Charles Dickens, *Bleak House* (1852/3)

Title is 'only a baronet', but to him high status matters.

Simile: dismissive attitude to nature, but also suggests they are ancient family.

His main concern is how others view him.

*Contradictory postmodifying adjectives and 'perfectly unreasonable' – almost an **oxymoron**.*

Glossary

baronet: the lowest hereditary British title; a baronet can use the title 'Sir'
gout: a disease causing joint pain, often associated with excessive consumption of rich food and drink

Task

4. **a)** Make notes on your first impressions of Sir Leicester Dedlock. Consider his family name and its associations.

   b) Now consider the character questions on the previous page. From the list, identify what information we are given and what at this stage, is missing.

   c) How do you think we are meant to respond to this character?

Key term

oxymoron: a figure of speech in which opposite or contradictory ideas or terms are combined (for example, 'sweet sorrow')

It is important to analyse the language the writer chooses to describe a character. Look at how one student has annotated the first paragraph of the Dickens extract above..

Task

5. Make notes on the use of different features to create character in the second paragraph.

   a) Which features are *external*, and which are *internal*?

   b) Why is Sir Leicester's exact age unclear?

   c) Why is so much information given about his clothing?

   d) Finally, does the information about 'my Lady' and his feelings for her alter our overall impression of his character?

Wider reading

Charles Dickens famously used unusual names to signal important qualities of his characters. Mr Gradgrind in *Hard Times* has a grindingly oppressive love of facts and figures, while the superficial Veneerings provide comic relief in *Our Mutual Friend*.

USING SETTING AND SYMBOLISM TO CREATE CHARACTER

Writers can also create powerful characters by describing places, objects or images that are somehow connected with them.

For example, in his novel *The Great Gatsby*, F. Scott Fitzgerald uses colour **symbolism** to create character. Gatsby, the self-made millionaire, longs for 'the green light' that glows across the bay. It becomes a **motif** that represents both Gatsby's hope of regaining his lost love Daisy Buchanan and also his jealousy. Daisy, on the other hand, is introduced using the colour white, which, rather than indicating purity, symbolises an emptiness or a moral blankness about her character.

Now read the following extract from the novel *Rebecca*, where the young narrator explores a room furnished and decorated by her predecessor in the house, the first Mrs de Winter.

> Somehow I guessed, before going to the window, that the room looked out upon the **rhododendrons**. Yes, there they were, blood-red and luscious, as I had seen them the evening before, great bushes of them, massed beneath the open window, encroaching on to the sweep of the drive itself. There was a little clearing too, between the bushes, like a miniature lawn, the grass a smooth carpet of moss, and in the centre of this, the tiny statue of a naked **faun**, his pipes to his lips. [...]
>
> This was a woman's room, graceful, fragile, the room of someone who had chosen every particle of furniture with great care, so that each chair, each vase, each small, infinitesimal thing should be in harmony with one another, and with her own personality. It was as though she who had arranged this room had said: 'This I will have, and this, and this,' taking piece by piece from the treasures in Manderley each object that pleased her best, ignoring the second-rate, the mediocre, laying her hand with sure and certain instinct only upon the best. There was no intermingling of style, no confusing of period, and the result was perfection in a strange and startling way, not coldly formal like the drawing-room shown to the public, but vividly alive, having something of the same glow and brilliance that the rhododendrons had, massed there, beneath the window.
>
> Daphne du Maurier, *Rebecca* (1938)

Key terms

symbolism: device where an object, image or action takes on a meaning within a story that is different from its literal sense

motif: an object, image or idea, used symbolically, that is repeated throughout a text

Glossary

rhododendron: a shrub with large clusters of bell-shaped flowers; rhododendrons were fashionable in formal gardens of English country houses

faun: a Roman rural god, represented as a man with a goat's horns, ears, legs, and tail

Task

6. Make notes on the information the narrator gives us about the room and its contents. How might this reveal the character of its previous occupant?

Now read what one student has written about how the imagery in the first paragraph relates to both the narrator and the character of the first Mrs de Winter.

The narrator notices the flowers outside of the window first. However, they are described in a way that makes them seem strangely threatening. The adjectives 'blood-red' and 'luscious' create menacing, rather than comforting imagery. The verbs 'massed' and 'encroaching' also suggest that they are in a military formation, almost planning an attack. The 'statue of a naked faun' also seems very sensual, which combined with the imagery of the 'luscious' flowers makes the view unsettling for the narrator who must now take over the space created by the first Mrs de Winter.

Task

7. **a)** What phrase does the student use to describe the overall effect of the room on the narrator?

b) Highlight where there is precise analysis of language.

c) Look up the verb 'to mass' and note down its connotations.

d) Do you agree that the 'statue of a naked faun' is 'unsettling' for the narrator? Why?

8. Write further paragraphs, modelled on the one above, commenting on the rest of the extract.

Begin by commenting on the adjectives used to describe the room:

The perfect taste and decorative skill of the first Mrs de Winter is shown by…

Comment on the effect of the rhododendrons inside the room:

The flowers are personified by their description as…

Comment, too, on how the flowers both inside and outside the room and the objects in the room could reveal the personality of the first Mrs de Winter.

Finally, what does this description also tell us about the narrator?

Thinking more deeply: **characters from the inside**

IN THEIR OWN WORDS: FIRST-PERSON NARRATION

The most direct way that we can access how a character feels and thinks is through **first-person narration**, as we follow a character's responses to people and events *in their own words*. You will need to consider, though, whether a first-person narrator is reliable in what they tell us.

Read the following passage from Charlotte Brontë's novel *Jane Eyre*. The orphan Jane has been taken to live with her aunt's family at Gateshead Hall. Here she reflects upon the family's harsh treatment of her.

> What a consternation of soul was mine that dreary afternoon!
> How all my brain was in tumult, and all my heart in insurrection!
> Yet in what darkness, what dense ignorance, was the mental battle
> fought! I could not answer the ceaseless inward question – *why*
> I thus suffered; now, at the distance of – I will not say how many
> years, I see it clearly.
>
> I was a discord in Gateshead Hall: I was like nobody there;
> I had nothing in harmony with Mrs Reed or her children, or
> her chosen **vassalage**. If they did not love me, in fact, as little
> did I love them. They were not bound to regard with affection
> a thing that could not sympathise with one amongst them; a
> heterogeneous thing, opposed to them in temperament, incapacity,
> in propensities; a useless thing, incapable of serving their interest,
> or adding to their pleasure; a noxious thing, cherishing the germs
> of indignation at their treatment, of contempt of their judgment.
>
> Charlotte Brontë, *Jane Eyre* (1847)

Key terms

first-person narration: where the narrator tells their own story using the pronouns 'I' and 'me'

Glossary

vassalage: a system or state where one person has power over another

Task

9. First consider what this passage reveals about the character of the narrator Jane.
   - Is she a mild-mannered woman who can forgive and forget?
   - Is she a strong-willed woman with a deep sense of injustice?
   - Is she a woman with very low self-esteem?

   How else might you describe her?

10. Now consider what we learn about the narrator's thoughts and feelings.

    In the first paragraph:

    a) What does the punctuation reveal or suggest?

    b) How does the narrator's choice of words and images reveal her strong feelings?

    In the second paragraph:

    a) What is the effect of the narrator's repeated use of the word 'thing'?

    b) What are her views of Mrs Reed and her children? What particular words reveal her intense feelings about them?

Wider reading

The novel *Jane Eyre* is a **bildungsroman**, a novel that follows the development of a character from youth through to adulthood and maturity. A popular genre in the 19th century, examples include Charles Dickens's *David Copperfield* and George Eliot's *The Mill on the Floss*. Twentieth-century examples include James Joyce's *Portrait of the Artist as a Young Man* and J.D. Salinger's *The Catcher in the Rye*.

HOW WRITERS USE DIALOGUE TO CREATE CHARACTER

In stories, a writer can use dialogue to:
- create or reveal aspects of a character
- develop or progress the narrative
- explore relationships between characters.

When analysing dialogue, it is useful to think about the context of the speech. Who is the character speaking to and why? Consider not just *what* a character is saying, but also how they say it. What might their words reveal, or even conceal?

In the following extract from Tsitsi Dangarembga's novel *Nervous Conditions*, the narrator discovers some surprising information about her aunt Maiguru's past.

'Is it true, Maiguru?' I asked later that afternoon when I went to the verandah to read and found my aunt marking her books there. 'Do you really have a Master's Degree?'

Maiguru was flattered. 'Didn't you know?' she smiled at me over the top of her glasses. How could I have known? No one had ever mentioned it to me.

'But Maiguru,' I answered immediately, emboldened by the thought of my aunt obtaining a Master's Degree, 'did you ever say?'

'Did you ever ask me?' she countered, and continued, 'Yes, we both studied, your uncle and I, in South Africa, for our Bachelor's Degrees and in England for our Master's.'

'I thought you went to look after Babamukuru,' I said. 'That's all people ever say.'

Maiguru snorted. 'And what do you expect? Why should a woman go all that way and put up with all those problems if not to look after her husband?'

Maiguru was more serious than she had ever been before. Her seriousness changed her from a sweet, soft dove to something more like a wasp. 'That's what they like to think I did,' she continued sourly. The lower half of her face, and only the lower half, because it did not quite reach her eyes, set itself into sullen lines of discontent. She bent over her books to hide them, and to prove she was not unhappy she made a chuckling sound, I think, she thought gaily, but sounding pained. 'Whatever they thought,' she said, 'much good did it do them! I still studied for that degree and got it in spite of all of them – your uncle, your grandparents, and the rest of your family. Can you tell me now that they aren't pleased that I did, even if they don't admit it? No! Your uncle wouldn't be able to do half the things he does if I didn't work as well!'

[…]

'What it is,' she sighed 'to have to choose between self and security. When I was in England I glimpsed for a little while the things I could have been, the things I could have done if – if – if things were – different – But there was Babawa Chido and the children and the family. And does anyone realise, does anyone appreciate what sacrifices were made? As for me, no one even thinks about the things I gave up.' She collected herself. 'But that's how it goes, Sisi Tambu! And when you have a good man and lovely children it makes it all worthwhile.'

Tsitsi Dangarembga, *Nervous Conditions* (1988)

Task

11. Think about how Dangarembga uses dialogue to present Maiguru's character in the extract:

   a) What does Maiguru reveal and what language does she use?

   b) How is Maiguru's speech described by the narrator?

   c) Which word or words best describe how the relationship between the two women is presented here?

   > competitive   respectful   uneasy   resentful   light-hearted

   d) What other words might describe their relationship?

A student has begun to analyse the extract here.

> Initially Dangarembga shows that Maiguru is pleased that her niece is finally asking her about her education. She uses the verb 'flattered' to describe Maiguru's satisfied reaction to her niece's questions about her past and the verb 'snorted' to indicate her incredulous response to the narrator's belief that she had only travelled to England for her husband and not to further her own education. Maiguru also frequently uses questions to challenge her niece's views and preconceptions. However, as the conversation continues, Dangarembga reveals another more serious side and possible regretful side to Maiguru's character…

— topic sentence and overview

— specific language references to support point

— point about punctuation and its effect

Task

12. Now continue the analysis focusing particularly on the writer's use of dialogue and its effects. Consider:

   a) the change in metaphors the narrator uses to describe Maiguru

   b) the use of the adverb 'sourly' and the phrase 'sullen lines of discontent'

   c) the punctuation used in Maiguru's speech

   d) the significance of the dashes in the last paragraph

   e) what this extract might reveal about Maiguru and her choices.

Thinking more deeply: **character development**

Once a main character has been introduced into a narrative, then perhaps the most significant way a writer can develop them is to present them with a challenging situation or dilemma. How do they react? And what do their reactions reveal about them?

Here are some questions you could ask:

- What exactly is the challenge or problem they face?
- Does their response surprise you, given what you have learned about them so far?
- Does the challenge or event change them? How is this shown?

Read the following extract from the late-Victorian novel *The Picture of Dorian Gray* by Oscar Wilde. This extract shows Dorian, reflecting upon his recent rejection of his lover, the actress Sibyl Vane.

Cruelty! Had he been cruel? It was the girl's fault, not his. He had dreamed of her as a great artist, had given his love to her because he had thought her great. Then she had disappointed him. She had been shallow and unworthy. And, yet, a feeling of infinite regret came over him, as he thought of her lying at his feet sobbing like a little child. He remembered with what callousness he had watched her. Why had he been made like that? Why had such a soul been given to him? But he had suffered also. During the three terrible hours that the play had lasted, he had lived centuries of pain, aeon upon aeon of torture. His life was well worth hers. She had marred him for a moment, if he had wounded her for an age. Besides, women were better suited to bear sorrow than men. They lived on their emotions. They only thought of their emotions. When they took lovers, it was merely to have someone with whom they could have scenes. Lord Henry had told him that, and Lord Henry knew what women were. Why should he trouble about Sibyl Vane? She was nothing to him now.

Oscar Wilde, *The Picture of Dorian Gray* (1890)

Third-person narration, but we are presented with Dorian's point of view and his internal conflicts.

Questions indicate his initial self-doubt.

Dorian justifies his rejection of Sibyl. The writer gives us access to Dorian's inner thoughts.

Reference to Lord Henry indicates the powerful influence of other characters upon him.

Simple declarative final sentence suggests he has reached a decision.

Task

13. Now consider the annotations. Make your own notes to support and extend these annotations.

14. Using your notes to the annotations above, which of the following adjectives do you think best describes the character of Dorian in this extract? Give reasons for your response.

| guilty | tortured | selfish | indecisive | callous | woman-hating | easily-influenced |

Final Task

Now read the following passage from E.M. Forster's Edwardian novel *A Room with a View*, which features George Emerson and Lucy Honeychurch, young people who have recently met while on a tour of Italy. Lucy faints, after witnessing a violent and fatal fight between two Italians in a square in Florence. She wakes up in George's arms; he has also seen the killing and comes to her aid. Shortly after, the pair walk back to the hotel together and reflect upon what they have seen.

Glossary

pension: a small Italian hotel
River Arno: the main river which runs through the city of Florence

'For something tremendous has happened; I must face it without getting muddled. It isn't exactly that a man has died.' Something warned Lucy that she must stop him.

'It has happened,' he repeated, 'and I mean to find out what it is.'

'Mr Emerson —'

He turned towards her frowning, as if she had disturbed him in some abstract quest.

'I want to ask you something before we go in.'

They were close to their **pension**. She stopped and leant her elbows against the parapet of the embankment. He did likewise. There is at times a magic in identity of position; it is one of the things that have suggested to us eternal comradeship. She moved her elbows before saying:

'I have behaved ridiculously.'

He was following his own thoughts.

'I was never so much ashamed of myself in my life; I cannot think what came over me.'

'I nearly fainted myself,' he said; but she felt that her attitude repelled him.

'Well, I owe you a thousand apologies.'

'Oh, all right.'

'And — this is the real point — you know how silly people are gossiping — ladies especially, I am afraid — you understand what I mean?'

'I'm afraid I don't.'

'I mean, would you not mention it to any one, my foolish behaviour?'

'Your behaviour? Oh, yes, all right — all right.'

'Thank you so much. And would you —'

She could not carry her request any further. The river was rushing below them, almost black in the advancing night. He had thrown her photographs into it, and then he had told her the reason. It struck her that it was hopeless to look for chivalry in such a man. He would do her no harm by idle gossip; he was trustworthy, intelligent, and even kind; he might even have a high opinion of her. But he lacked chivalry; his thoughts, like his behaviour, would not be modified by awe. It was useless to say to him, 'And would you —' and hope that he would complete the sentence for himself, averting his eyes from her nakedness like the knight in that beautiful picture. She had been in his arms, and he remembered it, just as he remembered the blood on the photographs that she had bought in Alinari's shop. It was not exactly that a man had died; something had happened to the living: they had come to a situation where character tells, and where childhood enters upon the branching paths of Youth.

'Well, thank you so much,' she repeated, 'How quickly these accidents do happen, and then one returns to the old life!'

'I don't.'

Anxiety moved her to question him.

His answer was puzzling: 'I shall probably want to live.'

'But why, Mr Emerson? What do you mean?'

'I shall want to live, I say.'

Leaning her elbows on the parapet, she contemplated the **River Arno**, whose roar was suggesting some unexpected melody to her ears.

E.M. Forster, *A Room with a View* (1908)

Task

15. Look first at the dialogue in the passage:

a) What differences do you notice in the way both characters speak after the event?

b) How does their dialogue reveal the different ways in which they react to what they have seen?

c) What is Lucy's immediate concern?

d) How would you describe George's state of mind? How does Forster use speech to reveal this?

16. Now consider the following questions:

a) Whose views or thoughts are presented in this sentence: 'There is at times a magic in identity of position; it is one of the things that have suggested to us eternal comradeship'?

b) Where in the extract are we given access to Lucy's thoughts and feelings?

c) What type of character does Lucy believe George to be?

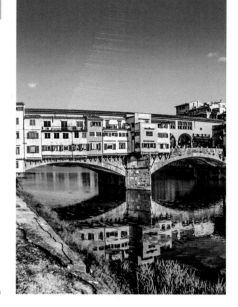

You are going to write a longer response to the task below.

> How does Forster present George Emerson and Lucy Honeychurch in this passage?

Follow the paragraph plan to organise your response.

Overview	Begin with an overall point about the narration, setting and characters featured in the passage.
Paragraph 1	Look at the opening of the extract and the differences in what each character says. How do both the content and tone of what they say differ? What might their responses reveal about them as characters?
Paragraph 2	Look at the long narrative paragraph. How are Lucy's thoughts and feelings presented here? How does Forster use language to present her concerns and her fears about George?
Paragraph 3	Comment on the final conversational exchange between Lucy and George. How does Forster use this dialogue to create an even greater contrast between the characters?
Paragraph 4	Comment on the final image of the River Arno. What might this image represent?
Conclusion	Summarise the overall impression Forster creates of both characters and make links to possible wider concerns.

Plenary

Choose a prose text that you know well and a character that you find interesting.

Copy this table, adding your own notes to explore how the writer presents the character.

How is the character first presented? Is the character described externally, internally or both?	How does the character respond to other characters in the text?	How does the character speak or act? What is significant or individual about their use of language?
How is the character presented at the end of the story? Has there been a change?	How does the character respond to conflict or difficulties? What does this tell you about them?	How are any wider themes and issues in the story linked to the character?

2.2 Exploring narration in prose fiction

Big question
- How and why do writers use different types of narrator?

EXPLORING DIFFERENT TYPES OF NARRATOR

Who is telling a story is often as significant as the story itself. It is often the writer's choice of **narrator** that gives a text its distinctive tone and feel.

Task

1. **a)** Think about a novel or short story that you know well. *Who* is telling the story? *Why* are they telling it? *How* is this story told?

   b) Now think about how different this story might be if told from the **perspective** of another character.

A writer may want to use a narrator as a guide, as an impartial observer or even as an active participant in the story itself. Ask yourself:
- what '**person**' does the narrator use?
- what is the narrator's relationship to the events of the story?
- is there more than one narrator?
- is the narrator rational and **reliable**?

Read the following two extracts:

> I was born in the year 1632, in the city of York, of a good family, though not of that country, my father being a foreigner of Bremen, who settled first at Hull.
>
> Daniel Defoe, *The Life and Adventures of Robinson Crusoe* (1719)

> For the most wild, yet most homely narrative which I am about to pen, I neither expect nor solicit belief. Mad indeed would I be to expect it, in a case where my very senses reject their own evidence. Yet, mad am I not – and very surely do I not dream. But tomorrow I die, and today I would unburthen my soul. My immediate purpose is to place before the world, plainly, succinctly, and without comment, a series of mere household events. In their consequences, these events have terrified – have tortured – have destroyed me.
>
> Edgar Allan Poe, 'The Black Cat' (1843)

Key terms

narrator: the person telling the story in a prose work

perspective: the point of view from which a story is told

person: the first person: '*I* left home'; second person: '*You* left home'; third person: '*He/she/Jo* left home'

reliable narrator: one that can be trusted (because they have the whole picture and/or do not intend to mislead)

Task

2. Look at one student's comments on the first style of narration:

> Defoe's narrator provides the reader with a series of facts set out like a careful explanation of events that cannot be disputed. The narrator therefore sounds plain-speaking and truthful. However, Poe's narrator

Continue this paragraph using these prompts:

a) How does Poe's narrator describe the tale he is about to tell?

b) What words or phrases set the tone for this narration?

c) What impression is created of Poe's narrator?

d) How does this compare with Defoe's narrator?

THIRD-PERSON NARRATIVE: OMNISCIENT, INTRUSIVE AND FOCALISED NARRATION

In third-person narration, writers can choose between the following modes of narration:

- **omniscient narration** – where events are recounted from an all-seeing perspective
- **intrusive** narration – where the narrator occasionally comments directly on events in the story
- **focalised** or **limited-vision narration** – where we see the events through a single character or from a restricted perspective.

Key terms

omniscient narration: where events are recounted from an all-seeing perspective

intrusive narration: where the narrator occasionally comments directly on events in the the story

focalised or limited-vision narration: where we see the events through a single character or from a restricted perspective

Task

3. Read the following passages. Is each narration omniscient, intrusive or focalised? Explain why.

> **Extract A**
> About thirty years ago, Miss Maria Ward, of Huntingdon, with only seven thousand pounds, had the good luck to captivate Sir Thomas Bertram, of Mansfield Park, in the county of Northampton, and to be thereby raised to the rank of a baronet's lady, with all the comforts and consequences of a handsome house and large income.
>
> Jane Austen,
> *Mansfield Park* (1814)

> **Extract B**
> And out of this shop came Mrs Hunter! She crossed to her carriage, followed by the shopman loaded with purchases for a party. The door was quickly slammed to, and she drove away; and Barton returned home with a bitter spirit of wrath in his heart, to see his only boy a corpse!
>
> You can fancy, now, the hoards of vengeance in his heart against the employers.
>
> Elizabeth Gaskell, *Mary Barton* (1848)

> **Extract C**
>
> Mrs. Manstey, in the long hours which she spent at her window, was not idle. She read a little, and knitted numberless stockings; but the view surrounded and shaped her life as the sea does a lonely island. When her rare callers came it was difficult for her to detach herself from the contemplation of the opposite window-washing, or the scrutiny of certain green points in a neighboring flower-bed which might, or might not, turn into hyacinths, while she feigned an interest in her visitor's anecdotes about some unknown grandchild.
>
> Edith Wharton,
> 'Mrs Manstey's View' (1891)

4. Copy and complete this table, adding your own notes and comments.

Extract	Details provided	Evidence	Narrative perspective and comment on effect
A	Social status Specific place details	'with only seven thousand pounds' 'baronet's lady' 'Mansfield Park'	Omniscient narration shown by reflection on past events 'about thirty years ago' and details of all characters' lives shown by…
B	Factory-owner's wife shopping Barton's response to his son's death (due to poverty)	'loaded with purchases' 'wrath'	Interruption of third-person pronouns with second-person 'you can fancy' shows the narrator is directing the reader to respond…
C	Mrs Manstey's daily life What she sees	'long hours spent at her window'	The window limits Mrs Manstey's view. It could also symbolise the narration, which is… The effect of this is…

5. Using the completed table as a guide, write a paragraph on narration in one passage.

DUAL OR MULTIPLE NARRATION

Writers may also choose to use two narrators in a work (**dual narration**) or even more than two (**multiple narration**) in order to create a range of effects.

For example, a writer might use multiple narrators to:
- present or develop characters more fully
- create suspense or enhance the plot by switching perspective at key moments
- influence the structure of the events or the time frame in a story
- make the reader question the credibility of the story or a character.

Here are three extracts from *The Woman in White* by Wilkie Collins. The novel is one of the first detective stories in the English language, and features a villain by the name of Count Fosco. It contains multiple narratives.

> **Key terms**
> **dual narration:** where a writer uses two narrators in a prose work
> **multiple narration:** where a writer uses three or more narrators in a prose work

The extracts all deal with the death of Lady Glyde in the story. The last three are printed as they appear, in order, in the book with these headings.

Extract A: from 'the narrative of Hester Pinhorn, cook in the service of Count Fosco.'

I let him in, and went upstairs along with him. 'Lady Glyde was just as usual,' says my mistress to him at the door; 'she was awake, and looking about her in a strange, forlorn manner, when I heard her give a sort of half cry, and she fainted in a moment.' The doctor went up to the bed, and stooped down over the sick lady. He looked very serious, all on a sudden, at the sight of her, and put his hand on her heart.

My mistress stared hard in Mr Goodricke's face. 'Not dead!' says she, whispering, and turning all of a tremble from head to foot.

'Yes,' says the doctor, very quiet and grave. 'Dead. I was afraid it would happen suddenly when I examined her heart yesterday.' My mistress stepped back from the bedside while he was speaking, and trembled and trembled again. 'Dead!' she whispers to herself; 'dead so suddenly! dead so soon!'

Extract B: The narrative of the Doctor

To the Registrar of the Sub-District in which the undermentioned death took place. – I hereby certify that I attended *Lady Glyde*, aged *Twenty-One* last Birthday; that I last saw her on *Thursday the 25th July* 1850; that she died *on the same day at No. 5 Forest Road, St. John's Wood*, and that the cause of her death was Aneurism. Duration of disease not known.

(Signed) ALFRED GOODRICKE.

Prof. Title. *M.R.C.S. Eng., L.S.A.*
Address, *12 Croydon Gardens*
St. John's Wood.

Extract C: The narrative of Jane Gould

I was the person sent in by Mr Goodricke to do what was right and needful by the remains of a lady who had died at the house named in the certificate which precedes this. I found the body in charge of the servant, Hester Pinhorn. I remained with it, and prepared it at the proper time for the grave. It was laid in the coffin in my presence, and I afterwards saw the coffin screwed down previous to its removal. When that had been done, and not before, I received what was due to me and left the house. I refer persons who may wish to investigate my character to Mr Goodricke. He will bear witness that I can be trusted to tell the truth.
(Signed) JANE GOULD.

Wilkie Collins, *The Woman in White* (1860)

Task

6. What types of text has Collins used? Why do you think these different narratives have been included?
7. Think more closely about each extract.
   - Who is speaking/writing?
   - What form of text is it?
   - What is distinctive about its tone?
   - What is distinctive about its use of language?

A student has begun to analyse Collins's use of narrators here, starting with Extract A.

> Collins's use of multiple narrators offers a range of perspectives on the same event, but equally importantly creates a rich variety of voices which play off each other to create effects. For example, the opening extract, written from the viewpoint of Hester Pinhorn, provides a fairly conventional dramatic narrative – with the heightened emotions of a Victorian mystery, such as the doctor's 'very quiet and grave' voice, and the repeated verb 'trembled' to describe the mistress's reaction. Hester is a witness, but one who is presenting the emotional, as much as the factual, context of the death.

— general topic sentence providing overview of the narrative

— comments on the specific type of narrative

— specific language references to support explanation

— concluding sentence drawing ideas together

Task

8. Now think about the effects of Collins's use of multiple narrators. Consider:
   - how the narratives reflect Victorian society in Britain over 150 years ago (think about social class, and the role and status of women)
   - why this choice of narration is effective in a detective story
   - which of the effects listed at the beginning of this section on multiple narration might apply to Collins's narrative.

EXPLORING NARRATIVE VOICE

As well as considering the form of narration – *who* is telling us the story – it is also important to think about *how* the story is being told – the narrative **voice**. This means identifying what is distinctive about the narrator's use of language:
- What words do they use or overuse?
- What literary features, such as imagery or metaphor, are present or absent?
- How formal, informal or mixed is the **register**?
- What is significant about their **lexicon**?

Key terms

voice: the characteristic way in which a story is told
register: the level of formality or informality in language use
lexicon: the stock of words or vocabulary of an individual
tone: in narration, the attitude that the author takes towards the concerns of the text, such as humorous, solemn or ironic

Read the following opening to a story aloud to get a sense of the narrative voice and its particular **tone** or perspective.

Fugu is a fish caught off the Pacific shores of Japan. The fish has held a special significance for me ever since my mother died through eating one. The poison resides in the sexual glands of the fish, inside two fragile bags. When preparing the fish, these bags must be removed with caution, for any clumsiness will result in the poison leaking into the veins. Regrettably, it is not easy to tell whether or not this operation has been carried out successfully. The proof is, as it were, in the eating.

Kazuo Ishiguro, 'A Family Supper'
(1982)

Task

9. Make some notes about the particular narrative voice.

a) Which person is the story told in?

b) What is the main tense the writer uses (for the first, third, fourth and fifth sentences)?

c) What tenses are used for the second sentence? To give what information?

d) What do you notice about the structure of the text?

e) What language devices or techniques have been used?

f) What is particular about their lexicon?

Exploring the text to understand how it is constructed will lead you to make some thoughtful judgements about narration and voice. Read what one student has written:

The narrator writes mostly in the present tense, beginning the story with a bland, factual piece of information about a particular type of fish. The use of the present tense in this sentence, and in the third and fifth sentences – if taken on their own – would not be out of place in an encyclopaedia or other nonfiction work. This, coupled with the lack of imagery and almost scientific description of the fish's physical properties ('the poison resides in the sexual glands') creates an almost cold, impersonal tone. The voice is one of a dispassionate observer.

describes the style of the first sentence

the style of the narration is further explained

further comment on the style used

reference to the text

summing up of the overall voice and tone

Task

10. Write a further paragraph on the conclusion of the passage.
Begin by commenting on the use of the word 'Regrettably' in the text:

A further sense of the voice is provided by the adverb
'Regrettably' which seems to suggest that…

Now, add a sentence commenting on 'as it were':

The idea of the calculated observer is also emphasised by…

Finally, comment on the final language device and how this adds a further, slightly different tone to the voice.

However, …

Thinking more deeply: **free indirect discourse**

In the following extract from Katherine Mansfield's short story 'Prelude', a young servant girl is preparing a meal.

> Alice was making water-cress sandwiches. She had a lump of butter on the table, a barracouta loaf, and the cresses tumbled in a white cloth.
>
> But propped against the butter dish there was a dirty, greasy little book, half unstitched, with curled edges, and while she mashed the butter she read [...].
>
> Oh, life. There was Miss Beryl. Alice dropped the knife and slipped the *Dream Book* under the butter dish. But she hadn't time to hide it quite, for Beryl ran into the kitchen and up to the table, and the first thing her eye lighted on were those greasy edges. Alice saw Miss Beryl's meaning little smile and the way she raised her eyebrows and screwed up her eyes as though she were not quite sure what that could be. She decided to answer if Miss Beryl should ask her: 'Nothing as belongs to you, Miss.' But she knew Miss Beryl would not ask her.
>
> Alice was a mild creature in reality, but she had the most marvellous retorts ready for questions that she knew would never be put to her. The composing of them and the turning of them over and over in her mind comforted her just as much as if they'd been expressed. Really, they kept her alive in places where she'd been that **chivvied** she'd been afraid to go to bed at night with a box of matches on the chair in case she bit the tops off in her sleep, as you might say.
>
> Katherine Mansfield, 'Prelude' (1918)

Task

11. Look first at the narrative perspective. Identify where in the passage:
    • we view Alice as if from the outside
    • we are given access to her thoughts and feelings.
12. Look at the highlighted sections. Which words or phrases appear to be Alice's, as opposed to the narrator's? How can you tell?

Sometimes a third-person narrative takes on the tone, lexicon and register of a character, rather than that of the narrator. This use of **free indirect discourse** can allow a writer to switch between different voices and viewpoints, even within a single passage.

Glossary

chivvied: harassed, bothered

Key term

free indirect discourse: a special type of third-person narration in which the narrator sometimes takes on the tone, lexicon and register of a character, thereby giving access to characters' thoughts and feelings

Final Task

Task

13. Write about what is distinctive about Mansfield's use of voice and narration in this extract. You could use these prompts:

In the opening paragraph, the form of narration is….

This is shown by….

In the third paragraph, Mansfield gives us insight into Alice's thoughts and feelings. This is shown by…

In the final paragraph, the narrative moves between third-person narration and free indirect discourse. This is shown where…

Plenary

Select a short passage from one of your prose texts and rewrite it using a different form of narration. What does this reveal to you about the writer's original choice of narration?

2.3 Exploring issues, concerns and ideas

Big question

- How do writers use fiction to explore issues, concerns and ideas?

In the world of a text, characters live, love and die. When you read a powerful work of fiction, you are first absorbed into a story about people and places, but, at a deeper level, you also engage with wider concerns, issues and ideas that emerge from the narrative.

These concerns may, in one sense, be considered 'universal'. For example, love, loss, conflict, death, faith and family are fundamental human concerns that affect us all, whoever or wherever we are. How a writer handles these concerns, however, is often very individual and needs to be considered not just within the world of the text, but also in relation to how, when and why a text is written.

EXPLORING CONCERNS, ISSUES AND IDEAS THROUGH SETTING

A choice of setting can be used to explore wider concerns and issues. To understand how setting can be used in this way, ask yourself these questions.

- Where is the story set?
- Is the story set in the same time it was written?
- Does the setting seem like a real place or an imagined one?
- How might the setting of the story explore wider themes and issues: or the **social and historical context**?

Key terms

social and historical context: important events and ideas in the real world outside of the story

sibilant: the characteristic soft or hissing sounds made by the consonants s, sh and z

Read the following passages, which both depict urban settings.

Passage A

It was a town of machinery and tall chimneys, out of which interminable serpents of smoke trailed themselves for ever and ever, and never got uncoiled. It had a black canal in it, and a river that ran purple with ill-smelling dye, and vast piles of building full of windows where there was a rattling and a trembling all day long, and where the piston of the steam-engine worked monotonously up and down, like the head of an elephant in a state of melancholy madness. It contained several large streets all very like one another, and many small streets still more like one another, inhabited by people equally like one another, who all went in and out at the same hours, with the same sound upon the same pavements, to do the same work, and to whom every day was the same as yesterday and tomorrow, and every year the counterpart of the last and the next.

Charles Dickens, *Hard Times* (1854)

The metaphor with its **sibilant** sound suggests that the industrial town is held tightly in the grip of the factories, which, like serpents, will eventually poison and destroy it.

The colour imagery of 'black' and 'purple' emphasises the unnatural urban setting.

Passage B

He sees the paving stone mica glistening in the pedestrianised square, pigeon excrement hardened by distance and cold into something almost beautiful, like a scattering of snow. He likes the symmetry of black cast-iron posts and their even darker shadows, and the lattice of cobbled gutters. The overfull litter baskets suggest abundance rather than squalor; the vacant benches set around the circular gardens look benignly expectant of their daily traffic – cheerful lunchtime crowds, the solemn studious boys from the Indian hostel, lovers in quiet raptures or crisis, the crepuscular drug dealers, the ruined old lady with her wild, haunting calls. Go away! She'll shout for hours at a time, and squawk harshly, sounding like some marsh bird or zoo creature.

Ian McEwan, *Saturday* (2005)

Task

1. Make some notes on your first impressions. What **mood** is created by each description of place?
2. Now, look more closely at setting. Copy and complete the grid for the second extract.

Key term

mood: the general feeling or atmosphere created by a writer's use of language – for example, gloomy, joyful, bitter, fearful, celebratory

	Text A Evidence	Text B Evidence
Where is the story set?	Industrial town: 'machinery', 'chimneys', 'piston', 'steam-engine'	
When is the story set?	References to 'steam-engine' and 'canals' suggest Victorian period	
Real or imagined place?	Description realistic but with more fantastical elements: 'serpent', 'elephants' and colour 'purple'	

HOW CONCERNS AND ISSUES ARE EXPLORED

So, how might the setting of the story reflect wider concerns and ideas?

Task

3. Find examples that reflect the following concerns or ideas in either passage:

    a) fears about pollution or waste

    b) the regular patterns of daily life

    c) the nature of urban communities

    d) the surprising beauty/shock of city living.

4. Look at the annotations on the previous page made by a student on how language creates meaning in the first part of Passage A. Continue through the passage, making notes on how the writer's language and literary techniques create a sense of the following:

    a) the strangeness of life in the industrial town

    b) daily life for the town's inhabitants.

5. What are your impressions of Dickens's views on life in the new industrial towns?

6. Now consider Passage B.

    a) Why do you think the writer has chosen to describe city life in this way?

    b) What wider ideas about modern city life might be reflected in this description of London?

7. Read this student's analysis of Passage B and then complete it, writing about the remainder of the passage.

    The tone of this description of modern city life is full of wonder about the incredible variety of this urban scene. The narrator sees a strange beauty in the modern city: the paving stones are 'glistening' in an almost jewel-like manner and even the white pigeon 'excrement' which covers everything is described with a delightful sibilant simile 'like a scattering of snow'. The street is empty but the narrator seems to miss the excitement of the daily crowds…

8. Finally, use your notes to discuss the following analysis of the passages:

    Dickens and McEwan both respond to the strangeness of urban life. Whereas Dickens presents monotony and oppression, McEwan is exhilarated by the sheer 'abundance' of London.

EXPLORING CONCERNS, ISSUES AND IDEAS THROUGH CHARACTER

Writers use characters to explore their concerns, issues and ideas. Putting a character in a particular situation or relationship in which they have to make a choice, or in which they are faced with a dilemma, allows the reader to empathise, understand or imagine what we might do in the character's place.

HOW WRITERS USE CHARACTERS TO EXPLORE MARRIAGE

Many writers have used female characters to explore the particular constraints and issues faced by women of their time.

Consider the female characters presented in these two passages:

It concerns the Story in hand very little to enter into the further particulars of the Family, or of myself, for the five years that I liv'd with this Husband; only to observe that I had two Children by him, and that at the end of five Year he Died. He had been really a very good husband to me and… left me a Widow with about **1200l** in my Pocket.

My two children were indeed taken happily off of my Hands by my Husband's Father and Mother, and that by the way was all they got by ***Mrs Betty***.

Daniel Defoe, *Moll Flanders* (1722)

As the devoted wife of a man who worshipped her, she felt she would take her place with a certain dignity in the world of reality, closing the portals forever behind her upon the realm of romance and dreams. But it was not long before **the tragedian** had gone to join the cavalry officer and the engaged young man and a few others; and Edna found herself face to face with the realities. She grew fond of her husband, realising with some unaccountable satisfaction that no trace of passion or excessive and fictitious warmth coloured her affection, thereby threatening its dissolution.

She was fond of her children in an uneven, impulsive way. She would sometimes gather them passionately to her heart; she would sometimes forget them. The year before they had spent part of the summer with their grandmother Pontellier in Iberville. Feeling secure regarding their happiness and welfare, she did not miss them except with an occasional intense longing. Their absence was a sort of relief, though she did not admit this, even to herself. It seemed to free her of a responsibility which she had blindly assumed and for which Fate had not fitted her.

Kate Chopin, *The Awakening* (1899)

— Edna's marriage – initially presented as ideal

— juxtaposition of reality (marriage) and dreams (romance)

— 'grew fond' – does not mention love; 'no trace of passion' – impression of no deep feelings for husband

Task

9. In what ways are the female characters presented in these extracts similar or different? Think about:
    - any details they provide about their marriage and children
    - how the details – or perhaps lack of them – reveal the characters' attitudes to marriage and motherhood.

10. Now look at how this student has explored the characterisation of Moll. Rewrite the highlighted final sentence to focus more on her attitude to marriage and motherhood.

    The character of Moll, despite being presented by Defoe in first-person narration, reveals very little about her marriage other than its length – 'five years' – and that she was left a widow with two children. She does not refer to her husband or her children by their names or any other details of the marriage other than 'he was a very good husband'. This makes the character of Moll seem very distant and detached.

11. Now write a further paragraph using your answers to the following questions:
    a) Why does Moll make a very precise reference to money?
    b) What might this reveal about her attitude to marriage?
    c) What does the word 'happily' reveal about Moll's attitude to her children?

Now look at the student annotations on the second passage. The focus is how the writer uses the character of Edna Pontellier to explore marriage in late-19th-century America.

Task

12. a) Reread the second paragraph of the passage, making notes on Edna's attitude to motherhood.

    b) Write a paragraph focusing on the characterisation of Edna and how the writer uses this to explore motherhood.

    Begin by commenting on the adjectives 'uneven' and 'impulsive'.

    A further sense of Edna's conflicted attitudes to motherhood is provided by contrasting words such as…

    Now add a sentence commenting on the word 'relief':

    Edna's unease about the responsibilities of being a mother is emphasised by…

Wider reading

Daniel Defoe's novel *The Fortunes and Misfortunes of the Famous Moll Flanders* (to give the book its full title) provides an early example of an **unreliable narrator**. Moll's accounts of her adventures are not always trustworthy, although they follow her five marriages, her life as a criminal and her final transportation to the American colonies where she repents for her past sins. What effects might be created by Defoe's use of Moll as an unreliable source for her own story?

Key term

unreliable narrator: not to be trusted (because they do not have the whole picture or intend to mislead)

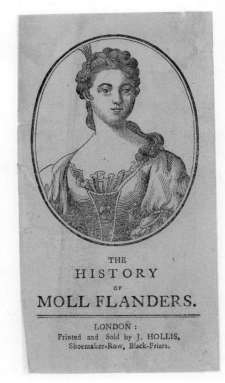

THE
HISTORY
OF
MOLL FLANDERS.

LONDON :
Printed and Sold by J. HOLLIS,
Shoemaker-Row, Black-Friars.

THE IMPORTANCE OF REBELLION

In the previous passages, the authors presented female characters facing social challenges or limitations on account of their gender. Writers also use moments when characters rebel to draw attention to wider concerns such as inequality or injustice.

'I tell you I must go!' I retorted, roused to something like passion. 'Do you think I can stay to become nothing to you? Do you think I am an automaton? – a machine without feelings? and can bear to have my morsel of bread snatched from my lips, and my drop of living water dashed from my cup? Do you think, because I am poor, obscure, plain, and little, I am soulless and heartless? – You think wrong! – I have as much soul as you, – and full as much heart! And if God had gifted me with some beauty and much wealth, I should have made it as hard for you to leave me, as it is now for me to leave you. I am not talking to you now through the medium of custom, conventionalities, nor even of mortal flesh; – it is my spirit that addresses your spirit; just as if both had passed through the grave, and we stood at God's feet, equal, – as we are!'

'As we are!' repeated Mr. Rochester – 'so,' he added, enclosing me in his arms. Gathering me to his breast, pressing his lips on my lips: 'so, Jane!'

Charlotte Brontë, *Jane Eyre* (1847)

In this passage, Jane's outburst relates to Mr Rochester's plans to marry. Although Jane has been employed as a governess, her feelings for Mr Rochester have clearly developed. She believes at this point in the novel that he intends to marry the wealthy, attractive Blanche Ingram.

Task

13. Discuss how the writer portrays Jane's rebellion. Consider:
    - the effect of the exclamatory sentence, and the repeated questions at the beginning of the passage
    - the imagery of the machine
    - the metaphors 'morsel of bread' and 'drop of living water', and what they reveal about Jane's feelings for Mr Rochester
    - the adjectives Jane uses to describe herself and why she focuses on her economic and social status and her appearance – and what this might say about Victorian expectations of women and of marriage in general.
14. Now write a paragraph about Jane's moment of rebellion and how this develops our understanding of the marriage and social expectation.

Thinking more deeply: **exploring perspectives**

An author might develop an idea or concern by making the reader look at events from a particular narrative point of view, or perspective. By choosing a different perspective from which a place or an event is usually described – away from the dominant perspective – a writer can draw particular attention to issues such as identity, inequality or injustice.

You are going to read two passages. The first, set in British-ruled colonial India before World War I, adopts a **dominant narrative perspective**. As you read, think about how this reflects colonialist views at the time.

> Except for the Marabar Caves – and they are twenty miles off – the city of **Chandrapore** presents nothing extraordinary. Edged rather than washed by the river Ganges, it trails for a couple of miles along the bank, scarcely distinguishable from the rubbish it deposits so freely. There are no bathing-steps on the river front, as the Ganges happens not to be holy here; indeed there is no river front, and bazaars shut out the wide and shifting panorama of the stream. The streets are mean, the temples ineffective, and though a few fine houses exist they are hidden away in gardens or down alleys whose filth deters all but the invited guest. Chandrapore was never large or beautiful, but two hundred years ago it lay on the road between Upper India, then imperial, and the sea, and the fine houses date from that period.
>
> E.M. Forster, *A Passage to India* (1924)

Key term

dominant narrative perspective: where a story is told from the perspective of the dominant culture

Glossary

Chandrapore: a fictional city, thought to be based on part of the city of Patna in the northern region of Bihar

Task

15. Look first at the perspective or viewpoint in this description.
    a) Identify what features of the city the narrator chooses to describe.
    b) What does this tell you about the position of the narrator in relation to the city? (Is he at street-level or above the city? Is he an Indian or an outsider to the country? Whom do you think he is addressing?)
    c) What effect does this have?
16. Now think about the tone of this description.
    a) What critical adjectives are used? What is their overall effect?
    b) What is the effect of the repeated use of 'no' in the third sentence?
    c) What aspect of the city appears to most concern the narrator?
    d) What evidence is there that the city, according to the narrator, may have once been grander?

NEW PERSPECTIVES

This second passage is told from the perspective of a narrator who is at the margins of the society she describes. Chika Okafor is a young bride who has newly arrived in New York from Lagos, Nigeria.

Our neighborhood was called Flatbush, my new husband told me the next day, as we walked to the bus stop, down a noisy street that smelled of fish left out too long before refrigeration. He wanted to show me how to do the grocery and how to use the bus.

'Look around, look around. You get used to things faster that way,' he said. I turned my head from side to side so he would see that I was looking around. Dark restaurant windows promised the Best Caribbean and American Food in lopsided print, a car wash across the street advertised $3.50 washes on a chalk board nestled among Coke cans and bits of paper. The sidewalk was chipped away at the edges, like something nibbled at by mice.

Inside the bus, he showed me where to pour in the coins, how to press the tape on the wall to signal my stop. This is not like back home where you shout out to the conductor, he said, sneering, as though he had invented the superior American system.

Inside Key Food, we walked from aisle to aisle slowly. I was wary when he put a beef pack in the cart. I wished I could touch it, to examine its redness, like back home where the butcher held up fresh-cut slabs buzzing with flies.

'Can we buy those biscuits?' I asked. The blue packets of Burtons Rich Tea were familiar, they were in every store in Lagos. I did not want to eat biscuits but I wanted something familiar in the cart.

'Cookies. Americans call them cookies,' he said.

I reached out for the biscuits (cookies).

'Get the store brand. They're cheaper, but still the same thing,' he said, pointing at a white packet. 'Okay,' I said. I put the store brand in the cart and stared at the blue packet on the shelf, at the familiar grain embossed Burtons logo, until we left the aisle.

'When I become an Attending, we will not buy store brands but for now we have to, they add up,' he said.

'When you become a Consultant?'

'Yes, but it's called an Attending here. An Attending Physician.'

The arrangers of marriage only told you that doctors made a lot of money in America. They did not add that before doctors started to make a lot of money, they had to do an internship and a residency program, which my new husband had not completed. My new husband had told me this during our short in-flight conversation, right after we took off from Lagos, before he fell asleep […]

[…] He stopped for a woman with her child tucked into her shopping cart to pass by.

'See how they have bars so you can't take the shopping carts out? In the good neighborhoods, they do not have them. You can take your shopping cart all the way to your car.'

'Oh,' I said. He did not know that my brows dipped low above my nose when I struggled to understand something, so I did not bother to look away. What did it matter that you could or could not take the carts out? The point was, there were carts.

I thought about the open markets back home, the traders who sweet-talked you into stopping at their zinc-covered sheds, who were prepared to bargain all day to add one single kobo to the price. They wrapped what you bought in plastic bags when they had them and when they did not have them, they apologized and laughed and offered you old hole ridden newspapers.

Chimanada Ngozi Adichie, 'The Arrangers of Marriage' (2003)

Task

17. Answer these questions on the perspective of the passage.

   a) What features of the city does the narrator choose to describe?

   b) What does this tell you about the position of the narrator in relation to the city? Is she at street-level or above the city? Does she know the city? Is she an American or an outsider to the country?

   c) What effect does this have?

If you compare the two extracts from Forster and Adichie, you can see that they are both written from the perspective of the outsider. Both describe encounters with new places and new cultures. Forster's omniscient narrator, however, literally and metaphorically *looks down* upon the city of Chandrapore from the perspective of the European coloniser. Adichie's narrator, in contrast, shifts the perspective to a much more personal one: that of a new migrant to a strange city. This shows us her vulnerability, her confusion and her longing for home.

Task

18. Now focus in on the language and style of the passage and how this creates meaning.

   a) Identify the adjectives and figurative language the narrator uses to describe the neighbourhood and impressions created.

   b) What do we learn about Chika's relationship with her 'new husband'? Look particularly at what he says, how he speaks to her and how she reacts.

19. Now look at paragraphs 3 and 4.

   a) Identify two references to 'back home'. Is there a difference in tone between Chika and her husband here?

   b) What is the effect of the verb 'sneering' and the reference to 'the superior American system'?

20. Look closely at the dialogue between Chika and her new husband in the supermarket.

   a) What does the apparently trivial conversation about biscuits reveal about Chika's feelings?

   b) How does her husband respond?

   c) The conversation moves on. What information are we given about the husband's job and his future prospects? Did Chika know this before the marriage?

21. **a)** What impression is created of the 'open markets' and the 'traders' back home?

   b) What is the effect of the verbs 'sweet-talked', 'apologized', 'laughed' and 'offered'?

22. Which words best describe Adichie's presentation of Chika? Add your own.

| lost | lonely | nostalgic | disorientated | nervous | confused | unhappy | anxious | self-contained | compliant |

Wider reading

The experience of immigration to America is also explored in Sandra Cisneros's *The House on Mango Street* (1984), set in a Latin-American district in Chicago, and Chimamanda Ngozi Adichie's novel *Americanah* (2013) with parallel stories of Nigerian immigration to America and Britain.

Final Task

You should now have an understanding of some of the different methods writers use to explore concerns, issues and ideas. You will be able to identify and analyse techniques, consider their effects and make links with wider themes and relevant contexts.

You are going to be writing a response to this task:

> How does Adichie present Chika and her impressions of her new American life in this passage?

Make sure you comment on:
- how the writer uses language and literary techniques to present Chika's impressions of her new life and her new husband
- what effects are created
- how these effects might link to wider issues about migrant experiences and also the role of women within marriage.

Use the notes you have made to complete this essay-planning grid.

Overview	Begin with an overall point about the narration, setting and tone of the passage.
Point 1	Look at the first two paragraphs of the extract. Comment on the description of the neighbourhood and the impressions created of both the setting and of the relationship between Chika and her new husband.
Point 2	Look at paragraphs 3 and 4. Comment on the characters' different views of 'back home' and how these are demonstrated.
Point 3	Look at the dialogue between Chika and her husband in the supermarket. What extra information does this give us about Chika's feelings and the background to their marriage?
Point 4	Look at the concluding paragraph. How does the writer use language to contrast the description of the Lagos market and Chika's supermarket experience. What effect does this create?
Conclusion	Conclude by making links with the general concerns of the passage. How do these impressions add to our understanding of Chika's experiences and of young women like her who, following an arranged marriage, are newly arrived in another, strange country?

Task

23. Now write a response to this final task. You could these prompts to help you:

In her short story 'The Arrangers of Marriage', Adichie employs the perspective of Chika, a new bride who has just arrived in America, to explore issues such as…

Through Chika, Adichie presents the experience of migration as…

Adichie's portrayal of the arranged marriage between Chika and her new husband shows…

Plenary

Consider any of the prose texts you have studied or are studying. Think carefully about when and where the story is set and when it was written. Make notes on any concerns, issues and ideas that are important in the text. Identify some of the techniques the writer uses to explore these concerns, particularly through character, setting or perspective.

2.4 Exploring prose forms and structures

Big question

- How do **form** and **structure** in novels and short stories shape meaning?

NARRATIVE STRUCTURES

It is important to consider carefully *how* writers organise their narratives and *why*. From your own reading experience, you will already know that there are many successful examples of narratives that are not organised in a straightforward way.

Task

1. Think of examples of the following types of story:
   - a story told backwards in time
   - a narrative which involves **flashbacks**
   - a story where important questions are left unanswered, even at the end
   - a surprising twist in a story which makes you rethink what's happened earlier.

The **plot**, or the way in which events are linked in stories, is often very complex. There may also be one or more **subplots**, which, in the early stages of a narrative, appear to have no connection to the main events or characters in the story. It is the task of the writer to bring all these events and characters together in a way that engages and surprises us.

Key terms

form: in prose this refers to the *type* of work such as short story, essay, novella or novel; form relates to the overall shape of a text and is therefore closely related to structure

structure: this covers all the different elements that give a prose text its distinctive shape, such as the organisation of chapters, different narrators, types of narrative as well as the order of events and actions that occur in the narrative

flashback: an interruption to the current events of a narrative, where a writer inserts past events in order to provide background or context

plot: the plan or pattern of a series of events in a work of fiction, organised in a way that creates interest. In *Aspects of the Novel*, E.M. Forster used this example to define the difference between story and plot: 'the king died and then the queen died' is a story, 'the king died and then the queen died of grief' is a plot. Plot, according to Forster, explores causality: not only what happens, but also how and why events occur and how they relate to each other.

subplot: a secondary plot in a story whose characters and events are connected in some way to the main plot

EXPLORING STRUCTURE

When we read a work of fiction, we generally expect events to unfold according to a basic pattern. Many writers and critics have tried to define and name the essential elements of plot structure. At a very basic level, these can include:

- introduction to the main character(s)
- challenging events
- complications that cause conflict
- events that reach a **climax**
- a **resolution**.

A summary of the plot of J.D. Salinger's novel *The Catcher in the Rye* is provided below:

Key terms
climax: the part in a story where a crisis point is reached
resolution: a solution or decision that occurs in a story in response to the crisis point

> The novel opens with the teenage narrator, Holden Caulfield, giving his views on 'phoneys' and adult life in general. [1] He recounts the circumstances leading up to him leaving his high school, Pencey Prep. [2] Holden does not want to admit to his parents what has happened, so he travels alone to New York to give himself time to think about what to do next. In New York he has an increasingly bizarre range of experiences. [3] In a final meeting with his younger sister, Phoebe, he appears incredibly vulnerable and emotionally fragile. [4] He suffers a mental breakdown and returns home for medical treatment, ready to begin at a new school after the summer. [5]

Introduction to main character through first-person narration

His expulsion from school: the most significant _challenging_ event

Series of _complications_ that escalate the difficulties faced by Holden

Task

2. Look at the student annotations above to the plot summary. Which elements of plot structure do you think are represented by the events in [4] and [5] above?
3. Now consider how the student has written about plot structure below:

   Through the complications faced by his teenage narrator, Holden Caulfield, Salinger explores the difficult transition between childhood and adulthood. Salinger begins with Holden's expulsion from school and his rejection of the adult 'phoney world' to start a chain of events in the narrative, which reaches a climax when…

   a) Where has this student identified and named different elements of plot structure?
   b) How do they link these to the wider concerns of the novel?
4. Using the example above, write a brief overview paragraph about the plot structure of a text you know.

Checklist for success
When writing about plot structure:
✓ identify and name the different plot elements
✓ analyse *how* these work to create effects
✓ make links to the wider concerns of the text
✓ avoid simply re-telling the main events in the story.

HOW WRITERS CREATE EFFECTIVE OPENINGS

The opening of a story or a novel is crucial — not just in terms of winning our attention — but also in setting up what might follow.

Task

5. Read the following opening lines. Which do you find the most intriguing? Why?

> **A** Emma Woodhouse, handsome, clever, and rich, with a comfortable home and happy disposition, seemed to unite some of the best blessings of existence; and had lived nearly twenty-one years in the world with very little to distress or vex her.
>
> **B** And after all the weather was ideal.
>
> **C** I was sick — sick unto death with that long agony; and when they at length unbound me, and I was permitted to sit, I felt that my senses were leaving me.
>
> **D** This is the saddest story I have ever heard.
>
> **E** To Sherlock Holmes she was always *the* woman.

6. For each of the examples, make notes on the following:
  • What information are you given/not given?
  • Who is speaking? How do you know?
  • Does the line set the scene or start in the middle of events?
  • What types of sentences are used?
  • What narrative tone do you expect from this opening line?
  • Are there any similarities between them?

Now read a student analysis of openings A and B.

> In the first opening, which is narrated in the third person, we are given important details about Emma Woodhouse, who we assume will be the main character. The list of adjectives used by the writer reflects not just the character's personal qualities, 'clever' 'handsome' and 'happy', but also her circumstances, which are described as 'rich' and 'comfortable'. The superlative 'best blessings of existence' further emphasises the character's fortunate life. However, the fact that very little had happened to 'distress or vex' her up until this point suggests that the narrative will focus on events that disrupt her life.
>
> In the second example, the sentence begins with a conjunction 'and' as if the reader is joining a conversation in the middle. The time adverbial 'after all' is also significant because it suggests that even though the weather is now perfect, there was concern about it previously. This element of concern creates a darker tone, which could be a feature of the narrative that follows.

Task

7. Identify the following features in the student's analysis:
  • focus on language with supporting evidence and analysis
  • link to possible events in the narrative
  • link to possible wider concerns and narrative development.

As you can see from the previous examples, the opening of a novel or story – even the first line – can raise as many questions as it answers. A writer's choice of language, sentence structure and imagery can also provide early clues as to what will follow.

Now read this longer opening passage:

> My father's family name being Pirrip, and my Christian name Philip, my infant tongue could make of both names nothing longer or more explicit than Pip. So, I called myself Pip, and came to be called Pip.
>
> I give Pirrip as my father's family name, on the authority of his tombstone and my sister – Mrs Joe Gargery, who married the blacksmith. As I never saw my father or my mother, and never saw any likeness of either of them (for their days were long before the days of photographs), my first fancies regarding what they were like, were unreasonably derived from their tombstones. The shape of the letters on my father's, gave me an odd idea that he was a square, stout, dark man, with curly black hair. From the character and turn of the inscription, 'Also Georgiana Wife of the Above,' I drew a childish conclusion that my mother was freckled and sickly. To five little stone **lozenges**, each about a foot and a half long, which were arranged in a neat row beside their grave, and were sacred to the memory of five little brothers of mine – who gave up trying to get a living, exceedingly early in that universal struggle – I am indebted for a belief I religiously entertained that they had all been born on their backs with their hands in their trousers-pockets, and had never taken them out in this state of existence.
>
> Charles Dickens, *Great Expectations* (1860/1)

Glossary

lozenge: a diamond shape but also a relatively archaic word for a medicine pill or tablet

Task

8. What do we find out about the narrator here? How might this relate to the possible concerns of the novel? How might the details here **foreshadow** events to come?
9. Make notes in response to the following questions:
   a) What person is the story told in?
   b) What is the main tense used here?
   c) What do you learn here about the narrator's family circumstances?
   d) What impression is created of the character's thoughts and feelings as he contemplates the graves of his immediate family?

Key term

foreshadow: when a writer gives a sign or warning that prepares the reader for what is to follow later in the narrative

Chapter 2 Studying prose fiction

Read how one student has analysed Dickens's use of language in this opening. What information might it suggest about character, situation, concerns and events later in the novel?

> This first-person narrative introduces the main character of 'Pip'. The immediate reference to the narrator's 'infant tongue' and his inability to pronounce his own name in full creates the impression of youth and vulnerability. This is further emphasised when Dickens explains that the narrator can only derive his family name on the 'authority' of a tombstone and his surviving sister. The narrator's confusion about his immediate family and origins is further highlighted by Dickens when the narrator states 'I never saw my father or my mother, and never saw any likeness of either of them.' The repetition of the adverb 'never' emphasises this confusion about his identity.

- correctly identifies the style of narration
- analysis of writer's choice of language in terms of characterisation
- reference to situation with further evidence and support
- detailed language analysis and link to possible wider concerns and events

Task

10. a) Now write a further paragraph, modelled on the one above, on the rest of the passage:

b) Comment on the use of the phrase 'first fancies', using these prompts:

> The narrator's youthful imagination is also shown by…
>
> His attitude to the loss of his siblings, however is…
>
> This is emphasised by…

c) Finally, comment on how these observations may point to some of Dickens's wider concerns and ideas in the novel.

Checklist for success

When analysing a novel opening, consider:
✓ narration and narrative voice
✓ use of language – tense, sentence structure, use of imagery
✓ situation – setting and initial events
✓ possible links to wider concerns or what might happen later.

ENDINGS

Although resolution is one of the key structural elements of a story, not all narratives come to an entirely neat conclusion, where the all the problems posed by the writer are 'solved'.

Now read through the plot summary below, which relates to the characters of Pip and Estella in *Great Expectations*.

- Both are orphans who meet as children, but Estella is scornful of the coarse village boy Pip.
- Pip is supported by an unknown benefactor to become a gentleman.
- Estella makes an unhappy marriage to a wealthy, but violent man.
- Estella's real origins as the adopted daughter of a criminal are discovered by Pip.
- Pip encounters Estella, now widowed, outside the house where they first met as children.

Now read the closing section of the novel.

'But you said to me,' returned Estella, very earnestly, "God bless you, God forgive you!" And if you could say that to me then, you will not hesitate to say that to me now, – now, when suffering has been stronger than all other teaching, and has taught me to understand what your heart used to be. I have been bent and broken, but – I hope – into a better shape. Be as considerate and good to me as you were, and tell me we are friends.'

'We are friends,' said I, rising and bending over her, as she rose from the bench.

'And will continue friends apart,' said Estella.

I took her hand in mine, and we went out of the ruined place; and, as the morning mists had risen long ago when I first left the forge, so the evening mists were rising now, and in all the broad expanse of tranquil light they showed to me, I saw no shadow of another parting from her.

Task

11. First make notes in response to the following questions:

   a) What do you notice about Estella's first speech? What evidence is there that she has changed?

   b) What is the effect of the characters repeating the word 'friends'?

   c) Comment on the final images of the setting and the weather in the last paragraph. What effects are created?

12. Look in detail at the last line 'I saw no shadow of another parting from her.' Consider two different readings of this ending:

   a) Pip has resolved to stay with Estella and they will never separate again.

   b) Pip would like to believe that he will never part from Estella, but he is still uncertain.

   Discuss these different interpretations. Can you find evidence to support each of them?

Wider reading

Dickens published *Great Expectations* in serialised form in weekly parts in his magazine *All the Year Round*. His original version of the ending of the novel was much darker in tone and suggested a final parting between the main characters. When he sent this version of the ending to another writer to be checked, he was told it was too disappointing for readers and was persuaded to change it to the one here.

RESOLUTION

Writers often use marriage as one way of achieving narrative resolution; the main characters overcome difficulties and can finally come together in celebration. This is particularly the case in many 19th-century realist novels.

Read the ending to Jane Austen's novel *Emma* (1815) and the annotations.

> The wedding was very much like other weddings, where the parties have no taste for finery or parade; and Mrs. Elton, from the particulars detailed by her husband, thought it all extremely shabby, and very inferior to her own. 'Very little white satin, very few lace veils; a most pitiful business! Selina would stare when she heard of it.' But, in spite of these deficiencies, the wishes, the hopes, the confidence, the predictions of the small band of true friends who witnessed the ceremony, were fully answered in the perfect happiness of the union.
>
> Jane Austen, *Emma* (1815)

Initially seems as if wedding is unexceptional, anticlimax

Critical view of another character adds to this effect

The use of the conjunction 'but' and the warm thoughts of 'true friends' lift the tone to one of hope and celebration

The final noun phrase 'the perfect happiness of the union' completes this joyful resolution

Task

13. Compare the two endings – from *Great Expectations* and *Emma*. Which of the following student statements do you think best applies to these endings? Give reasons to support your response.

a) A good ending is one where there is hope for us all.

b) The best endings are those where the characters have grown and changed.

c) An ending should still leave some questions unanswered.

d) The end should almost be the beginning of a new story.

14. Consider what, in your opinion, makes a satisfying ending to a story. Weigh up the suggestions below. Can you add any others?

- Characters or events surprise you.
- Good overcomes evil.
- Characters are seen to be reflect their 'true' selves.
- Secrets, questions or plot lines are tied up.
- Key concerns are illuminated or new questions emerge.

How well do some or any of these factors fit to the ending of a short story or novel you have studied?

TIME, EVENTS AND NARRATIVE STRUCTURE

A writer often chooses not to relate the events of a story in the order in which they occur. It is often much more effective to reorder and be selective about events. As a reader, you should therefore always consider whether there is any difference between a story's **chronological order** and its **narrative order**.

Whether you are writing about a complete text or a passage, remember to consider the treatment of time as a key element of its structure. Ask yourself:

- Over what time period do the events of the story occur?
- Do the main events follow time order, or is this order changed in the narrative?
- How are events reordered and what effect does this have?
- If there is more than one narrator or narrative point of view, do these occupy the same timeline?
- How does the writer indicate a time shift? Tense change? Section break?
- Are there any time gaps in the narrative? If so, what are their effects?
- Does the story return to key moments? Or have a circular structure?

Key term

chronological order: ordering events according to the time at which they happened, with the earliest coming first, and the latest coming last

narrative order: the order in which events in a story are told

TIME SHIFTS

For example, in this passage below from a short story by Katherine Mansfield, Ma Parker has arrived at her cleaning job and has told her employer that her little grandson Lennie has died. However, her memories of Lennie keep interrupting what she is doing now.

> Ma Parker drew the two jetty spears out of her toque and hung it behind the door. She unhooked her worn jacket and hung that up too. Then she tied her apron and sat down to take off her boots. To take off her boots or to put them on was an agony to her, but it had been an agony for years. In fact, she was so accustomed to the pain that her face was drawn and screwed up ready for the twinge before she'd so much as untied the laces. That over, she sat back with a sigh and softly rubbed her knees…
>
> 'Gran! Gran!' Her little grandson stood on her lap in his button boots. He'd just come in from playing in the street.
>
> 'Look what a state you've made your gran's skirt into – you wicked boy!'
>
> But he put his arms round her neck and rubbed his cheek against hers.
>
> […] The old woman sprang up, seized the iron kettle off the gas stove and took it over to the sink. The noise of the water drumming in the kettle deadened her pain, it seemed.
>
> Katherine Mansfield, 'Life of Ma Parker' (1921)

Task

15. **a)** What punctuation mark does Mansfield use to indicate the start of a flashback?

    b) How does the tone of the flashback section contrast with her account of her cleaning work?

    c) Look at the two highlighted declarative sentences. What similarities do they have in terms of structure? Which verb is repeated?

    d) Why do you these two sentences almost mirror each other? What effect does this have?

    e) Why does Mansfield state, after the flashback, that Ma Parker 'sprang up' and 'seized the kettle'? What is her character trying to do?

16. What are the effects of Mansfield's use of flashback in this passage?

    a) Does it present a softer, more sympathetic side to Ma Parker's character?

    b) Does it explore the way all of our minds move constantly between the past and the present?

    c) Does it show how Ma Parker cannot stop painful memories intruding into her daily life?

    d) Which effect do you think is most significant? Can you think of any others?

Thinking more deeply: **moments of epiphany**

Looking back to the basic plot structure outlined at the opening of this unit you can see that, in a short narrative, it could be difficult to fully develop even the most basic sequence of character – challenge – complication – climax – resolution. In short stories or novellas, therefore, writers often compress time and are very selective about key events.

   One such key event can be a moment of **epiphany** – where the main character has a sudden change of heart or realisation which alters their view of the world.

Key term

epiphany: in literature, this term describes a character's moment of discovery, revelation or realisation

Now read a passage from the ending of the short story 'Life of Ma Parker'.

It was cold in the street. There was a wind like ice. People went flitting by, very fast; the men walked like scissors; the women trod like cats. And nobody knew - nobody cared. Even if she broke down, if at last, after all these years, she were to cry, she'd find herself in the lock-up as like as not.

But at the thought of crying it was as though little Lennie leapt in his gran's arms. Ah, that's what she wants to do, my dove. Gran wants to cry. If she could only cry now, cry for a long time, over everything, beginning with her first place and the cruel cook, going on to the doctor's, and then the seven little ones, death of her husband, the children's leaving her, and all the years of misery that led up to Lennie. But to have a proper cry over all these things would take a long time. All the same, the time for it had come. She must do it. She couldn't put it off any longer; she couldn't wait any more... Where could she go?

- simple sentences
- dramatic similes
- use of colloquial word 'lock-up'
- free indirect speech
- shift in time frame
- final question is moment of epiphany

Task

17. Read the annotations above. Then make your own notes to explore the effect of these features.

Now read the beginning of one student's analysis.

The extract from just before the end of the story opens with two simple sentences that emphasise not just the inhospitable cold weather outside, but also the emotional coldness of the city and perhaps even the other people on the streets who do not understand Ma Parker's suffering. Mansfield's use of the dramatic first simile, where men are described as 'like scissors' also emphasises the alien nature of other people – metaphorically cutting through the crowds without care or thought.

Task

18. Using your notes and the paragraph above as a guide, continue the analysis of the language used in the rest of passage. Consider:
- how this passage might reflect a key moment or epiphany for the character
- how effective it might be as an ending or resolution to the story.

Now read this concluding section of a short story by Chinua Achebe. In this story Nnaemeka goes against his father's wishes and marries Nene, a woman not chosen for him by his family or from his own Ibo tribe. For eight years, Nnaemeka has no contact with his father, Okeke, who continues to refuse to accept him or his wife.

The story eventually got to the little village in the heart of the Ibo country that Nnaemeka and his young wife were a most happy couple. But his father was one of the few people who knew nothing about this. He always displayed so much temper whenever his son's name was mentioned that everyone avoided it in his presence. By a tremendous effort of will he had succeeded in pushing his son to the back of his mind. The strain had nearly killed him but he had persevered, and won.

Then one day he received a letter from Nene, and in spite of himself he began to glance through it perfunctorily until all of a sudden the expression on his face changed and he began to read more carefully,

…Our two sons, from the day they learnt that they have a grandfather, have insisted on being taken to him. I find it impossible to tell them that you will not see them. I implore you to allow Nnaemeka to bring them home for a short time during his leave next month. I shall remain here in Lagos…

The old man at once felt the resolution he had built up over so many years falling in. He was telling himself he must not give in. He tried to steel his heart against all emotional appeals. It was a re-enactment of that other struggle. He leaned against a window and looked out. The sky was overcast with heavy black clouds and a high wind began to blow filling the air with dust and dry leaves. It was one of those rare occasions when even Nature takes a hand in human fight. Very soon it began to rain, the first rain in the year. It came down in sharp drops and was accompanied by lightning and thunder which mark a change of season. Okeke was trying hard not to think of his two grandsons. But he knew he was now fighting a losing battle. He tried to hum a favourite hymn but the pattering of large rain drops on the roof broke up the tune. His mind immediately returned to the children. How could he shut his door against them? By a curious mental process he imagined them standing, sad and forsaken, under the harsh angry weather – shut out from his house.

That night he hardly slept, from remorse – and a vague fear that he might die without making it up to them.

Chinua Achebe, 'Marriage is a Private Affair' (1952)

Task

19. First make notes on the following:
    - The different time lines mentioned. Where are there references to the past, present and the future?
    - How does Achebe indicate that Okeke's views of his son's marriage may have changed over time?
    - Achebe uses the noun 'remorse' at the end of this extract. Look up its precise meaning. What other words might be used to describe the main concerns of this story?
20. Now think about the structure of the narrative. Make notes on the following key structural elements:
    - memory/flashback
    - epistolary narrative
    - epiphany
    - resolution.
    Are there any other structural elements evident in this passage?

Final Task

You should now be able to identify and comment upon the different ways writers choose to structure narratives and the effects of these choices.

You are going to write a longer response to the task below:

> How effective is this passage as an ending to a story?

Make sure you comment closely on:
- the writer's use of language throughout the passage
- the overall structure of the extract
- how the father's changing views are represented
- the effect of the final line.

Task

21. Begin by making notes on the points above.

Now look at the following sentence starters from student responses.

> In this concluding extract, Achebe initially presents the character of the father as still determined to maintain his rejection of his son. This is emphasised by…

> Achebe then creates a time shift and an event that disrupts the father's life; this occurs when…

> The language used in Nene's letter is effective because…

> It is clear that the father is undergoing a change. This is emphasised by…

> Achebe uses the image of the storm to symbolise…

> The image of the grandchildren 'sad and forsaken, under the harsh angry weather' is effective because…

> The final line should present resolution to the story, however, because…

> Overall, the effect of this concluding passage is…

Task

22. Using your notes and, if you wish, the sentence starters above, write a response to this final task.

Plenary

Consider any prose text you are currently studying or have studied recently. Choose two of the following key concepts: opening, climax, resolution, time-shift or epiphany and explain how effectively they are presented to the reader.

2.5 Exploring context in pre-1900 prose

Big question
- How does knowledge about the context of a prose text help you understand its impact?

WHAT IS CONTEXT?

When creating a work of fiction, a writer can draw upon many different sources, experiences and outside influences. Writers are shaped by the world around them, yet fiction does more than just reflect life; sometimes it can affect the way we see the world or even how we live in it. As a student of literature, therefore, it is important not just to analyse how a writer uses language, structure and narrative, but also to connect your analysis to the wider contexts of a literary work.

But what do we mean by 'contexts'?

Task

1. Think about a prose text you have studied recently and consider:

a) the social and historical context
- What important events were occurring around the time the text was written?
- How might these events have impacted upon the writer?

b) the literary context
- Who or what were the writer's main literary or artistic influences?
- How did the text's first readers and critics respond to it?

EXPLORING PRE-1900 PROSE TEXTS

Social and historical context: concerns in pre-1900 prose texts

Creative works can make us think about how we, as individuals, live, die, love or interact with those around us. They can also tackle more *time-specific* issues. The issues and concerns listed on the right were often explored by writers of prose fiction, particularly in the 18th and 19th centuries, and can be related directly to social and historical context. It is important, however, that we do not see fiction as a simple reflection of these concerns or as a direct product of a writer's biography. You should always follow the text-context-text rule: always use the text you are studying and your detailed analysis of meaning as the starting and end-point for your analysis.

industrialisation
social class
urban versus rural life
slavery and race   imperialism
crime and punishment
marriage and divorce
working conditions and pay
education
poverty and social justice
the role and rights of women
the natural world
political representation
religion versus science
duality of human nature

Task

2. Think of a pre-1900 prose text you know or are studying. Which of the concerns listed in the margin on the right are relevant to it?

HOW TO INCLUDE CONTEXT IN YOUR ANALYSIS

This passage is from a Victorian novel, and describes a slum area called 'Tom-all-Alone's' in the city of London. The passage comes after the character of Jo, a poor vagrant child, has been introduced in the novel.

> Jo lives – that is to say, Jo has not yet died– in a ruinous place known to the like of him by the name of Tom-all-Alone's. It is a black, dilapidated street, avoided by all decent people, where the crazy houses were seized upon, when their decay was far advanced, by some bold vagrants who after establishing their own possession took to letting them out in lodgings. Now, these tumbling tenements contain, by night, a swarm of misery. As on the ruined human wretch vermin parasites appear, so these ruined shelters have bred a crowd of foul existence that crawls in and out of gaps in walls and boards; and coils itself to sleep, in maggot numbers, where the rain drips in; and comes and goes, fetching and carrying fever and sowing more evil in its every footprint than Lord Coodle, and Sir Thomas Doodle, and the Duke of Foodle, and all the fine gentlemen in office, down to Zoodle, shall set right in five hundred years – though born expressly to do it.
>
> Charles Dickens, *Bleak House* (1852/3)

Task

3. What are your first impressions of this setting?

   a) What mood does the name 'Tom-all-Alone's' create?

   b) What do you notice about the adjectives used to describe the area? Can you identify any semantic fields?

   c) What are the effects of the two highlighted metaphors?

   d) Why is there a list of 'fine gentleman' at the end of the extract? What effect does it create?

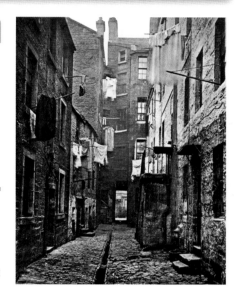

It is also important to consider the following *social and historical* contextual information relevant to this text.

- 'Tom-all-Alone's' is a fictional setting drawn from several of London's Victorian slum areas of poor, insanitary housing and great poverty.
- Outbreaks of epidemic diseases such as typhoid, cholera and smallpox occurred in urban areas throughout the 1840s and 1850s. The precise causes of these diseases, often just termed 'fevers', were still unknown. They were thought to be spread by filth and bad air, or 'miasma'.

Now consider the following *literary* context:

- Throughout the 1850s, Charles Dickens supported campaigns for the improvement of slum areas like Tom-all-Alone's. He wrote articles about sanitation and housing in his magazine *Household Words*.
- Many Victorian writers and politicians wanted to draw attention to the plight of the urban poor and the 'two nations' divide between the rich and the poor.

Task

4. In what ways has this contextual information changed your ideas about this passage? How has it developed your understanding?

Chapter 2 Studying prose fiction

Read this student analysis, along with the teacher's annotations.

Student A

Dickens's family spent time in Marshalsea Debtors' Prison when Dickens was a child. This experience meant that Dickens wanted to write about poverty and the poorest areas of the city. In this extract he is shocked by the poverty in Tom-all-Alone's, one of the worst slum areas in London in the Victorian period. This can be seen with the negative nouns he uses such as 'misery', 'vermin' and 'swarm'. There is also reference to disease such as 'fever', which led to the residents dying in great numbers. The reference to the 'fine gentlemen' is to those who ignore the poverty.

— biographical details not relevant to this passage

— basic overview

— unclear about point of view and narration; some understanding of setting

— comment not very specific

— some support

— some support and basic observations

Now compare it with the following, much stronger, student analysis with the teacher's annotations.

Student B

The extract opens with Dickens's reference to the character of Jo, the child vagrant, to both humanise and personalise the shocking description of Victorian slum conditions for middle-class readers unaware of the full extent of urban poverty. It is clear that Jo's life is one where mere survival is everything and his only achievement is that 'he has not yet died'. The use of the adverb 'yet' here is significant, suggesting that death for Jo, as for all the residents of the slum area Tom-all-Alone's, is always near. The lexis of decay is also prominent here as Dickens emphasises the abandoned, forgotten nature of the area, which is 'avoided by all decent people' and is now a 'dilapidated street' of 'tumbling tenements'. The 'ruined shelters' of this slum area then become personified as both the body of a 'ruined human wretch' and emblematic of epidemic disease and 'fever' such as typhoid which was prevalent throughout the mid-19th century. Dickens connects this decay to the emotive word 'evil', which is then juxtaposed with a list of ridiculously named 'fine gentleman in office' to emphasise what he and other writers considered to be a growing divide between rich and poor.

— effects linked to social and literary context

— detailed analysis of language

— analysis linked directly to social and historical context

— specific link between text and relevant example of literary context

Task

5. Using the teacher's annotations, write a brief commentary on the strengths of the second student's paragraph.

Final Task

Read the following passage from a short story first published in 1898 by Charles Chesnutt.

> The ball was to take place on Friday night. The house had been put in order, the carpets covered with canvas, the halls and stairs decorated with palms and potted plants; and in the afternoon Mr Ryder sat on his front porch, which the shade of a vine running up over a wire netting made a cool and pleasant lounging-place. He expected to respond to the toast 'The Ladies,' at the supper, and from a volume of Tennyson – his favourite poet – was fortifying himself with apt quotations. The volume was open at A Dream of Fair Women…
>
> […] He weighed the passage a moment, and decided that it would not do. Mrs Dixon was the palest lady he expected at the ball, and she was of a rather ruddy complexion, and of lively disposition and buxom build…
>
> […then] he heard the latch of his gate click, and a light footfall sounding on the steps. He turned his head, and saw a woman standing before the door.
>
> She was a little woman, not five feet tall, and proportioned to her height. Although she stood erect, and looked around her with very bright and restless eyes, she seemed quite old; for her face was crossed and recrossed with a hundred wrinkles, and around the edges of her bonnet could be seen protruding here and there a tuft of short gray wool. She wore a blue calico gown of ancient cut, a little red shawl fastened around her shoulders with an old-fashioned brass brooch, and a large bonnet profusely ornamented with faded red and yellow artificial flowers. And she was very black – so black that her toothless gums, revealed when she opened her mouth to speak, were not red, but blue. She looked like a bit of the old plantation life, summoned up from the past by the wave of a magician's wand, as the poet's fancy had called into being the gracious shapes of which Mr Ryder had just been reading.
>
> He rose from his chair and came over to where she stood.
>
> Charles Chesnutt, 'The Wife of his Youth' (1898)

Task

6. First consider the presentation of the characters:
   a) What impression is created of Mr Ryder in the first paragraph?
   b) What do we learn about the event he is planning?
   c) What information are we given about the visitor's clothes, her appearance and her skin colour?
   d) Why might this be significant?
7. Now consider the social and historical information relevant to this text.
   - In 1865, after the Civil War, slavery was abolished throughout the United States.
   - In 1898, racial discrimination was still rife. Black and mixed-race people continued to live their lives segregated from white people.
   - Light-skinned people of mixed race could sometimes 'pass' as white and so avoid discrimination.

   Consider also the literary context:
   - Charles Chesnutt was an African-American lawyer and writer who wanted to highlight problems with race relations after the Civil War.
   - The story's title is 'The Wife of his Youth'.

   How does this information affect your reading of the passage?
8. Write two paragraphs on how the author presents Mr Ryder and his visitor. Link your analysis of meaning to your contextual knowledge using the text-context-text model.
   Points for you to think about include:
   - Mr Ryder's social status as indicated by the setting
   - the significance of the Tennyson poem
   - the effect of the details provided about the visitor
   - the possible significance of the story's title.

Plenary

Now think about a prose text that you have studied or are studying. In what ways has your understanding of context shaped your understanding? You can use the following prompt to help you respond:

> My knowledge of contexts has developed my understanding of the novel in a number of ways. For example…

2.6 Exploring context in post-1900 prose

Big question

- How do you use your knowledge of the context of a post-1900 prose text?

When commenting on social, historical or literary context, you need to make sure your discussion is relevant to the text and emerges directly from your own detailed analysis of a text's language and structure. Following the text-context-text structure in your paragraphs will help you get the balance right.

SOCIAL AND HISTORICAL CONTEXT: ISSUES AND CONCERNS IN POST-1900 TEXTS

Since 1900, the world has seen immense social and cultural change, and prose fiction has therefore had to confront a wide new range of issues and ideas. The following are some of the most significant areas of concern:

war and global conflict	role and rights of women
social class and mobility	racial discrimination
violence and crime	global migration	totalitarianism
colonialism/post-colonialism	science and technology
environmental destruction	psychological damage
identity	oppression	alienation

Task

1. **a)** Are there any other areas of concern that you consider significant?

   b) Can you link any of these concerns with a post-1900 prose text you know?

LITERARY CONTEXT: FORM AND STRUCTURE IN POST-1900 PROSE TEXTS

The modern era has been shaped by uncertainty and instability. This has led to increased experimentation in fiction, particularly evident in the works of **modernist** writers such as Joseph Conrad, Virginia Woolf, William Faulkner, Katherine Mansfield and James Joyce.

These early 20th-century writers broke away from the traditions of the plot-driven, realist novels, in which characters were represented mostly from the *outside*. Instead, they created new, often unsettling, forms of narrative in which characters' internal selves and their very thought processes were laid bare.

Modernist prose fiction can include:

- unreliable or self-conscious narrators
- non-linear or non-chronological narratives
- narrative fragmentation
- **stream of consciousness** techniques.

Key terms

modernism: term used to describe movement of writers who broke away from older prose forms and narrative structures, such as the realist novel, to experiment with language, the representation of time and of consciousness

stream of consciousness: a narrative technique that presents the free flow of random thoughts, feelings and perceptions inside a character's mind

Read the following passage:

> For, if for me we were four people with the same tastes, with the same desires, acting – or, no, not acting – sitting here and there unanimously, isn't that the truth? If for nine years I have possessed a goodly apple that is rotten at the core and discover its rottenness only in nine years and six months less four days, isn't it true to say that for nine years I possessed a goodly apple? So, it may well be with Edward Ashburnham, with Leonora his wife and with poor dear Florence. And, if you come to think of it, isn't it a little odd that the physical rottenness of at least two pillars of our four-square house never presented itself to my mind as a menace to its security? It doesn't so present itself now though the two of them are actually dead.
>
> I don't know….
>
> I know nothing – nothing in the world – of the hearts of men. I only know that I am alone – horribly alone.
>
> Ford Maddox Ford, *The Good Soldier* (1915)

Task

2. How is the narrator's uncertainty indicated in this passage?

  a) Comment on the writer's use of:
   * punctuation
   * tense changes and time shifts
   * elements of a spoken voice
   * the repeated conditional 'if'
   * negatives and 'nothing' in the last line.

  b) What are the overall effects of these features on the tone of the extract?

  c) Which word, in your view, best describes this narrative voice?
   * ambiguous
   * unreliable
   * non-linear

  d) Are there any other words you would use to describe it?

  e) Look again at the definition of modernism and the list of features of modernist fiction on the previous page. In what ways can this extract be considered a modernist text?

SOCIAL AND HISTORICAL CONTEXTS: CONCERNS IN POST-1945 TEXTS

In this extract, a young Nigerian woman, Chika Okafor, joins her new husband, Ofodile, in New York.

> My new husband carried the suitcase out of the taxi and led the way into the brownstone building, up a flight of brooding stairs, down an airless hallway with frayed carpeting and stopped at a door. The number 2B, unevenly fashioned from yellowish metal, was plastered on it.
>
> "We're here," he said. He had used the word "house" when he told me about our home. I had imagined a smooth driveway snaking between cucumber-colored lawns, a door leading into the hallway, walls with sedate paintings. A house like those of the white newlyweds in the American films that NTA showed on Saturday nights.
>
> He turned the light on in the living room, where a beige couch sat alone in the middle, slanted, as though dropped there by accident. The room was hot; old musty smells hung heavy in the air.
>
> Chimamanda Ngozi Adichie, 'The Arrangers of Marriage' (2003)

Task

3. What are your first impressions of the setting and the narrator's reaction to it?

- Comment on the adjectives used to describe the apartment in the first and third paragraphs.
- Comment on the adjectives used to describe the narrator's imaginary 'house'
- What is the effect of the reference to the 'white newlyweds in the American films'?

4. Now read the information about the social and historical context and the literary context relevant to this text in the margin. How does this context influence your ideas about the narrator and the setting she describes?

5. a) Read the student paragraph below. How does the student link context to analysis?

In this extract Adichie contrasts the narrator's dreams of her new American life with its reality. She is shown her new home by her 'new husband' who at this stage remains un-named, perhaps to reflect the emotional distance between the couple, who it appears are not familiar with each other and have been brought together in a traditional, Nigerian arranged marriage. The disappointment in her surroundings is evident from the adjectives used by the narrator as she approaches the apartment door: 'brooding stairs' 'airless hallway' and 'frayed carpeting', which creates an oppressive atmosphere and a sense of neglect. This is then sharply contrasted with the narrator's dreams of her American 'house'…

b) Complete the paragraph using further points of context relevant to your own analysis.

6. How might this passage reflect wider concerns about the experiences of young immigrant women coming to the United States for the first time?

Social and historical context

- The setting of this story is Flatbush, Brooklyn – a very diverse area of New York City.
- Since the 1980s, Flatbush has also become home to many African immigrants from countries such as Ghana, Zimbabwe, Nigeria and Kenya.
- Lagos is Nigeria's largest city.
- Traditional marriages in Nigeria are generally arranged between families, rather than individuals.

Literary context

- Chimamanda Ngozi Adichie was born in Nigeria and lives in both the USA and Lagos.
- Her short fiction often explores Nigerian immigration to the USA through the eyes of young female characters.

Wider reading

A significant feature of late-20th-century and 21st-century prose fiction is its concern with the complexity of modern identity. Concerns with gender, ethnicity, sexuality, culture, social class, religion and nationality are frequently central elements of these narratives.

Final Task

Read this passage from the ending of the novel *1984* by George Orwell.

The voice from the telescreen was still pouring forth its tale of prisoners and booty and slaughter, but the shouting outside had died down a little. The waiters were turning back to their work. One of them approached with the gin bottle. Winston, sitting in a blissful dream, paid no attention as his glass was filled up. He was not running or cheering any longer. He was back in the Ministry of Love, with everything forgiven, his soul white as snow. He was in the public dock, confessing everything, implicating everybody. He was walking down the white-tiled corridor, with the feeling of walking in sunlight, and an armed guard at his back. The long hoped-for bullet was entering his brain.

He gazed up at the enormous face. Forty years it had taken him to learn what kind of smile was hidden beneath the dark moustache. O cruel, needless misunderstanding! O stubborn, self-willed exile from the loving breast! Two gin-scented tears trickled down the sides of his nose. But it was all right, everything was all right, the struggle was finished. He had won the victory over himself. He loved Big Brother.

George Orwell, *1984* (1949)

Task

7. a) What impression is created of Winston's state of mind?

b) What do you think happened to Winston in the Ministry of Love?

c) In the last paragraph, what do you think the word 'struggle' could relate to?

Now consider the following points of context:

* George Orwell's **dystopian** novel, *1984*, was published in 1949, four years after the end of the Second World War.
* Orwell feared the rise of new repressive, totalitarian political regimes in Europe and Russia.
* The phrase 'Big Brother' has now entered popular culture. It is associated with any form of surveillance or control over thought and expression.

Read the following student paragraph examining Orwell's depiction of the character of Winston at the end of this novel.

> **Key term**
>
> **dystopian:** a genre where dysfunctional imaginary human societies are presented in the form of alternative futures or histories

Orwell emphasises the way in which Winston, and others, are entirely unmoved and disconnected from the suffering and oppression that surrounds them. The triadic listing of 'prisoners and booty and slaughter' which details the events on the telescreen should be genuinely disturbing, but instead the waiters 'turn back to their work' and both they, and Winston, reach instead for the 'gin bottle.' Orwell shows Winston retreating into alcohol and to a 'blissful dream'; yet this dream is one which, for the reader, appears instead to be a nightmare of confession and submission. Despite 'implicating everybody' Winston can assert, with the shockingly simple simile, that his soul is now 'as white as snow'. Winston is finally broken by tyranny and the type of repressive totalitarian forces that Orwell himself feared would rise to power in Europe and Russia in the decades after the Second World War.

— clear overview

— analysis with support

— effect on reader

— reference to literary feature

— links relevant context to analysis

Task

8. Using the student response and context points above, continue to analyse the rest of the passage. Comment on:

* the imagery of 'the armed guard' and 'long hoped-for bullet'
* the use of free indirect discourse
* the last two simple sentences.

Plenary

Choose a prose text written in the last 50 years. Does it explore any of the following common concerns: gender, race, sexuality, culture, social class, religion and nationality? Using a spider diagram, make notes about how these and other related concerns are explored in the text.

2.7 Developing different interpretations

Big question
- How can prose texts be interpreted in different ways?

DIFFERENT RESPONSES

There are as many different responses to texts as there are readers – *that* is often what makes the study of literature so interesting and so challenging. For example, every individual reader will interpret a text in a way that reflects their own personal response to it. There are also, however, alternative readings of texts that reflect differing critical and theoretical perspectives.

RESPONSES TO SOCIAL CLASS

In this section, you will explore different perspectives on texts, beginning with responses to the representation of social class.

To help you to explore different interpretations and readings in relation to social class, it can be useful to ask challenging questions:
- Who or what holds most power in the narrative?
- Is power connected to wealth, social class, gender, race, nationality or some other factor? Does it ever change hands?
- Are there any conflicts or struggles – either within characters or across the wider narrative?
- Are there any recurrent symbols or narrative patterns?
- Are the conflicts or struggles resolved by the end of the story?

Task

1. Now apply these questions to any prose text you have studied. Do your findings change your response to the text in any way?

Read the passage from the opening chapter of Charles Dickens's novel *Our Mutual Friend*. Gaffer Hexam and his daughter Lizzie are in a small boat on the Thames scavenging what they can. Gaffer has just discovered a body.

His arms were wet and dirty, and he washed them over the side. — references to dirt and washing
In his right hand he held something, and he washed that in the river
too. It was money. He chinked it once, and he blew upon it once, and
he spat upon it once, – 'for luck,' he hoarsely said – before he put it
in his pocket.

'Lizzie!'

The girl turned her face towards him with a start, and rowed in — imagery of the 'roused bird of prey'
silence. Her face was very pale. He was a hook-nosed man, and with
that and his bright eyes and his ruffled head, bore a certain likeness
to a roused bird of prey.

'Take that thing off your face.'

She put it back.

'Here! and give me hold of the **sculls**. I'll take the rest of
the **spell**.'

'No, no, father! No! I can't indeed. Father! – I cannot sit so near it!' — punctuation in Lizzie's speech and use of pronoun 'it'

He was moving towards her to change places, but her terrified
expostulation stopped him and he resumed his seat.

'What hurt can it do you?'

'None, none. But I cannot bear it.'

'It's my belief you hate the sight of the very river.'

'I–I do not like it, father.'

'As if it wasn't your living! As if it wasn't meat and drink to you!'

At these latter words the girl shivered again, and for a moment
paused in her rowing, seeming to turn deadly faint. It escaped his
attention, for he was glancing over the stern at something the boat — use of indefinite pronoun 'something'
had in tow.

Charles Dickens, *Our Mutual Friend* (1865)

Task

2. a) Using spider diagrams, examine the features highlighted in the annotations, making notes of their connotations.

b) Now share and compare your responses with another person's. Are there any similarities? Or points of difference?

Glossary

scull: one of two small oars used to propel a boat
spell: shift, period of work

In the study of literature, it is important to recognise that there are many ways of responding to a text. These different interpretations are only valid, however, if they are based securely on evidence from the text.

Now consider some more challenging questions to deepen your response to the extract.

Task

3. How does Dickens:
- focus on money and making a living in the extract?
- demonstrate Lizzie's horrified reaction to the corpse?
- use language to heighten the shock of what Gaffer Hexam is actually doing?

4. What do you think this passage suggests about the Hexams and their way of making a living?

Look at how one student has responded to the passage.

> At the opening of the extract, Dickens twice refers to washing,
> before indicating in a short, simple sentence that the 'something'
> Gaffer Hexam has found is money. The initial association of dirt
> with money and the deliberate lack of clarity regarding exactly
> what has been scavenged suggest that Gaffer's livelihood is
> somehow metaphorically unclean. This is further emphasised
> by Dickens use of the imagery of the 'roused bird of prey' to
> describe Gaffer…

Task

5. Using your own notes and the student response above as a model,
   create your own response to the scene Dickens describes in the
   extract. Conclude with what you think Dickens is saying here about
   the Hexams and, in wider terms, about the lives of the poor in
   Victorian London.
6. Next consider one critic's response, which follows a **Marxist
   reading** of the text. Remember, it can be helpful to consider different
   critical or theoretical perspectives, but it is not essential. Different
   personal interpretations are equally useful to include and explore.

> 'Dickens highlights new and disturbing ways in which the poor are
> forced to scrape a living in Victorian London. Discarded objects
> floating in the Thames are scavenged by the Hexams, but, although
> it is never directly mentioned, the scavenging now extends to looking
> for corpses. Gaffer Hexam, therefore, pickpockets the dead and
> through him Dickens shows how the human body has become a
> valuable commodity in a capitalist society.'

7. Do the ideas above develop or challenge your own response? Now
   add a final sentence to your response to integrate these ideas into
   your own analysis. If you wish, choose one of the following sentence
   starters, which all use interpretative language:
   It could be argued, however, that…
   Alternatively, it could said that…
   By extension, it could be stated that…

RESPONSES TO GENDER

Another perspective to consider when responding to a text focuses
on gender and the ways in which male and female characters are
represented. Read the following extract from a novel in which Mr
Pontellier is visiting Dr Parbleu to discuss his wife, Edna Pontellier.

'Ah, Pontellier! Not sick, I hope. Come and have a seat. What news do you bring this morning?' He was quite portly, with a profusion of gray hair, and small blue eyes which age had robbed of much of their brightness but none of their penetration.

'Oh! I'm never sick, Doctor. You know that I come of tough fiber – of that old Creole race of Pontelliers that dry up and finally blow away. I came to consult – no, not precisely to consult – to talk to you about Edna. I don't know what ails her.'

'Madame Pontellier not well,' marvelled the Doctor. 'Why, I saw her – I think it was a week ago – walking along Canal Street, the picture of health, it seemed to me.'

'Yes, yes; she seems quite well,' said Mr Pontellier, leaning forward and whirling his stick between his two hands; 'but she doesn't act well. She's odd, she's not like herself. I can't make her out, and I thought perhaps you'd help me.'

'How does she act?' inquired the Doctor.

'Well, it isn't easy to explain,' said Mr Pontellier, throwing himself back in his chair. 'She lets the housekeeping go to the dickens.'

'Well, well; women are not all alike, my dear Pontellier. We've got to consider – '

'I know that; I told you I couldn't explain. Her whole attitude – toward me and everybody and everything – has changed. You know I have a quick temper, but I don't want to quarrel or be rude to a woman, especially my wife; yet I'm driven to it, and feel like ten thousand devils after I've made a fool of myself. She's making it devilishly uncomfortable for me,' he went on nervously. 'She's got some sort of notion in her head concerning the eternal rights of women; and – you understand – we meet in the morning at the breakfast table.'

The old gentleman lifted his shaggy eyebrows, protruded his thick nether lip, and tapped the arms of his chair with his cushioned fingertips.

'What have you been doing to her, Pontellier?'

'Doing! Parbleu!'

'Has she,' asked the Doctor, with a smile, 'has she been associating of late with a circle of pseudo-intellectual women – super-spiritual superior beings? My wife has been telling me about them.'

'That's the trouble,' broke in Mr Pontellier, 'she hasn't been associating with any one. She has abandoned her Tuesdays at home, has thrown over all her acquaintances, and goes tramping about by herself, moping in the street-cars, getting in after dark. I tell you she's peculiar. I don't like it; I feel a little worried over it.'

Kate Chopin, *The Awakening* (1899)

Task

8. Make notes in response to the following questions:

   a) Why does Pontellier correct himself over his use of the word 'consult'?

   b) What example does Pontellier give to illustrate his wife not acting 'well'?

   c) What is the effect of the doctor's use of the pronoun 'we'?

   d) How are Edna's actions affecting her husband?

   e) What is the doctor's initial explanation?

   f) How do you respond to Pontellier's more detailed description of his wife's behaviour?

> **Key term**
>
> **feminist reading:** literary criticism that challenges representations of women in texts and questions prevalent attitudes and assumptions about women and women writers (for more information, see the 'Introduction to literary critical theory' at the end of this book)

9. What does this passage show about views of women in late 19th-century America? Consider:

   - the absence of a female voice in the extract – two men talking about an absent woman
   - the reference to 'pseudo-intellectual women' and links to late-19th-century context
   - the verbs used by Pontellier to describe his wife's behaviour at the end of the extract.

10. a) Here are a range of responses to this question. Can you find evidence in the text to support each view?

    - Men often displayed extreme concern and care about their wives.
    - A wife's behaviour was only seen in terms of how it affected her husband.
    - Women who neglected their domestic roles were viewed as a problem.
    - A wife's actions were seen as her husband's responsibility.
    - Support for the 'rights of women' campaign was viewed as a form of sickness.

    b) Looking at the evidence, which of the responses to the text do you agree with? To what degree?

11. Now use the following to structure a longer response. Use embedded quotations throughout to support your analysis.

    At the opening of the extract Pontellier's unease is shown by...

    The initial words he uses to describe her behaviour are...

    Pontellier's own response to his wife's actions is shown by...

    His reference to the 'eternal rights of women' and the doctor's to 'pseudo-intellectual women' reflect wider late-19th-century concerns such as...

    The verbs used by Pontellier to describe Edna's solitary behaviour are...

    When Pontellier describes this behaviour as 'peculiar', this might suggest that Chopin is highlighting...

    Overall, in this passage, it could be argued that Chopin is exploring...

12. Finally, consider how one student has used the highlighted point in question **10a** as a **feminist reading** and integrated it into their own analysis.

    From a feminist point of view, it could also be argued that Chopin shows Edna's behaviour here is not only labelled by her husband as 'odd' and 'peculiar', but also that her rebellion and support for 'the eternal rights of women' is actually diagnosed as a sickness that must be symbolically 'cured' by men.

    Now use any of the other bullet point responses in a similar way to challenge or develop a different interpretation.

Thinking more deeply: **responses to patterns and symbols**

Read the opening to a novel in which the unnamed narrator – a very young woman who marries a much older, wealthy widower – recounts a dream of Manderley, the grand house the couple once lived in together.

Last night I dreamt I went to Manderley again. It seemed to me I stood by the iron gate leading to the drive, and for a while I could not enter for the way was barred to me. There was a padlock and a chain upon the gate. I called in my dream to the lodge-keeper, and had no answer, and peering closer through the rusted spokes of the gate I saw that the lodge was uninhabited.

No smoke came from the chimney, and the little lattice windows gaped forlorn. Then, like all dreamers, I was possessed of a sudden with supernatural powers and passed like a spirit through the barrier before me. The drive wound away in front of me, twisting and turning as it had always done, but as I advanced I was aware that a change had come upon it; it was narrow and unkempt, not the drive that we had known. At first I was puzzled and did not understand, and it was only when I bent my head to avoid the low swinging branch of a tree that I realised what had happened. Nature had come into her own again and, little by little, in her stealthy, insidious way had encroached upon the drive with long, tenacious fingers. The woods, always a menace even in the past, had triumphed in the end. They crowded, dark and uncontrolled, to the borders of the drive. The beeches with white, naked limbs leant close to one another, their branches intermingled in a strange embrace, making a vault above my head like the archway of a church. And there were other trees as well, trees that I did not recognise, squat oaks and tortured elms that straggled cheek by jowl with the beeches, and had thrust themselves out of the quiet earth, along with monster shrubs and plants, none of which I remembered.

The drive was a ribbon now, a thread of its former self, with gravel surface gone, and choked with grass and moss. The trees had thrown out low branches, making an impediment to progress; the gnarled roots looked like skeleton claws. Scattered here and again amongst this jungle growth I would recognise shrubs that had been land-marks in our time, things of culture and of grace, hydrangeas whose blue heads had been famous. No hand had checked their progress, and they had gone native now, rearing to monster height without a bloom, black and ugly as the nameless parasites that grew beside them.

Daphne du Maurier, *Rebecca* (1938)

Annotations (right margin):

- dream sequence and imagery of gates and locks
- mood created by adjective 'forlorn' and supernatural reference
- retrospective narration
- natural world personified and presented as menacing
- sensual imagery along with religious simile
- plants become monstrous and threatening
- references to death and decay

Chapter 2 Studying prose fiction

Task

13. What do you think this imagery from the opening of the novel suggests about the state of mind of the narrator? What concerns or ideas might it foreshadow in the rest of the story?

14. One interpretation of this passage focuses on how du Maurier's description of the dream might reveal the narrator's hidden feelings about her marriage to a much older, wealthier man – and her thoughts regarding her own restricted role as a woman and wife among the upper classes in 1930s Britain.
Using this interpretation, makes notes on:
 a) the imagery of barriers
 b) the menacing woodland setting
 c) references to death and darkness/decay.

Character–based **psychoanalytical criticism** could explore how this dream reveals what the female narrator is repressing and how her unconscious desires, wishes and fears, which might be socially unacceptable or even forbidden, emerge through patterns in language and the use of symbols and imagery.

Key term

psychoanalytical criticism: approach to literary criticism that uses the theories of Sigmund Freud (1856–1939) and his followers (for more information, see the 'Introduction to literary critical theory' at the end of this book)

Wider reading

Sigmund Freud in *The Interpretation of Dreams* (1900) suggested that dreams provide valuable clues to the workings of our unconscious mind and that they can be primarily interpreted as a form of wish fulfilment. In dreams, according to Freud, our hidden desires are subject to *condensation* (where two or more ideas become one), *displacement* (where our real concerns are transferred onto or transformed into something or someone else) and the use of *symbolism* (where our real desires and fears are represented by other, less troubling, objects).

Task

15. In what ways could this critical reading be applied to the passage on the previous page? Are there any other ways in which you can interpret the significance of her dream?

Read part of a student response below, which uses a psychoanalytical approach to analyse du Maurier's description of the dream:

The narrator makes clear at the outset that this is a dream narrative where she is returning to a transformed and newly threatening Manderley. The passage opens with many references to barriers; the 'barred' 'iron gate' and the 'padlock' and 'chain' initially prevent the narrator's entry to the estate and could symbolise that what she will later discover within the dream has been similarly 'barred' within in her own mind.

112

Final Task

Task

16. Using the notes and the student response, continue with the psychoanalytical analysis.
You can use the following sentence starters and possible responses to help structure your analysis:

The decay and abandonment of the Manderley estate is shown by…

This could represent…

> *…a decay of hope?*

> *…or the abandonment her own wishes and desires?*

> *…or…?*

The effect of the time reference and the change of pronoun in 'we had known' is…

The imagery of nature becomes increasingly threatening. This is emphasised by…

This nature imagery is contrasted with more passionate language – for example…

This could suggest…

In a psychoanalytical reading of this passage, it could be argued that the dream represents a displacement of the narrator's real fears…

> *…of some form of death?*

> *…or of her future role as a wife?*

> *…or of her loss of identity?*

> *…or of her transition to adulthood?*

> *…or …?*

Du Maurier might therefore be using this dream narrative to present contemporary concerns…

> *…about women's roles?*

> *…marriage and loss of female identity?*

> *…or…?*

Plenary

Think of a prose text you have studied and a significant character within it. Now think about how the writer represents this character and how you have responded to them. Use the table below to help you gather notes on your own and other responses to this character.

How did you first respond to this character? Why?	How might other readers respond differently to them?	Are there any other critical or theoretical perspectives that might be useful when considering this character?
What do you think might be their significance in the story?	How might this character link to any wider context and concerns in the text?	What evidence is there in the text to support these other readings and/or interpretations?

Checklist for success
✓ Lead with your own reading and interpretation.
✓ Include detailed language analysis and support from the text.
✓ Be careful to select other suitable interpretations that are based on evidence.
✓ Use other interpretations to extend and develop your own analysis.
✓ Make links to wider context or issues where relevant.

2.8 Writing about a whole prose text

Big question
- How do you plan a response to a discursive question on a whole prose text?

UNDERSTAND THE TASK (AS/A LEVEL)

When approaching a discursive essay question at AS or A Level, it is important to make your points across the text as a whole. In Units 2.1–2.7, you have explored the key elements of prose texts, which means you can now draw on your understanding of:
- the writer's choice of narrative methods and setting
- how far the text fits into existing genres or challenges them
- the structural features such as opening, closing, climax and resolution
- how characters are created and how their thoughts and feelings are conveyed
- what is distinctive about the writer's style and use of language
- how meaning is shaped by the writer's choices
- the writer's wider concerns, ideas and issues.

Your task now is to relate your understanding of these elements to the focus of the question.

Discursive questions can be worded in a number of ways. These examples are based on Edith Wharton's short story 'A Journey'.

A full version of 'A Journey' by Edith Wharton is provided in the Teacher Resource.

> **A.** Discuss the ways in which Wharton presents the character of the husband in 'A Journey' and consider his significance to the story as a whole.
> **B.** Discuss the effects that Wharton creates using a particular point of view in 'A Journey'.
> **C.** Discuss the effects that Wharton creates using the setting of the railway carriage in 'A Journey'.
> **D.** Discuss the ways in which Wharton presents marital disillusion in 'A Journey'.

Look at the highlighted parts of the questions:
- **A.** This is a character focus question, where you will need to explore the presentation, development and significance of the character in the whole text.
- **B.** This is a narrative focus, where you need to analyse the writer's choice of narrative method and the effect this has across the story as a whole.
- **C.** This setting focus question is asking you to think about how the particular choice of setting impacts upon the development of the narrative.
- **D.** This concern focus question is asking you to explore the presentation, development and significance of this concern or issue in the whole text.

Task

1. Look at two further questions. Identify the question focus for each.

> **E.** Discuss the effects that Wharton creates by shifting forwards and backwards in time in 'A Journey'.
> **F.** Discuss the ways in which Wharton presents death and illness in 'A Journey'.

Now look in detail at the first discursive essay question:

> **A.** Discuss <u>the ways</u> in which Wharton presents the character of the husband in 'A Journey' and consider <u>his significance</u> to the story as a whole.

It is important to identify what this question is asking you to do. It is a character-based question, but you should discuss:
- the narrative methods Wharton uses to present the character of the husband
- the effects of these methods
- the impression created of his character
- how this might relate to wider concerns and issues in the story as whole.

GATHER YOUR IDEAS AND EVIDENCE

To answer this question, you need to discuss how Wharton presents the character *throughout* the narrative.

> Task

2. Locate the following sections of the text. Make notes on how the character of the husband is presented in each:
- **a)** the opening of the story where the husband's response to his illness is described
- **b)** the description of couple's life together and his character before the illness
- **c)** other characters' reactions to him as an invalid
- **d)** where there is extensive use of dialogue
- **e)** descriptions of him after death
- **f)** the ending of the story.

Are there other parts of the story that might be helpful?

PLAN YOUR RESPONSE

Having selected relevant sections of the text, you can begin to formulate your argument. You can use the *tracking* approach, where you work through the text from beginning to end, or you could organise your response according to the *different methods* the writer uses to present the character.

In the tracking approach, your points should come in order as they do in sections **a)** to **f)**. If you are focusing on the different methods, you could use the following structure:

Discuss the overall **structure** of the text – point of view, narrative structure, time, setting – and analyse how this contributes to the presentation of the character of the husband.	Discuss the use of **language and imagery** to describe the husband.	Discuss sentence **structures, patterns and other literary devices** that contribute to the presentation of his character.

However, with the methods-based approach, you must be careful not to lose sight of how meaning develops across the text.

Now gather together your notes and consider:
- the significance of the character to the text as a whole
- how the presentation of this character might reflect wider concerns and issues.

You can incorporate the two points above in your conclusion and/or introduction, but you could also refer to wider points throughout the essay where relevant.

For example, here is a sample student paragraph and commentary.

> As the journey progresses, the husband is presented as increasingly frail and burdensome. It is, however, the reactions of other passengers to him that are emphasised as the journey progresses. Their reactions range from curiosity through to unease. Wharton states that the 'freckled child hung about him like a fly' with a simile indicating that she could not be dislodged whereas the actions of the 'nervous man' and other 'philanthropic passengers' reflect a growing sense of panic among the group. Wharton therefore presents the character of the husband as a symbol of our own problematic response when faced with mortality and serious illness.

— clear point but could develop in terms of point of view

— sense of wider structures of text

— support and analysis that could be further developed

good link to wider significance of character; could develop with reference to late-19th-century context

WRITE YOUR RESPONSE

Now plan and write your response to the task below in **1 hour**.

> Discuss the ways in which Wharton presents the character of the husband in 'A Journey' and consider his significance to the story as a whole.

UNDERSTANDING YOUR TASK (A LEVEL ONLY)

When you are approaching a whole text question for A Level, your response should follow *all* the guidelines given above. However, there is one *additional* area to develop:

• incorporate different interpretations in your analysis.

The format of the question may be different to reflect this additional skill:

> **1.** Discuss some of the ways in which Wharton presents women's roles and choices in 'A Journey'.
>
> **2.** 'At all costs she must conceal the fact that he was dead.' Discuss the impact on the wife of her husband's death in the light of this quotation from the middle of the story.
>
> **3.** By what means and with what effects does Wharton present a woman's view of marriage in 'A Journey'?

Now consider in detail this discursive whole-text A Level-style question:

> Discuss some of the ways in which Wharton presents women's roles and choices in 'A Journey'.

To answer this question, you will need to:

• focus on the language and techniques used by Wharton
• relate these to the presentation of female characters in the text
• take the opportunity to make reference to wider social, cultural and historical contexts
• consider different interpretations.

Task

3. The final sentence in the student's paragraph touches upon concerns and issues in the text as a whole, relating them to the character of the husband.

How could you develop this point further? For example, how might Wharton's characterisation of the husband and his illness also relate to:

• the commitments or sacrifices of marriage?
• gender roles and responsibilities at this time?

Task

4. Match each of the questions 1–3 above left with either type **a)**, **b)** or **c)**.

a) This form of question uses a direct quote from the text to stimulate your response.

b) This question makes direct reference to wider concerns and contexts.

c) In this question, the form of narration is foregrounded.

GATHER YOUR IDEAS AND EVIDENCE

As you collect evidence for a discursive whole-text A Level response, take these additional areas into account in your planning:

- gender roles and societal expectations of women at this time
- how these are reflected in Wharton's choice of language and narrative techniques
- how to incorporate other interpretations into your analysis.

PLAN YOUR RESPONSE

Whichever method of planning you choose, you will need to incorporate these additional features in a response at A Level.

When thinking about gender roles and relationships, you could consider:

- when the story was written
- the social class of the main female character
- the presentation of the main female character's life before and after marriage
- her behaviour in the story
- the presentation of other female characters and their attitudes.

When thinking about other interpretations, it is also useful to reflect upon:

- different ways in which readers might respond to the character and actions of the wife (with sympathy? shock? condemnation?)
- how contemporary or modern readers might respond differently.

Read the sample paragraph from an A Level-style response below.

> Wharton presents the main female character as 'restless' and increasingly desperate to arrive home to reconnect with the other members of her family. The journey, therefore, is a symbolic escape from the isolation of marriage and a role as wife and care-giver. This relationship is one that Wharton describes with the simile 'like two faces looking at each other through a sheet of glass'. In this image the couple cannot connect and, although the barrier between them is initially presented as the husband's illness, it appears to be much more. Wharton, whose early stories according to one biographer, relate frequently to 'marital misery' is arguably using the husband's invalid status and the wife's changed role to emphasise the social constraints upon married women forced to behave in acceptable ways. The wife's apparent lack of care and her deceptions after her husband's death challenge these constraints on women in late-19th-century America.

Task

5. Now highlight where in this response there is:
   - insightful analysis of deeper meaning
   - reference to a different interpretation
   - links to wider literary, social and historical contexts.

WRITE YOUR RESPONSE

Task

6. Now using the support from the sections above, plan and write your response to the discursive whole-text task in **1 hour**.

   When you have completed your response, turn to Unit 2.9, Evaluating responses to a whole prose text.

Discuss some of the ways Wharton presents women's roles and choices in 'A Journey'.

2.9 Evaluating responses to a whole prose text

Big question

- How should you evaluate your response to a whole prose text?

SAMPLE RESPONSES TO A WHOLE-TEXT TASK (AS/A LEVEL)

In this section, you will explore two discursive essay responses to the task in Unit 2.8. This will enable you to evaluate what makes a strong response and, using these responses and commentaries as a guide, help you to improve and develop your own whole-text answers.

> ### Task
>
> 1. Using the sample paragraph in Unit 2.8 as a model, read through your own response carefully, paragraph by paragraph, and complete an initial annotation (covering aspects such as assessment of overview, structure of response, analysis of language, form and structure, support from text, reference to context where relevant, strength of conclusion).
> 2. Read the following response. As you read, think about:
>   - what this response does well
>   - how the response might be improved.

> Discuss the ways in which Wharton presents the character of the husband in 'A Journey' and consider his significance to the story as a whole.

Response I

In Edith Wharton's 1899 short story 'A Journey', the reader is given insight into a middle-class marriage under strain. The strain is caused by the illness of the husband, who is presented throughout from the point of view of his wife. Through the narrative, which takes place during a two-day train journey across America, we are shown surprising events that lead to the wife concealing her husband's death to avoid being removed from the train. — *sound overview*

Wharton uses the character of the husband to explore expectations and roles within marriage. Initially the wife's disappointment in their situation is the focus of the story as she describes their 'estrangement'. This is due to the husband's 'irritability' and his 'increasing childish petulance'. Here Wharton shows that the husband is not coping with his poor health and that his response has led to the growing divide between them. Wharton shows this divide with the simile 'like two faces looking at one another through a sheet of glass'. — *some appreciation of language choices and effects*

The disappointment with her husband's loss of power is also evident when his wife describes him before his illness as 'strong, active, gently masterful'. These admiring adjectives suggest his masculine power and thus contrast with his weak state where his wife looks at him like 'a strange animal'.

— some analysis and support

Later in the story as the journey progresses, the husband, who is initially 'revived' by the journey, is presented as becoming increasingly bad tempered and 'weary', He then becomes more fragile and ill, and the rest of the train carriage become concerned that 'something must be done' about him. The husband and wife exchange some words, although very little is said. Wharton uses the dialogue to show that he is so weak, he just echoes her words: 'We'll be there soon now'; 'Yes very soon.' This increasing weakness provides an indication of what follows, as before the night is over, the husband is dead. He then becomes no longer a person but 'a dead thing', and this phrase is repeated by Wharton as she presents the wife's shock when she discovers his death. This is the climax of the story, and the husband's body is shown by Wharton to be a burden and a problem to be solved. This presents a very shocking impression to the reader and could relate to Wharton's wider views about the nature of marriage for women at this time – as something that is like a burden.

— some analysis and support

— some appreciation of contexts

Wharton also shows other people's reactions to the sickness of the husband in the story. While the wife disguises his death and pretends that he is still sleeping, other passengers ask questions and offer advice. A 'motherly' woman offers to give him medicine and a 'fat man' offers her spiritual support in the form of a religious pamphlet. Thus, Wharton uses these other characters to reveal the problems in the couple's marriage, which lacks care and religious feeling. Wharton does however show the wife as becoming increasingly fearful of discovery, and her thoughts become more terrifying as she imagines she sees her husband's face as 'like a waxen mask against a red curtain'. Wharton uses this simile and the imagery of the red curtain possibly to foreshadow the violent end to the narrative.

— personal response and support

— appreciation of language choices and effects

The resolution of the story occurs as the train pulls into the station at New York where the wife plans to pretend that she has only just discovered her husband's death. Wharton states 'the journey was over' and at this point the porter brings her husband's hat. This hat, which appears to remind the wife of her husband as a living person, brings on a fainting fit and she collapses, striking her head as she does so. Thus, Wharton shows that the end of the journey becomes not only the end of the lie, but also the end for both characters and their marriage. Wharton therefore uses the metaphor of the journey to present the challenges of marriage. The character of the husband becomes a symbol of the wife's disappointment with the 'match' she has made and with her experience of marriage in general.

— personal response and support

— effective communication: sound organisation and conclusion

COMMENTARY

This is a competent response, coherent and supported with relevant evidence from the text. There is some awareness of context and some relevant analysis of language choices. Expression is clear, and the organisation of the response covers the text as a whole and follows the general shape of the story.

Task

3. Now read a second response to the same question. As you read, think about what has been done to develop and improve upon the previous response.

Response 2

The characterisation of the husband may in some ways seem peripheral to Edith Wharton's 1899 short story 'A Journey', given that the third-person narrative exclusively follows the point of view and experiences of his unnamed wife throughout. This journey, however, can be read both literally and metaphorically. As well as the couple's two-day train ride across America, the journey is a reflective one for the wife in which she considers her former hopes of marriage and her disappointment as she faces the prospect of her husband's severe illness and her new role as his nurse. Wharton's presentation of the character of the husband through the eyes of his wife becomes a means to explore not just the wife's thoughts and feelings, but also the very nature of marriage itself for middle-class women at the end of the 19th century.

— very good understanding of structure

— different readings (for A Level-style responses)

— appreciation of methods linked to contexts

Throughout the story the reader must understand that everything is filtered through the wife's consciousness. The 'shadows' that form at the beginning of the story as the couple travel through the darkness, mirror those that, from the wife's point of view, have now appeared in their marriage. The husband is accused of 'childish petulance' and 'irritability' as a means of explaining the couple's 'imperceptible estrangement'. He is presented as a man adversely transformed by his ill health and the oxymoronic reference to his 'helpless tyrannies' also indicates how the power has shifted between them. Wharton then uses antithesis to emphasise this further as the wife's energy 'still bounded ahead' while his 'lagged behind', and the contrast between these two verb phrases is evident.

— sustained and detailed language analysis

The husband is also presented symbolically as a source of economic freedom for the wife who had built up 'such arrears of living' as a teacher to 'reluctant children'. The function of the husband as a provider of materialistic comforts – someone who can settle these 'arrears' - is again emphasised by Wharton with references to the 'pretty house' and the 'wedding presents', 'new furniture' and 'new dresses' that were abandoned to allow him to convalesce in Colorado. This loss of social status or of anyone to 'envy' their fortune is also mirrored by the husband's loss of physical power. He is no longer able to conform to the masculine stereotype of a 'strong, active, gently masterful' individual: an idealised romantic 'good match'.

Key term

antithesis: the juxtaposition of contrasting ideas, phrases, or words so as to produce an effect of balance

The loss of status and physical health is therefore shown by Wharton to render him less of a man. ⌐——— perceptive personal response

This depersonalisation of the husband continues into the narrative as he recedes to become an increasingly shadowy figure. There is only a brief exchange of dialogue presented between them and it is not used by Wharton to reveal anything more about either character. ⌐——— good understanding of writer's use of language
He can only echo her words: 'We'll be there soon.' – 'Yes very soon.' Significantly, no names or terms of affection are used between them and Wharton adds, with a short compound sentence, that 'He nodded and they sat silent.' The husband, however, is silent for the rest of the narrative as his death follows soon after. Wharton's presentation of this romantic anticlimax – he delivers no meaningful last words – arguably presents their marriage and marriage itself as a source of profound disappointment. Yet the most significant emotional response to the husband occurs not when he is living but when he is dead. When he is transformed into 'a dead thing' – and the noun phrase is repeated to mark the wife's horror – he becomes the focus for her fears and for the opinions and views of others. His body becomes an obstacle for the wife, one that must be concealed, and a source of fascination for other passengers. ⌐——— personal and perceptive reading

Wharton uses the narrative complication of the wife concealing the body to introduce a darker almost comic element to the story. A motherly lady fusses over his treatment of him and a 'fat man' delivers a sermon about 'sickness' offering a religious pamphlet. It is as if these characters, who subtly criticise the wife's lack of care for his physical and spiritual needs, operate on the husband's behalf as instruments of his 'helpless tyrannies'. In this way Wharton shows the powerful influence of social norms of behaviour in this period, particularly regarding female, caring roles. ⌐——— detailed analysis and relevant link to contexts

To conclude, Wharton shows that the husband asserts his greatest power as the train draws into New York and the wife collapses senselessly into the 'dead man's berth'. Although the husband is never named and, at the end of the story, he is simply 'the dead man', his character is used symbolically in the narrative by Wharton to reflect the inescapable pressures and constraints of marriage and monogamy both for women and for men. ⌐——— confident and perceptive conclusion

COMMENTARY

This is a very fluent and perceptive response, which ranges confidently across the text as a whole. There is sustained analysis of the writer's use of language, structure and form along with perceptive and insightful readings linked effectively to context.

EXTRACTS FROM SAMPLE RESPONSES TO A WHOLE-TEXT TASK (A LEVEL)

Remind yourself of the A Level-style task below:

> Discuss some of the ways Wharton presents women's roles and choices in 'A Journey'.

Your response to this discursive task should include all the elements you have explored in the AS/A Level-style responses above, but in addition it should feature:

- further references to wider social, cultural and historical contexts
- different interpretations as part of your analysis.

Task

4. Read through your response and annotate it. Initially you can use the sample AS/A responses above as a guide.

5. To help you evaluate the additional A Level elements required, read through the extract from a sample analysis below.

As you read, think about:

- what this response has done well
- how the response might be improved.

Response 3

Wharton presents the wife's dilemma after the husband has died as the climax of the narrative. The wife remembers what she saw happening to a couple whose child had died on a train journey: '[they] had been thrust out at some chance station… and this is what would happen to her'. The strong verb 'thrust' here reflects the wife's fears about how harsh her treatment might be if she reveals her husband has died. This incident can be read psychologically. Wharton shows that the wife does not want to acknowledge not only her husband's death, but also her own fears perhaps about life and death. Her fear is expressed as being 'alone with her husband's body…Anything but that! It was too horrible –'. Wharton uses the ellipsis and dash here to indicate the wife's disgust at death and her inability to express her terror. The hiding of his body could symbolise hiding her deepest fears from others. Wharton could also be suggesting the wife fears a loss of social status too. This is because, as a widow, she would have a more restricted and difficult role as part of middle-class, late-19th-century society.

sound awareness of structure, sound analysis and support

considers other opinions

relevant support from text

sound awareness of contexts

COMMENTARY

This is a sound response with relevant support from the text. There is also sound awareness of the structure of the text as whole plus relevant language analysis and support. There is some relevant consideration of other opinions, supported by evidence from the text. Some focus on the question.

Task

6. Now read the extract from a second response to the same question. Think about what has been done to develop and improve upon the first response.

Response 4

Following the husband's death, the wife has difficult encounters with other passengers. Through these encounters, Wharton explores societal expectations of women and their roles as wives and as carers. Wharton shows how the wife is challenged first by the porter with his offer of milk and then by 'a motherly woman with an intimate smile'. It is during the encounter with the unnamed 'motherly woman', however, that the wife's own shortcomings as a nurse and wife are most emphasised. Wharton shows the wife's unease in their exchange of dialogue – the wife's is repeatedly marked by repetition and dashes, indicating her anxiety: 'Oh, no–no, please!' and 'I–I let him sleep.' The motherly woman, however, subjects her to question after question about her nursing regime – 'What do you do when your husband's taken this way?' and 'When does he take the next dose?' – and Wharton suggests that each one of these questions is a subtle reproach. Next a 'lantern-jawed man', 'a freckled child' and 'fat man' with an 'apostolic smile' who offers religious pamphlets all challenge the wife – each one is, arguably, used symbolically by Wharton to accentuate the wife's strange un-motherly, un-Christian and un-female behaviour. In this way, Wharton shows the extreme social pressures placed upon women in the period to conform. A feminist reading of the story might suggest, therefore, that the wife's collapse and injury at the end of the story provides a brutal and punitive resolution for a character who defies conventions.

very good focus on question and overview

personal and fully supported point

perceptive reading

varying views considered, persuasively argued

COMMENTARY

This is a perceptive, fluent and focused response. Confident and detailed analysis that ranges across the text. A strong sense of overview, with very good awareness of contexts plus wider concerns. Persuasive use of other views and readings.

Final Task

Now that you have considered the sample responses for either AS/A or A Level-style discursive questions, reflect again upon your own response.

Task

7. **a)** Use the guidance in the tables on the final page of this chapter (page 136) to assess whether you think your response could be classed as 'competent' or 'very good'.

  b) What do you think were the strengths of your response? What could you do to improve upon and develop your own whole-text discursive essays?

  c) Write a brief commentary at the end of your own essay with action points for development.

2.10 Writing about a passage from a prose text

Big question

• How do you plan a response to a passage-based prose question?

UNDERSTAND THE TASK (AS/A LEVEL)

When approaching a passage-based question at AS Level, it is important to consider:

• the writer's style and choice of language
• their choice of narrative methods, structure and form
• how meaning is shaped by the writer's choices
• how the extract relates to the text as a whole
• how the extract might relate to wider concerns and contexts of the text.

You also need to understand the focus of the question so that your essay has a clear and purposeful structure.

First read the short story 'A Journey' by Edith Wharton. Now look more closely at the passage below from the opening of the story.

As she lay in her berth, staring at the shadows overhead, the rush of the wheels was in her brain, driving her deeper and deeper into circles of wakeful lucidity. The sleeping-car had sunk into its night-silence. Through the wet window-pane she watched the sudden lights, the long stretches of hurrying blackness. Now and then she turned her head and looked through the opening in the hangings at her husband's curtains across the aisle… [1]

She wondered restlessly if he wanted anything and if she could hear him if he called. His voice had grown very weak within the last months and it irritated him when she did not hear. This irritability, this increasing childish petulance seemed to give expression to their imperceptible estrangement. Like two faces looking at one another through a sheet of glass they were close together, almost touching, but they could not hear or feel each other: the conductivity between them was broken. She, at least, had this sense of separation, and she fancied sometimes that she saw it reflected in the look with which he supplemented his failing words. Doubtless the fault was hers. She was too impenetrably healthy to be touched by the irrelevancies of disease. [2] Her self-reproachful tenderness was tinged with the sense of his irrationality: she had a vague feeling that there was a purpose in his helpless tyrannies. The suddenness of the change had found her so unprepared. A year ago their pulses had beat to one robust measure; both had the same prodigal confidence in an exhaustless future. Now their energies no longer kept step: hers still bounded ahead of life, pre-empting unclaimed regions of hope and activity, while his lagged behind, vainly struggling to overtake her. [3]

When they married, she had such arrears of living to make up: her days had been as bare as the whitewashed school-room where she forced innutritious facts upon reluctant children. His coming had broken in on the slumber of circumstance, widening the present till it became the encloser of remotest chances. But imperceptibly the horizon narrowed. Life had a grudge against her: she was never to be allowed to spread her wings. [4]

At first the doctors had said that six weeks of mild air would set him right; but when he came back this assurance was explained as having of course included a winter in a dry climate. They gave up their pretty house, storing the wedding presents and new furniture, and went to Colorado. She had hated it there from the first. Nobody knew her or cared about her; there was no one to wonder at the good match she had made, or to envy her the new dresses and the visiting-cards which were still a surprise to her. And he kept growing worse. She felt herself beset with difficulties too evasive to be fought by so direct a temperament. She still loved him, of course; but he was gradually, undefinably ceasing to be himself. The man she had married had been strong, active, gently masterful: the male whose pleasure it is to clear a way through the material obstructions of life; but now it was she who was the protector, he who must be shielded from importunities and given his drops or his beef-juice though the skies were falling. The routine of the sick-room bewildered her; this punctual administering of medicine seemed as idle as some uncomprehended religious **mummery**. [5]

Edith Wharton, 'A Journey' (1899)

Glossary

mummery: a ridiculous or overcomplicated performance or ceremony

Here is an example of a passage-based question.

Comment closely on the passage, paying particular attention to the ways in which Wharton presents the relationship between the couple in the passage.

Task

1. Look closely at this first sample question. Highlight key words and phrases that would help to shape your response.
   - Which key words tell you to focus on details?
   - Which key words ask you to explore the how the writer uses language and techniques?
   - Where is the question focus indicated?

Now look at how a student has annotated another passage-based question below:

Comment closely on the passage, paying particular attention to the ways in which Wharton presents the wife's thoughts and feelings in the passage

need to analyse writer's use of language, structure and form

must include a number of ways and methods used by the writer and focus on how, not what

link all points to the presentation of the character of the wife and her thoughts and feelings

GATHER YOUR IDEAS AND EVIDENCE

Before you begin to write, you should collect the relevant points and support that you will need to complete a response. You can then include these in an outline plan.

This question asks you to focus closely on the writer's methods and use of language to create effects. It is therefore important to consider general points about the structure and organisation of the passage. You can refer back to Units 2.1 to 2.4 to help you.

Task

2. Here are a number of questions to help you make notes on the passage. Highlight supporting examples from the text and annotate these with your own notes.

   a) What is the form of narration? Whose point of view are we being offered here?

   b) How is time referenced in the extract? Are there any time shifts? How are these indicated?

   c) Where is the extract set? How is this setting described? What mood is created?

   d) What sentence structures are being used? Is there any pattern or change in the use of particular sentence structures or functions? What effects are created in terms of tone and pace?

   e) What devices does the writer use to indicate the character's thoughts and feelings?

   f) Do these change in the course of the extract? How is this indicated?

3. Next read these annotations on the passage, which track its different phases. Can you find examples from the text that support these phases? Make notes on the effects created.

   [1] imagery of journey and tone created

   [2] the wife's responses to the onset of her husband's illness

   [3] how she views the changes in their relationship

   [4] references made to past and present

   [5] increasing reflection on how illness affects her

PLAN YOUR RESPONSE

Use your notes and annotations to create a structured plan for the exam-style question that focuses on the wife's thoughts and feelings.

You can approach this in a number of ways. One way is to track your way through the extract from beginning to end, including relevant selections and analysis as you go along. Another involves ordering your points according to the *methods* that the writer uses to convey the thoughts and feelings of the character of the wife.

In the tracking approach, you could use the notes on the annotations [1]–[5] above to organise your response.

In the methods-based approach, you could organise your response as follows:

- Comment on *structure* – narration, time, setting. Write an analysis of these features with support relating them to the focus of the question.
- Comment on use of *imagery* and other *figurative language*. Write an analysis of these features with support relating them to the focus of the question.
- Comment on other *language choices, sentence structures* and *patterns*. Write an analysis of these features with support relating them to the focus of the question.

With this approach there is, however, a danger of just feature-spotting and losing a sense of what the passage is about. Be sure, therefore, to link your points to how *meaning* develops in the passage.

You can of course approach the question in another way, but whatever form of organisation you choose, make sure you:

- consider the *effects* of the *form* of narration
- discuss the *beginning* and *ending* of the extract
- keep a tight focus throughout on how the *techniques* you have identified relate directly to the question
- comment briefly on how the extract relates to the *text as a whole* – this is not compulsory for AS Level but can be helpful.

To help you plan, here is an AS/A Level-style paragraph to guide you.

> At the opening of the extract, Wharton uses the description of the railway carriage at night to explore the mood of the unnamed female character, a wife of a man who is seriously ill. The sibilant description of the carriage refers to 'shadows' and the 'sleeping-car sunk into its night-silence'. This restful imagery contrasts with the character's state of mind, which is described by Wharton as both 'wakeful' and 'restless'. Her feelings of unease are therefore foregrounded by Wharton and further developed later in the extract as we learn more about her difficult relationship with her husband.

Task

4. Highlight where in the paragraph there is:
   - an effective overview
   - analysis of language choices and effects
   - further development of point with support
   - link to focus of question and extract as a whole.

WRITE YOUR RESPONSE

Now plan and write your response to the task below in **1 hour**. Remember: a strong response needs to be clearly structured, relevant and have support from the text throughout.

> Comment closely on the passage, paying particular attention to the ways in which Wharton presents the wife's thoughts and feelings in the extract.

UNDERSTANDING YOUR TASK
(A LEVEL ONLY)

When you are approaching a passage-based question for A Level, your response should follow *all* the guidelines given above for AS. However, there are two *additional* areas where you should develop your response:
- Relate the passage to the text as a whole.
- Incorporate different interpretations in your analysis.

The format of a passage-based question for A Level will reflect these additional expectations. For example, consider the question below:

> Paying close attention to language, tone and imagery, write a critical appreciation of the following extract, relating them to Wharton's presentation of the character of the wife in 'A Journey' as a whole.

Look at the highlighted parts of the question. You are being asked to:
- analyse the writer's use of language, structure and form in detail in the extract
- link your analysis to the presentation of the character of the wife in the extract
- make wider links to the presentation of the character of the wife in the text as a whole

GATHER YOUR IDEAS AND EVIDENCE

As you collect your evidence for a passage-based A Level response, you need to take these two additional areas into account in your planning. This means thinking about how:
- the extract forms the opening of the short story
- the extract relates to the development of the narrative and the character in the *story as a whole*
- how you might incorporate *other interpretations* into your analysis.

PLAN YOUR RESPONSE

Whichever method of planning you choose, you will again need to incorporate these additional features in a response at A Level.

When considering the text as whole, these questions will help you in your planning:
- How does Wharton develop the character of the wife as the story progresses?
- What challenges face her and how does she respond?
- What happens to her by the end of the story?
- How might readers respond differently to the character of the wife? Might they sympathise with her behaviour on the journey? Or find her actions bizarre or selfish? Or be shocked or even horrified by what she does?

When thinking about *other interpretations*, it is useful to reflect upon:
- power, gender and class issues that might be relevant to the text
- when the story was written
- your understanding of the wider concerns of Wharton as a writer.

Read the sample paragraphs from A Level-style responses in Tasks **5** and **6**. These demonstrate ways in which the two additional A Level elements can be incorporated into an extract analysis.

Task

> In this extract, Wharton demonstrates the wife's increasing irritation with her husband's invalid status and her new role as his nurse and carer. This reaches a climax later in the story when he dies suddenly. At this point Wharton's narrative becomes darker as the wife's reaction to the death is extremely unusual: she decides to conceal the death, it appears, fearing an awkward scene and removal from the train. Her reaction, however, is not entirely surprising given what Wharton has indicated about the character in the opening extract, for example…

5. In the response above, highlight where there is:

   a) focus on extract

   b) link to events later in the whole text

   c) reference to structure of the whole text

   d) link back to evidence and analysis from the extract.

> Wharton demonstrates the wife's mounting frustration regarding her husband's illness. Although this appears heartless, it could be argued that her disappointment is as much an economic one as it is a marital one. Her marriage and her husband's financial support freed her from her work as a teacher, which she depicts as barren: 'as bare as the white-washed school room'. This suggests that in late-19th-century America, all relationships have been somehow commodified and assigned a monetary value.

6. In the response above, highlight where there is:

   a) focus on question

   b) the introduction of an alternative reading

   c) support for this alternative reading

   d) development.

   Finally, what words or phrases are used in this paragraph to introduce different readings of the text?

WRITE YOUR RESPONSE

Task

7. Now, using the support from the AS/A and A Level sections above, plan and write your response to the passage-based task in **I hour**.

> Paying close attention to language, tone and imagery, write a critical appreciation of the following extract, relating them to Wharton's presentation of the character of the wife in 'The Journey' as a whole.

When you have completed your response, turn to Unit 2.11, Evaluating a passage-based response.

2.11 Evaluating responses to a passage-based question

Big question

- How do you evaluate your response to a passage-based question?

SAMPLE RESPONSES TO A PASSAGE-BASED TASK (AS/A LEVEL)

In this section, you will explore two responses to the passage-based task in Unit 2.10. This will enable you to evaluate what makes a strong response and, using these responses and commentaries as a guide, will help you to improve and develop your own answers.

Task

1. Using the sample paragraph in Unit 2.10, read through your own response carefully, paragraph by paragraph, and complete an initial annotation (covering aspects such as assessment of overview, structure of response, analysis of language, form and structure, support from text, reference to context where relevant, strength of conclusion).
2. Read the following response. As you read, think about:
   - what this response does well
   - how the response might be improved.

> Comment closely on the passage, paying particular attention to the ways in which Wharton presents the wife's thoughts and feelings in the passage.

Response 1

The short story 'A Journey' was written at the end of the 19th century and takes place during a train journey across America from Colorado to New York. The story, by the author Edith Wharton, focuses on the relationship between a husband and wife and how this has been changed by his illness. This extract from the beginning of the story emphasises how much this relationship has changed as the wife thinks back to how her life was before her husband's illness and the ways in which they have grown apart from each other.

sound overview, with some sense of relationship of passage to rest of text

Firstly, Wharton presents the wife's thoughts and feelings through the language choices and sentence structure used. At the beginning of the extract, Wharton makes it clear that the wife thinks the connection between herself and her husband is broken. This is shown with the simile 'like two faces looking at one another through a sheet of glass' and her use of the noun 'estrangement'. Wharton shows that the illness has created a barrier between the couple. This is also shown with the simple sentence 'doubtless the fault was hers' and the reader can see that the wife blames herself for their separation. Wharton also emphasises that the wife is still full of energy and ready to live her life while her husband is 'helpless'. This adjective emphasises how the wife is now the husband's carer.

some appreciation of writer's choice of language and effects

focus on question and understanding of writer's methods

There is a tone of disappointment in this extract. Wharton shows how the wife had high hopes for her marriage. She had been in a teacher in 'a white washed school-room' and after her marriage she had been able to leave this work as it would not have been acceptable for a married woman to keep this job at the time. She is disappointed by what has happened in her marriage and this is shown in the complex sentence 'Life had a grudge against her; she was never to be allowed to spread her wings.' Here Wharton personifies 'life' and uses the emotive noun 'grudge' to emphasise the wife's disappointment. The reader can see that the wife is resentful of the husband's weak state when he was so strong previously.

some appreciation of contexts

personal response supported from text

Wharton shows that the wife also feels sorry for herself and the reader may form a critical opinion of her because of this. This is shown when the wife describes leaving their 'pretty house' and wedding presents behind to go to Colorado to help him recover. Wharton shows the wife resented this move with the simple sentence 'She had hated it there from the first.' The wife is also sad that no one could appreciate her presents and new dresses and therefore Wharton is presenting her here as rather selfish and self-centred. This could reflect the fact that money was important to make a good marriage at this time. Wharton also uses the verb 'envy' when she describes how the wife would like her friends to see what a 'good match' she has made emphasising again the importance of money.

some analysis and support

some link to context

Wharton also emphasises that the wife's feeling towards her husband have changed. She uses a list of approving adjectives such as 'strong, active, gently masterful' to describe him before the illness and this shows how much he has changed and the wife's disappointment with this. This could reflect what was expected of men in the 19th century and now that he is weak he is no longer considered masculine. The wife's changed feelings also explain what happens later in the story when she is too ashamed to admit her husband has died and behaves in a way that is very uncaring and shocking.

personal response

awareness of relationship of passage to rest of text

The theme of love and caring is also highlighted in this extract as the wife finds nursing her husband difficult. Wharton shows this when she states 'the routine of the sickroom bewildered her'. The use of the word 'bewildered' here shows that she is not a natural nurse and is not comfortable with this form of caring and loving. Later in the story, other female passengers also make her feel bad about her lack of care. Wharton is therefore concerned with different forms of love between men and women and shows this through the character of the wife.

competent selection and analysis but slight loss of focus

To conclude, through Wharton's use of language and sentence structure and the contrast between the time before the illness and after it, she shows that the wife is disappointed with her marriage as it is no longer a 'good match' that others would envy. The reader can view the wife as uncaring, but by the end of the story, she also suffers injury, which is an effective resolution.

effective communication, sound organisation and conclusion

COMMENTARY

This is a competent response with relevant knowledge and use of appropriate support. Understanding is sound, but a little underdeveloped in places. There is analysis of some of writer's choices and some appreciation and reference to contexts. Expression is clear and straightforward. There is some sense of the extract's relationship to the text as a whole.

Task

3. Now read a second response to the same question. Think about what has been done to develop and improve upon the previous response.

Response 2

Wharton uses the opening of the short story 'A Journey' to exemplify the divide between illusion and reality in middle-class marriage in late-19th-century America. With the use of third-person focalised narration, from the point of view of the unnamed character of the wife, she explores the wife's growing frustration with her role as a carer to her terminally-ill husband. — very effective overview showing very good understanding of narrative structure

The opening of the story, in the berth of the railway carriage, creates an oppressive tone from the outset. The reference to the 'shadows' and the motion of the train, described with the soft sibilance of 'the sleeping car had sunk into its night silence' is in contrast to the wife's 'wakeful lucidity'. Wharton also uses the adverb 'restlessly' to describe the wife's wonderings. — detailed and sustained analysis of language choices and support

Wharton demonstrates that although, on the surface, her concerns are for her husband's needs, their underlying relationship is increasingly fractured. Wharton indicates this with the use of judgemental abstract nouns such as 'irritability' and 'petulance': although these are ascribed to the husband from the narrative, the wife's point of view suggests that the 'irritability' is more on her own side as she loses patience with her transformed spouse. This is further emphasised by Wharton — perceptive reading

with the comparison of their recent 'estrangement' as being 'like two faces looking at one another through a sheet of glass'. This simile suggests an invisible barrier between the couple, but Wharton develops this sense of separation later in the passage to emphasise that the barrier, in terms of the wife, is not between herself and her ill husband but between her hopes of marriage and its disappointing reality. — further perceptive development

This aspect is developed by Wharton when there is time-shift in the narrative when the wife reflects upon her life before marriage. — detailed understanding of form and structure

The imagery of her pre-marriage life as a schoolteacher is one that is 'bare' and 'white' and this stark, virginal description is followed by the use of harsh 'f' consonants as she 'forced innutritious facts upon reluctant children'. It appears that marriage, for the young teacher, would 'widen the present' and bring the 'remotest chances' within her reach. It is here that the wife's disappointment reaches its fullest expression in the passage with the bitter tone of the forceful statement: 'Life had a grudge against her: she was never to be allowed to spread her wings.' Here Wharton uses these metaphors to reduce the wife, rather than the husband, to a 'petulant' child, while also suggesting that for women, marriage represented a liberation from limited economic and social opportunity.

————— thoughtful reference to contexts

This is made clearer in the next part of the extract with Wharton's use of a financial and materialistic vocabulary, which mirrors the wife's earlier reference to her 'arrears of living.'

————— sustained analysis of language choices

Marriage, as Wharton suggests here, was for the wife defined by the 'pretty house' 'wedding presents', 'new furniture', 'new dresses' and 'visiting cards.' It then becomes clear that the economic advantages she acquired as a result of the 'good match' are now lost due to her husband's illness and their forced relocation. The overriding sense of disappointment and even anger felt by the wife in this extract is primarily associated with the loss of her new economic status. Wharton's use of language here conveys the uneasy reality of marriage for many middle-class women in late-19th-century America, where financial motivations outweighed emotional ones.

————— perceptive reading and relevant context

The extract concludes with Wharton's description of the wife's sense of frustration with her new role as a nurse and 'protector', which is presented with a bitter tone as if it is a subtle breach in this fiscal contract. Her role as nurse 'bewildered' her and Wharton's use of this verb followed by the image of 'uncomprehended religious mummery' reveals the wife's impatience and dismissive rejection of the more convention female caring role. Wharton's coupling of the adjective 'uncomprehended' with the noun phrase 'religious mummery' also suggests the wife is an outsider who has not been initiated into the feminised rituals of caring and nursing which, later on in the narrative, become a focus for others' criticism of her.

————— good knowledge of text as whole

In conclusion, therefore, Wharton presents the wife's feelings through this focalised narration as defined by disappointment. Her sense of betrayal of the promises of marriage is palpable and underscores her later actions which, though shocking, are a logical extension of the thoughts and feelings Wharton presents in this opening extract.

————— very coherent structure with very effective conclusion

COMMENTARY

This is a strong and perceptive response, which is supported by sustained analysis of language, structure and form throughout and thoughtful links made to the passage's relationship to the text as a whole. Very good appreciation of literary features and good knowledge of contexts of the work.

EXTRACTS FROM SAMPLE RESPONSES TO A PASSAGE-BASED TASK (A LEVEL)

Remind yourself of the A Level-style task below from Unit 2.10:

> Paying close attention to language, tone and imagery, write a critical appreciation of the following passage, relating them to Wharton's presentation of the character of the wife in 'A Journey' as a whole.

Your response to this A Level task should include all the elements you have explored in the AS/A responses above, but in addition it should feature:

- wider reference to the text as a whole
- different interpretations as part of your analysis.

Task

4. Read through your response to this question and annotate it. Initially you can use the sample AS/A Responses 1 and 2 in this unit as a guide.
5. To help you evaluate the additional A Level elements required, read through the extract below. As you read, think about:
   - what this response does well
   - how the response might be improved.

Response 3

As the opening extract develops, Wharton shows the wife as bitter and disappointed. She had high hopes of the marriage, but these have been crushed. This is shown with the simple sentence 'But imperceptibly the horizon narrowed' and this image creates a feeling of enclosure and oppression for the character. — sound analysis and relevant support

This is also evident later, in the climax of the narrative, when the wife behaves in such a strange way when her husband dies suddenly on the journey. — relating passage to whole text

Here again she is frightened of what his death will mean for her. Wharton does not even release the character from these feelings at the end of the story as she collapses and falls into the 'dead man's berth' and is therefore still trapped. — reference to different constituent parts of text with some support

This could reflect Wharton's own experiences, and it could be said that she presents a critical view of marriage at this time. Wharton's own first marriage ended in divorce and 'A Journey' explores what marriage could mean for women at the end of the 19th century. — considers other opinions

---

COMMENTARY

This is a sound and relevant response with support from the text. There is evidence of engagement with the text as a whole and a consideration of the relationship between this extract and the later development of the narrative. There is some consideration of other opinions, although this is underdeveloped. The biographical reference and link to the wider 19th-century context is rather generalised.

Task

6. Now read the extract from a second response to the same question. Think about what has been done to develop and improve upon the first response.

Response 4

Wharton's story and this extract open with the image of the train berth at night, with the character of the wife watching the 'sudden lights' and 'long stretches of hurrying blackness' through the window. Her 'wakeful' worried state, which is set against the imagery of light and dark, establishes the uneasy tone for the extract and the surprising development of the wife's character through the narrative as a whole. Wharton, through focalised third-person narration, subsequently presents the thoughts and feelings of the unnamed wife as she reflects upon the hopeful early stages of her marriage, 'the sudden lights' and also, in contrast, upon the 'hurrying blackness', which could symbolise his increasing weakness and her fears for the future. This light/dark antithesis in the opening of the story mirrors the ending of the narrative. Here the joy of reaching her destination of New York without her husband's death being discovered is soon dispelled by her fall into the darkness of the 'dead man's berth'. The story therefore has no clear resolution and remains ambiguous. Arguably, one interpretation of this symbolic journey – with light and dark in equal measure – could reflect the nature of marriage for women in the 19th century. Wharton shows that for many women, economic promise could soon be dashed by oppressive domestic reality and that, even as a widow, a wife might be unable to escape from the power of 'the dead man's berth'.

- very good selection of support and sensitive analysis
- very good analysis of the extract and its structure
- thoughtful consideration of a text as a whole
- perceptive consideration of other views with persuasive support

COMMENTARY

This is a very confident and perceptive analysis, with clear and thoughtful consideration of the passage's relationship to the text as a whole and how the character of the wife develops across the narrative. Very good consideration of other views, which are confidently explored and supported.

Final Task

Now that you have considered the sample responses for either AS/A or A Level passage-based questions, reflect upon your own response.

Task

7. a) Use the guidance in the tables on the final page of this chapter (page 136) to assess whether you think your response could be classed as 'competent' or 'very good'.

  b) What do you think were the strengths of your response? What could you do to improve upon and develop your own passage-based essays?

  c) Using the example commentaries in this unit, write a brief commentary at the end of your own essay with action points for development.

PROSE

What should you aim for in a competent response to the question?

Knowledge and understanding	You should show knowledge of your text and understanding of its concerns by making clear references to relevant episodes and events. Some use of quotations will make this even better. Try to include some reference to context, making sure it's relevant to what you have to say.
Analysis	You should try to say something about the effects of the writer's choices of words, images or structure with most quotations that you use.
Personal response	You should offer something of your own interpretation. How does the writer's expression of ideas help you understand the characters, plot events and the concerns of the text?
Communicating effectively	You should aim for a clear opening to your essay, showing you understand the question, and work towards a conclusion that returns to it. Make connections between your paragraphs and write clearly.
Literary criticism (A Level only)	You should show that you are aware that works of literature are not fixed and can be read in different ways. You might be able to quote a critic, but you can also use phrases such as 'This could be read as…' or 'A reader might respond to this by…'.

What should you aim for in a very good response to the question?

Knowledge and understanding	You need to show a detailed knowledge of the text and a subtle understanding of its concerns. Do this by making particular references to key parts of the text that are relevant to the question, and by focusing your points with accurate quotations. Show some precise knowledge of context, made directly relevant to the particular point you are making.
Analysis	You should build your essay on exploration of how the writer expresses their ideas. Focus on the writer, the presentation of concerns, events and characters. Think about how the narrative is shaped to guide the reader's response.
Personal response	You should communicate your own interpretation of the text, supported with clear evidence from it. Show how you read and respond to characters and events from the way that they have been written.
Communicating effectively	Address the question consistently throughout the essay, so that every paragraph is clearly directed and relevant. Don't be afraid of having your own voice in your essays.
Literary criticism (A Level only)	You should show how your reading of the text has been influenced by different readings, whether these are from particular critics, critical movements, or just hypothetical different ways in which the text, or parts of it, might be read. Think about the implications of these differences.

This chapter explores in depth the essential concepts and skills required when studying poetry as part of Literature in English at an advanced level. You will learn how to approach poems by engaging with examples of poetry from different periods and cultures. You will also explore a variety of different styles and forms.

The chapter will develop your skills and confidence in analysing the language, structure and form of poems, in order to write effectively about concerns, contexts and wider issues. You will also develop your own personal responses to texts, learning how to link poems, appreciate a poet's style, and engage meaningfully with alternative readings and interpretations.

In addition, you will develop and extend your own writing skills, building towards full exam-style responses at the end of the chapter. You will have the opportunity to evaluate your progress against a range of sample responses.

3.1 Exploring language and imagery in poetry

Big question

- How do poets use words and images to convey their ideas and create effects?

WORDS AND IMAGES

Poets use language to shape and communicate their meanings. Word choices, the use of **imagery**, personification, patterns, contrasts and symbols are used to build and develop ideas and concerns.

Moniza Alvi, a poet, was born in Pakistan and moved to England when she was a few months old. Her father was Pakistani and her mother was English. The speaker of her poem, 'Presents from my Aunts in Pakistan', looks back on her childhood and how she felt about her dual heritage.

Key term

imagery: a general term used to describe powerful language that draws vividly on the senses; it also includes techniques such as simile and metaphor

Task

1. Read the poem, 'Presents from my Aunts in Pakistan'. Begin by exploring what the poem is about and the ideas it appears to be including.

   a) What events and objects are described?

   b) Who might the speaker be?

   c) What we can tell about her thoughts and feelings about Pakistan and her aunts?

   d) What we can tell about her thoughts and feelings about England?

   e) What is the significance of the clothes mentioned in the poem, and why does Alvi focus on them?

You have a cultural heritage. This is the beliefs and behaviours of the life you are born into and grow up in. It can include language, religion, history, politics, fashion, food, festivals, sports and music. Some of these things will affect your daily life in an obvious way (for example, if you practise a religion or support a football team), while others make a smaller but still significant contribution to how you behave and view the world around you.

Task

2. Identify five things from your own life that are part of your cultural heritage.

Many of Moniza Alvi's ideas and concerns are conveyed through imagery, using the following:

- simile
- metaphor
- personification
- recurring images.

Presents from my Aunts in Pakistan

They sent me a **salwar kameez**
    peacock-blue,
      and another
glistening like an orange split open, [1]
embossed slippers, gold and black
    points curling.
    Candy-striped glass bangles
      snapped, drew blood.
    Like at school, fashions changed
      in Pakistan —
the salwar bottoms were broad and stiff,
    then narrow.
My aunts chose an apple-green **sari**,
    silver-bordered
      for my teens.

I tried each satin-silken top —
    was alien in the sitting-room.
I could never be as lovely
    as those clothes —
    I longed
for denim and corduroy.
    My costume clung to me
      and I was aflame,
I couldn't rise up out of its fire,
    half-English,
      unlike Aunt Jamila.

I wanted my parents' camel-skin lamp —
    switching it on in my bedroom,
to consider the cruelty
    and the transformation
from camel to shade,
    marvel at the colours
      like stained glass.

My mother cherished her jewellery —
    Indian gold, dangling, **filigree**,
      But it was stolen from our car.
The presents were radiant in my wardrobe.
    My aunts requested cardigans
      from **Marks and Spencers**.

My salwar kameez
    didn't impress the schoolfriend
who sat on my bed, asked to see
    my weekend clothes.

But often I admired the mirror-work,
    tried to glimpse myself
      in the miniature
glass circles, recall the story
    how the three of us
      sailed to England.
Prickly heat had me screaming on the way.
    I ended up in a cot
in my English grandmother's dining-room,
    found myself alone,
      playing with a tin-boat.

I pictured my birthplace
    from fifties' photographs.
    When I was older
there was conflict, a fractured land
    throbbing through newsprint. [2]
Sometimes I saw **Lahore** —
    my aunts in shaded rooms,
screened from male visitors,
    sorting presents,
      wrapping them in tissue.

Or there were beggars, sweeper-girls
    and I was there —
      of no fixed nationality,
staring through **fretwork**
    at the **Shalimar Gardens**.

Moniza Alvi,
(1993)

[1] simile shows colour; verb 'glistening' – bright, shining;
    split – violent?

[2] metaphor – newspapers report of battles,
    explosions; verb 'throbbing' – suggests alive,
    shocking, almost tangible.

Glossary

salwar kameez: national dress of Pakistan, combining loose-fitting trousers and a long shirt
sari: a long garment, wrapped around the waist and draped over the shoulder
filigree: ornamental design combining fine gold or silver wires
Marks and Spencers: a traditional British department store
Lahore: a city in Pakistan, the capital of the Punjab province
fretwork: a decorative design made by cutting ornate holes into panels of wood
Shalimar Gardens: a famous garden complex in Lahore

Task

3. **a)** At what points in the poem does the speaker seem proud or comfortable with her Pakistani heritage? Find an image that suggests this.

   b) Where in the poem does she seem uncomfortable or ambivalent about her Pakistani heritage? Find an image that suggests this.

   c) Identify an example of imagery that expresses pride or comfort, and one that expresses ambivalence or discomfort.

In the poem, similes are used to describe aspects of the poet's Pakistani heritage: her *salwar kameez*, fashion trends and her parents' lampshade.

Look at the simile describing the orange *salwar kameez* with a student's annotations:

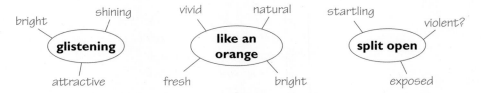

Read how the simile is explored in the student's analytical writing:

> The simile shows the intense colour of the salwar kameez, with the verb 'glistening' suggesting it has a bright, shining appearance that attracts the speaker, though the fact that the orange is 'split open' may indicate that the fascination has an edge to it.

Notice that the student has considered explicit meanings (the colour) and implied meanings (the appearance of the *salwar kameez* and the impression it has made on the speaker). The observations are linked to effects and possible meanings.

Task

4. **a)** Now unlock the associations and meanings created by the following metaphor, by making your own notes or annotations.

> When I was older
> there was conflict, a fractured land
> throbbing through newsprint. [2]

   b) Now write about this metaphor using the example above and the following prompts:

   The metaphor describes…

   This may suggest…

Although the speaker is drawn to her Pakistani heritage, she also feels that it intrudes on her life: she experiences a dual attraction and pain. In order to develop this idea, Moniza Alvi uses personification to describe the aunts' presents.

Looking at the lines, 'Candy-striped glass bangles / snapped, drew blood.' a student might write:

> Despite the first adjective seeming innocent and pretty, when the poet describes how the snapped bangles 'drew blood', it sounds as if her jewellery is deliberately hurting her. This use of personification suggests that, although she was attracted to and proud of her Pakistani heritage, she also felt uncomfortable or pained by it when it jarred with her normal life.

Task

5. Identify where the student has:

a) made a clear point about the poem

b) embedded a quotation as evidence

c) used subject terminology to specify a feature of language

d) analysed how the quotation conveys the poet's thoughts and feelings.

6. Using the student's paragraph as a model, write a brief explanation of how the poet might be using personification to convey her feelings in the line, 'My costume clung to me'. You could use these prompts:

The poet uses personification to describe…

The verb 'clung' suggests…

The choice of the noun 'costume' implies…

SYMBOLS AND ALLUSIONS

Poets use **symbols** such as objects or colours to develop their meanings and ideas. At a simple level, doves can be seen as symbols of peace, for example. But symbolism can also open up multiple or ambiguous meanings.

Key term

symbol: in literature, when an object, image or action takes on a meaning within a story beyond its literal sense

Task

7. Looking back at the lines where Moniza Alvi personifies the glass bangles, what different things could 'blood' symbolise here?

Towards the end of the poem, Moniza Alvi mentions 'beggars, sweeper-girls' who would live in poverty as social outcasts. As a child, the speaker seems to feel that she wasn't fully English and wasn't fully Pakistani, so she perhaps didn't fit in anywhere. Alvi uses the image of the 'beggars, sweeper-girls' to symbolise how the speaker also felt like she was an outsider.

Task

8. How might this idea of being excluded also be symbolised by the 'fretwork' in the lines, 'staring through fretwork / at the Shalimar Gardens.' towards the end of the poem?

9. Now look back at the lines:

> But often I admired the mirror-work,
>   tried to glimpse myself
>   in the miniature
> glass circles,

    a) What do you think mirrors can be used to symbolise?

    b) What does the symbolism suggest here about heritage and identity? Consider:
- the fact that there are many mirrors
- that the images are tiny and hard to see.

Poets sometimes create symbols that allude to stories or ideas beyond the poem. The second stanza of Alvi's poem contains an **allusion** to the legend of the phoenix.

Key term

allusion: a word or phrase that makes reference to another place, person, story or event, thereby bringing to mind other, related ideas

Task

10.   **a)** What is the legend of the phoenix? What is the symbolic meaning?

    b) If you recognise this allusion, how does it add to your understanding of the following lines?

> My costume clung to me
>   and I was aflame,
> I couldn't rise up out of its fire,
>   half-English,
>   unlike Aunt Jamila.

11. Look at these two examples of student writing about symbols and allusions. Which do you think is better and why? Think about the following:
- How the symbol is analysed. Is there a close focus on its meanings and allusions? Is the analysis detailed and precise? Is subject terminology used to show understanding?
- Does the student connect the close analysis to the overall concerns of the poem?
- Do you think the interpretation of the poem presented is justified and well supported?

Example 1:

The poet uses many symbols to present the speaker's conflicted feelings about her cultural heritage. In the line, 'I admired the mirror-work', the verb suggests that the speaker is attracted to her Pakistani heritage, whilst the mirrors are used to symbolise the way her heritage makes her feel like more than one person, or that she has many identities. The idea of a reflection suggests she feels she can never be truly Pakistani, and this concern is developed further through the symbols of 'fretwork' and 'beggars, sweeper-girls', which create an impression of her as an outsider only looking in. The 'fretwork' suggests there may be barriers to her heritage that she (as a 'beggar') would like to break down but cannot.

Example 2:

When Alvi writes, 'I was aflame, / I couldn't rise up out of its fire', she is making an allusion to the myth of the phoenix. The lines show the brightness of the clothes, suggesting that the speaker found her Pakistani heritage exciting. However, the negative words also indicate that this heritage made her uncomfortable: putting the clothes on made her feel strange. In the myth, the phoenix bursts into flames and dies, only to be reborn from its own ashes. It comes from Greek mythology and the phoenix is associated with the sun, but it isn't a real bird. The speaker also hopes to be reborn but it doesn't work.

Task

12. Reread the example that you thought was less successful and improve it. You may present an alternative interpretation of the poem, but make sure you focus closely on the symbols and how they relate to the poem's overall concerns.

LOOKING AT CONNOTATIONS OF CONNECTED WORDS AND IMAGERY

Now you have a stronger understanding of the key concerns in the poem and how they are conveyed through individual words or images, you should begin to trace and explore recurring images or patterns of language that are being used to develop meaning. This is a key skill at AS and A level.

The clothes in the poem are clearly important and reflect the two cultures. Make a list of all the different words that are used to describe the clothes that the aunts send from Pakistan.

Task

13. a) Make your own copy of the table on the following page. First group the words under the headings in the left-hand column.

b) Then fill in the right-hand column, considering the effect that these recurring images have on the poem. How do they help to convey the speaker's thoughts and feelings about having a dual heritage?

Recurring imagery	Effect
colours peacock-blue like an orange	
natural images peacock-blue like an orange	By associating her Pakistani clothes with animals and fruit that aren't originally English, Alvi highlights the perceived foreignness of her cultural heritage. However, these images also reinforce the idea that her heritage is a natural part of her that she finds excitingly exotic and (specifically the peacock images) wants to show off.
decorative, attractive glistening	
valuable	
vibrant	
unsettling	

Read this paragraph, analysing the effect of patterns of imagery and how they reveal the poet's feelings.

Moniza Alvi uses recurring images of nature to show that the speaker feels her Pakistani heritage is an essential part of her and that for her it represents something fresh, alive and appealing. For example, she includes the phrase 'satin-silken' to make the top sound natural rather than artificial. These words suggest delicacy and beauty, reflecting how she values her heritage, although the fact that she then felt 'alien' wearing this finery also implies that while attracted to it, she isn't completely comfortable with, or feels unequal to, her heritage. She shows concern or anxiety about how to handle her dual heritage. Similarly, Alvi draws on natural imagery to describe one salwar kameez as 'glistening like an orange split open' and another 'peacock blue'. Here the natural imagery suggests a vibrancy, splendour and lusciousness associated with Pakistan. The fact that blue peacocks originally came from the Indian subcontinent, also suggests its inherent importance to the speaker, and that if she was to wear this garment, she would express this side of her identity and show it off. Together, these natural images express the allure of her Pakistani heritage and its incongruity with her ordinary English life: 'the sitting room', the more workaday fabrics of 'denim and corduroy'.

- a clear point about how connected imagery is used in the poem to communicate an aspect of the poem's concerns
- an embedded quotation as evidence
- analysis of the overall effect of the quotation
- development of analysis, considering additional meanings and effects
- if relevant, could also consider any alternative meanings that link to other aspects of the poem's concerns
- further analysis to highlight the connotations of patterns of imagery
- draws the detail together to consider the overall effect

Task

14. Choose one of the other groupings from the table and write a paragraph about how the patterning shapes our understanding. Use the paragraph above as a model to help you structure your response.

CONTRAST

Your notes from task **13** may have identified a different type of pattern in the poem: that of contrast.

Task

15. a) Read stanza 4. Comment on the words used to describe her mother's jewellery: 'cherished', 'dangling', 'filigree'.

b) These words are followed by the contrasting, harsh and everyday 'But'. Comment on the effect here.

c) How are the English cardigans described? What is the effect of this contrast?

d) Now consider another contrast in stanza 6 between the language and imagery of the voyage on the ship and the image of herself as a child with the 'tin-boat' in her grandmother's dining room?

e) What other contrasts can you find in the poem, and what effect do they have?

16. Why do you think Alvi uses contrast throughout the poem? How does this reflect the wider concerns of the poem?

Final Task

Read this student paragraph analysing one of the ways in which Moniza Alvi uses contrasts in her poem.

> Moniza Alvi uses contrasts to build a picture of the speaker's mixed feelings about her country of birth. In the phrase, 'I pictured my birthplace / from fifties photographs', she seems nostalgic and happy. The verb 'pictured' shows her imagining what it was like, and the noun 'birthplace' implies joy and pride. However, this is a frozen moment and contrasts with the metaphor, 'there was conflict, a fractured land / throbbing through newsprint' – the speaker's feelings about Pakistan turn to shock and anxiety as more wars break out as the partition of India and Pakistan in 1947 continues to reverberate. The verb 'throbbing' makes the news sound urgent and horrifying, while the adjective 'fractured' suggests violent splintering.

Task

17. Add a line to the end of the paragraph that draws together the building effect of the use of contrast in the poem.

18. Using the paragraph as a model, write your own paragraph, explaining how Alvi uses contrast in the poem, but this time working with other examples. Make sure you focus closely on the language and imagery used and how this develops the concerns of the poem.

Plenary

Thinking back to the poem as a whole, and the work that you have done exploring language and imagery, what do you think is the most effective feature of language that Alvi has used in the poem? Why does it have such an impact on the poem?

3.2 Exploring sound and rhythm in poetry

Big question

- How do poets use sound and rhythm to emphasise and contribute to meaning in poetry?

METRE AND RHYTHM

'Sonnet 2', by William Shakespeare, is about the idea of getting old and losing your youthful looks. Shakespeare suggests that you can't keep your energy and beauty, but you can create a copy of it by having children.

Sonnet 2

When forty winters shall besiege thy brow,
And dig deep trenches in thy beauty's field,
Thy youth's proud **livery**, so gazed on now,
Will be a tatter'd **weed**, of small worth held:
Then being ask'd where all thy beauty lies,
Where all the treasure of thy lusty days,
To say, within thine own deep-sunken eyes,
Were an all-eating shame and **thriftless** praise.
How much more praise deserved thy beauty's use,
If thou couldst answer 'This fair child of mine
Shall sum my count and make my old excuse',
Proving his beauty by succession thine:
This were to be new made when thou art old,
And see thy blood warm when thou feel'st it cold.

William Shakespeare (1609)

Glossary

livery: distinctive outfit or uniform
weed: archaic word for clothes
thriftless: wasteful

The **metre** of a poem is best described as the length and rhythm of each line. As well as making a poem enjoyable to read and listen to, the poet's metrical choices can be used to reflect and emphasise the different concerns established by their language choices.

The rhythm of a poem is based around sets of syllables. Each set is usually a pair of syllables but is sometimes three syllables. The most familiar rhythm in English is **iambic**. This is a repeated pattern where an unstressed syllable is followed by a stressed syllable. For example, the word 'besiege' is an iamb: you pronounce it be-SIEGE rather than BE-siege.

Task

1. a) To make sure you are really clear about the progression of meaning, write a 14-line translation of 'Sonnet 2' in modern English. The opening lines can seem quite insulting, so don't be afraid to have some fun with your version!

    b) Mark your translation with an asterisk each time you focus on a different idea.

2. Read the poem all the way through twice. Make notes or annotations to show the following language patterns:
    - military and natural images to describe an attractive face
    - military and natural images to suggest becoming ugly
    - metaphors to suggest that having a child will rejuvenate you, physically and mentally.

The first line of 'Sonnet 2' is iambic:

> when FOR-ty WIN-ters SHALL be-SIEGE thy BROW

This creates a de-DUM, de-DUM rhythm in the lines of the poem.

Task

3. In pairs, reread the poem aloud, deliberately emphasising the iambic rhythm so you can hear where Shakespeare has placed his unstressed and stressed syllables.
4. Look back at the annotations you made in task **2** about how language conveys the poet's ideas. Can you see any points where the stresses in the lines fall on key words in order to emphasise what the poet is saying?

   For example, in the first line, the iambic rhythm emphasises the idea of turning 40 (FOR-ty), the idea that old age is inevitable (SHALL), and the focus on how age affects beauty (BROW).
5. Write an explanation of how the iambic rhythm has been used to emphasise ideas in one line of the poem. Use the example below to help you. (Notice how the student phrases their exploration of how sounds *emphasise* meaning – highlighted here.)

   The iambic rhythm is used in the final line of 'Sonnet 2' to emphasise Shakespeare's belief that having a child can rejuvenate you. One of the stresses falls on 'blood' to highlight the significance of the word and its dual meanings of family (the bloodline) and the life source (blood is vital for health and a youthful appearance). The stresses also help to make the line sound persuasive, with 'see' and 'when' urging the reader to imagine the future and the inevitability of ageing.

In addition to stressing important words or features, the *overall effect* of the metre of a poem can be important to its meaning.

A set of syllables, such as an iamb or an **anapaest**, is also called a **metrical foot**. The length of a line of poetry is measured in these feet. If there are three sets of feet, the length of the line is called a **trimeter**; four sets create a **tetrameter**; five sets a **pentameter**; six sets a **hexameter**, and so on. Therefore, the metre of a line containing four sets of iambs is called iambic tetrameter.

Sometimes poets use a set metre simply because it creates a familiar rhythm. However, this metre can sometimes be used to create a particular effect.

The pattern of de-DUM, de-DUM, de-DUM, de-DUM, de-DUM that is created by iambic pentameter can suggest steadiness, endurance, a heartbeat, cycles or uniformity; equally, it might imply boredom, routine, feeling trapped or inevitability.

Sometimes, variations on or deviations from an underlying rhythm can be used to create particular effects and emphasise key ideas.

Key terms

metre: the length and rhythm of a line of poetry

iambic: an unstressed beat followed by a stressed beat

anapaest: a pattern of unstressed, unstressed, stressed (a three-syllable group)

metrical foot: a group or set of syllables, such as an iamb

trimeter: three sets of metrical feet

tetrameter: four sets of metrical feet

pentameter: five sets of metrical feet

hexameter: six sets of metrical feet

Other types of metrical feet:

trochaic: a stressed beat followed by an unstressed beat

pyrrhic: two unstressed beats

spondaic: two stressed beats

dactylic: a pattern of stressed, unstressed, unstressed (a three-syllable group)

Note: you will not be expected to use all of these terms, and it is possible to comment on rhythm without using the precise technical terminology.

Task

6. Quickly count the number of iambs in each line of 'Sonnet 2' and work out the poem's metre.

Task

7. Use some of the words above to explain how the iambic pentameter brings out the concerns of 'Sonnet 2' (becoming old and ugly, or procreation).

The use of metre in 'Sonnet 2' emphasises the concern(s) of…

because the iambic pentameter suggests…

The metre of a poem can be used to emphasise key images. You have already identified how the concern of becoming old and ugly is conveyed in the poem through military language. You could develop an exploration of such images by adding a comment about metre. For example:

> *Shakespeare's military metaphors are emphasised through the way the iambic pentameter creates a uniform rhythm, like an army marching.*

Task

8. The use of rhythm in poetry is very deliberate. Try writing a four-line poem in iambic pentameter. Use the metre accurately so that the iambic stresses fall naturally on words (remember the example of how you say be-SIEGE not BE-siege).

Start by choosing a theme to write about, such as love, war, food or football. Decide what you want to communicate about that theme before you begin writing.

To really challenge yourself, try to organise your writing so that the metre emphasises your meaning by stressing important words or linking to key images.

SOUND PATTERNS

As mentioned above, poems sometimes break out of a familiar metre in order to emphasise certain words and ideas.

Read these opening lines of Robert Greene's poem 'Farewell to Folly' (1591), about settling down and living a quiet life:

> Sweet are the thoughts that savour of content;
> The quiet mind is richer than a crown;
> Sweet are the nights in careless slumber spent;

Notice that the trochaic substitution also creates two consecutive unstressed syllables.

> SWEET are the THOUGHTS that SA-vour OF con-TENT

Poets often do this (it can also be achieved through dactyls and anapaests) in order to create a gentler rhythm.

Task

9. a) The poem is written in iambic pentameter, but the first iambs of lines 1 and 3 have been substituted for a different type of foot. Look back at the key terms on page 147 and identify how the rhythm (the type of foot) is different.

b) What word has the change of rhythm emphasised?

c) Thinking about the subject of the poem, why might Greene have wanted to emphasise this word?

Task

10. a) How might these unstressed syllables reflect the concerns of Greene's poem?

b) Complete the paragraph below, choosing the most suitable words from the box.

'Farewell to Folly' is concerned with the joys of living a _____ life. In line 1, the poet's use of _____ creates consecutive _____ syllables on the words 'are the'. This gives the line a more _____ rhythm that reflects the speaker's wish to settle down.

aggressive	calm	gentle	iambic pentameter
stressed	stressful	trochaic	substitution
	unstressed	urgent	wild

Key terms

phonology: the way in which sounds are organised in language or text
prosody: the patterns of rhythm and sound used in poetry, including stress and intonation
alliteration: repetition of sounds at the beginning of words
assonance: repetition of vowel sounds within words
consonance: the use of similar-sounding consonants in close proximity
sibilance: repetition of sibilant sounds (s, sh, z)
plosive: a consonant produced by the release of a sharp burst of air when spoken (such as p, b or k)

Poets make use of a variety of **phonological** or **prosodic** patterns, from rhyme and **alliteration** to **assonance** and **consonance**, **sibilance** and **plosives**. Sounds don't create meaning, but they are an effective way of emphasising meaning.

Rhyme is one of the most evident features of prosody, and many poems choose to work with a set rhyme scheme (see Unit 3.3 for more detail). For example, 'Sonnet 2' has an alternating rhyme scheme with a rhyming couplet at the end, with each phase of the rhyme scheme relating to a phase of meaning in the sonnet. The rhyme scheme can be described using a letter for each new rhyme:

abab, cdcd, efef, gg

Although not all rhymes are used for an effect, you should look at the words being rhymed and consider whether they are highlighting any of the ideas or images in the poem. For example, the rhyming of 'brow' and 'now' links the subject's physical beauty to the current moment in time, emphasising the idea that this beauty is transitory and will not last.

Task

11. a) Look back and identify this rhyme scheme in Shakespeare's 'Sonnet 2'.

b) Comment on how the progression of ideas is linked to the rhyming groups here. The main focus of lines 1–4 is that the subject of the poem will get old and lose their beauty. What do lines 5–8, 9–12, and 13–14 focus on?

Task

12. Find other rhymes used to emphasise the ideas of beauty and ageing in 'Sonnet 2'.

13. Poets use many different sound techniques. Copy and complete the table below, inserting a definition and the correct example from a)–e) on the right, for the technique. Write an example of your own of each technique.

a) The snake slithered gracefully across the grass
b) They haggled over the big bag of goods.
c) Crash! Bang! Pop!
d) The thin girl was as slim as a pin.
e) The dreadful darkness descended like death.

Technique	Definition	Examples
alliteration		
assonance		
consonance		
plosives		
sibilance		

Thinking more deeply: **writing about sound effects**

Task

14. Comment on the effect of alliteration and plosives in the opening lines of 'Sonnet 2'.
How do these sound effects convey the idea of ageing and the loss of beauty?
Think about how they help to foreground the military images.

> When forty winters shall besiege thy brow,
> And dig deep trenches in thy beauty's field,

Write up your ideas in a couple of sentences using one or two of these words:
reflects, emphasises, highlights, conveys, foregrounds, accentuates.

15. a) Identify a sound technique in lines 1 and 3 of 'Farewell to Folly':

> Sweet are the thoughts that savour of content;
> Sweet are the nights in careless slumber spent;

b) How does the technique reflect the idea of living and calm and quiet life? Write sentences
linking the technique to the meaning of the lines. Again, include one or two of these words
from task **14**.

When you write about rhythm, metre, phonology or prosody, remember to focus on how they
emphasise meaning in a poem. Individual features of sound are often used to highlight specific images
or moods, while overall sound patterns can reflect or even shape the main concern of the poem.

Task

16. Look at this example of a student's work, exploring the opening lines of 'Sonnet 2'.

> The opening lines of 'Sonnet 2' present ageing as an unavoidable horror. Shakespeare's use of
> military imagery in the line 'Forty winters shall besiege thy brow' suggests that time destroys
> beauty. The personification makes it seem like a physical attack, and a correspondingly harsh
> tone is created by the plosives towards the end of the line. The military images continue
> with 'dig deep trenches in thy beauty's field', and Shakespeare uses alliteration to highlight
> the depiction of wrinkles. Shakespeare also makes references to nature's seasons, using
> the modal verb 'shall' to emphasise that the ugliness of ageing is inevitable. These ideas are
> reflected in the constant, uniform rhythm created through the poem's iambic pentameter, like
> the ticking of time or the constant beat of a heart as life passes by.

a) Where has the student focused on the ways in which sound can be used by a poet to
emphasise or reflect ideas?

b) Where have they explored how sound can create a mood or tone?

c) Look at the way these ideas have been expressed in the paragraph. How has the
student chosen words to make their ideas clear and how have they maintained the
focus on meaning?

Final Task

Now apply your understanding of sound and rhythm in poetry to a different poem.

In this poem, Thomas Wyatt explores unrequited love; he exaggerates the agony of not having his love returned by describing how nearly dying from an illness wasn't as painful.

The Enemy of Life

The enemy of life, decayer of all kind,
That with his cold withers away the green,
This other night me in my bed did find,
And offer'd me to rid my fever clean;
And I did grant, so did despair me blind:
He drew his bow with arrow sharp and keen,
And **strake** the place where love had hit before;
And **drave** the first dart deeper more and more.

Thomas Wyatt (1503–42)

Task

17. Read the poem twice; then answer these to establish a first understanding:
    a) What is being described in line 1?
    b) What is death described as doing in line 2?
    c) What single word is used to describe the pain of love in line 4?
    d) What emotion does the pain of love cause the speaker in line 5?
    e) How is death made to sound dangerous in line 6?
    f) What does death offer to do in lines 4–5 and why does the speaker agree?
    g) Instead of the speaker dying, what actually happens to his feelings of unrequited love in the last two lines?
18. Rhythm:
    a) What is the poem's metre?
    b) How is the first line slightly different?
    c) How might this choice of rhythm reflect what the speaker is feeling in the poem?
    d) How might the poem's rhythm also link to a traditional symbol of love or to what happens when you have a fever?
19. Sounds:
    a) What words (and what feeling of the speaker) does the alliteration emphasise?
    b) Comment on the use of plosives in line 7. How do they affect the tone of the poem?
    c) What is the poem's rhyme scheme?
    d) What is the effect of the rhyming couplet at the end of the poem? What idea or feeling does it emphasise?
    e) How do the sounds in a poem help create tone and mood?
20. Now complete this final task on the poem.

> Write two or three paragraphs on how rhythm and sound contribute to the meaning of Thomas Wyatt's poem 'The Enemy of Life'.

Begin by examining how the ideas and concerns of the poem are conveyed through Wyatt's use of language and imagery; then go on to consider how these concerns are emphasised by (or reflected in) his use of rhythm, metre and sound. You may want to use the student response in task **16** as a model.

Wider reading

If you would like to read more of William Shakespeare's sonnets, try 'Sonnet 12'. As you read, think about rhythm and metre, and how Shakespeare uses sound patterns in the poem to help convey his ideas.

Glossary

strake: struck
drave: drove

Plenary

In a group, discuss your work on Shakespeare's 'Sonnet 2', Greene's 'Farewell to Folly', and Wyatt's 'The Enemy of Life'. What features of sound and rhythm in the poems do you find most interesting? Why?

3.3 Exploring poetic form, genre and structure

Big question
- How do poets use form, genre and structure to emphasise and communicate their ideas?

SONNETS

Task

1. What elements do you think make up a poem? Are there any 'rules'?

There are many different forms of poetry, from **odes** and **ballads**, through **elegies** and **lyric poems**, to short verses such as **haikus**. The shape and structure of these forms often contribute to the way in which the poet conveys their concerns and ideas.

One of the most popular **poetic forms**, appearing throughout literature in English, is the **sonnet**. The sonnet originated in Italy and Italian sonnets, made famous by Francesco Petrarch (1304–74), were structured in two parts, like an argument: an **octave** (which set up a problem or a proposition, using an *abbaabba* rhyme scheme) and a **sestet** (which provided resolution, with either a *cdcdcd* or a *cdecde* rhyme scheme).

English writers, including Edmund Spenser (1552–99), began to adapt the form, using three **quatrains** and a **couplet**; recurring rhymes were used to link and develop ideas throughout the sonnet (such as *abab, bcbc, cdcd, ee*), and a **volta** or 'turn' was added at line 9 to develop or twist its meaning.

When Shakespeare popularised the English sonnet in the late 1500s, he used a simpler alternating rhyme scheme (*abab, cdcd, efef, gg*) and placed his volta at line 13.

Task

2. a) Look back at Shakespeare's 'Sonnet 2' on page 146. In what way is the poem about love?

b) Identify where the volta alters the focus of the poem. What is the new twist of meaning?

c) As well as a sonnet's specific use of metre and rhyme, its poetic form can be used to communicate the poet's concerns. With only 14, relatively short, condensed lines, the sonnet's form can add to the intensity of feeling in the poem. What intense feelings or ideas can you see in 'Sonnet 2'? Can you link the progression of these ideas and feelings to the form of the poem?

Edmund Spenser (1552-99)

Writing about the form of a poem can be difficult. It is easy to describe what a poem looks like and make vague references to aspects of form, but more challenging to provide a precise interpretation of how the form contributes to the meaning of the poem.

Task

3. Read the example of a student's work below exploring the effect of poetic form in 'Sonnet 2'.

   a) What makes this analysis successful?

   b) How does it link the poem's concerns to its form?

   c) How does it use specific terminology when exploring form?

The tight formality of the sonnet form provides a framework for the development of Shakespeare's ideas. Shakespeare uses the sonnet's rhyming structure to provide shifts in focus: at line 9, as a new quatrain begins, the focus on ageing and ugliness shifts to the suggestion that, because of this, the lover should create a 'fair child' in order to continue their beauty. The closing rhyming couplet provides a further development in the progression of ideas, but with the volta's anticipated 'twist'. The effect is to highlight and emphasise with the resounding rhyme the persuasion to have children, by juxtaposing the joys of having a child with the threat of being 'old' and 'cold'.

Just as the fixed rhyme scheme brings out the progression of ideas, the formal regular iambic rhythm and line lengths also serve to emphasise the concerns of the poem. The repeated military imagery is highlighted, for example, with stress placed on 'besiege', 'deep' and 'trenches' comically highlighting their inevitable onslaught. This sense of the rhythm's regularity, like a heartbeat, could also be said to echo Shakespeare's sense that ageing is inevitable; it cannot be escaped or changed.

Wider reading

Having explored a Shakespearean sonnet, you could also read a Spenserian sonnet (for example, 'Ice and Fire' by Edmund Spenser) and a Petrarchan sonnet (such as 'Sonnet 43' by Elizabeth Barrett-Browning).

Thinking more deeply: **experimenting with the sonnet form**

Although there are different forms of poetry that follow particular rules, some poets deliberately break or experiment with rules or decide not to follow formal rules at all. Some poems are written in **blank verse**, with a regular rhythm but no rhyme scheme, while some poets avoid rules altogether and write in **free verse**. An early example of a poet experimenting with the rules of form is Gerard Manley Hopkins's sonnet, 'The Windhover', which conveys his enjoyment of watching a falcon in flight.

Task

4. Read 'The Windhover' and decide which rules of a sonnet the poem follows and which it breaks. Pay extra attention to lines 1, 7 and 14 when considering how far Hopkins is using the sonnet form.
   Think about:
   - subject matter
   - rhyme
   - rhythm
   - metre.

Key terms

blank verse: a poem written in a regular metre (usually iambic pentameter) but without rhyme
free verse: an open form of poetry that doesn't use a regular metre or rhyme scheme

The Windhover

I caught this morning morning's minion, king-	1
dom of daylight's **dauphin**, dapple-dawn-drawn Falcon, in his riding	2
Of the rolling level underneath him steady air, and striding	3
High there, how he rung upon the rein of a wimpling wing	4
In his ecstasy! then off, off forth on swing,	5
As a skate's heel sweeps smooth on a bow-bend: the hurl and gliding	6
Rebuffed the big wind. My heart in hiding	7
Stirred for a bird, – the achieve of, the mastery of the thing.	8
Brute beauty and valour and act, oh, air, pride, plume, here	9
Buckle! AND the fire that breaks from thee then, a billion	10
Times told lovelier, more dangerous, O my **chevalier**!	11
No wonder of it: sheer plod makes plough down **sillion**	12
Shine, and blue-bleak embers, ah my dear,	13
Fall, gall themselves, and gash gold-**vermilion**.	14

Gerard Manley Hopkins (1877)

Glossary

dauphin: a prince
chevalier: a knight
sillion: thick, shiny soil turned over by a plough
vermilion: bright red

Task

5. The poem is concerned with a love of nature. It focuses on how spectacular the falcon is in flight and how this makes the speaker feel. Copy and complete the table below, identifying the words and images used to convey the bird's movement and how impressive it is.

Words and images that make the falcon sound impressive or powerful	Words and images that show the falcon's movement
dauphin	riding / of the rolling

Although Hopkins is writing a sonnet, many of his lines do not use iambic pentameter. They lack the iambic rhythm, or feature more than ten syllables, or both. Hopkins called this 'sprung verse', and it was an attempt to make poetry sound more like natural speech.

Task

6. Looking at lines 2, 3, 4 and 6, why do you think Hopkins breaks out of the restrictions of the sonnet form? What is he conveying? To help you, count the initial ten syllables of each line and then decide what the extra words are describing.

In much traditional pre-20th-century poetry, lines in a poem were often **end-stopped**. This traditional feature of a poem's structure could be achieved with any punctuation (full stop, comma, colon, dash, ellipsis) to create a small pause between the lines, reining the sentence in rather than allowing it to run straight on. This can have the effect of separating or clarifying ideas within the poem. When a line isn't end-stopped, and the meaning flows on, the poet has used a device called **enjambment**.

Key terms

end-stopped: when a line of poetry ends with a punctuation mark

enjambment: when a line or stanza of poetry is not end-stopped, allowing the sentence to run straight on into the next line

caesura: punctuation used inside lines of poetry to create a pause

Task

7. a) Are the majority of Hopkins's lines end-stopped or do they run on? Does this restrict the sentences or make them continue more freely?

b) Why does Hopkins choose to structure his poem like this? How does it relate to what he wants to convey about the falcon? Can you link your ideas back to your exploration of rhythm and metre in task **6**?

When you look at the structure of a poem, punctuation within the lines (not just at the end) is also important. This is called a **caesura** and it creates a small break or pause in the poem's rhythm. Traditionally, poets used these sparingly to emphasise an idea either side of the punctuation mark. In 'Sonnet 2', Shakespeare uses just three.

Task

8. a) Reread 'The Windhover' and identify the caesuras used by Hopkins. How many are there? Which line features the most caesuras?

b) Thinking about Hopkins's concerns in his poem, why does he include so many caesuras in his lines? Consider how they might link to:
- the falcon's movement (look particularly at lines 3–6)
- his fascination with the bird (look particularly at line 10).

NARRATIVE POEMS

> **Task**
>
> **9. a)** What are the key elements of a story?
>
> **b)** Think of any poems that you have previously read, or songs that you have listened to, that aim to tell a story. What setting, characters, events and emotions did those narratives contain?

The earliest examples of literature are **narrative poems**. This type of poetry is often much longer than other forms and tells a story in verse, creating settings, developing characters, and exploring problems, decisions, and powerful emotions.

One of the earliest narrative poems is *The Odyssey* by the Greek poet Homer, which dates back to the 8th century BCE, and the oldest surviving narrative poem in English is *Beowulf*, written around 1000 CE. This form has been popular in many eras: for example, Chaucer's *The Canterbury Tales* in the 14th century, Spenser's *The Fairie Queen* published in the 1590s, *Don Juan* by the **Romantic** poet Lord Byron, *Idylls of the King* by the **Victorian poet laureate** Alfred Lord Tennyson, and more modern works such as Carol Ann Duffy's *The Laughter of Stafford Girls' High*.

Key terms

narrative poem: a form of poetry that tells a story, often presenting the voices of a narrator as well as different characters

Romantic movement: a Western artistic movement, from around 1800–1850, that focused on the truthful representation of emotions and nature

Victorian period: the period of time in Britain when Queen Victoria reigned (1837–1901)

poet laureate: a great poet, officially appointed by a government to compose poems for special occasions and events

omniscient narration: where events are recounted from an all-seeing perspective

> **Task**
>
> **10.** Read the opening of *The Eve of St Agnes*, a 42-stanza narrative poem, written by John Keats in 1819. On St Agnes' Eve, it was believed that a young girl could see her future husband in a dream. As the poem opens, we follow the 'Beadsman' as he moves around the castle. Start thinking about how the poem tells a story:
>
> **a)** What character are we introduced to as the poem opens?
>
> **b)** What happens in these opening stanzas?
>
> **c)** The story is set in an old castle, home to a wealthy established family. How might this be reflected in the choice of form used to frame the narrator's words? Is it formal and traditional, or free and modern?
>
> **d)** What different things can you work out about the setting?
>
> **e)** Do you notice a change in focus and atmosphere? At what point?
>
> **11.** All stories, whether they are written as a novel or a poem, need a narrator.
>
> **a)** Although the narrator doesn't take part in the poem, what do you notice about how the first line is written?
>
> **b)** How does the opening line act as a narrative hook? Think about what we are told, how we are told it, the use of the caesuras, and the effect of an **omniscient narrator** writing in the past tense.

The Eve of St Agnes

St Agnes' Eve – Ah, bitter chill it was!
    The owl, for all his feathers, was a-cold;
    The hare limped trembling through the frozen grass,
    And silent was the flock in woolly fold:
    Numb were the **Beadsman**'s fingers, while he told
    His rosary, and while his frosted breath,
    Like pious incense from a **censer** old,
    Seemed taking flight for heaven, without death,
Past the sweet Virgin's picture, while his prayer he saith.

    His prayer he saith, this patient, holy man;
    Then takes his lamp, and riseth from his knees,
    And back returneth, meagre, barefoot, wan,
    Along the chapel aisle by slow degrees:
    The sculptured dead, on each side, seem to freeze,
    Emprisoned in black, purgatorial rails:
    Knights, ladies, praying in dumb orat'ries,
    He passeth by; and his weak spirit fails
To think how they may ache in icy hoods and mails.

    Northward he turneth through a little door,
    And scarce three steps, ere Music's golden tongue
    Flattered to tears this aged man and poor;
    But no – already had his deathbell rung;
    The joys of all his life were said and sung:
    His was harsh **penance** on St Agnes' Eve:
    Another way he went, and soon among
    Rough ashes sat he for his soul's reprieve,
And all night kept awake, for sinners' sake to grieve.

    That ancient Beadsman heard the **prelude** soft;
    And so it chanced, for many a door was wide,
    From hurry to and fro. Soon, up aloft,
    The silver, snarling trumpets 'gan to chide:
    The level chambers, ready with their pride,
    Were glowing to receive a thousand guests:
    The carved angels, ever eager-eyed,
    Stared, where upon their heads the cornice rests,
With hair blown back, and wings put cross-wise on their breasts.

John Keats (1819)

Glossary

Beadsman: a religious man, looked after by a rich family in return for his regular prayers for them
censer: a container for burning incense during a religious ceremony
penance: a punishment undertaken to make up for bad or sinful behaviour
prelude: an introduction to something

Task

12. a) As it is a narrative poem, Keats spends plenty of time building up a picture of the Beadsman. Reread the poem and highlight or note the lines that describe him.

b) Write a few sentences about the Beadsman, supporting each of your points with a quotation and commenting on the effect of specific words used to convey the character. Include comments about the Beadsman's appearance or physical state, his behaviour, his beliefs and how he feels about his life.

13. Make a list of all the words and images that link to the cold and death. Write a paragraph analysing how Keats creates a bleak atmosphere.

a) Look at the different descriptions of winter in stanza 1. Decide which you think is the most powerful description. Write a brief paragraph, analysing how Keats creates his setting.

b) Now find a description from stanza 1 that shows how cold it is down in the castle's vaults. Extend your paragraph, analysing how Keats moves the poem's setting from outside to inside.

c) Finally, select a description from stanza 2 that you think is good at conveying a gloomy or sinister atmosphere. How do the stressed beats of the iambic pentameter emphasise the atmosphere that the poet conveys? Write about how this is used to develop the setting of the poem.

Like all stories, narrative poems seek to create an atmospheric setting or tone. You are going to look at how Keats achieves this in *The Eve of St Agnes*.

The poem is set on a winter night and begins in the vaults of a castle, full of old statues of dead family members.

Narrative poems quickly develop aspects of setting, plot, character and theme, just as in a novel. In order to develop his narrative, Keats begins to change the atmosphere of his poem.

Task

14. Now track how Keats builds a contrasting atmosphere in stanzas 3 and 4. Identify words, sounds and images linked to brightness and liveliness as heard by the Beadsman.

15. As the poem is about St Agnes' Eve, the story is likely to be linked to love.

a) What happens in stanza 4 and how might this suggest the possible direction of the storyline?

b) In terms of building up a storyline, why might Keats have decided to begin his poem with so many references to death (such as the statues of dead 'knights, ladies')? What might this foreshadow?

16. Write a paragraph analysing how Keats uses foreshadowing in his poem to suggest that the love story will be tragic. You might start:

The title of Keats's narrative poem indicates that it will feature a love story, as St Agnes' Eve was a time when young girls were said to have a vision of their future husband. Images of brightness are used to build up a possible romantic setting, such as the metaphorical 'glowing' of the rooms. Personification is used in, 'Music's golden tongue', to suggest happiness, or enchantment, with the adjective 'golden' perhaps being included for its associations with love and marriage.

However, Keats uses foreshadowing at the start of the poem to suggest…

DRAMATIC MONOLOGUES

A dramatic monologue is a form of poetry in which the poet takes on a character's voice. This poetic voice describes a powerful feeling or event from a particular point of view, allowing the reader to construct a psychological portrait of the character. A dramatic monologue is usually written as if the speaker is taking part in a conversation, resulting in the reader almost becoming part of the poem.

The dramatic monologue became particularly popular as a form during the Victorian period, with poems such as 'My Last Duchess' and 'Porphyria's Lover' by Robert Browning. Dramatic monologues are still popular today and modern poets have made use of the form to give a 'voice' to people they see as ignored in society or forgotten by history.

Stealing

The most unusual thing I ever stole? A snowman.
Midnight. He looked magnificent; a tall, white mute
beneath the winter moon. I wanted him, a mate
with a mind as cold as the slice of ice
within my own brain. I started with the head.

Better off dead than giving in, not taking
what you want. He weighed a ton; his torso,
frozen stiff, hugged to my chest, a fierce chill
piercing my gut. Part of the thrill was knowing
that children would cry in the morning. Life's tough.

Sometimes I steal things I don't need. I joy-ride cars
to nowhere, break into houses just to have a look.
I'm a mucky ghost, leave a mess, maybe pinch a camera.
I watch my gloved hand twisting the doorknob.
A stranger's bedroom. Mirrors. I sigh like this – Aah.

It took some time. Reassembled in the yard,
he didn't look the same. I took a run
and booted him. Again. Again. My breath ripped out
in rags. It seems daft now. Then I was standing
alone among lumps of snow, sick of the world.

Boredom. Mostly I'm so bored I could eat myself.
One time, I stole a guitar and thought I might
learn to play. I nicked a bust of Shakespeare once,
flogged it, but the snowman was the strangest.
You don't understand a word I'm saying, do you?

Carol Ann Duffy

Task

17. Read 'Stealing' by Carol Ann Duffy and consider the speaker:
  a) What in the poem suggests this is a dramatic monologue – a conversation?'
  b) Does anything about the speaker seem contradictory?
  c) Do you think the speaker is male or female? Why?
18. Now explore what we find out about the character and how he/she feels and acts by completing the table.

Characteristic	Quotations	Key features of language and structure	Effect
lonely	'He looked magnificent; a tall, white mute / beneath the winter moon. I wanted him, a mate' 'alone among lumps of snow'	'Mate' and the verb 'wanted'. Personification – snowman described as if it's alive. Enjambment. Image of a quiet, night-time setting and the adjective 'alone'.	Creates a sense of yearning. The speaker is desperate, turning to objects for friends Could suggest speaker can't stop wanting the snowman. Emphasises speaker's solitary life.
unfeeling	'Part of the thrill was knowing / that children would cry in the morning. Life's tough.'		

19. Read the poem aloud to get a sense of the narrative **voice** and its particular **tone** or perspective.
20. What makes the speaker's voice distinctive? Think about:
  • level of formality
  • word choices that create a brash, aggressive impression
  • word choices that create a different impression
  • sentence forms
  • any interesting formal features, such as rhythm, sound, enjambment or endstopping, caesuras.

Key terms

voice: the characteristic way in which the story is told
tone: the mood or feeling created in a text

Final Task

Dramatic monologues often create a character without a direct sense of judgement from the poet. Instead, the poet guides the reader to draw their own conclusion about the speaker through their choice of language and style.

Task

21. Prepare a debate to consider how Duffy's choices make us respond to the character created in the poem 'Stealing'. You will need to come up with two sides to the argument:
- One half should argue that Duffy's choices of language and style make the reader sympathise with the speaker.
- The other half should argue that that Duffy's choices of language and style create an unsympathetic character.

To find your evidence, you will need to look at ways in which Duffy creates the voice of the speaker and through that voice tells the reader about the speaker's activities and attitudes, thereby helping the reader make judgements perhaps about the character and their environment.

Make sure that your points are supported by quotations, and that you can link the effect of specific words, images, sentence structure and aspects of form to your viewpoint. Spend 15 minutes preparing your side of the argument.

Plenary

In this chapter, you have explored three different poetic forms: sonnets, narrative poems and dramatic monologues.
Using the sentence starters below, write a summary paragraph about each of the three poetic forms. Support your comments with examples, quotation and analysis.

> A sonnet is a particularly powerful way of conveying intense personal feelings.
>
> A narrative poem conveys the poet's ideas through evocative settings and an engaging storyline.
>
> A dramatic monologue presents an interesting poetic voice by taking the reader into a character's mind.

Wider reading

Read some more narrative poems (such as 'The Teacher's Tale' by Wendy Cope) and dramatic monologues (such as 'Mrs Midas' by Carol Ann Duffy). Then explore some other forms of poetry. Try John Keats's ode 'To Autumn', 'Elegy' by Edna St Vincent Millay, and William Wordsworth's lyric poem, 'I Wandered Lonely as a Cloud'.

3.4 Exploring poetic concerns in pre-1900 contexts

Big question

- How do poets present their ideas and concerns, and how is this affected by the context in which the poem is written?

Task

1. Why do people write poetry? What is the point of it?

People write poetry for many reasons: to convey a feeling or experience, to describe a scene, to evoke a particular emotion, to tell a story. Poems also explore a wide variety of ideas, from the very personal (such as falling in love) to more abstract or universal concerns (such as faith, politics, and life and death). Often a poet will explore a broader concern by focusing on something that initially seems individual to them.

   When studying poetry, you need to learn to identify the central concerns of a poem, explore its subtleties and consider how these ideas are conveyed by the poet. You should also consider how ideas can change over time; for example, a poet's attitude to marriage in the 16th century might be very different to our attitudes today.

LOVE

Task

2. The topic of love is one of the most familiar concerns in poetry, and poets explore many different aspects of love. Look up the following types of love and write a definition of each one: courtly, familial, patriotic, platonic and unrequited.

3. Read 'The Passionate Shepherd to His Love' by Christopher Marlowe.

   a) What type of love is the poet exploring?

   b) What does the speaker want to achieve? (What is the purpose of his words?)

4. In this poem, Christopher Marlowe takes on the persona of a shepherd. **Pastoral poetry** was a popular feature of **Classical literature** and this style of writing was revived in the late 16th century.

   a) Identify the words in the poem that link to the speaker being a shepherd.

   b) Does the poem appear to describe a realistic picture of the life of a shepherd or an idealised, romanticised one? In what way does this choice suit the concern of the poem?

   c) What form of poetry is Christopher Marlowe using? (If you're unsure, look back at Unit 3.3.)

   d) The poem can also be considered a lyric poem, meaning that it expresses strong feelings through a first-person speaker. Which lines convey love in a particularly powerful way?

Key terms

pastoral poetry: a tradition of poetry idealising rural life and landscape, often drawing a contrast between the innocence of a simple life and the corruption of urban or court life; typically, pastoral poems followed highly conventional forms

Classical literature: the literature of Ancient Greece and Rome (from around 1200 BCE to 455 CE)

The Passionate Shepherd to His Love

Come live with me and be my love,
And we will all the pleasures prove,
That Valleys, groves, hills, and fields,
Woods, or steepy mountain yields.

And we will sit upon the Rocks,
Seeing the Shepherds feed their flocks,
By shallow Rivers to whose falls
Melodious birds sing **Madrigals**.

And I will make thee beds of Roses
And a thousand fragrant **posies**,
A cap of flowers, and a **kirtle**
Embroidered all with leaves of Myrtle;

A gown made of the finest wool
Which from our pretty Lambs we pull;
Fair lined slippers for the cold,
With buckles of the purest gold;

A belt of straw and Ivy buds,
With Coral clasps and Amber studs:
And if these pleasures may thee move,
Come live with me, and be my love.

The Shepherds' **Swains** shall dance and sing
For thy delight each May-morning:
If these delights thy mind may move,
Then live with me, and be my love.

Christopher Marlowe (1599)

Having identified what the poem is about, you can start exploring specific features of language, structure and form used by the poet.

Glossary

Madrigal: songs requiring several different voices
posies: small bunches of flowers
kirtle: a woman's gown
Swain: a young man

Task

5. Copy and complete the table, analysing how Marlowe shows the shepherd's love for the woman and presents the speaker trying to convince the woman to be with him. First identify the features in the poem; then, using the hints, complete the analysis.

Feature	Analysis
Hyperbole Hint: What is he suggesting about the extent of his love? How does this link to the context of pastoral poetry?	The rhyming couplet, 'And I will make thee beds of Roses / And a thousand fragrant posies', uses **hyperbole** to suggest he loves her more than other men would and will prove this through actions not just words. The natural images that are familiar motifs in pastoral poetry also suggest his love is purer than that of others, while drawing on the senses to evoke his love in a more powerful way.
List Hint: What is he offering her and why? How does this link to the context of pastoral poetry?	
Repetition of **modal verbs** Hint: What is the relevance of promises and why are they in the future tense?	
Repetition at the start and the end Hint: What is the purpose of his speech?	
Rhyming couplets Hint: What might arranging the lines in couples or pairs represent in this poem?	
A series of quatrains in iambic tetrameter Hint: What might the regular, steady rhythm symbolise about his love?	

Task

6. Read the following paragraph, written by a student about Marlowe's use of superlative adjectives. Does the student:
   * establish an idea about the poem?
   * provide evidence?
   * analyse the effect being achieved?
   * link analysis to an aspect of the poem's context?
   * develop the response further?

   In his dramatic monologue, 'The Passionate Shepherd to His Mistress', Marlowe uses **superlative adjectives** *to show the shepherd trying to convince the woman to be with him. The words 'finest' and 'purest' try to tempt her and prove his love by suggesting he will give her the best things he can. In particular, his offer of the 'finest wool' links to the idealised setting of the pastoral style that Marlowe has used in order to emphasise the romantic atmosphere. The superlatives also represent the shepherd's love, by implying that he is an honourable and faithful man, as well as praising what he sees as the woman's attractive qualities.*

7. Now choose a different feature and write a paragraph about how its use contributes to the concerns of the poem.

8. How might this pastoral poem be seen as a rejection of the limitations and corruptions of the 16th-century English court?

Key terms

superlative adjective: the most something can be (such as 'best', 'coldest', 'finest')

hyperbole: language exaggerated for effect

modal verb: a verb that changes another by adding a sense of possibility or necessity, such as 'could', 'may', 'would'

DEATH

Task

9. The subject of life and death appears again and again in literature across the centuries.

   a) Thinking about different cultures or times, what different attitudes do people have to death? For example, you could think about Aboriginal tree burial, Catholic beliefs in the last rites, and the pyramids of Ancient Egypt.

   b) Make a list of synonyms for the feeling of grief and rearrange them in order of intensity (for example, you might have 'sadness' at one end of the list and 'agony' at the other).

Read 'On My First Son'. The poem concerns the poet's grief at the death of his firstborn son.

On My First Son

Farewell, thou child of my right hand, and joy;
My sin was too much hope of thee, lov'd boy.
Seven years tho' wert lent to me, and I thee pay,
Exacted by thy fate, on the just day.
O, could I lose all Father now! For why
Will man lament the state he should envy?
To have so soon 'scap'd world's and flesh's rage,
And if no other misery, yet age?
Rest in soft peace, and, ask'd, say, 'Here doth lie
Ben Jonson his best piece of poetry.'
For whose sake henceforth all his vows be such,
As what he loves may never like too much.

Ben Jonson (1616)

To help you build up an understanding of a poem, start by identifying key concerns and exploring how features of language, structure and form convey meaning.

 Task

10. **a)** Note down different words or phrases that show the speaker's grief at losing his son.

    b) Poems often contain different feelings or subtle variations of one feeling.

      Look at line 10, where the poet describes his dead son as his 'best piece of poetry'. What type of imagery is this and what does the image suggest about his feeling for his child?

Key term

elegy: a formal poem reflecting on, and lamenting, someone's death. The form, based around rhyming couplets, has its roots in Western classical literature where it was often used to convey individual loss or aspects of war. The elegy began to be used in English literature in the 16th century, with poets seeing its formal use of rhyme and metre as a suitable medium for serious meditations on grief.

When you start to link your ideas to other parts of the poem, you will see patterns in the way that language is used.

Task

11. **a)** Can you find words, phrases or images related to loans and money? What meaning is suggested here? How might this relate to contemporary theological ideas about God, life and death?

    b) What other patterns or semantic fields can you identify?

12. The poem is written in the form of an **elegy**, using iambic pentameter and rhyming couplets.

    a) Why might this formal and precise use of form be suitable for the subject or concerns of the poem?

    b) Could the idea of pairs created by the rhyming couplets symbolise anything in the poem?

    c) Some critics have suggested that the poem reads like a sonnet that has been cut short. Thinking back to your understanding of sonnets, why might this form of poetry also be suitable for Jonson's subject?

    d) How might ending the sonnet on 12, rather than 14, lines reflect some of the ideas in the poem?

Task

13. a) Read this contextual information about the time at which Jonson wrote his poem.

> 'On My First Son' was written in 1603 by a man with strong religious beliefs. Jonson believed that a soul left Heaven, lived on Earth for an amount of time decided by God, and then returned; he also believed that Heaven was a better place than Earth, and that God punished sins such as greed, anger, and self-regard.

b) Look at lines 2, 3–4, and 5–7. How does the context help you to understand more about Ben Jonson's thoughts and feelings surrounding the death of his son? Think about how they show Jonson dealing with his grief and wanting the best for his child.

c) Identify where and how the contextual information is worked into the following analysis.

*The opening of the poem establishes the speaker's grief at the death of his child. The words, 'Farewell, thou child of my right hand', **directly address** his son as if he hopes he can still be heard. The arguable futility of this, along with the finality of the first word, increases the line's **pathos**. The 'right hand' metaphor refers to his son being part of him and successfully conveys his painful sense of loss. On the other hand, given the time and culture in which the poem was written, the use of 'farewell' could present the speaker's acceptance of his son's death and his belief that the child is going to a better place.*

14. Write two sentences about the imagery of money and lending in the poem, making contextual links to contemporary views on death and or sin.

PASSION

Another familiar theme in poetry is passion, clearly linking to the concerns of love and life.

Attitudes to love and passion are different across the world and have changed through time, so understanding the context of a poem such as 'To His Coy Mistress' by Andrew Marvell is vital. The poem was written in England, around the middle of the 17th century. At the time, it was expected that a man would 'court' a woman for a long period of time in order to gain her love. The young couple would not sleep together until they had married. The poet was drawing on the tradition of **courtly love**.

In this poem, the speaker is more eager than contemporary morality would allow. He believes in the Latin saying 'carpe diem', which means 'seize the day', so he doesn't want to wait for marriage before he can be close to the woman he is attracted to.

Key terms

direct address: when a speaker directs his words towards a specific reader (often using 'you')

pathos: a sense of pity or sadness

courtly love: a concept of love that originated in Medieval European literature, based around the noble and chivalric behaviour of knights towards ladies. The term explores the idea that a man should persuade a woman of his true affection through his continued devotion, acts of wooing, heroic deeds and feelings of lovesickness. After the Medieval period, the notion of courtly love remained popular in literature, particularly during the 16th century, with some writers also exploring ways in which the modes of courtly love could be subverted or satirised.

Task

15. Before you read the poem, look up the meaning of the word 'coy'. Does the speaker think the woman he is courting feels the same way that he does?

16. Read the poem and, pick out words and phrases that link to love, death, and having energy.

17. When you have finished reading and making notes, decide which of the following descriptions best fits each stanza.
- He is urging her to seize the day.
- He is telling her how much he loves her.
- He is warning her that their youth will not last.

Because the poem is structured in three clear stages, creating a persuasive argument, it will help to explore the poem stanza by stanza.

Task

18. In Stanza 1, the speaker tries to be romantic and convince the lady of his love. Look at how the he constructs his argument using conditionals and modal verbs.

a) The speaker uses the following arguments. Identify the modal verbs that he uses in each case. How do the modals help his argument?
- Love is eternal so a relationship doesn't have to be rushed.
- His love is centuries old.
- He doesn't mind how long she makes him wait.
- His love is always increasing.
- He's happy to take his time courting her.
- He respects her enough to go slowly.

b) The poem's opening line sets up a conditional form that operates throughout the first stanza ('Had we... we would'). What is the effect of this conditional and how does it undercut the romantic promises and ideals?

To His Coy Mistress

Had we but world enough, and time,
This coyness, lady, were no crime.
We would sit down, and think which way
To walk, and pass our long love's day.
Thou by the Indian Ganges' side
Shouldst rubies find; I by the tide
Of Humber would complain. I would
Love you ten years before the flood,
And you should, if you please, refuse
Till the conversion of the Jews.
My vegetable love would grow
Vaster than empires, and more slow;
An hundred years should go to praise
Thine eyes, and on thy forehead gaze;
Two hundred to adore each breast,
But thirty thousand to the rest;
An age at least to every part,
And the last age should show your heart.
For, lady, you deserve this state,
Nor would I love at lower rate.

But at my back I always hear
Time's winged chariot hurrying near:
And yonder all before us lie
Deserts of vast eternity.
Thy beauty shall no more be found;
Nor, in thy marble vaults, shall sound
My echoing song; then worms shall try
That long-preserved virginity,
And your quaint honour turn to dust,
And into ashes all my lust:
The grave's a fine and private place,
But none, I think, do there embrace.

Now therefore, while the youthful hue
Sits on thy skin like morning dew,
And while thy willing soul transpires
At every pore with instant fires,
Now let us sport us while we may,
And now, like amorous birds of prey,
Rather at once our time devour
Than languish in his slow-chapped power.
Let us roll all our strength, and all
Our sweetness, up into one ball,
And tear our pleasure with rough strife
Through the iron gates of life:
Thus, though we cannot make our sun
Stand still, yet we will make him run.

Andrew Marvell (1661)

Task

Glossary
vault: tomb
strife: conflict

19. In stanza 2, the speaker changes tack, attempting to convince the lady that they should 'seize the day' and be together. Copy and complete the table below focusing on how the speaker creates his argument.

Stanza 2	Quotations	Specific techniques and effects
Imagery Hint: Look for impactful images and recurring images.		
Structural features Hint: Which specific type of word is repeated?		
Voice/tone Hint: How does the speaker's voice alter to emphasise certain images?		
Rhyme and metre Hint: How might the speaker be using these to urge her to be with him? What is different about lines 2 and 4?		

20. a) Moving on to the conclusion of the speaker's argument in stanza 3, identify a metaphor that reminds us that the speaker is burning with passion for the girl.

  b) Find four phrases that show the speaker urging the girl to be with him (look for active verbs)?

  c) Of your four phrases, which do you think is the best to show he wants the two of them to join together? Why?

21. a) Does Marvell present the speaker as very courtly? How is courtly love presented as something frustrating or difficult to achieve?

  b) In what ways might we respond differently to the poem today?

22. Using your notes and annotations, write an analysis of how Marvell's speaker constructs and develops his argument. Write one paragraph about each stanza.

You might begin:

In the first stanza, Marvell presents the poem's concern of passion through the way the speaker tries to convince the girl to be with him. In stanza 1, the speaker begins by expressing his love for her, '_____', with Marvell using…

You should also aim to include some exploration of how your understanding of context affects the poem's meaning. For example, you could start with:

Although the first stanza contains a lot of romantic images, the opening of the poem shows that Marvell is focusing on passion by subverting 17th-century ideals of courtly love. Instead of offering romantic constancy and patience, the line, '_____', suggests…

Thinking more deeply: **a different context**

You should now be ready to explore a pre-1900 poem much more independently, applying context to your analysis as you consider how meaning is conveyed.

'Cousin Kate' was written by the English poet Christina Rossetti in 1859. Marvell's poem 'To His Coy Mistress' showed a man trying to convince a woman to be with him; Rossetti was interested in the lives of the women who gave in to men and ended up pregnant outside marriage. Men had greater social power in Victorian society as they were still seen as more important than women. Similarly, there were clear class distinctions, and people of a higher class held more social power than the working classes. The 19th century was in some ways a very strict, religious and moral time, with an emphasis on the importance of appearance and reputation. Therefore, so-called 'fallen women' were often shunned by the rest of society, including the men who had made them pregnant.

Task

23. Read the poem 'Cousin Kate' and make a note of the thoughts and feelings of a fallen woman.

Cousin Kate

I was a cottage maiden
Hardened by sun and air,
Contented with my cottage mates,
Not mindful I was fair.
Why did a great lord find me out,
And praise my **flaxen** hair?
Why did a great lord find me out
To fill my heart with care?

He lured me to his palace home —
Woe's me for joy thereof —
To lead a shameless shameful life,
His plaything and his love.
He wore me like a silken knot,
He changed me like a glove;
So now I moan, an unclean thing,
Who might have been a dove.

O Lady Kate, my cousin Kate,
You grew more fair than I:
He saw you at your father's gate,
Chose you, and cast me by.
He watched your steps along the lane,
Your work among the rye;
He lifted you from **mean estate**
To sit with him on high.

Because you were so good and pure
He bound you with his ring:
The neighbours call you good and pure,
Call me an outcast thing.
Even so I sit and howl in dust,
You sit in gold and sing:
Now which of us has tenderer heart?
You had the stronger wing.

O cousin Kate, my love was true,
Your love was writ in sand:
If he had fooled not me but you,
If you stood where I stand,
He'd not have won me with his love
Nor bought me with his land;
I would have spit into his face
And not have taken his hand.

Yet I've a gift you have not got,
And seem not like to get:
For all your clothes and wedding-ring
I've little doubt you fret.
My fair-haired son, my shame, my pride,
Cling closer, closer yet:
Your father would give lands for one
To wear his **coronet**.

Christina Rossetti (1859)

Task

24. Make notes on how Rossetti uses language, form and structure to develop the poem's concern with fallen women. Consider:
- the voice and tone of the speaker and how this changes
- the form of the poem
- the effect of all stanzas being the same length with a regular rhyme, rhythm, and metre throughout
- the poet's use of time and tense
- the use of language and imagery
- the speaker's account of life before and after the 'great lord'
- the lord's behaviour and attitudes
- the poet's use of **interrogatives**
- how Cousin Kate is presented and why the lord liked her
- what the speaker thinks Kate should have done when the lord asked to marry her and why
- the differences between the speaker and Kate
- how the speaker feels about her **illegitimate** son.

Glossary

flaxen: golden or pale yellow
mean estate: a poor life
coronet: a small crown
illegitimate: a child born outside marriage

Key terms

interrogatives: questions

Task

25. Read through your ideas and consider whether any have been affected by the 19th-century context in which the poem was written. Think about:
- traditions of love (as shown in the previous poems in this chapter)
- idealised love and the how love is presented in this poem
- the use of a female voice
- the depiction of the lower and upper classes
- attitudes to premarital sex and illegitimacy.

Final Task

Now use your work on 'Cousin Kate' and 'To His Coy Mistress' to begin to link the concerns of the poems together.

Task

26. Write a response to this task:

Discuss some of the ways in which the poets present courtship in two of the poems.

You could choose an essay structure that:
- links the poems' concerns in an opening paragraph
- then goes on to focus on poem 1
- then goes on to focus on poem 2
- concludes by drawing the linked poems together.

Checklist for success
✓ Comment on specific features of each poet's language, structure and form.
✓ Focus on the issues and concerns, referring to relevant contextual ideas.
✓ Explain the impact of the writers' choices in relation to the issues identified.

Wider reading

To further investigate how Victorian poets explored the concern of fallen women, you could read Christina Rossetti's narrative poem 'Goblin Market', the dramatic monologue 'A Castaway' by Augusta Davies Webster, or Thomas Hardy's duologue 'The Ruined Maid'.

Plenary

Read back over your final task. Evaluate the success of each paragraph, checking that there is a clear point, well-chosen evidence and detailed analysis. Decide whether the paragraph could be improved through more detailed analysis or consideration of how context affects meaning.

Add a conclusion to your work on 'Cousin Kate' and 'To His Coy Mistress'. Comment clearly on the initial argument that you were exploring. Summarise the ways in which Rossetti and Marvell have presented their ideas and concerns, and how this presentation is affected by the contexts in which they were writing.

3.5 Exploring poetic concerns in post-1900 contexts

Big question

- How do modern poets present their ideas and concerns, and how is this affected by the context in which the poem is written?

MODERNISM AND A BREAK WITH THE PAST

By the start of the 20th century, writers were trying to make a break from the traditions of the past and look at new ways of conveying meaning. This found expression through **modernism**, which peaked between 1910 and 1945.

Modernist writers were particularly concerned with the new uncertainties of an increasingly industrialised world with its rapidly growing cities; they often rejected religion and explored the horror of the First World War and how it changed our perceptions of ourselves. Modernist writers expressed themselves by experimenting with a variety of new forms and approaches to language. Though diverse, modernist poetic techniques included the use of free verse with natural rhythms and open rather than end-stopped lines, fragmented stanzas, multiple speakers, **juxtaposition**, **intertextuality**, and word choices that were precise and exact rather than unnecessarily descriptive.

As modernism evolved, **postmodernism** emerged, with its greater emphasis on questioning the world and critiquing universal notions of morality and truth, along with greater scepticism, irony, and **self-referentiality**.

Key terms

modernism: term used to describe movement of early 20th-century writers who broke away from older traditions and concerns, to experiment with new ideas, forms, structures and language

juxtaposition: the act of placing two things side by side to create an effect through comparison or contrast

intertextuality: shaping a text's meaning by using another text; this can be a whole text (rewriting something from a different perspective), borrowing words or lines from another text, or making allusions to another text

postmodernism: a late 20th-century style and concept that represents a departure from modernism, characterised by a distrust of theories, the self-conscious use of earlier styles as well as a mixing of different artistic styles and media

self-referentiality: when a writer refers to themselves or their own work in a text, or draws attention to their writing as something crafted and constructed

Task

1. Read this Modernist poem. What immediately strikes you?

> **In a Station of the Metro**
>
> The apparition of these faces in the crowd;
> Petals on a wet, black bough.
>
> Ezra Pound (1913)

What meanings are conveyed by the poem, and how is this achieved? Comment on the following aspects:

- Modernity. How is the poem exploring an aspect of the modern world?
- Intertextuality. The form and its images relate to a much older form from a different culture (defined on page 146). What is deliberately jarring about this choice?
- Juxtaposition. How and why have images been juxtaposed?
- Metre. Is it iambic? Are the lines the same length?

- Phonology. Is there rhyme? Are any sound patterns used to link the images?
- Fragmentation. What word types are missing from the poem, stopping it reading as a complete sentence?
- Clarity. What is clear? What is left unanswered? Can we identify the speaker?

FORM AND IDENTITY

Modern poetry is often concerned with aspects of identity and how it is shaped both by individual experience and broader influences such as gender, ethnicity, family relationships, politics and nationality. These concerns can be explored through modern forms, such as free verse, or through more established forms.

GENDER IDENTITY AND ESCAPING TRADITION

Task

2. Find out about the Classical myth of Orpheus and Eurydice, and then consider the following questions:
   - In what way is the myth a love story?
   - How does Orpheus come across as a hero and the most important character in the story?
   - What does Orpheus's lyre represent?
   - When does Orpheus look back and how does he feel at the end of the story?
   - How would you feel, at the end of the story, if you were Eurydice? Why?

Writers find inspiration from a huge range of sources, and one source is literature itself. Poets have often created their own versions of older stories, especially through narrative poems, such as Shakespeare's use of Roman myth in 'Venus and Adonis' and Tennyson's use of Arthurian legend in 'The Idylls of the King'.

Modern poets continue to be inspired by other authors' works but often try to present a new perspective, reshaping ideas and subverting meanings to reflect modern concerns such as identity, conflict or family. Frequently, these ideas are expressed through reworked forms that break free from traditional constraints in order to more fully represent the complexity of our modern world. This is a form of intertextuality, a key feature of modernist and postmodern literature.

Task

3. Read this extract from H.D.'s poem, 'Eurydice'. How does the focus of the poem appear to be different from the original Greek myth? How might this relate to changing attitudes to women since the original was composed in 70 BCE?

Eurydice

So you have swept me back,
I who could have walked with the live souls
above the earth,
I who could have slept among the live flowers
at last;

so for your arrogance
and your ruthlessness
I am swept back
where dead lichens drip
dead cinders upon moss of ash;

so for your arrogance
I am broken at last,
I who had lived unconscious,
who was almost forgot;

if you had let me wait
I had grown from listlessness
into peace,
if you had let me rest with the dead,
I had forgot you
and the past.

Here only flame upon flame
and black among the red sparks,
streaks of black and light
grown colourless;

why did you turn back,
that hell should be reinhabited
of myself thus
swept into nothingness?

why did you turn?
why did you glance back?
why did you hesitate for that moment?
why did you bend your face
caught with the flame of the upper earth,
above my face?

what was it that crossed my face
with the light from yours
and your glance?
what was it you saw in my face?
the light of your own face,
the fire of your own presence?

H.D. (1917)

The poem can be read as a **feminist** revision of the original myth.
Rather than Orpheus being a tragic figure that the reader sympathises
with, the focus is on the woman's feelings of being betrayed by her lover.

Key term

feminist: literary approach that
challenges representations of women in
texts and questions prevalent attitudes
and assumptions about women

Task

4. Select a word, a phrase and a sentence structure that show the female speaker criticising the man who has let her down. Explain your three choices.
   How does H.D. make the female speaker sound stronger or fiercer than the male?

5. Now explore, in more detail, how the text presents a revision of Orpheus and Eurydice's story through the following features:
   * Free verse. How might this help to reflect the speaker's feelings? How might it contrast with everything that Orpheus represents?
   * Natural rhythms rather than a fixed metre. How does this affect the voice of the speaker?
   * Enjambment and non-standard grammar. How might these reflect the speaker's feeling and circumstances?
   * Word choices. How do these show Eurydice's feeling towards Orpheus? How are traditional symbols of love used in the poem?
   * Repetition and **anaphora**. How do these emphasise her feelings and challenge the concept of patriarchy?
   * Allusion. What reason (very different from that in Classical literature) is suggested for why Orpheus looked back? Is the poem just about Orpheus and Eurydice, or could it represent the modern world in any way?

6. How might the extract from 'Eurydice' show a Modernist exploration of love and gender?

> **Key term**
>
> **anaphora:** a structured use of repetition where the same words or phrases appear at the beginning of lines

IDENTITY AND THE IMMIGRANT EXPERIENCE

'Hurricane Hits England', by Grace Nichols, is another poem that explores identity in a modern context. Grace Nichols was born in Guyana in 1950 and emigrated to England in 1977. In the poem, she explores how a series of hurricanes in 1987 made her feel less homesick and reconnected her with her Guyanese heritage.

Migration is a key feature of modern societies, as many people move to a new country for a variety of reasons: to find work or earn more money, to have greater educational opportunities, to live safely away from conflict or to join a loved one.

After 1945, many different peoples from the former British Empire (such as India, Nigeria, and the Caribbean) emigrated to the UK. Although they expected a bright future, they often met with racial prejudice and missed the sense of community and belonging that they had left back home. They also discovered that British weather was regularly grey and miserable.

Task

7. What difficulties or challenges do you think you would encounter if you moved to a completely different country?

Now read the poem.

Hurricane Hits England

It took a hurricane, to bring her closer
To the landscape
Half the night she lay awake,
The howling ship of the wind,
Its gathering rage,
Like some dark ancestral spectre,
Fearful and reassuring:

Talk to me Huracan
Talk to me Oya
Talk to me Shango
And Hattie
My sweeping, back-home cousin.

Tell me why you visit
An English coast?
What is the meaning
Of old tongues
Reaping havoc
In new places?

The blinding illumination,
Even as you short-
Circuit us
Into further darkness?

What is the meaning of trees
Falling heavy as whales
Their crusted roots
Their cratered graves?

O why is my heart unchained?
Tropical Oya of the Weather,
I am aligning myself to you,
I am following the movement of your winds,
I am riding the mystery of your storm.

Ah, sweet mystery,
Come to break the frozen lake in me,
Shaking the foundations of the very trees within me,
Come to let me know
That the earth is the earth is the earth.

Grace Nichols (1987)

Task

8. Discuss your impressions of how the speaker's identity is related to the landscape around her and the weather. Where does she seem at ease in the poem and where does she seem unsettled?
9. Now identify where the text explores:
   - the hurricane
   - the speaker's response to the hurricane
   - the identity of the speaker.

   Consider how these concerns are explored through the writer's choices of language, structure and form.

   For example, look at the lines: 'trees / Falling heavy as whales'. What does this image suggest about the power of the hurricane? What type of image has the poet used? Why has the poet chosen to link the hurricane to a creature that is rarely seen around the English coast?
10. Think about what the poet is conveying at the end of the poem:
    - What does the speaker mean by her 'foundations' and how does the hurricane help her to feel them?
    - How would it feel to have a 'frozen lake' inside you and what does this suggest about the speaker?
    - What does the hurricane allow the speaker to understand about Guyana and England and how is this emphasised to the reader?
    - What might the poet want her readers to understand about the immigrant experience?

MODERN FAMILY AND IDENTITY

Of course, the concerns of modern poets are often very similar to those of poets writing before the 20th century, from love to family relationships. However, the ways in which modern poets express these concerns can be very different, both because of the social, historical and cultural context in which they are writing and because of the different poetic forms and structures that are popular today.

Task

11. **a)** You are going to read a recent poem exploring family relationships. Thinking about your own life, what are the best and worst things about family? How has your family, and your position in your family, shaped your identity? (Think, for example, things you have embraced and things you have reacted against.)

    b) How could you use the symbols of an anchor or a kite to represent the pros and cons of family? (Think about what each object is for, and what it can and cannot do.)

Task

12. Read the following poem in which the speaker has just moved to a new house. What are the speaker and the mother doing in the poem?

Mother, Any Distance

Mother, any distance greater than a single span
requires a second pair of hands.
You come to help me measure windows, pelmets, doors,
the acres of the walls, the prairies of the floors.

You at the zero-end, me with the spool of tape, recording
length, reporting metres, centimetres back to base, then leaving
up the stairs, the line still feeding out, unreeling
years between us. Anchor. Kite.

I space-walk through the empty bedrooms, climb
the ladder to the loft, to breaking point, where something has to give;
two floors below your fingertips still pinch
the last one-hundredth of an inch… I reach
towards a hatch that opens on an endless sky
to fall or fly.

Simon Armitage (1993)

13. What do you learn about the mother and speaker, and their relationship in the poem?

14. Which words and images do you think are most striking or revealing about the mother and speaker's relationship? Explain your answer.

15. a) In the poem, Armitage uses the measuring of the new house as an **extended metaphor** for the speaker's relationship with his mother. Copy and complete the grid to track the metaphor as it extends throughout the poem.

Key term

extended metaphor: a single metaphor that is introduced and then further developed throughout a poem or text

	Where is the speaker?	**Where is the mother and what is she doing?**	**What might this suggest about their relationship or this stage in the speaker's life?**
Stanza 1			
Stanza 2			
Stanza 3			

b) What does the metaphor communicate about the speaker's relationship with the mother as the poem progresses? Find quotations and explain your observations.

Task

16. **a)** Do you recognise the form of this poem? Is it a traditional sonnet, or is it written in more modern free verse, or do you think there are aspects of both?

    b) Using the two headings below, make a list of features relating to rhyme, metre and structure that you can see in the poem.

Traditional	Modern
Some iambic rhythm but…	No fixed metre or a mixture of different metres

    c) How might Armitage be using the phrase 'fall or fly' to explore the idea of independence? Comment on its placement in the poem.

17. Why do you think the pre-1900 poem that you explored about family (Jonson's 'On My First Son') was so much more formal and constrained than Armitage's poem? Think about the time in which it was written, the subject matter of the poem, and the relationship between the speaker and the family member.

18. Write three or four paragraphs examining how Armitage presents the relationship between mother and child in 'Mother, Any Distance'. Include references to language, structure and form in your response. You might begin:

    In 'Mother, Any Distance', the poem opens by showing how the speaker needs his mother. In the lines…

Final Task

Task

19. Explore how identity is presented in two of the poems from this chapter.
    Start by considering what is being said about identity in each poem and what things are affecting identity.
    Then explore how this is conveyed through the writers' choice of language, structure and form. Try to draw links between any similar methods being used by your chosen poets.

Checklist for success
✓ Identify an idea, or ideas, about identity in each poem.
✓ Support your ideas with quotations from each poem.
✓ Analyse how identity is being presented through the writer's choices of language.
✓ Analyse how the writer's ideas are emphasised by their choices of structure and form.

Wider reading

If you liked the poets' work in this chapter, you could also read 'Cassandra' by H.D., 'Island Man' by Grace Nichols and 'About His Person' by Simon Armitage.
If you enjoyed the particular concerns in this chapter, you might try 'Medusa' by Carol Ann Duffy, 'I Like Them' by Musaemura Zimunya, 'My Message' by Cecil Rajendra, 'I Cannot Remember My Mother' by Rabindranath Tagore and 'The Road Not Taken' by Robert Frost.

3.6 Exploring different interpretations

Big question

- How can you interpret poetry in different ways?

INTERPRETING A POEM

One of the things that makes the study of literature so interesting is that a text can be read, or interpreted, in multiple ways. The meaning of a text can also work on a number of levels, from an immediate surface understanding to a deeper, more complex appreciation on closer reading. When you read and explore a poem, keep an open mind and build your interpretation through close analysis.

Task

1. You are going to explore a poem called 'Eden Rock'. Start by thinking about the title:

   a) What different connotations do the words 'Eden' and the word 'Rock' suggest to you? Draw spider diagrams like the ones shown here on the right.

   b) Now think about the effect of placing these two words together. Think about what the title suggests to you now.

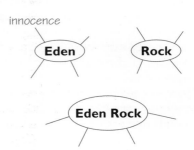

Eden Rock

They are waiting for me somewhere beyond Eden Rock: 1
My father, twenty-five, in the same suit
Of Genuine Irish Tweed, his terrier Jack
Still two years old and trembling at his feet.

My mother, twenty-three, in a sprigged dress   5
Drawn at the waist, ribbon in her straw hat,
Has spread the stiff white cloth over the grass.
Her hair, the colour of wheat, takes on the light.

She pours tea from a Thermos, the milk straight   9
From an old H.P. sauce-bottle, a screw
Of paper for a cork; slowly sets out
The same three plates, the tin cups painted blue.

The sky lightens as if lit by three suns.   13
My mother shades her eyes and looks my way
Over the drifted stream. My father spins
A stone along the water. Leisurely,

They beckon to me from the other bank.   17
I hear them call, 'See where the stream path is!
Crossing is not as hard as you might think.'

I had not thought it would be like this.   20

Charles Causley (1988)

Task

2. Read 'Eden Rock'. Start thinking about the poem and its concerns.

   a) What do you think 'Eden Rock' is about?

   b) What does the speaker convey about himself and his family?

   c) How do you respond to the poem personally?

When expressing your different interpretations, use tentative language (such as 'might', 'could', 'perhaps', 'can be', 'suggests', 'implies', 'appears'). However, make sure that your ideas are rooted in evidence from the text, so your interpretations are also confident.

Task

3. Discuss and compare your interpretations of 'Eden Rock'.

   a) Did you and your classmates come up with the same or different interpretations?

   b) Could all the interpretations be evidenced by the language in the poem?

   c) Was any one interpretation more valid than the others?

4. a) Identify which lines are about his father and which are about his mother. How does the speaker describe them? How are their actions described?

   b) At lines 2–4, the speaker sees his father as he might have seen him as a child. How might these lines suggest that the speaker has a fond memory of his father?

   c) Alternatively, are there any words or phrases that could suggest he doesn't have fond memories of his father?

5. On one level, the poem might seem to be an account of a family picnic as remembered by the speaker. Can you find any evidence for this interpretation? To what extent do you agree with it?

6. The most ambiguous part of 'Eden Rock' is the ending. Reread the last four lines of the poem.

   a) In many cultures, the traversing of a river is associated with death or deliverance. This has its roots in classical literature (rivers like Lethe and Styx leading to the underworld) and the Bible (crossing the River Jordan into the Promised Land). How could these allusions alter your reading of the poem?

   b) What might the words 'beckon', 'see', 'crossing', and 'not as hard' suggest the speaker is feeling at this point?

7. How do you respond the last line of the poem?

   a) What is the 'it'?

   b) What do you think he had 'thought'?

   c) All the previous stanzas are **quatrains**, but the final line of the poem is split off to create a **tercet** and a single-line stanza. Why might the poet have done this? Does it affect how we interpret the ending of the poem?

Key terms
quatrain: a four-line stanza
tercet: a three-line stanza

APPLYING LITERARY THEORY

When interpreting a poem, you may also want to draw on different theoretical perspectives and consider how they illuminate the text in different ways. You will find a useful 'Introduction to literary critical theory' at the end of this book (pages 312–6) that you could refer to as you explore 'Eden Rock' further.

Autobiographical information, showing the relationship between a poet and their poem, can also help to illuminate a text. However, such information should be used with caution: the first person or speaker in poetry, as in prose, is a construct and should not be confused with the author. Use such information only as an element of interpretation with the focus still on the effects of language, structure and form to convey ideas and meaning.

For example, a student might use historical criticism and autobiographical reference to comment:

> Causley wrote the poem when he was in his seventies and a key concern seems to be reflecting on the past. Lines like 'From an old H.P. sauce-bottle, a screw / Of paper for a cork' create a relaxed image, and the noun phrases present no criticisms of the family's humble life, suggesting the speaker is looking back at the past in a nostalgic manner.

Task

8. How might the following autobiographical and historical information help you to interpret specific images from the poem?
   - Charles was 7 when his father died in 1924; his mother died in 1971.
   - Charles had a good relationship with his parents; he never married or had children.
   - Eden Rock is not a real place.

9. Read the explanation of psychoanalytical theory on page 313. How might this information allow you to explore a psychoanalytical approach to the poem?

   a) Does the poem appear to be a memory of the speaker's or something else?

   b) How might the depiction of the speaker's parents be described as idealised or dreamlike rather than realistic?

   c) What other descriptions or details seem dreamlike or unrealistic?

   d) In a dream, objects often work on a symbolic level. You have already considered the different meanings of the river, but what could the rock represent?

   e) If the poem is interpreted as the speaker remembering his dead parents, how might you explore the extent to which their deaths have affected him in the text?

10. Read the explanation of feminist theory on page 312. Looking at the poem from a feminist perspective, you might consider what the poem reveals about the role of women in England in the early 20th century.

Copy and complete the table below.

Evidence from the poem	What this could suggest about the role of women in early-20th-century England
'My mother […] / pours tea from a Thermos […] / slowly sets out / The same three plates, the tin cups painted blue.'	
'My father, twenty-five, in the same suit / Of Genuine Irish Tweed […] / My mother, twenty-three, in a sprigged dress / Drawn at the waist, ribbon in her straw hat'	
Father is introduced first (in stanza 1), then Mother (stanza 2).	

11. **a)** Read the explanation of Marxist theory on pages 312–3. A Marxist exploration of the poem might help you consider more about the parents' lives. What might the following details from the poem be suggesting about their economic status?

> the same suit
>
> her straw hat
>
> the milk straight from an old H.P. sauce-bottle
>
> a screw of paper for a cork
>
> tin cups

   b) What might these details from the poem suggest about how the parents respond to their economic status?

> suit of Genuine Irish Tweed
>
> ribbon in her straw hat
>
> spread the stiff white cloth over the grass
>
> slowly sets out
>
> cups painted blue

Thinking more deeply: **writing about different interpretations**

When you analyse a poem, you should not just list all the different interpretations that you can think of. Instead, start by developing your own clear view of the poem; you can then use different interpretations to develop that view or to present a contrasting perspective. You could make use of sentence starters such as:

> It might be considered that the line ..._suggests ..._because ...
> However, ...
> Alternatively, ...

Read this student response to the question: 'How does Eden Rock present the speaker's attitudes towards his parents?'

> The speaker displays clear affection for his mother. When Causley describes her, the natural images ('sprigged dress', 'straw hat', 'hair, the colour of wheat') create a mood of calm around her. The metaphorical description of her hair, with its symbolism of light, suggests goodness and beauty. His mother's attractiveness is also implied by the use of ornament ('sprigged', 'ribbon') and the suggestion of her slimness through her dress being 'drawn at the waist'.
>
> Given the early-20th-century context, the poem also seems to present her as a dutiful wife. When she 'pours tea from a Thermos / [...] slowly sets out / The same three plates', we see her playing the role that was expected of her at the time. There is perhaps some sympathy in the choice of the adverb 'slowly', showing the care she takes but also implying that these things may have been important to her because her life revolved around the domestic and she had little else.

Task

12. a) What is the main point that the student develops about the speaker's attitude towards his parents?

b) What evidence is provided for this and what language features are analysed?

c) How does the student use historical context to help develop their main point?

d) How does the student use feminist perspective to add a different aspect to the main point?

e) Do you agree with the interpretations suggested here? Explain why.

Final Task

Task

13. Using the paragraphs above as a model, write a response to the question:

> In what ways and with what effects does Causley present the speaker's attitudes towards his parents in 'Eden Rock'?

Plenary

Think about the different interpretations of 'Eden Rock' that you have encountered today.
- Which interpretations and critical perspectives of 'Eden Rock' did you find most interesting?
- Were some interpretations easier to evidence from the text?
- Did any interpretations arise that you disagreed with? Based on the text, what made you disagree?

Checklist for success
✓ Establish a clear point (it may be the same as in the sample paragraph).
✓ Analyse how that point is conveyed through specific aspects of language, structure, or form.
✓ Develop your point using alternative interpretations (historical and/or Marxist perspectives may be particularly useful).

3.7 Writing about a single poem for AS Level

Big question

- How do you plan a response to a question on a single poem? (AS Level)

UNDERSTAND THE TASK

When approaching a single-poem question at AS Level, it is important to consider:

- the writer's style and choice of language
- their choices of structure and form
- how meaning is shaped by the writer's choices
- how the poem presents different concerns and issues.

You also need to understand the focus of the question so that your essay has a clear and purposeful structure.

Read the poem 'This Room' by Imtiaz Dharker.

This Room

This room is breaking out
of itself, cracking through
its own walls
in search of space, light,
empty air.

The bed is lifting out of
its nightmares.
From dark corners, chairs
are rising up to crash through clouds.

This is the time and place
to be alive:
when the daily furniture of our lives
stirs, when the improbable arrives.
Pots and pans bang together
in celebration, clang
past the crowd of garlic, onions, spices,
fly by the ceiling fan.
No one is looking for the door.

In all this excitement
I'm wondering where
I've left my feet, and why

my hands are outside, clapping.

Imtiaz Dharker (2001)

Now read an example of a question on a single poem:

> Comment closely on the poem 'This Room', discussing the ways in which Imtiaz Dharker presents a change of routine.

Task

1. Look closely at this first sample question. Highlight key words and phrases that would help to shape your response.
  - Which key words tell you to focus on details?
  - Which key words ask you to explore how the writer uses language and techniques?
  - Where is the question focus indicated?
2. The question can be phrased in different ways. Repeat the steps in task **1**, using the following sample questions:

> Comment closely on the poem 'This Room', discussing the ways in which Imtiaz Dharker creates contrasting moods.

> Comment closely on the poem 'This Room', discussing the ways in which Imtiaz Dharker expresses a response to a change of routine.

GATHER YOUR IDEAS AND EVIDENCE

Before you begin to write, you should explore the poem in relation to the question, identifying clear points and evidence to help you to complete your response. You can then include these in an outline plan.

This question expects you to focus closely on how the writer has used language, structure and form to create effects. You can refer back to Units 3.1 to 3.3 to help you.

Task

3. Start by noting down the words and phrases that are about routine and those that are about a change of routine.
  What ideas about routine do these words and phrases suggest to you? For example, what is the poet suggesting about routine and what is she suggesting about a change of routine?
4. Once you have got a feel for the poem, you can start exploring it in more detail and considering the different methods that the poet has used in order to convey meaning.
  With the focus of the question in mind (in this case, how Dharker presents a change of routine), consider how the following aspects of poetry are being used:
  - the speaker's voice or tone
  - the poem's setting and mood
  - the poet's use of sentence structure
  - the way the poem is structured as a whole to develop ideas or create patterns
  - the poem's form, rhythm and metre
  - the poet's choices of imagery.
  Gather more ideas about 'This Room' by taking notes based on these prompts.

PLAN YOUR RESPONSE

You can now use your notes to create a structured plan for the question
The main aim is to identify your points and the order in which you are
going to present them so you can develop your argument.

Task

5. Look at the table below. Put the points about 'This Room' into a
coherent order so there is a sense of development. Then decide
which of the two quotations allows the most sophisticated analysis.

Point	Quotation 1	Quotation 2
A change of routine is presented as exciting.	'Pots and pans bang together / in celebration, clang / past the crowd of garlic, onions, spices'	'In all this excitement'
A change of routine is presented as scary.	'The bed is lifting'	'This room is breaking out / of itself, cracking'
However, change is also liberating and uplifting.	'in search of space, light, / empty air'	'chairs / are rising up to crash through clouds'
The excitement of change can be almost overwhelming.	'I'm wondering where / I've left my feet, and why / my hands are outside, clapping.'	'the crowd of garlic, onions, spices, / fly by the ceiling fan. / No one is looking for the door.'
Routine is presented as restrictive and depressing.	'its nightmares. / From dark corners'	'its own walls'

6. As well as preparing to analyse language, consider how the poet has
used structure and form in order to emphasise her ideas. Look at
your chosen quotations, alongside the poem as a whole and add to
your notes. You could focus on the effects of short sentences, lists,
enjambment and free verse.

7. Before you begin writing your paragraphs of analysis, your response
will need an introduction that clearly shows your engagement with
the questions set. Look at the two examples of students' writing.
What are the strengths of each introduction and how could each
be improved?

Introduction 1

Imtiaz Dharker, in her poem 'This Room', conveys different responses to
a change to routine, presenting it as an ultimately positive experience.
Initially exploring the negative aspects of routine, she then focuses on
how change can be frightening and liberating, exciting and overwhelming.

Introduction 2

'This Room' by Imtiaz Dharker conveys different responses to a change
to routine. Her poem explores how routine can be restrictive and
depressing before explaining that changes to this routine can seem
scary. She goes on to say that a change of routine can be exciting
and liberating. However, she also acknowledges that change can be
overwhelming. Imtiaz Dharker's poem uses different poetic techniques
to look at all these different responses to a change to routine.

The first introduction is clear and concise, offering a point of view about the poem that is clearly linked to the exam question; it also provides an overview of the poem, although the last sentence is a little rushed. The second introduction gives a clear overview of the poem, but it could be more concise and also offer a specific viewpoint; the last sentence is too general and doesn't add anything to the paragraph.

As well as starting with an introduction, you should remember to close your essay with a clear conclusion. This should refer back to the argument that you established in the introduction and draw together the different threads of your essay in order to make a final, confirming point.

Task

8. As guidance on how to construct your individual paragraphs, here is an annotated student paragraph. Read the comments below and consider whether the paragraph could be improved in any way.

> Dharker begins by presenting routine as restrictive and depressing. In lines like 'its nightmares. / From dark corners', she uses the extended metaphor of a room to represent how we can trap ourselves in routines. The use of the word 'corners' suggests an inability to escape while darkness is used to symbolise unhappiness and a lack of hope. The personification of the room adds to the sense of misery, with a short three-syllable line emphasising this image to convey the constricting effects of routine on the speaker.

- clear point linked to the question focus
- embedded quotation as evidence, with accurate use of quotation marks and forward slash showing the end of a line
- analysis of language
- closer analysis, focusing on specific details
- link to focus of the question

You should always consider whether you can develop your idea by analysing a related quotation; only do this if it allows you to deepen and extend, rather than repeat, your point.

Task

9. Fill in the blanks to complete the paragraph of analysis below. Then continue the paragraph by selecting an additional quotation that allows you to extend your analysis.

Dharker presents a change in routine as liberating and uplifting. In the surreal image of 'chairs / [...] rising up to crash through clouds', she uses powerful _____ to suggest _____. The enjambment creates _____ to highlight the change of routine, and the onomatopoeic '_____' is particularly effective because the alliteration of the 'c' plosive adds _____. This idea...

WRITE YOUR RESPONSE

Task

10. Now plan and write your response to the task below in **1 hour**.

> Comment closely on the poem 'This Room', discussing the ways in which Imtiaz Dharker presents a change of routine.

3.8 Evaluating responses to a single poem for AS Level

Big question

- How do you evaluate a whole-text response to a single poem for AS Level?

SAMPLE RESPONSES TO A SINGLE-POEM TASK

In this unit, you will explore two discursive essay responses to the task in Unit 3.7. This will enable you to evaluate what makes a strong response and, using these responses and commentaries as a guide, help you to improve and develop your own single-poem responses.

Task

1. Using the sample paragraph in Unit 3.7 as a model, read through your own response carefully, paragraph by paragraph, and complete an initial annotation (covering aspects such as assessment of overview, structure of response, analysis of language, form and structure, support from text, reference to context where relevant, strength of conclusion).
2. Read the following response. As you read, think about:
   - what this response does well
   - how the response might be improved.

Response 1

Imtiaz Dharker presents different responses to a change to routine in 'This Room'. At first, she presents routine as limiting and depressing before exploring how a change to that routine can be frightening as well as liberating, exciting and overwhelming.

> A clear and straightforward introduction. Writing could be more sophisticated with more sense of an overview.

At the start of the poem, Dharker presents routine as something that holds you back and upsets you. She uses personification to describe the room's 'nightmares. / From dark corners'. This creates a sense of being trapped, as 'corners' implies a lack of escape. This links to the short sentences. Mentioning 'nightmares' suggests that breaking out of a routine can be frightening, while the word 'dark' creates an unhappy mood, which suggests that routine eventually weighs people down and ruins their lives.

> Clear topic sentence, but language could be more precise and the use of the second person is clumsy.

> Some good analysis of language; a feature of structure is identified but impact not explored. Quotation not well embedded.

Dharker writes, 'This room is breaking out / of itself, cracking'. She is exploring how a change to routine can be frightening and the two verbs create a sense of danger, which is heightened by the harsh plosive sounds of the b and c. The metaphor creates an image of walls collapsing, which implies danger and also explains why people might avoid a change to routine: it seems unsafe and creates a feeling of vulnerability.

> The lack of topic sentence means the next point is unclear — no sense of the essay's discussion developing.

This image opens the poem and it contains enjambment and a pause before 'cracking', both of which create a feeling that the poem is in some way broken, so it seems like there is something wrong from the beginning.

The poem becomes more positive and Dharker presents a change of routine as something liberating and uplifting rather than something frightening that holds people back: 'in search of space, light, / empty air'. The verb 'search' makes a change to routine sound valuable, like a treasure, suggesting it should be looked far rather than avoided. The pattern of three nouns creates a feeling of freedom, suggesting that without a routine there is a new beginning where you can live your life and develop as a person without feeling weighed down.

Dharker also presents a change to routine as exciting. In the third stanza, she writes 'In all this excitement' to convey her mood when she escapes her daily routine. The word 'excitement' shows that she is feeling full of happiness and adventure as if the change has motivated her to do more with her life. The word 'all' increases this by suggesting that this feeling of exhilaration is all around her.

The last lines read:

> I'm wondering where
> I've left my feet, and why
> my hands are outside, clapping.

This also creates a mood of happiness and excitement. The descriptions are unusual as she seems to have left her body and this is emphasised by the way the final line is separated by enjambment into a single line in its own stanza. This could be a metaphor for feeling uplifted and having no sense of burden in life. It also creates a sense of ecstasy as if she's completely caught up in the joy of living her life rather than following a routine. The poem ends with the verb 'clapping', which is how good things usually end, creating an idea that a change of routine is something that should be celebrated.

The poet uses metaphor, verbs and other techniques to present the change to a routine in different ways. Dharker shows that people get trapped in routines and this makes them unhappy. The poem appears to encourage people to escape their routines, showing that although it can be frightening, it will lead to a happier life. The poem builds up a real sense of freedom and escape that contrasts with the mood at the beginning.

Some good analysis of language and an attempt to offer a personal interpretation. A less confident, vague consideration of the effect of structure.

Some good language analysis, but it is rather generalised instead of being specific. Vocabulary choices could be more sophisticated and precise.

A poor quotation choice doesn't allow much specific analysis of the writer's methods, although there is some attempt to interpret meaning.

A good attempt to convey how the poem's structure has been used to emphasise meaning.

This is an adequate conclusion. The list of techniques isn't useful but there is an attempt to draw together the different aspects that the essay has explored.

COMMENTARY

This is a sound response that is clearly focused on the question. Writing could frequently be more precise and sophisticated, but there are good attempts to present an interpretation of the poem and some sense of development between paragraphs. Quotations are usually well chosen and analysis of language is generally good, although exploration of structure is much less successful. Some subject terminology is used effectively, but the essay would benefit from a greater range. The response could have looked in more detail at form, rhythm and the poetic voice.

Task

3. Now read a second response to the same question. As you read, think about what this student has done that develops and improves upon the previous response.

Response 2

In her poem, 'This Room', Imtiaz Dharker, uses the extended metaphor of a room to present different and sometimes conflicting responses to a change to routine. Initially exploring the limiting aspects of routine, Dharker then conveys how change can be frightening and liberating, exciting and overwhelming.

> Clear overview is established. Writing is accurate and sophisticated.

In the first two stanzas of the poem, Dharker explores how routine can be restrictive and stultifying. Personifying the room, she describes 'its nightmares / From dark corners' to create a sense of entrapment. 'Corners' is used symbolically to imply a lack of movement or direction, and the comparatively short sentences in stanza 2 add to this sense of enclosure. The reference to 'nightmares' perhaps explains the lack of change through the idea that, once someone gets into a routine, the prospect of breaking out of it can be frightening. The context of nightmares also links to Dharker's use of the adjective 'dark' to create a despondent mood, which is heightened by the way the personification seeks to make the room seem like a living, feeling organism.

> Topic sentence introduces the first part of the argument.

> Analysis is clear and sophisticated with subject terminology.

The notion that a change of routine is scary can also be seen in the opening lines. When Dharker writes, 'This room is breaking out / of itself, cracking', she is focusing on the change rather than the mere prospect of change. The enjambment and the subsequent caesura create unusual pauses that indicate dislocation, instantly bringing uncertainty to the poem. The two verbs create a sense of danger, heightened by the multiple plosive sounds that are emphasised through consonance, but the image also has connotations of an egg hatching, underpinning the danger with a feeling of anticipation via a sense of rebirth and new beginnings.

> Topic sentence uses a connective and refers back to a previous comment in order to begin developing the argument.

> Analysis is detailed and nuanced, offering interesting interpretations and exploring structure alongside language.

As Dharker's exploration of a change of routine develops into something more positive, she begins to present it as also liberating and uplifting. Describing the room as 'in search of space, light, / empty air', she evokes a sense of freedom through the trio of abstract nouns. Each carries a related symbolic meaning, with 'space' implying room to grow, 'light' linking to hope and new beginnings, and 'air' suggesting a lack of impediment (or emotional baggage) and the chance to breathe freely. The verb 'search' makes it clear that such a change to routine is to be desired and valued, rather than feared and avoided.

> Clear, detailed analysis refers back to previous – develops discussion. Answer is specific, considers effects of individual words. Precision and sophistication in language used.

The excitement of a change to routine is most apparent in the third stanza. Incorporating a mixture of onomatopoeia, plosives, personification and powerful verbs, Dharker uses a list, to build up a feeling of euphoria, all summarised in the word 'celebration':

> Pots and pans bang together
> in celebration, clang
> past the crowd of garlic, onions, spices.

The stanza is full of noise, life and action, creating a stark contrast to the dullness of lines 7–8 and reflecting the poet's use of free verse: all tradition, formality and rules can be happily broken.

Impact of form explored.

This excitement seems almost overwhelming at the end of the poem. The last lines build on the early images of liberation to create an almost out-of-body experience through the way in which the speaker is caught up in the sheer ecstasy of change:

> I'm wondering where
> I've left my feet, and why
> my hands are outside, clapping.

Symbolically, the action of the poem now moves to 'outside' as opposed to the confining interior that opened the poem, representing how the speaker has escaped her own self-constraints. The enjambment and the final single line stanza highlight the mood of elation, as does the use of the caesura to emphasise the verb 'clapping' in order close the poem with connotations of applause and approval.

Thoughtful analysis creates an effective final point.

Despite admitting that change can be frightening, Dharker makes the need to escape the constraints of routine very clear. Through her extended metaphor of a room, she presents a change of routine as exciting, liberating and, ultimately, life-affirming.

A good conclusion, drawing together different aspects of the discussion, offering closing viewpoint.

COMMENTARY

This is a strong essay with regular, detailed analysis that explores a range of features of language, structure and form. Quotations are well selected and successfully embedded into the essay. Each paragraph establishes a clear point that builds upon its predecessor to develop the overall argument. The essay ends with a secure conclusion. Writing is accurate and sophisticated with a wide range of subject terminology. The essay would benefit from more specific discussion of the narrative voice.

Final Task

Now that you have considered the sample responses for discursive question based on a single poem, reflect upon your own response.

Task

4. **a)** Use the guidance in the tables on the final page of this chapter (page 214) to assess whether you think your response could be classed as 'competent' or 'very good'.

   b) What do you think were the strengths of your response? What could you do to improve upon and develop your own whole-text discursive essays?

   c) Using the examples above, write a brief commentary at the end of your own essay with action points for development.

3.9 Writing about linked poems

Big question

- How do you plan a response to a discursive essay question linking two poems?

UNDERSTAND THE TASK (AS/A LEVEL)

At AS level, you will be asked to consider how **two** poems written by the same poet might be linked, focusing, for example, on how the poems develop ideas or characters, or on how they use particular techniques. When it comes to A Level, you will be asked to consider how a poet's concerns and techniques compare, this time referring to **three** poems.

When approaching a question that links poems at AS level, it is important to consider:

- the writer's choices of language, form and structure
- how far the poems fit into existing genres or challenge them
- how voice, tone and mood are created
- what is distinctive about the writer's style
- how meaning is shaped by the writer's choices
- the writer's wider concerns, ideas and issues
- links between the poems.

You then need to relate your understanding of the elements above to the focus of the linked question.

Read this example of an AS Level-style question, asking you to discuss and link two poems.

Discuss the ways in which Blake presents places. You should refer to **two** poems in your answer.

Look at the highlighted parts of the question. You are being asked to:

- analyse the poet's use of language, structure and form in detail
- directly link your analysis to the presentation of place in two poems.

Task

1. Questions can be phrased in a number of ways. What is the focus of each of the following questions?

'I wander through each chartered street'. Discuss Blake's presentation of place in **two** poems.

Discuss Blake's presentation of the natural world in his poetry, making detailed reference to **two** poems.

You would need to start by deciding which poems to write about. Choose poems that share the concern focused on in the question (in this case, place) and present that concern in a powerful way. Your choice of poems will affect how you structure your essay. If you choose similar poems, this will lead to a continuing development of ideas; if you select contrasting poems, this will invite consideration of the differences. Either approach is fine so long as you keep focused on the question.

Read the poems 'London' and 'Holy Thursday' by William Blake and the context box below.

Historical and social context

By the end of the 18th century, England had been significantly changed by the Industrial Revolution. The new production factories had made a small section of society rich. However, while the cities rapidly grew, their infrastructures hadn't been developed by the government, leading to poor housing, hygiene and working conditions, as well as social problems such as child-labour (doing jobs such as sweeping chimneys), crime and poverty. The Church and the monarchy were also criticised for their lack of help, although **Holy Thursday** was a day when the Church would hold services for poor children and give them food.

London

I wander through each **chartered** street,
Near where the chartered Thames does flow,
A mark in every face I meet,
Marks of weakness, marks of woe.

In every cry of every man,
In every infant's cry of fear,
In every voice, in every ban,
The mind-forged **manacles** I hear:

How the chimney-sweeper's cry
Every blackening church appals,
And the hapless soldier's sigh
Runs in blood down palace-walls.

But most, through midnight streets I hear
How the youthful harlot's curse
Blasts the new-born infant's tear,
And blights with plagues the marriage hearse.

William Blake (1794)

Holy Thursday

Is this a holy thing to see
In a rich and fruitful land, -
Babes reduced to misery,
Fed with cold and **usurous** hand?

Is that trembling cry a song?
Can it be a song of joy?
And so many children poor?
It is a land of poverty!

And their sun does never shine,
And their fields are bleak and bare,
And their ways are filled with thorns,
It is eternal winter there.

For where'er the sun does shine,
And where'er the rain does fall,
Babe can never hunger there,
Nor poverty the mind appal.

William Blake (1794)

Glossary

Holy Thursday: the Thursday immediately before the Christian festival of Easter
chartered: documented by the government to show rights and ownership
manacles: chains for restraining a person's wrists or ankles, similar to handcuffs
usurous (an old version of 'usurious'): immorally lending money in order to unfairly make yourself richer

GATHER YOUR IDEAS AND EVIDENCE

Once you have got a feel for the poems and places, you should start exploring them in more detail and considering the different methods that the poet has used in order to convey meaning.

Task

2. With the focus of the question in mind (in this case, how Blake presents places), consider how the following aspects of poetry are being used:

   a) the speaker's voice or tone

   b) the poem's setting and mood

   c) the poet's use of sentence structure

   d) the way the poem is structured as a whole to develop ideas or create patterns

   e) the poem's form, rhythm and metre

   f) the poet's choices of imagery

   g) links between the poems, in terms of the poet's concerns and the methods used.

   Gather more ideas about 'London' and 'Holy Thursday' by taking notes based on these prompts.

   You will then need to identify links between what aspect of 'place' is explored by the poem and how the poet uses techniques to present this.

PLAN YOUR RESPONSE

You can now use your notes to create a structured plan for your answer. The main aim is to identify your points, the order you are going to present them in order to develop your argument, and the best quotations that will allow you plenty of analysis. You could use a mind map, a table or a Venn diagram.

Task

3. Copy and complete the table below to establish your points about, and links between, the two poems.

	Holy Thursday	**Link**	**London**
Intro	Late-18th-century England, Industrial Revolution	Same place	Late-18th-century England (specifically the capital, London), Industrial Revolution
Section 1			Nature lost and England longer free
Section 2	A place of misery and poverty		
Section 3		Focus on the plight of children	
Section 4		Metaphor	

Then decide which of your quotations match each section and will allow the most sophisticated analysis.

You can use different methods to structure your essay when linking poems; there is no need to compare poems throughout a response, although you could do this.

- You could choose an approach with a linked introduction, tracking poem A, tracking poem B, then linked conclusion as a way to plan.
- Alternatively, you can plan your essay in a more integrated way, tracking poem B with what you have said about poem A clearly in mind, so that development of your argument is clearer.

Task

4. To help you to decide how to construct your individual paragraphs, read this student's response and the annotated comments. How could the paragraph be improved?

> 'Holy Thursday' presents England as a place of unhappiness due to poverty. The lines 'Is that trembling cry a song? / [...] And so many children poor?' convey the misery in which children live through the use of the adjectives 'trembling' and 'poor'. The adverb phrase 'so many' emphasises the intensity of the problem, while the repeated rhetorical questions criticise what Blake saw as a lack of government intervention. His use of metre deliberately resembles a nursery rhyme to create a scathing tone of **irony** about innocent children being brought up in such a terrible place.
>
> There is a similar presentation of England as an unhappy place in 'London'. In the lines…

— clear point linked to the question focus

— embedded quotation as evidence

— analysis of language

— analysis developed through additional focus on language and structure

— analysis developed further through exploration of form

— link to the second poem through similarity of poetic concerns

You will see that this student has adopted an approach to planning that focuses on Poem A, and then links to Poem B in a following paragraph. This approach is fine, but there is a danger that the essay could become rather 'bitty' and not develop a coherent reading of each poem.

Key term

irony: conveying your meaning by pointedly saying the opposite of what you actually intend to say

Task

5. Now construct a linked paragraph that analyses how Blake presents England as an unhappy place in 'London'. If you notice any similarity in the methods Blake employs in 'London' and 'Holy Thursday', point them out during your analysis.

WRITE YOUR RESPONSE

Task

6. Now plan and write your response to the exam-style task below in **1 hour**.

> Discuss the ways in which Blake presents places. You should refer to **two** poems in your answer.

Checklist for success

✓ Begin with a clear concise introduction that gives a brief linked overview of the two poems or establishes an initial link to be explored.

✓ Then focus on paragraphs of detailed yet concise analysis.

✓ Use topic sentences to show how the direction of your essay's discussion is developing from paragraph to paragraph.

✓ Finish with a brief conclusion that draws together the threads of your discussion and considers the key links between the two poems.

UNDERSTANDING YOUR TASK (A LEVEL ONLY)

When you are approaching a discursive linked poetry question for A Level, your response should follow *all* the guidelines given above.

There is also one *additional* area where you should develop your response:

• incorporate different interpretations in your analysis.

For example, in 'London', when Blake refers to the 'mind-forged manacles', he could be using this metaphor to suggests that England doesn't value education so its people are ignorant. It could also suggest that the harsh living conditions eventually wear people down until they don't even value themselves and then give up on life. Alternatively, a Marxist perspective might suggest that the metaphor is a criticism of different political or religious ideologies that the country encourages its people to believe in so that it can enslave them.

Read this A Level-style question, asking you to discuss and link three poems:

Discuss some of the ways in which Blake presents place. You should refer to **three** poems in your answer.

The question format here reflects the A Level skill of incorporating different interpretations.

This is the focus for comparison.

You will need to discuss three – rather than two – poems.

Here are some more A Level-style questions that could be asked about linked poems:

Discuss some of the ways in which Blake presents attitudes towards children. You should refer to three poems in your answer.

Discuss some of the ways in which Blake presents the loss of the countryside. You should refer to three poems in your answer.

Task

7. What do you notice about the wording and focus of the questions?
8. Reread 'Holy Thursday' and consider how the following lines could be interpreted in different ways:
   • 'In a rich and fruitful land,'
   • 'And their sun does never shine,'
   • 'It is eternal winter there.'

Task

9. Read 'The Chimney Sweeper' by William Blake, keeping focused on the task:

> Discuss some of the ways in which Blake presents place. You should refer to **three** poems in your answer.

The Chimney-Sweeper

A little black thing among the snow,
Crying! 'weep! weep!' in notes of woe!
'Where are thy father and mother? Say!' –
'They are both gone up to the church to pray.

'Because I was happy upon the heath,
And smiled among the winter's snow,
They clothed me in the clothes of death,
And taught me to sing the notes of woe.

'And because I am happy and dance and sing,
They think they have done me no injury,
And are gone to praise God and His priest and king,
Who made up a heaven of our misery.'

William Blake (1794)

GATHER YOUR IDEAS AND EVIDENCE

Task

10. Now, work through the three poems, making notes on their exploration of 'place', how this is presented using a range of techniques, and considering the different interpretations you might want to explore.
   You may want to consider voice, tone, setting, mood, form, structure and patterning, language and imagery.

PLAN YOUR RESPONSE

Task

11. Look back at your notes on 'The Chimney-Sweeper', 'London' and 'Holy Thursday', and decide how you can draw links between them, focusing on how they present 'place'.
   Put an asterisk by any quotations that will allow you to include alternative interpretations.

WRITE YOUR RESPONSE

Task

12. Now plan and write your response to the task on the right in **1 hour**. For guidance, use the 'Checklist for success' in Task **6**, but with reference to three poems instead of two.

> Discuss some of the ways in which Blake presents place. You should refer to **three** poems in your answer.

3.10 Evaluating responses to linked poems

Big question

- How do you evaluate a whole-text response to linked poems?

SAMPLE RESPONSES TO A LINKED-POEM TASK (AS/A LEVEL)

In this section, you will explore two discursive essay responses to the task in Unit 3.9. This will enable you to evaluate what makes a strong response and, using these responses and commentaries as a guide, help you to improve and develop your own whole-text answers.

Task

Discuss the ways in which Blake presents places. You should refer to **two** poems in your answer.

1. Using the sample paragraph in Unit 3.9 as a model, read through your own response carefully, paragraph by paragraph, and complete an initial annotation (covering aspects such as assessment of overview, structure of response, analysis of language, form and structure, support from text, links between poems, reference to context where relevant, strength of conclusion).

2. Read the following response. As you read, think about:
   - what this response does well
   - how the response might be improved.

Response 1

Blake criticises 18th-century England by focusing on London. He shows sympathy with the working classes and particularly children born into poverty. Attacking the lack of compassion shown by the Establishment, Blake predicts its effect on the future of the country.

At the start of 'Holy Thursday', Blake asks, 'Is this a holy thing to see / In a rich and fruitful land'. He uses a rhetorical question to say that England should be a prosperous place. The words 'rich' and 'fruitful' link to the country's natural resources. 'Rich' has a double meaning – having abundant resources and being a wealthy person - implying that wealth is not distributed as evenly as it should be. In 'London', the opening lines suggest that a land that once belonged to everyone has been divided up amongst the wealthy: 'I wander through each chartered street, / Near where the chartered Thames does flow'.

A competent introduction, focusing on the essay question, but doesn't specify which poems.

There would be a stronger sense of analysis and links between the poems if the opening sentence established a clear point about both texts. The quotation could be embedded more carefully.

There is some good analysis but it could be expressed in a more sophisticated way, developing nuance and making use of subject terminology.

This sentence would benefit from a connective (such as 'Similarly') to highlight links between the poems.

The word 'chartered' is repeated for effect to show his disapproval of this dividing up. This is highlighted through the metaphorical image of water being allocated different owners, suggesting that England is everyone's and everyone should benefit from it, not just the few.

Blake presents England as an unhappy land. 'Holy Thursday' has the phrase 'trembling cry'. The adjective describes a child and this creates sympathy. He links this distress to a lack of money in the short sentence, 'It is a land of poverty!' The exclamation mark creates a tone of shock that things have become so bad in England. Blake also expresses the population's distress by using the word 'cry' in 'London': 'In every cry of every man, / In every infant's cry of fear'. The repetition of 'every', and the mention of both adult and child, suggests that all the people in England are unhappy. He adds to this by linking it to a lack of personal freedom. The metaphor 'mind-forged manacles' suggests a nation restricted mentally because the country has made them feel worthless and like things cannot change.

Linking is stronger in this paragraph because of the topic sentence and the use of a connective.

Analysis is a little more developed and sophisticated; however, the quotation could be placed in the context of the whole poem in order to make the analysis clearer.

The Church is criticised in 'Holy Thursday'. Blake satirises the religious festival by implying it is the only day when the Church is actually charitable. The religious leaders are described as having a 'cold and usurous hand'. This suggests charity is given out to the poor unwillingly, with the word 'usurous' implying the poor are forced to believe in God in return for charity. This creates an image of a church that is only superficially good: it lacks real moral values and is tricking or exploiting the poor. The Church is also criticised in 'London' when Blake writes, 'the chimney-sweeper's cry / Every blackening church appalls'. The description shows that the Church has done nothing to change social injustices, and the symbolism of black is used to say the Church should be ashamed of itself. He makes another attack on the establishment, 'the hapless soldier's sigh / Runs in blood down palace-walls'. This is also a metaphor. The monarchy is responsible for the deaths of innocent men, which is partly conveyed through the adjective 'hapless'. The soldiers are fighting in wars that only benefit the rulers.

Links are established at the start of the paragraph, but are only explicitly expressed later on in the paragraph through a connective. Clear topic sentences to show how the discussion is developing would create a much stronger essay structure.

There is some good analysis, but it could be more precise and coherent. Sentences aren't crafted in order to link and develop ideas. The isolated reference to metaphor looks like feature spotting: any terminology should be integrated with analysis.

Blake also suggests in both poems that England is a place without hope or future. 'Holy Thursday' uses anaphora to build up a sense of desperation. The metaphor 'bleak and bare' and saying there is no sunshine make the country sound desolate and hopeless. These images imply that there is an absence of goodness in the country. In 'London', Blake describes how

> The youthful harlot's curse
> Blasts the new-born infant's tear,
> And blights with plagues the marriage hearse.

The opening sentences of the paragraphs have generally focused on the question and created a sense of an argument being developed.

This metaphor is about sexual immorality, a major social problem in the cities at the time when Blake was writing. This is another suggestion that there is a lack of goodness in the country, shown in the unkind way the woman treats her child. The harsh verb 'blasts' shows this, as well as the word 'curse' to show she's swearing at an innocent baby. Blake also includes many images linked to death, such as blights, plagues and hearse, which suggest that England is dying and losing all its goodness.

Both poems present places. 'London' deals with the whole city, while 'Holy Thursday' looks at a specific part of the city. They both show Blake's pessimistic view of England, as London represents the whole country because it is the capital city. Through his choices of language and structure, and by focusing on key figures such as religious leaders, soldiers and harlots, Blake portrays England as a place where the poor are unhappy and badly treated.

Language and sentence structure could be more sophisticated.

A fair conclusion, giving a brief overview of the poems and referring very generally to the methods used by Blake. The argument could be concluded in a more deliberate manner.

COMMENTARY

This is a sound response that is clearly focused on the question. There is balanced coverage of the two poems and regular links are made, although these are sometimes only implied. The answer would benefit from more specific consideration of the poet's methods, particularly the use of form, rhythm and meter to show a secure grasp of how the texts are working as poems. Quotations are well chosen but could be more skilfully embedded into sentences. Analysis is sound but could be more precise and nuanced. Writing is accurate but not sophisticated; sentences are sometimes disjointed and there could be more accurate use of subject terminology.

Task

3. Now read a second response to the same question. As you read, think about what this student has done that develops and improves upon the previous response.

Response 2

In 'Holy Thursday' and 'London', Blake presents a social critique of 18th-century England. Sympathising with the working classes, and particularly children born into poverty, he depicts their suffering in an industrialised world. Blake attacks the lack of compassion shown by the Establishment, predicting the effect it will have on the country's future.

Blake's poems begin by establishing a problem in England. In the opening stanza of 'Holy Thursday', he uses a rhetorical question, 'Is this a holy thing to see / In a rich and fruitful land', to critique the nation and imply that England should be a prosperous place. The adjectives 'rich' and 'fruitful' link to the country's natural resources, but the former has an important double

Clear argument and links established.

Topic sentence introduces the first part of the argument and sets out link.

meaning, linking also to personal wealth, that suggests there is a problem with the distribution of wealth. Similarly, in 'London', the opening lines, 'I wander through each chartered street, / Near where the chartered Thames does flow', suggest through the repetition of 'chartered' that a land that once belonged to everyone has been divided up amongst the wealthy. He emphasises his disapproval with the metaphorical image of water (a similar reference to a natural resource) being allocated different owners. Both of these openings blame England's problems on its establishments: the Church ('holy') and monarchy ('chartered').

Analysis is clear and sophisticated with subject terminology.

The connective highlights a link and further connections are made during the paragraph, considering similar imagery as well as similar ideas.

Blake develops his exploration of England by presenting it as an unhappy land. Both poems repeat the noun 'cry' – 'In every cry of every man, / In every infant's cry of fear' and 'trembling cry' – in order to depict a place of perpetual misery. The repetition of 'every', combined with the image of it affecting both adult and child, is particularly effective. 'Holy Thursday' links this distress to a lack of money in the second stanza's short exclamative sentence, 'It is a land of poverty!', altering the stanza's rhythm at this point to emphasise the speaker's shocked and critical tone. 'London' presents a more complex image of a lack of personal freedom, describing the population as enchained by 'mind-forged manacles' and using this metaphor to suggests a nation restricted mentally, through a lack of education and a sense of worthlessness arising from being poor. The formal nature of Blake's verses, with their regular metre, fixed rhyme scheme and traditional end-stopped lines, can be seen as reflecting the restricted minds of the populace.

Comparison of methods as well as ideas.

Analysis is developed through an interpretation of the poet's use of form.

The Church is criticised in both poems for its role in shaping a country that lacks true morality and charity. As a whole, 'Holy Thursday' satirises the religious festival by implying it's the only day when the Church is actually charitable. The description of a 'cold and usurous hand' is particularly scathing, suggesting charity is given unwillingly. The adjective 'usurous' suggests that the poor are forced to believe in God in return for charity, with Blake deliberately referring to a biblical sin in order to accuse the Church of hypocrisy. Similarly, he asserts that religious leaders should be ashamed of their lack of social intervention in the metaphor, 'the chimney-sweeper's cry / Every blackening church appals', using traditional colour symbolism to portray the Church as evil. Blake's notion that England is a place where the establishment does not care about its people is developed through the powerful metaphor, 'the hapless soldier's sigh / Runs in blood down palace-walls', and its suggestion that the monarchy is responsible for the deaths of innocent men fighting in wars that only benefit the ruling minority.

The overall style of the poem is considered in addition to specific language features.

The two poems end with Blake suggesting England is a place without hope or future. The third stanza of 'Holy Thursday' uses anaphora to build up a sense of desperation:

> And their sun does never shine,
> And their fields are bleak and bare,
> And their ways are filled with thorns.

As well as suggesting the loss of nature heralded by the Industrial Revolution, the images work at a metaphorical level to imply the country's moral desolation. The speaker's denunciation of this situation is subtly highlighted by the almost incongruous use of a nursery rhyme style, with the additional anapaest that opens each line also producing a gentleness that is contrastingly lacking in society. This immorality can also be seen in 'London' in Blake's description of how

> the youthful harlot's curse
> Blasts the new-born infant's tear,
> And blights with plagues the marriage hearse.

Here he uses metaphor to expose the rise in social problems and their effects on the city. Immorality is presented as something contagious ('blights... plagues'), spreading through London and killing the family unit ('hearse'), while a loss of love is pictured in the young woman's reaction to her crying child through the harsh verb 'blasts'. However, she can also be seen as being sympathised with through the double meaning of 'curse', referring to her inappropriate language as well as an acknowledgement that she is trapped in an immoral life by a lack of money, linking to Blake's image of 'ways... filled with thorns'.

Throughout the two poems, and perhaps most effectively in the wider-ranging images of 'London', Blake presents a country on the verge of disaster. Levelling the blame at the Church and the monarchy, he depicts England as a place filled with poverty, desperation, sin, and hypocrisy, offering little hope for the future.

Again, links are being made between methods not just ideas.

Sophisticated analysis, making use of subject terminology and drawing connections between the poems

A good conclusion, summarising the argument and evaluating which poem is most successful.

COMMENTARY

A very good essay. There are regular, integrated connections and comparisons between the two poems. Unlike the first essay, each paragraph clearly develops the overall argument, and there is a secure conclusion with some evaluation. Quotations are well selected, and analysis is detailed and precise. The student discusses a range of poetic methods (exploring language, form and structure), presents original responses and interpretations, and draws on context to add depth to the analysis. Writing is accurate and often sophisticated with a wide range of subject terminology.

SAMPLE RESPONSE TO A LINKED-POEM TASK (A LEVEL)

 Task

4. Now read this extract from a response to an A Level-style question. As you read, think about how the student has made links to three poems and incorporated alternative interpretation.

> Discuss some of the ways in which Blake presents place. You should refer to **three** poems in your answer.

Response 3

Blake develops his exploration of England by presenting it as an unhappy land. All three poems use a reference to the people's cries – 'In every cry of every man, / In every infant's cry of fear', 'trembling cry', and 'Crying! weep! weep!' – in order to depict a place of perpetual misery. The repetition of 'every' in 'London', combined with the image of it affecting both adult and child, is particularly effective. The poems link the causes of distress to a sense of absence, with 'Holy Thursday' focusing on a lack of money in the short exclamative sentence, 'It is a land of poverty!' and 'The Chimney-Sweeper' creating particular pathos through its portrayal of a lack of love for the 'thing' deserted in the snow by his parents. 'London' presents a more complex image of a lack of personal freedom. Blake describes the population as being enchained by 'mind-forged manacles', using the metaphor to suggests a nation restricted mentally, perhaps through a lack of education, a sense of worthlessness arising from being poor, or a misplaced allegiance to the Church and monarchy. Blake could additionally be using this slave image to focus on the workers of the Industrial Revolution and suggest that they are being exploited by the rich factory owners.

Final Task

Now that you have considered these sample responses to exam-style questions, reflect upon your own response.

Task

5. a) Use the guidance in the tables on the final page of this chapter (page 214) to assess whether you think your response could be classed as 'competent' or 'very good'.

b) What do you think were the strengths of your response? What could you do to improve upon and develop it?

c) Using the examples above, write a brief commentary at the end of your own essay with action points for development.

3.11 Writing a critical appreciation of poetry for A Level

Big question
- How do you plan a response to a critical appreciation question?

UNDERSTAND THE TASK (A LEVEL)

When approaching a critical appreciation question at A Level, it is important to consider:
- the writer's choices of language, form and structure
- how voice, tone and mood is created
- what is distinctive about the writer's style
- the writer's wider concerns, ideas and issues
- links between the poems
- alternative interpretations
- the context in which the texts were written and received.

You also then need to relate your understanding of the elements above to the focus of the critical appreciation question.

Read this example of an A Level exam-style question.

> Paying close attention to the effects of the writing, discuss 'The Chimney-Sweeper', showing what it contributes to your understanding of Blake's poetic methods and concerns.

Look at the highlighted parts of the question. You are being asked to:
- analyse the poet's use of language, structure and form in detail
- directly link your analysis to 'The Chimney-Sweeper' and other poems by Blake.

Start by deciding which poems to write about. Ideally, you should refer to *four* other poems (two in detail and two briefly) to demonstrate a broad yet detailed understanding.

Here, the focus will be on the named poem plus 'Holy Thursday' and 'London' (both in Unit 3.8) as well as 'The Schoolboy' and 'Infant Sorrow'. These poems are provided in the Teacher Resource.

GATHER YOUR IDEAS AND EVIDENCE

Task

1. **a)** Next, explore the named poem in relation to the question, identifying clear points about concerns and methods with evidence to support them.

    b) While exploring the named poem, make links to other poems that display similar concerns and/or methods.

    When looking for links, focus on concerns, language, style, and imagery, as well as form and structure (for example, sentence functions such as exclamatives, the use of dialogue to present a character's voice, and whether the poem has a set rhyme scheme and metre).

PLAN YOUR RESPONSE

Use your notes to create a structured plan.

Task

2. You could complete a table to establish the main concerns in the named poem and to make links with other poems. For example, a plan about 'The Chimney-Sweeper' might begin:

Key concerns in 'The Chimney-Sweeper'	Quotation	Notes for analysis and relevant links to context	Links to concerns and methods in other Blake poems
The mistreatment of children	'A little black thing among the snow,'	Adjective 'little' evokes sympathy. Contrasting symbolism of snow and black = innocence and corruption. Use of 'thing' to suggest objectification.	More direct criticism of mistreatment in 'London'. Similar use of 'black' and contrasting symbolism of innocence and experience.
Children's unhappiness and loss of innocence	'They clothed me in the clothes of death, / And taught me to sing the notes of woe.'	Repetition of 'woe' in poem to emphasise unhappiness. Metaphor to show the dangers of chimney-sweeping.	Mistreatment of children in 'Holy Thursday'. Repeated images of crying and use of metaphor in 'Holy Thursday' and 'London'.

3. Although you need solid links to the concerns and methods of other poems, your analysis of the named poem should dominate.
Read this annotated student paragraph that demonstrates one approach to linking and consider whether it could be improved.

'The Chimney-Sweeper' displays one of William Blake's key concerns: the plight of children in England's newly industrialised cities. By having the chimney-sweeper describe how he has been treated by his parents, 'And taught me to sing the notes of woe', Blake focuses on the harm done to children. The verb 'taught' suggests that children are mistreated by their elders, but it could also be implying that children are being prepared for a future life of misery. Blake's use of an anapaest as its second metrical foot ('me to sing', with the happy connotations of 'sing' being ironic) creates a gentler rhythm that suggests how a child should live compared to the life actually being described. The reference to 'woe' is repeated later in the poem and this, like 'crying' in line 2, is a familiar motif used by Blake to show the mistreatment of the young, for example the children's 'trembling cry' in 'Holy Thursday' and their 'marks of woe [...] cry of fear' from 'London'.

- clear point linked to the question focus
- embedded quotation as evidence
- analysis of language and alternative interpretation
- analysis of the named poem is developed further through exploration of form
- key concerns and the methods used to convey them are linked to other poems

WRITE YOUR RESPONSE

Task

4. Now plan and write a response to the task below in **1 hour**.

> Paying close attention to the effects of the writing, discuss (*a poem of your choice*), showing what it contributes to your understanding of (your *chosen poet's*) poetic methods and concerns.

3.12 Evaluating a critical appreciation of poetry for A Level

Big question

- How do you evaluate a critical appreciation of poetry?

SAMPLE RESPONSES TO A WHOLE-TEXT TASK THAT LINKS A POEM TO THE POET'S METHODS AND CONCERNS (A LEVEL)

In this section, you will explore two critical responses to poems that are linked to the poet's methods and concerns in a wider range of poems. These responses follow the task in Unit 3.11. This will enable you to evaluate what makes a strong response and, using these responses and commentaries as a guide, help you to improve and develop your own critical appreciation.

Task

Paying close attention to the effects of the writing, discuss 'The Chimney-Sweeper', showing what it contributes to your understanding of Blake's poetic methods and concerns.

1. Using the sample paragraph in Unit 3.11 as a model, read through your own response carefully, paragraph by paragraph, and complete an initial annotation (covering aspects such as assessment of overview, structure of response, analysis of language, form and structure, support from text, links between poems, reference to context where relevant, strength of conclusion).

2. Read the following response. As you read, think about:
   - what this student has done well
   - what they might need to do to improve the response.

Response 1

'The Chimney-Sweeper' explores one of Blake's key concerns: the mistreatment of children. It also presents the importance of nature and criticises authority. All these concerns appear in other poems by Blake.

Blake is concerned that children are losing their innocence. He presents this by starting with the situation that the chimney-sweeper is in, having been placed in the world of adulthood much too quickly. The opening line describes him as 'A little black thing among the snow'. Blake is using contrast symbolism to present

Introduction establishes some concerns of named poem, but style needs to be more sophisticated and precise. Chosen linking poems not mentioned.

Clear point focusing on named poem, introducing its key concern. Quotation could be embedded more successfully.

a loss of innocence. The white snow represents purity and the black soot suggests that this innocence has been lost because of his job. This can also be seen as a criticism of economic power, if viewed from a Marxist perspective, as the chimney-sweeper doesn't have any money and that is the cause of all the problems. A sense of innocence being lost is also created by the way Blake has written the poem: it sounds like a song or nursery rhyme and this contrasts with all the harsh images inside the poem.

Good analysis of the named poem.

Some attempt to offer alternative reading.

Some attempt to explore form.

'The Chimney-Sweeper' explores the poor treatment of children by introducing the child's speech. The metaphor, 'They clothed me in the clothes of death', shows how the child feels he has been pushed into an unhealthy, and sometimes deadly, trade by his parents. By giving over the narrative voice of the poem to the chimney-sweeper, Blake creates a more immediate impression of the child's life to increase the reader's sympathy. To show the effect of mistreatment on children, Blake also has the chimney-sweeper 'crying' in line 2 and this powerful verb adds to the sad mood of the poem.

Some good analysis of the named poem, including consideration of voice.

'The Chimney-Sweeper' also shows that Blake is concerned about nature and its importance in a child's successful upbringing. We are told how the boy 'was happy upon the heath, / And smiled among the winter's snow'. The words 'happy' and 'smiled' have positive connotations and suggest that nature enriches a person's life. However, use of past tense suggests this natural environment has been taken away from the child. The historical context is important here because Blake was writing in the 18th century when there was an Industrial Revolution in Britain. Large parts of the countryside were built on to create big factories and cities, which Blake appears to see as the wrong environment for a child to be brought up in. So this poem could also be concerned with the Industrial Revolution's effects on England not just the chimney-sweeper.

Clear analysis of how methods convey concerns.

Use of historical criticism to present alternative interpretation. Could be more strongly linked to analysis of the named poem.

Blake also criticises the Church in the 'The Chimney-Sweeper'. When the boy refers to 'God and His priest and king, / Who make up a heaven of our misery', Blake is accusing the Church and the monarchy of spoiling the country. The verb phrase and the contrasting images of 'heaven' and 'misery' suggest that the Church only pretends to care about the poor.

Blake also shows his concern about children's lost innocence in the poem 'London'. When Blake depicts the 'harlot' swearing at her baby to stop it crying, the word 'curse' shows that some children are not brought up with enough love. This is similar to how the chimney-sweeper's parents have sent him off to work so young.

Clear link to another of Blake's poems.

There is some analysis and linking but not enough awareness of Blake's methods.

The poor treatment of children can also be seen in poems like 'The Schoolboy'. Blake describes the harsh discipline of the educational system as a 'cruel eye outworn'. As in 'The Chimney-Sweeper', Blake is using a metaphor to show mistreatment. It implies that children aren't free and happy: they are constantly watched and then punished if they do anything wrong. Like 'The Chimney-Sweeper', Blake shows the effect of mistreatment of children in 'The Schoolboy'. He uses the word 'anxious' when the boy is stuck inside the classroom and contrasts this with 'joy' when he's outdoors. This also links to Blake's belief that nature is important in a child's upbringing.

More successful linking of concerns and methods to another poem.

Blake's concerns about society also appear in 'Holy Thursday'. He uses the metaphors, 'And their sun does never shine, / And their fields are bleak and bare' to accuse the Church of not looking after children and creating a word that is without love, hope, and charity. This idea appears in 'London' as well.

Undeveloped linking of a third poem to the named poem.

'The Chimney-Sweeper' shows Blake's concerns about children, innocence and how the establishment is destroying nature and ruining society. Similar concerns appear in other poems by William Blake such as 'London', 'Holy Thursday' and 'The Schoolboy'. Some of his key methods in 'The Chimney-Sweeper' are metaphor, symbolism and contrasting images, and these are also used by Blake in other poems to convey his concerns.

Straightforward summary of how poem shows familiar concerns of Blake, with some awareness of poetic methods.

COMMENTARY

This is a competent essay with continual focus on the question. The balance between the named poem and other poems by Blake is quite successful. There is light-touch comparison, with the poems dealt with one at a time, rather than integrated linking. There is some good discussion of 'The Chimney-Sweeper' with clear understanding of Blake's main poetic concerns. The essay is less successful when making links about Blake's poetic methods, but there are some attempts to spot patterns. The essay includes some alternative interpretations and tries to relate analysis to context, but this lacks sophistication.

Task

3. Now read a second response to the same question. As you read, think about what this student has done that develops and improves upon the previous response.

Response 2

'The Chimney-Sweeper' depicts the plight of a child and a sense of innocence lost, key concerns of Blake's Songs of Innocence and Experience. The poem also shows Blake's concerns about nature, liberty, and the individual, linking to his place in the Romantic movement.

'The Chimney-Sweeper' shows Blake's key concern that changes in society were removing children's innocence. The opening line describes the chimney-Sweeper's circumstances through the image of, 'A little black thing among the snow', using the non-specific noun 'thing' to show how this child isn't valued (perhaps that he isn't valued as an individual, only as a resource). The line features a contrast of traditional symbolism, using the white snow to represent purity and innocence, while the black soot – which can also be seen as a reference to the factories of the Industrial Revolution – suggests the evil and immorality of the adult world that the child is plunged into. This concern is shown more vividly in 'London', where symbolism of immorality reappears in 'midnight streets' before Blake describes the 'curse' of the 'harlot' on her baby. The literal meaning is her swearing, but it is also another example of Blake's using metaphor, suggesting that the child is doomed to the same career and (when combined with references to 'blights' and 'plagues') already infected with disease. It is deliberately ironic that 'The Chimney-Sweeper', like all the poems in this collection, has a childish sing-song rhythm, regularly adopting anapaests to create a gentler metre that contrasts with the actual content.

'The Chimney-Sweeper' develops Blake's concerns about the poor treatment of children by introducing dialogue and letting the child's voice take over. This more personal perspective creates greater sympathy for the child's circumstances. When describing how he has been treated by his parents, the metaphor, 'They clothed me in the clothes of death,' shows the child has been forced into an unhealthy, and sometimes deadly, trade. Blake regularly employs metaphor to describe oppression of children, such as the 'cruel eye outworn' used in 'The Schoolboy' to portray the harsh discipline of the education system. Blake also has the chimney-sweeper 'crying' and this is a recurring motif in many of his poems to convey the misery that he saw in children's lives.

Good introduction, establishing main concerns of named poem and placing it in wider contexts of collection and Romantic movement.

Begins by identifying a key concern of named poem.

Successful discussion focusing on named poem then linking to other poems. Some evaluation and form well handled.

Good focus on specific methods, followed by links with another poem.

This can also be seen as a criticism of economic power in the late 18th century as Blake focuses on a working-class family and the effects of an unfair distribution of wealth and resources upon their lives.

Another concern that Blake presents in 'The Chimney-Sweeper', which he links directly to innocence, is the importance of nature. In the second stanza, the young chimney-sweeper looks back on his past and says he, 'was happy upon the heath, / And smiled among the winter's snow', with the joyous language implying that nature creates contentment. Blake uses similar language to the same effect in many of his poems, such as 'The Schoolboy' where an 'anxious' classroom is contrasted with the 'joy' of the outdoors, and children are even compared to 'buds… and blossoms'. The Romantic poets viewed nature as a place of ultimate truth and beauty, so Blake's use of part tense in the phrase 'was happy' from 'The Chimney-Sweeper' could be an allusion to how the destruction of the environment both causes and reflects the decline of civilisation.

'The Chimney-Sweeper' presents clear social criticism, and this was a key feature of the Romantic movement. The final **tricolon**, 'God and His priest and king, / Who make up a heaven of our misery', attacks the Church and the monarchy that were a major part of the establishment in 18th-century England. The verb phrase 'make up' implies that the Church is fraudulent, pretending to be more moral and charitable than it truly is. The lines could be suggesting that the poor are always promised a better future if they do as they are told, but that this never materialises. Blake's use of structural devices like the tricolon to highlight his criticisms of society can also be seen in 'Holy Thursday', where the third stanza's use of anaphora builds up an image of a morally desolate and hopeless country. That poem's title is steeped in an irony, another of Blake's powerful tools that can be seen in the reference to 'heaven' in 'The Chimney-Sweeper'.

'The Chimney-Sweeper' typifies Blake's concerns about society not safeguarding children nor valuing their innocence, subjects also explored in poems like 'Holy Thursday', 'London', and 'The Schoolboy'. The poem also explores wider Romantic concerns about nature and the Industrial Revolution, making particularly strong use of symbolism and irony to convey Blake's ideas. Perhaps his most effective method is his use of metre, seen in 'The Chimney-Sweeper' and throughout The Songs of Innocence and Experience, creating a gentle, almost childish rhythm that highlights the contrast between Blake's beliefs about how life should be and the reality that he presents in his poetry.

Clear alternative interpretation.

Topic sentences link discussion effectively. Style is sophisticated.

Successful alternative interpretation, drawing on Blake's place in Romantic movement.

Key term

tricolon: a rhetorical device that employs a series of three parallel words, phrases or clauses

Some consideration of structure, in linked poems.

Clear conclusion, drawing together concerns and evaluating methods.

COMMENTARY

A proficient, well-balanced discussion of how 'The Chimney-Sweeper' shows Blake's concerns and methods. The essay shows a secure understanding, regularly analysing the named poem's use of language, structure and form, before making insightful links with other poems. Alternative interpretations and context are used effectively. The discussion is well structured, linking and developing points throughout. Writing is accurate and often sophisticated with a wide range of subject terminology used to heighten the analysis.

Final Task

Now that you have considered the sample responses for an A level-style critical appreciation question, reflect upon your own response.

Task

4. **a)** Use the guidance in the tables on the final page of this chapter (page 214) to assess whether you think your response could be classed as 'competent' or 'very good'.

    b) What do you think were the strengths of your response? What could you do to improve upon and develop it?

    c) Using the examples above, write a brief commentary at the end of your essay with action points for development.

POETRY

What should you aim for in a competent response to the question?

Knowledge and understanding	You should show knowledge of your poems and understanding of their concerns by making specific references to the poetry. Some use of quotations will make your points firmer. Try to include some reference to context, making sure it's relevant to your argument.
Analysis	Try to say something about the effects of the poet's choices of language, images or structure with most quotations that you use. Say something about the structure of the whole poem as well.
Personal response	You should offer something of your own interpretation. How does the poet's writing of the poem help you understand its meaning and concerns?
Communicating effectively	Aim for a clear opening to your essay, showing you understand the question, and work towards a conclusion that returns to it. Write clearly and make sure your paragraphs are connected.
Literary criticism (A Level only)	You should show that you are aware that works of literature are not fixed and can be read in different ways. You might be able to quote a critic, but there will be opportunities to use phrases such as 'This could be read as…' or 'A reader might respond to this by…' In this way, you can explore some of the ways different readers might respond to the poem.

What should you aim for in a very good response to the question?

Knowledge and understanding	You need to show a detailed knowledge of the poems and a subtle understanding of their concerns. Do this by making specific references to key parts of a poem's development that are relevant to the question, and by focusing your points with accurate quotations. Show some precise knowledge of context, made directly relevant to the particular point you are making.
Analysis	You should build your essay on exploration of how the poet expresses their ideas. Write about the poet and the presentation and development of their concerns in the poem. Think about how the poem is structured to guide the reader's responses.
Personal response	You should communicate your own interpretation of the poem, supported by clear evidence from it. Show how you read and respond to its concerns from the way that the poem is written.
Communicating effectively	Address the question consistently throughout the essay, so that every paragraph is clearly directed and relevant. Don't be afraid of having your own voice in your essays.
Literary criticism (A Level only)	You should show how your reading of the poems has been influenced by alternative readings, whether these are from particular critics, critical movements, or just hypothetical different ways in which the poem, its language and imagery might be read. Think about the implications of these differences.

Chapter 4 Studying drama

This chapter explores in depth the key concepts and skills required when studying drama as part of Literature in English at an advanced level. You will learn how to approach a range of drama texts, issues and dramatic focuses, applying both personal and critical interpretations, including how performative aspects can be brought to bear on your responses.

You will develop and extend your writing skills, building towards full exam-style responses at the end of the chapter, and you will have the chance to evaluate your progress against a range of sample responses.

4.1 Exploring key ideas about drama

Big question
- What are the key ideas to keep in mind during your drama study and why are they important?

WHAT ARE THE KEY IDEAS IN YOUR DRAMA STUDY?

There are three core ideas to keep in mind during your study of plays, namely:
- dramatic action: not only the wider plot events (the death of a king), but also specific gestures, movements or developments (the entrance of a character at a particular moment, an argument, a slap in the face)
- dramatic language: *what* characters say (the information they reveal or conceal), but also *how* it is said (tone, pace, rhythm); this might also encompass particular *forms* of language (**soliloquy**, songs, dialect, **utterances**)
- dramatic effects: how the action and the language affect the audience – producing emotions, interest, suspense, joy, laughter, empathy or **alienation**.

You should also be aware of **staging** and other aspects of production, such as the use of a specific prop or item of clothing, but *only* where these influence how an audience views character or particular issues.

Look at this extract from an early scene in William Shakespeare's *Macbeth*. A powerful lord (Macbeth) has decided with his wife that he will murder the king, who is staying at his castle. Here he reflects on what he is about to do.

> **Key terms**
>
> **soliloquy:** a speech given by a character speaking their thoughts aloud, either alone or oblivious of any possible hearers
>
> **utterance:** any single unit of speech, which might include sighs, cries, gasps, and so on
>
> **alienation:** when sympathy is removed or distance created
>
> **staging:** information given about how the stage should look at various times in the play

---

Macbeth: [*To Servant*] Go bid thy mistress, when my drink is ready,
        She strike upon the bell. Get thee to bed. [1]

                              Exit Servant [1]

        Is this a dagger that I see before me,
        The handle toward my hand? [2] Come, let me clutch thee: [1]
        I have thee not, and yet I see thee still.
        Art thou not [2], fatal vision [2], sensible
        To feeling as to sight? Or art thou [2] but
        A dagger of the mind [2], a false creation…?

              William Shakespeare, *Macbeth* (1606)

Task

1. The annotations numbered [1] all relate to actions – the movements or gestures of characters.
   • What does Macbeth tell the servant to do?
   • What happens next? What does he see, and how does he react?
2. The second set of annotations [2] relate to language – what is said and how it is said.
   • What sorts of lines are these: statements, exclamations, questions?
   • What does Macbeth wonder about the object he sees?
   • What is unusual in how he speaks to the object?

WHY DO THESE THINGS MATTER?

Here is what one student has written about the action and language:

> Macbeth sends the servant away and makes sure he goes to bed. He doesn't want anyone around when he kills the king. He seems clear-headed, but then sees a 'vision' of a dagger, which is very real as he tries to 'clutch' it – he even speaks to it, calling it 'thou' as if it were a living thing. Such a powerful vision might suggest that Macbeth is losing his mind or cannot face the reality of what he has decided to do. The audience can't see the dagger, but Macbeth's fear makes it real.

Task

3. Which parts of this paragraph deal with the 'effect' – what the language and action tell us about Macbeth, and the reaction these produce from the audience?

IDENTIFYING LANGUAGE AND ACTION

If you identify 'what happens' and 'what is said' in a particular scene in a play, it can often reveal important things. As you have seen, though, you will still need to go further and explore what the impact or effect is.

Much later in the play, Macbeth is cornered by his enemies after committing several murders with his wife's help in order to become king and stay in power.

Enter Seyton (a servant)

Macbeth: **Wherefore** was that cry?

Seyton: The queen, my lord, is dead.

Macbeth: She **should** have died **hereafter**.
There would have been a time for such a word.
Tomorrow, and tomorrow, and tomorrow,
Creeps in this **petty** pace from day to day
To the last syllable of recorded time,
And all our yesterdays have lighted fools
The way to dusty death. Out, out, brief candle!
Life's but a walking shadow, a poor player
That struts and frets his hour upon the stage
And then is heard no more. It is a tale
Told by an idiot, full of sound and fury,
Signifying nothing.

William Shakespeare, *Macbeth* (1606)

Glossary

Wherefore: why
should: would
hereafter: later
petty: small or little

Task

4. Read through the scene with a partner to get a sense of the dramatic action – what has happened:
   - Who enters the scene?
   - What does Macbeth ask him? What makes him ask the question?
   - What news does the man bring?

5. Now, look closely at the dramatic language.

   a) How does Macbeth respond initially to the news?
   - Does he express sadness or shock? Does he rage and curse, or race off the stage in tears?
   - When he says, 'She should have died hereafter', he means 'She would have died later anyway'. Is this what you would expect from a husband speaking about the death of his wife?

   b) In the second part, Macbeth seems to switch to talking about time and life in general.
   - What does he say about time passing?
   - What does he say life is like? What does he compare someone's life to?

EXPLORING DRAMATIC EFFECT

Looking at this short scene in this way allows you to 'map' how it works, but 'effect' requires you to go further in a number of ways. For example, to decide:

- *what it tells us* – how our understanding of plot, issue or character is advanced by what we have read or seen on stage
- *how it affects us* – perhaps altering our viewpoint, changing our sympathies, or making us feel tense, happy, angry or sad.

Look at these notes made by one student:

> Tomorrow, and tomorrow, and tomorrow,
> Creeps in this petty pace from day to day

repeated words and commas drag out line

moves very slowly

slow speed

more repetition

Task

6. What does this tell us about:
   a) how Macbeth views time passing?
   b) how Macbeth might view his life?
7. How might Macbeth deliver these lines? Try reading them aloud, or even acting them out to give a sense of his tone of voice, the speed at which he speaks, and so on.
8. What is likely to be the effect on the audience? Think not only about how we see Macbeth (for example, with sympathy or anger), but also about the tone created (whether these lines create tension or excitement, or create a different sort of feeling).

Final Task

Write about the second extract from *Macbeth*.

Task

9. In what ways, and with what effects, does Shakespeare present Macbeth's state of mind at this point?

Checklist for success
✓ Comment on details of language and action.
✓ Interpret or explain the effects of the details you have identified.

Plenary

Work with a partner to answer these questions:
- What do the terms 'dramatic action', 'dramatic language' and 'dramatic effects' mean to you?
- Give one example of each from the text you have looked at in this unit or in your own study.

4.2 Exploring dramatic characterisation

Big question
- In what ways do writers present characters and relationships in their plays?

WHAT IS CHARACTERISATION IN DRAMA?

Playwrights have two main tools with which to convey character: a) speech, and b) gesture or movement. In some scripts, aspects of staging and design can also contribute to **characterisation**. However, none of these exist in isolation; you need to consider how they operate together to create character.

Task

1. Think about any single character in a play you are studying. You will already have formed an idea of what they are like, but what *specific* things have created this idea in your mind?
Using a diagram, add information about your character – the evidence, if you like, that creates the picture of them on the stage.

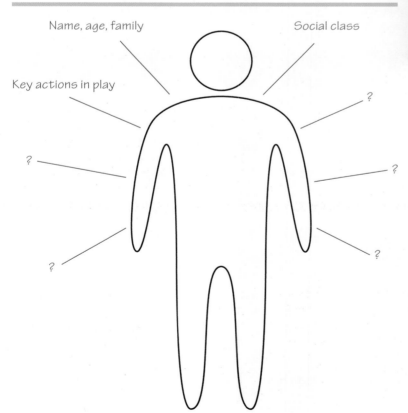

Name, age, family

Social class

Key actions in play

?

?

?

?

?

Task

2. Look at your diagram. Check whether it answers all the questions below about your chosen character.

a) What is their *role in the story*? (How do they affect the action – or how are they affected by it? How central are they to the main events?) Are they the protagonist or a more minor or supporting character?

b) What is their *history or background*? (Is there anything the writer reveals about their life before the play began?)

c) What is their ***status***? (Do they have power? If so, what sort: emotional, financial, physical? Or do they lack power? And if so, why?)

d) What is their ***motive***? (What do they want – either across the whole play, or at specific points within it?)

e) What is their *journey/development*, if any? (What is their situation when we first see them and when we last see them? How do they change in response to events?)

f) What is *distinctive* about them in terms of their appearance, manner of speaking such as **dialect**, and gestures or movements?

g) What do we learn about them from their *interactions* with others?

3. How these things are revealed is characterisation. Go back to your diagram and add in any of the missing details raised by these questions.

Key terms

status: the level of power a particular character has, which can be external (for example, 'king' as opposed to 'servant'), or emotional or physical (stronger speech in an argument, for example); status can fluctuate in a play – a king may fall from power and then regain it; someone can be losing an argument and then win it

motive: in drama, the emotional goals or objectives of a character, such as the need to be loved or admired, or aims related more closely to the action, such as to become king or gain revenge on a rival

dialect: language and grammar specific to a particular race, group or culture

Now read the following paragraph, in which a student further explores the characterisation of Macbeth based on the scene in Unit 4.1 when Macbeth learns his wife is dead.

> The highly elevated language Macbeth employs in exploring the nature of life itself as a metaphorical 'poor player' constructs him as a tragic hero struggling to make sense of mortality. He seems weary, as if he desires life to end quickly, not be dragged out forever. Although his servant is still present when Macbeth speaks, he might as well be invisible – he is either terrified of his tyrant king, or realises Macbeth is in his own world.

Task

4. At least four 'character pointers' from the list have been used in this short paragraph: motive (or motives), distinctive language, interaction with others, and status/position. Identify where they have been used – and what each tells us about Macbeth.

SELECTING AND INTERPRETING EVIDENCE ABOUT CHARACTERS

As you have already seen, conflict is a vital element in characterisation. It can take many forms from the inner, emotional conflict a character experiences, to direct disagreement or violent rivalry with others. Macbeth struggles with ambition and the terrible acts it leads him to commit, but he also faces real conflict in terms of people who wish to remove him from power. In this next passage, the conflict is more subtle, reflecting milder disagreements or clashes of personality.

Read the opening to a play called *A Hero's Welcome* by Winsome
Pinnock. As you read, consider how Len and Nana (his grandmother) are
presented, and what, if any conflict seems to exist between them.

Setting: Small district on an island somewhere in the West Indies,
1947.

Act I Scene I

*Outside LEN's house. Daytime. LEN with the sleeves of his white
shirt rolled up, is washing clothes in a tin bath. NANA sits on a chair.
CHARLIE, a young boy, sits on the ground a short distance from them
staring at LEN.*   — house is Len's

— Nana sitting watching Len

LEN: You made up your mind to stay or what?
NANA: I'm thinking about it.   — Nana making her mind up
LEN: I'm making your favourite dinner, Nana. Ackee and saltfish.
NANA: How am I going to eat ackee and saltfish with no teeth?   — Len wants to please her?
LEN: You don't need teeth for ackee and saltfish.
NANA: You need teeth for everything.
LEN: What's that you reading?
NANA: Mind you business. (*Slight pause*) Boy, why didn't you just
leave me alone?
LEN: One day, Nana, I ain't going to come and look for you.
Next time I'm going to sit down, put me feet up, smoke a
cigarette and just wait for you to come running back.
NANA: I din ask you to come look for me. I mean it ain't like I get
lost or something.
LEN: Anything could happen to you out there.
NANA: Like what? I know this place like the back a me hand.
I don't know why you just can't leave me alone. Just
because I'm an old woman it don't mean that I don't
want a life a me own, telling me what to do all the time.
LEN: Nobody telling you what to do, Nana. Hey, look at this
shirt, Nana, nice and clean. Look at that white. Watch the
way the sun shine on it. (*Slight pause*) Is about time you ge
a new set ennit.
NANA: Set a what?
LEN: Teeth. Those old teeth won't last much longer.
NANA: Neither will I if you don't leave me alone.
LEN: I'm only trying to help.
NANA: Most of the old people round here does die from too
much kindness. Look at poor Mrs B., the strongest woman
I know. Everybody say she can't look after herself, sen'
her to live with she daughter. Within two months the
woman stone cold dead. Couldn't cope with the strain of
pretending to be a poor helpless old woman.
LEN: That won't happen to you, Nana.

Winsome Pinnock, A Hero's Welcome (1989)

Task

5. What do the annotated points tell us about the relationship between Len and Nana?

    a) Is everything fine, or are there any hints about conflict between them?

    b) Where does the power – or status – seem to lie? Think about the first annotated point about the house, for example.

6. Now, work through the rest of the text and select 3–4 further things said by Len and/or Nana that could:
- tell us something about Nana's character
- tell us something about her relationship with Len.

Checklist for success

✓ Select words, phrases or shorter lines for direct quotation (examples you could include as they stand in your own work).

✓ Make a note of longer sections that you will need to **paraphrase** later, such as Nana's long final story about her friend.

Key term

paraphrase: sum up in your own words

Now, consider what the evidence you have selected tells us about the distinctive way in which the author has presented Nana. Some of this may be straightforward – and can probably be taken at face value: For example:

> 'I know this place like the back a me hand' – she knows the land and local environment well

However, other statements may be open to interpretation. For example, you will need to consider what might be her real feelings – her actual motives. *How* Nana speaks – her manner or tone – might help. For example:

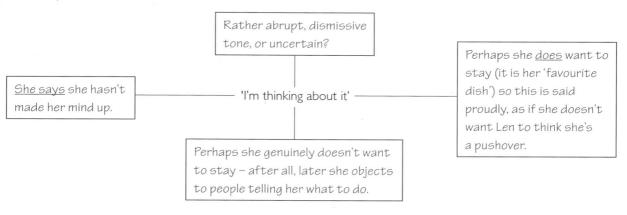

Task

7. Take each of the quotations or references you have selected and:
- make notes in a similar way
- include a comment on Nana's tone or mood.

As you can see, there is no 'right' answer here, but based on the whole of the extract, you might be able to draw your own conclusions. For example, one student has written:

> Nana states, somewhat abruptly, that she's 'thinking about it' when asked by Len about staying for dinner. This might suggest that, while secretly she is keen to have her 'favourite' dish, she has a more fundamental motive to present herself as independent, despite her age, something which she alludes to in her later account of her friend who died through an excess of kindness from her daughter.

— direct quotation embedded in statement

— paraphrase (not direct quotation) of what Nana says at end of extract

The final piece of the jigsaw in developing an understanding of Nana is the *interaction* between the characters. In this scene, Len:

- is shown cooking and cleaning
- makes Nana her favourite food
- questions her about what she's reading
- warns her he won't search for her when she disappears into the countryside
- tells her she ought to get some new teeth
- says he is 'only trying to help'.

Task

8. How does Nana respond in each case to these actions/statements? Who seems to have the power or status in these exchanges?

9. What does this tell us about their relationship? Think about each of these possibilities – which seems most convincing? Why?

   a) Nana angrily resents her grandson's interference in her life and rejects his attempts to control her.

   b) Nana is compliant and grateful to Len for caring for her and making sure she has all the home comforts she needs.

   c) Nana finds it difficult to accept her lack of independence and proudly questions Len's attempts to care for her.

   d) Nana presents herself as a helpless old woman who wishes Len would do more for her.

10. Take one of Nana's reactions to Len (such as when she tells him to 'Mind you business'), and write a paragraph similar to the model above.

   Start by explaining what Nana does or says; then explore what this suggests about her feelings or motives. As you write, bear in mind your overall thoughts about Nana (as in **a)**–**d)** above).

> **Key concept: Naturalistic language** Note how Nana's characterisation is also developed through her naturalistic language – speech that is not flamboyant or elevated in style, but reflects the realities of life. When she says, 'I know this place like the back of me hand', the understated dialect in using 'me' rather than 'my' is truthful to the Caribbean context while the idiom as a whole reminds us of Nana's grounded and 'no-nonsense' persona.

TRACING CHARACTER ACROSS A PLAY

In your literary study, you will often be asked to trace a character's development across a play or explore characterisation in a number of scenes.

Read this later passage from the same play. Here, Len has married a woman called Minda, whom the audience know has already had an affair with a married man.

NANA:	I ain't happy Len.
LEN:	Whas' wrong Nana?
NANA:	That little girl. Ever since she came her she tek over the whole house.
LEN:	Don't be silly.
NANA:	This morning she throw me out, tell me to stay out here.
LEN:	Only because she want to clean the place up.
NANA:	The place clean already. Marriage gone to the girl head, I tell you. I thought she woulda calm down by now but she ain't tired a playing wife yet.
LEN:	What's wrong with that? She's happy.
NANA:	Happy? She? Thas' all you know boy.
LEN:	What you saying Nana?
NANA:	Nuttin'. I ain't sayin' nuttin'. She can't even do things properly. You ever taste food like she cook last night?
LEN:	She's young. She'll learn. *(MINDA comes out holding a large basket full of clothes, she puts them down quickly, panting)* You all right Min?
MINDA:	All I've done since I came here is cook and wash clothes.
LEN:	I help you don't I Min?
MINDA:	You? You more get in the way than help me Len.
LEN:	I try darling.
MINDA:	Funny how you use to be able to do those things before an' now all of a sudden you all fingers and thumbs.
NANA:	So what? You thought you were going to live like a queen here or something? We're simple people Minda.
MINDA:	Simple not the word.

Task

11. How is the audience's understanding of Nana advanced by this later scene? In particular, it is worth thinking about how:
    - her personal **allegiances** shift or change
    - how conflict between her and others develops or is resolved, or how new conflicts arise
    - how her status (emotional, financial, social) changes.

12. Make notes on:
    - how she seems to feel about the house compared with the earlier scene
    - what she says and how she speaks to Len – in what way does she seem to have more knowledge than him about Minda?
    - what she says and how she speaks to Minda directly.

13. What conclusions can you draw about Nana based on the evidence you have gathered so far in both scenes? Write 125–150 words about her characterisation by the writer. You could use these prompts:

    In the opening scene, Nana is presented as someone who…

    She is uneasy about…

    In the later scene, there has been a shift in her attitude to the house and also in her relationship with Len…

Glossary

allegiance: loyalty to a person or group

Checklist for success
- ✓ Comment on what Nana says and how she says it.
- ✓ Comment too on how others respond to her.
- ✓ Support what you say with direct quotation or paraphrase longer sections of text.

SPEECHES AND SOLILOQUIES

Extended passages of speech by one character can give us a greater insight into their character. In Shakespeare's works, characters often give a speech while alone on stage. This convention – the soliloquy – is used as a way of revealing a character's inner thoughts which are spoken aloud.

In the following soliloquy, Macbeth is considering whether he should murder the king (Duncan), who is staying at his castle, and take his crown.

> If it were done when 'tis done, then 'twere well
> It were done quickly. If the assassination
> Could **trammel** up the consequence, and catch
> With his **surcease** success; that but this blow
> Might be the be-all and the end-all here,
> But here, upon this bank and **shoal** of time,
> We'd jump the life to come. But in these cases
> We still have judgment here, that we but teach
> Bloody instructions, which, being taught, return
> To plague th' inventor: this even-handed justice
> Commends the ingredients of our poisoned **chalice**
> To our own lips. He's here in double trust:
> First, as I am his **kinsman** and his subject,
> Strong both against the deed; then, as his host,
> Who should against his murderer shut the door,
> Not bear the knife myself. Besides, this Duncan
> Hath borne his **faculties** so meek, hath been
> So clear in his great office, that his virtues
> Will plead like angels, trumpet-tongued, against
> The deep damnation of his **taking-off**;
> And pity, like a naked newborn babe,
> Striding the blast, or heaven's **cherubim**, horsed
> Upon the sightless couriers of the air,
> Shall blow the horrid deed in every eye,
> That tears shall drown the wind. I have no **spur**
> To prick the sides of my intent, but only
> **Vaulting** ambition, which o'erleaps itself
> And falls on th' other.
>
> William Shakespeare, *Macbeth* (1606)

Glossary

trammel: sweep up or away
surcease: ending (here 'death')
shoal: could mean 'school' here – or group of fish, but it is not clear!
chalice: large cup
kinsman: usually means relative, but here might mean close friend or member of same 'tribe'
faculties: abilities
taking-off: death
cherubim: a winged angel
spur: sharp point worn on heel to dig into a horse to make it move
Vaulting: leaping, jumping

Thinking more deeply: **the power of the soliloquy**

Although a soliloquy is by definition a speech given by a character on their own, a rehearsal technique actors often use is to speak a soliloquy to a listener, perhaps sitting on a chair next to them.

Task

14. Try doing this with this speech, or another soliloquy from a play you are studying. The act of speaking it as if explaining thoughts to a person can help make those thoughts clearer. The listener should not comment but could say words such as 'Really?' or 'Right, I see…' as an encouragement.

15. How is Macbeth's indecision – his reluctance to go ahead with the murder – shown? Reread the speech and identify the sections of the speech that deal with these thoughts:

a) He wishes that in killing the king, everything would be sorted out and no further problems would follow.

b) He fears that this won't be the case and that the violence he shows will only teach others to behave in the same way towards him.

c) He feels that killing the king is a double betrayal.

d) He feels that the king is a virtuous and decent person.

e) His only motivation is ambition, which rushes people into disaster.

These are the thoughts Macbeth has, but you need to look more closely at the *how* – the manner in which they are expressed. For example, in speaking about Duncan being a good man, he uses the following imagery:

[…] his virtues
Will plead like angels, trumpet-tongued, against
The deep damnation of his taking-off;

— his good points

— simile comparing his virtues to angels crying out

— alliterative adjective suggesting strength of their cries

— powerful, alliterative phrase describing Macbeth's crime

Task

15. How would you sum up the way Macbeth is presented here? A student has begun to write an explanatory paragraph – copy and complete it.

Macbeth's turmoil is shown through his use of religious imagery to describe the murder of the king. His main concern is that…

16. What other simile does Shakespeare use to describe 'pity'? In what way is it also linked to religious ideas about innocence and virtue?

Final Task

Task

17. Write a short report (250–350 words) on the way that playwrights present characters based on the different extracts you have read. You should address a range of points and give detailed examples.

Plenary

Go back to your 'stick figure' from task **1** in this unit. Taking into account what you have learned about characterisation, select a short section of the play and write notes on the different ways the writer conveys the character here.

Checklist for success

Aspects of characterisation to cover include:

✓ how characters act or behave
✓ how they interact with other characters
✓ how they speak
✓ how they talk about themselves or their feelings
✓ how they develop across the play.

4.3 Exploring issues and concerns in drama

Big question
- What methods do writers use in drama to convey issues or concerns that interest them?

WHAT ARE 'ISSUES' AND 'CONCERNS'?

Read this opening to the play, *The Shape of Things* by Neil Labute, first performed in 2001.

> **A MUSEUM**
>
> *silence. darkness.*
>
> *a young woman stands near a stretch of velvet rope.*
> *she has a can in one hand and stares up at an enormous human sculpture. after a moment, a young man (in uniform) steps across the barrier and approaches her.*
>
> ADAM
> . . . you stepped over the line. miss? / umm, you stepped over . . .
>
> Neil Labute, *The Shape of Things* (2001)

Task

1. What questions does this opening raise in your mind? One might be: 'Who is the woman?' What other question can you think of?

When any play begins, it engages an audience to ask questions.

The questions at the forefront of your mind are likely to be related to character and action, but each line or stage direction begins to touch on much more.

The play is set in a museum, and the woman looks as if she has a spray can – is she going to deface the painting? This 'plot' question might lead us to ask:

- Is this a play about the value of art?
- Is this a play about how best to protest or make a stand?
- Is this a play about transgression – doing something society deems 'wrong'?

These questions could be described as the 'concerns' of the play.

In the same way, *Macbeth* may present the rise and fall of a violent man who reacts to supernatural forces and wants to be king, but it too raises other questions. For example:

- Are we in charge of our own fate, or are our futures **predetermined**?
- How does 'ambition' damage or corrupt people?
- What makes a good king?
- Are the forces of darkness real or imagined?

Phrasing concerns as questions can help to direct your exploration of such themes more effectively.

Wider reading

There is more from *The Shape of Things* in the next unit, but to really find out about what it is about, it is best to check out the play for yourself.

Glossary
predetermined: already decided

HOW ARE ISSUES AND CONCERNS DRAMATISED?

As you saw from the opening to *The Shape of Things*, a playwright's exploration of a particular concern can emerge through:

- the story – or stories – they tell through the plot
- the speech and actions of particular characters
- the ways in which those characters interact
- the settings or contexts that provide a backdrop to, or have a specific role in, the drama.

Read the following opening to a play by South African writer Beverley Naidoo. A number of elements of the staging have been highlighted as potentially relevant to the writer's concerns. In this extract, Rosa, a young black girl is walking past a school on her way to work.

SCENE 1

Winter 1994. Early afternoon. A small rural town. A fence surrounds the playground of the whites-only Oranje Primary School – Laerskool Oranje. Rosa, age 10, in black school tunic and white shirt, enters. She is outside the fence. She carries a school bag and a plastic bag carrying a kleinmeid's uniform. This is her first day coming into the town to work for the van Nierkerk family. She is both curious and anxious as she approaches the fence. Her journey is accompanied by singing off-stage.

Hennie van Nierkerk, age 10, barefoot, in khaki shirt and shorts enters the playground with Jannie, age 9. They are absorbed in a game of rugby, cheered on by Marie, age 9. Rosa watches Hennie but he does not see her. Jannie falls. He spots Rosa. He whips himself up, making his hand into a mock pistol.

JANNIE: Pioouu! Pioouu!… Hey, got her, man!

Rosa is startled. Her bag spills open. Explosions of laughter from Jannie and Marie.

JANNIE: D'you see that, Hennie! Jiss man!

Jannie and Marie go, laughing. Hennie glances uneasily at Rosa before he goes. Shaken, Rosa picks up the kleinmeid's uniform that has fallen out of her bag.

PAPER BOY: Dumela Sis.

The Paper Boy lifts his hand in a furtive, sympathetic wave. Rosa acknowledges the gesture. The Paper Boy goes.

ROSA (to audience):   Imagine… That is the school Mama wants
            me to attend!

Beverley Naidoo, *The Playground* (2003)

Is the date relevant? It is **post-apartheid**.

The school is fenced off – why?

Rosa is 'outside'.

A *kleinmeid* is a little servant/maid.

She's a 10 year old working for a white family.

Glossary

post-apartheid: after the formal repeal of most laws in South Africa separating black and white people

kleinmeid: little maid

Dumela: Good morning

Chapter 4 Studying drama

Each of the four elements of the drama is exemplified here: story, character speech, interactions and setting/context.

The opening stage directions (up to the first line of speech) certainly provide setting and context, and also provide some initial information about the characters.

> **Task**

2. A key concern of the play is racial segregation. In what ways do the staging, stage directions and information provided about characters in the opening directions foreshadow this concern? Think about:
- how details about the school both symbolise and tell the audience directly about social and racial separation
- how details about Rosa emphasise the separation even further
- how details about the children in the playground further emphasise the separation between their lives and hers (think about what they are doing in contrast with her)
- how Jannie's gestures suggest a further, more serious level of division.

The issue of racial segregation is further explored in the remainder of the scene through the actions and speeches of the characters.

> **Task**

3. Look at the following table, which lists some of the key detail from the rest of the scene. What does it add to our growing understanding of the writer's concerns? Here, it is important to distinguish between what such details suggest about a character or the plot (for example, ideas about how friendly or aggressive someone might be) and the wider issues that are raised.
Copy the table and complete the rows.

Information from scene	Element/aspect of writer's craft	What this tells us about character or plot	Wider issues or concerns suggested
JANNIE: Pioouu! Pioouu!... Hey, got her, man!	Character speech	Suggests Jannie's childish pleasure in frightening Rosa.	That children's prejudices are embedded early in life? That violence, humiliation and fear might still characterise the relations between black and white South Africans?
Rosa is startled. Her bag spills open. Explosions of laughter from Jannie and Marie	Stage direction/ character actions		
Jannie and Marie go, laughing. Hennie glances uneasily at Rosa before he goes			
PAPER BOY: Dumela Sis. *The Paper Boy lifts his hand in a furtive, sympathetic wave.*			

LINKING ISSUES OR CONCERNS TO DRAMATIC IMPACT

Everything you have learned about identifying elements of the text and exploring how they suggest wider issues is true, to some extent, of all texts. However, it is important you show that issues and concerns do not exist in the abstract – they have dramatic impact on the stage, and on the audience.

For example, the issue of racial segregation only has *dramatic* impact at the point at which it affects individual characters or relationships.

Here, a student has written about the dramatic impact of the opening stage directions.

> The initial dramatic impact is made through the staging. The significance of the 'fence' around the all-white school in the period just after apartheid was supposed to have ended and Rosa's position 'outside' it all reflect the undercurrent of racial and social segregation to the play.
>
> However, it is the dramatic gesture of Jannie firing an imaginary gun at Rosa, and symbolically wounding her – she drops her bag in fright – that the external themes of racial conflict become personal: Rosa is identified as alien, a thing to be hunted, perhaps not quite human. Jannie and Rosa are set in opposition, mirroring the power of the white state and black oppression.

— topic sentence introduces an overview of one dramatic element of the play

— specific details of that staging

— the wider issue

Task

4. **a)** What dramatic elements does the student comment on in the second paragraph?

   b) What does the student infer from this new element? In what way is the concern now personal?

   c) How are the external themes of racial segregation and the personal one of character conflict brought together?

5. In what ways does Naidoo also foreshadow the impact of race on characters or relationships in this scene? Think about the following points:
   - How Hennie reacts to Jannie's play-shooting. What adverb suggests he might have a slightly more **nuanced** view of Rosa than Jannie?
   - What Rosa says about her mother's plans for her. Who or what might this bring Rosa into conflict with?
   - How Naidoo signals the personal connection and solidarity between the paper boy and Rosa.

Wider reading

Take care when you are reading plays with a strong **polemic** or political theme that you do not reduce characters to **ciphers**, unless that is how the dramatist intended them to be seen. Here, Rosa and Jannie become interesting at the point at which their lives intersect and we begin to care about what happens to them as people. Sometimes, **flat characters** serve the dramatist's message, but they rarely interest us as people.

Key terms

polemic: a powerful attack on someone or some thing
cipher: code for an idea rather than something to be taken at face value
flat character: an uncomplicated character who doesn't develop or change over the course of a play, or exists only to advance the plot
nuanced: having shades of meaning rather than one single clear idea

Task

6. Write up your thoughts on one of these ideas in a paragraph, using the following prompts. Remember to refer to specific words or phrases – or sum up what happens – as evidence of your point.

The reaction of… To…

when the writer states that…

suggests that [name of character] will…

It might also suggest that…

Thinking more deeply: **tracing issues across a text**

It can be challenging to trace how issues develop across a text. This is particularly the case when the playwright plays around with time, as Naidoo does in *The Playground*.

   Now read this passage from the next scene of the play. The play has gone back in time, and the audience has just learned that Nelson Mandela is about to be released from prison. We also find out that Rosa is the daughter of Mama, the black servant in Hennie's parents' house. Meneer (a property developer) and Mevrou are Hennie's parents. Hennie is playing with Rosa.

HENNIE: Let's play Tag now! Kom! Kom! You can't catch me!

Their game involves tumbling, laughing, giggling. They move on to playing a game of pebbles in the background where we can see them but no longer hear them. Meneer enters side stage into the street.

PAPER BOY: Die Star! Die Star! Hot news, sir!
MENEER: Give me a paper, boy! (he goes off reading)
PAPER BOY: Your change Meneer!

Meneer ignores him. Paper Boy shrugs and goes.
Inside the house, Afrikaans music is playing softly on the radio in the sitting room (something with an accordion and a strong dance beat e.g. Die Laste Dans). Mevrou enters with a vase and a bunch of winter flowers. Mama assists as Mevrou arranges the flowers. Mama plays the obedient servant but we sense her independent character.

MEVROU: Haven't these flowers lasted well? Mooi, ja!
MAMA: Yes, Madam. They look fresh like when the Master brought them.
MEVROU: I didn't think he would remember our anniversary this year. All this trouble in the country. It's not good for business… (*Mama shakes her head and makes sympathetic noises*)… No one wants to build new properties these days.

Beverley Naidoo, *The Playground* (2003)

Task

7. Make your own notes on the issues and concerns explored here. Copy and complete the table below to record your ideas.
   - Focus on character actions, speech and interactions, as well as anything else related to the setting or context.
   - Consider in what ways, if at all, some of the issues/concerns of the opening scene are developed, or whether new ones are introduced.

Key term

juxtaposition: the particular presentation of two or more related elements so as to raise questions or create effects

Point	What happens	How does it advance the issue or concern?	Dramatic impact
Hennie and Rosa's behaviour	They play without thought – 'tumbling' and 'laughing'.	Children's apparent innocence of racial difference?	The **juxtaposition** of this with the opening scene provides a stark contrast – absence of racial conflict.
How Meneer speaks to the paper boy	He orders him, calls him 'Boy'.	Emphasises…	
How Mevrou speaks to Mama			
How Mama and Mevrou interact			

Final Task

Task

8. Write about the two scenes from the play in response to this task:

How and in what ways does Naidoo dramatise issues of relations between black and white South Africans in the two scenes from *The Playground*?

Checklist for success
✓ Comment on the specific things Naidoo does or presents.
✓ Focus on the issues and concerns.
✓ Explain the dramatic impact of specific moments or lines in relation to the issues identified.

Plenary

Consider any play you are currently studying or have studied recently. Choose two of the key issues or concerns in the play and explain the different ways these issues are conveyed to the audience/reader.

4.4 Understanding dramatic context and genre

Big question
- How does knowledge about a play's genre or its context help you understand its impact?

WHAT IS CONTEXT?

In Unit 4.3, some knowledge of apartheid in South Africa would undoubtedly help in exploring the concerns of Beverley Naidoo, the author of *The Playground*. For example, knowing that South Africa had been a segregated society divided along racial lines for many years would help you understand the motives of the characters: white Afrikaaners in the play worry about losing power; black characters are aggrieved about the oppression they are still facing.

Context is complex, however. While the general issue of apartheid is the backdrop, it is the specific context of the issue of mixed schools that drives the action and has an impact on the personal.

Task

1. Think about the play you are studying. Draw a similar set of circles.
   - What is the *personal context* in your play? Note down the particular personal situation or set of events that your main character or characters face.
   - What is the *specific context*? Is there one event, problem or conflict that affects the main characters or is a key part of the action of the play?
   - What is the *overarching context* or *backdrop*? Does the play take place during a particular historical period, or during a time when particular movements were gaining momentum, such as first-wave feminism in the 60s and 70s in the USA?

   As you did for issues and concerns, keep in your head this idea of the *internal and personal* (what the main character faces and tackles) and the external (the forces and ideas that impact on the personal).

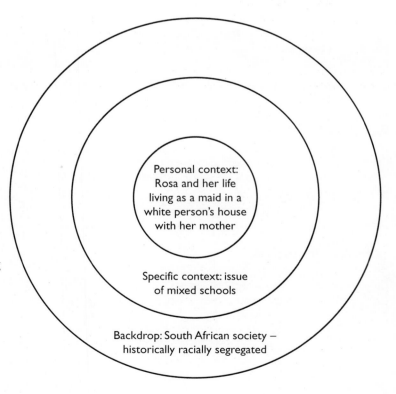

Personal context: Rosa and her life living as a maid in a white person's house with her mother

Specific context: issue of mixed schools

Backdrop: South African society – historically racially segregated

EXPLORING A DIFFERENT CONTEXT IN A PLAY

Writers are products of their environments, so it is not surprising that the contexts in which the plays are created or produced have an impact on how they are perceived.

For example, in **Jacobean** England, Shakespeare was writing at a time of huge political and religious upheaval. Conflict between Catholics and Protestants had resulted in numerous uprisings both before James's reign and during it. The Gunpowder Plot of 1605 was an attempt led by Robert Catesby and Guy Fawkes and other Catholics to blow up **Parliament** while the Protestant King James was in attendance.

There was also the issue of legitimacy: was James the rightful king? He was not the son of the previous queen, Elizabeth I; she had died childless. James himself believed in the 'Divine Right of Kings', the notion that kings were chosen by God.

Within this broad historical context, Shakespeare wrote *Macbeth*, a play in which a lord who is not the son of the King, murders him, seizes power and rules by terror before being brought down by forces led by the King's son. It was a play almost certainly performed in front of James I.

Key terms

Jacobean: referring to the reign of King James I of England (1603–25)
Parliament: place of government, but also those who are in government at the time

Task

2. Write a paragraph explaining how Shakespeare responds to the historical context in *Macbeth*. You could comment on:
- what Macbeth does
- what happens to him at the end.

If you do not know the full story of the play, you can easily access it online – either the original play script or a summary of the plot.

Wider reading

In Unit 4.2, you read a speech in which Macbeth agonised over whether to kill the king or not. Reread it and try to identify any references to Duncan (the King) that link him to heaven/ the afterlife and thus God. How do you think James would have responded to this speech?

Now read this scene from *Macbeth*. It comes directly after the murder of King Duncan by Macbeth. There are no specific references to the murder – at this point no one knows that Macbeth is the killer – but the discussion nevertheless reflects some of the contextual ideas about kingship mentioned above.

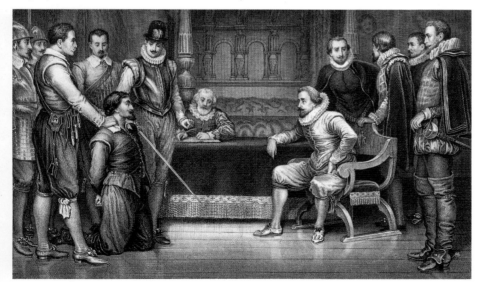

Act 2 Scene 4. Outside Macbeth's castle.
Enter ROSS and an old Man

OLD MAN: Threescore and ten I can remember well:
Within the volume of which time I have seen
Hours dreadful and things strange; but this sore night
Hath **trifled** former knowings.

ROSS: Ah, good father,
Thou seest, the heavens, as troubled with man's act,
Threaten his bloody stage: by the clock, 'tis day,
And yet dark night strangles the travelling lamp:
Is't night's **predominance**, or the day's shame,
That darkness does the face of earth entomb,
When living light should kiss it?

OLD MAN: 'Tis unnatural,
Even like **the deed that's done**. On Tuesday last,
A falcon, towering in her pride of place,
Was by a **mousing owl** hawk'd at and kill'd.

ROSS: And Duncan's horses – a thing most strange
and certain –
Beauteous and swift, the **minions** of their race,
Turn'd wild in nature, broke their stalls, flung out,
Contending 'gainst obedience, as they would make
War with mankind.

OLD MAN: 'Tis said they eat each other.

ROSS: They did so, to the amazement of mine eyes
That look'd upon't.

William Shakespeare, *Macbeth* (1606)

Glossary

Threescore and ten: seventy (a 'score' = twenty)
trifled: beaten or made unimportant
predominance: dominance, power over something/one
the deed that's done: murder of the king
mousing owl: owl that normally catches mice
minions: the best, favourites
Contending 'gainst: battling against, or refusing

Task

3. A key idea of kingship in James's time was that kings represented the natural order – they were part of God's creation. In what way are the recent events described here *unnatural*? Think about:
- how unusual the night was according to the 'old man' in his experience
- how the day is unnatural – what does Ross say about light/dark?
- how the actions of the owl on 'Tuesday last' were strange
- how the behaviour of the king's horses was surprising.

Taken on their own merits, these images are extremely powerful, but their impact is heightened by:
- the specific context: reflecting the murder of the king by one of his lower-ranked lords
- the wider historical context: reminding the audience of the moral framework of Jacobean society – the social order that must be maintained.

A student has written about one of the images in the speech on the previous page.

> The idea of the breakdown of social and political order is alluded to through the image of the king's own horses who seem to change character. Normally, 'beauteous' and the 'minions of their race', which would suggest they are obedient and well-behaved, they destroy their 'stalls' and escape, the verb 'flung' suggesting the sudden and aggressive action. In this way, they 'make war' with mankind, their masters, and this reflects Macbeth 'making war' against Duncan. In addition, it suggests Macbeth's actions may have caused this disobedience. It's as if the act of murder affects not just individual people, but the fabric of life itself – nature.

Task

4. This is a very effective paragraph. Can you identify:
- the first, general point about context made by the student?
- the quotations selected to support the point?
- the explanation that summarises the idea of 'war'?
- the further interpretation that introduces a new, related point?

5. Now, write your own paragraph about one of the other images.
- Begin with a topic sentence outlining the main contextual point. (It might be similar to the one above, but you will need to rephrase in your own words.)
- Comment on particular words or phrases by way of explanation.
- Continue with a summary explanation beginning: 'So, we can see…' or 'Thus it can be seen that…'.
- Finish with a further interpretation of the language you have selected.

Exploring: **dramatic genre**

On its own, the social or historical background may not be interesting enough to engage an audience. It is when the external contexts intersect with the personal that the dramatic impact is felt. Macbeth's anxieties about killing the king are given added weight because *he* and the audience understand the moral transgression he is going to commit, not only killing a man but killing a king, chosen by God.

The literary context of a play is also important. Playwrights often respond to dramas that were written before or at the same time as theirs – either in imitating or breaking with their conventions. Such conventions help to connect plays, which can be seen to belong to a broadly similar 'family'.

Shakespeare's main dramatic modes, and those of some of his contemporaries and followers, are often expressed as **genres**.

> **Key term**
>
> **genres:** in drama, the different types of play (such as tragedy, comedy, history) and their different characteristics and conventions

Genre	Example	Key conventions
Tragedy	*Othello, Hamlet*	The rise and fall of a noble figure brought down by a character weakness such as 'jealousy' or 'lust for power', or by some fatal mistake. Ends with the death(s) of the main character(s).
Comedy	*A Midsummer Night's Dream, Much Ado about Nothing*	Usually a main plot revolving around love and/or marriage with humorous events (such as mistaken identities) and characters. Ends with misunderstandings sorted out, order restored and often a marriage.
History	*Henry V, Richard III*	Deals with actual events, usually from English history, particularly the conflict between noble families or nations, and often involving succession rights (the struggle for the crown).

Task

6. Where would *Macbeth* fit within the grid above? You may need to check out the plot before you respond.

> **Wider reading**
>
> Other categories have been used to classify Shakespeare's plays such as 'problem plays' and the 'late romances'. Which plays might fit into these categories?

As with context, genre can be a lens through which you view the play, and by considering the extent to which a play matches a well-known genre, you can explore its nuances. If we see *Macbeth* as a *history* play (as it does deal with some real events – Macbeth did replace Duncan as king in Scotland in 1040), this shifts the play from being a character study of one man's tragic rise and fall, to a study of political allegiances and kingship.

Why does this matter? Read this extract from a study of *Macbeth* by the critic, A.C. Bradley. Here he writes about Macbeth and his wife, Lady Macbeth.

> 'These two characters are fired by one and the same passion of ambition; and to a considerable extent they are alike. The disposition of each is high, proud, and commanding. They are born to rule, if not to reign. They are **peremptory** or **contemptuous** to their inferiors. They are not children of light, like Brutus and Hamlet; they are of the world. We observe in them no love of country, and no interest in the welfare of anyone outside their family. Their habitual thoughts and aims are, and, we imagine, long have been, all of **station** and power.'

> **Glossary**
>
> **peremptory:** off-hand, dismissive
> **contemptuous:** looking down on
> **station:** social position or level

Task

7. Where does Bradley stand on the issue of whether *Macbeth* is more of a tragedy than a history play?

8. a) In what way do Macbeth and Lady Macbeth fit more closely with characters from plays in the *tragic* genre than history?

   b) Why does any of this matter? Write a sentence or two explaining how viewing *Macbeth* as a tragedy might change our response to the characters.

Interestingly, then, plays that seem to be 'about' one thing, or fit into a particular genre, often defy expectations and play around with some of the conventions. For example, in some of Shakespeare's works, clowns or fools are the mouthpieces of truth or wisdom, whereas noble characters behave in foolish or unwise ways.

Thinking more deeply: **the problem with comedy**

Whilst it is generally relatively easy to say what is tragedy, comedy can be more difficult to define and to write about. There can be a number of reasons for this:

- Comedy in performance may often be **non-verbal** and immediate: writing about it analytically some time later can make you forget what was funny about it in the first place. Restoration comedy, for example, often depends on visually ridiculous scenes and behaviour.
- Comedy is very dependent on context: what might be humorous in the past (making fun of a fiery woman and assaulting or abusing her as in Shakespeare's *Taming of the Shrew*) may provoke anger and criticism now. Equally, comedy that arises out of mild social or class embarrassment (as might be the case in some of the plays of Oscar Wilde) may seem tame and irrelevant to a modern audience.
- Conversely comedy can be by nature **subversive**: it is sometimes used to poke fun at or criticise the prevailing social norms, or even mock drama conventions itself, so it can actually be quite serious; plays by writers such as Beckett and Pinter which formed part of the movement that came to be known as the **Theatre of the Absurd** can be funny simply because they don't conform to the usual well-shaped play. They might feature tragic or grim situations but presented in unconventional ways, with language that is unheroic or full of cliché, or with plots which have no resolution, go round in circles or which are full of nonsense.
- Comedy (like the Theatre of the Absurd) often draws on what is ridiculous – characters making fools of themselves in which they are made to look ill-at-ease or embarrassed. This can be funny, but it can also be unnerving if an audience recognises their own weaknesses or finds themselves laughing at someone who they might otherwise feel sympathy for.
- Comedy often uses **word-play** or jokes which we enjoy because of their cleverness or because they create silly or unusual images in our minds, but which can be difficult to decode or unpick.

Key terms:

non-verbal: not to do with words; in this case, coming from the actors' physical performance rather than what they say

subversive: intended to weaken or destroy a particular aspect of society or to go against social or literary conventions

The Theatre of the Absurd: A movement in European theatre which started after World War 2, but was only named by critic Martin Esslin in 1960. Many of the plays were a response to political and social upheaval and conflict which made it difficult to rationalise life. Playwrights such as Samuel Beckett, Albert Camus and later Harold Pinter produced dramas which seemed to explore the meaningless of existence, with people threatened by invisible forces over which they had no control.

word-play: word-play can be the use of **puns** – words with more than one meaning ('What did the cheese say when it looked in the mirror? Halloumi (Hallo me)') or simply clever dialogue between characters. In *The Taming of the Shrew* Petruchio calls Katherina a 'wasp', to which she replies that if she's a wasp he'd better 'beware my sting.'

Read the following extract, taken from a play called *Watching Brief*, which draws on some of these elements:

Scene 2

A coffin lies on a table. Two men, MANT and VOSS, are sitting in chairs nearby. They are drinking tea. Both are wearing long winter coats.

MANT: Is the tea ok?

VOSS: It's fine.

MANT: Not too much sugar?

VOSS: No.

MANT: I expect you'd like some more milk…

VOSS: There's plenty of milk.

MANT: Is it too weak?

VOSS: It's fine.

MANT: You would say, wouldn't you?

VOSS: Of course I would. Why should I lie?

MANT: People do.

VOSS: Not me.

MANT gets up: looks at coffin.

MANT: She looks like she could do with a nice cuppa.

VOSS: Bit late for that now.

MANT: I'm just saying. A cup of tea perks you up.

VOSS: Not when you're dead.

MANT: No. Of course.

VOSS: Anyway, she didn't drink tea.

MANT: Didn't drink tea? That's unbelievable! *Everyone* drinks tea.

VOSS: She didn't. They told me.

MANT: They?

VOSS: *(ignores the question)* Drank lemonade apparently. Bottles of the stuff.

MANT: If she'd had a nice cuppa everyday, maybe she'd still be alive.

VOSS: I doubt it. Life is more than what you drink. Death is more than what you drink.

Mike Gould, *Watching Brief*

Wider reading

We might think that older plays have fewer absurdist elements, but you may find that they are present, if in a reduced form. For example, in the *Importance of Being Earnest* by Oscar Wilde, in Act 2, Cecily and Algernon have a talk about their past engagement which is entirely invented by Cecily, but which Algernon readily accepts as real.

Task

9. In what ways could this be said to be a 'comedy'? Read back over the bullet points on page 239 and consider to what extent the comedy depends on any of the factors mentioned. You could think in particular about the visual and absurd elements of the piece. For example:
- What, if anything, do we learn about the characters? (Do we have access to their inner thoughts and motives?)
- In what way might the situation seem unusual or strange?
- In what way might the visual element of the scene be shocking or unnerving?
- In what way does the language of the characters clash or subvert what we might expect to hear?
- In what way are there any 'jokes' or funny comments made by the characters?
- In what way are there hints of 'outside forces'?

In writing about these elements, it is as important as when you are writing about tragedy to consider the *effects* on the audience – whether these are to make them feel uncomfortable, or to laugh out loud at something incongruous or silly.

Final Task

Task

10. Consider the context and genre of a play you are studying. Draw a Venn diagram (like the one below done for *Macbeth*) and fill it with details relevant to the play.

Context:
- Scotland under threat from rebel forces (in play)
- Divine Right of Kings
- Ideas about the supernatural
- The rule of James I
- Catholics vs Protestants
- Gunpowder Plot

the rise and fall of an ambitious man and his wife

Genre:
Tragedy:
- Macbeth is noble and has a tragic weakness: ambition.
- His bravery in battle meant he could have had respect but he lost it.
- He initially struggles with his conscience.

History:
- Macbeth and Duncan were real kings.
- Conflict between nations: Scotland v England.
- Ideas about kingship.

Plenary

Write up or explain your ideas about your play. You could begin:
My knowledge of contexts has modified my understanding of the play in some key areas…

4.5 Exploring dramatic form and structure

Big question
- How do the form and structure of plays contribute to their impact?

WHAT ARE DRAMATIC FORM AND STRUCTURE?

Dramatic form is what makes a play distinct from other types of writing such as novels and poetry. In particular, it refers to those elements that indicate its **performative** aspects:
- how actions and speech are conveyed, including any distinctive ways of presenting voice or dialogue
- how time and settings are presented dramatically.

Dramatic structure refers to the organisation of a dramatic text or passage, its shape or development. This includes:
- how time is structured over the course of a play or scene
- how and in what order events, information, concerns or characters are revealed
- the particular stages of the plot that build humour, tension, and so on.

In this unit, you are going to read two extracts from a play by Stephen Vincent Benét called *The Devil and Daniel Webster*. It takes place in 1841 in a small farming town in the USA. The main characters are Daniel Webster, a respected local lawyer, and Jabez Stone and his wife Mary. The play opens with a dance on the Stones' wedding day.

> **Key term**
>
> **performative:** relating to the nature or essence of dramatic performance

EXPLORING FORM

Read this extract, paying attention to the *form*. As you read, think about how the speech and events have been presented.

FIDDLER:	[...] Set to your partners! Scratch for corn! (*The dance resumes, but as it does so the CROWD chants back and forth*)
WOMEN:	Gossip's got a sharp tooth.
MEN:	Gossip's got a mean tooth.
WOMEN:	She's a lucky woman. They're a lucky pair.
MEN:	That's true as gospel. But I wonder where he got it.
WOMEN:	Money, land and riches.
MEN:	Just came out of nowhere.
WOMEN AND MEN (*together*):	Wonder where he got it all – But that's his business.
FIDDLER:	Left and right – grand chain! (*The dance rises to a pitch of ecstasy with the final figure – the fiddle squeaks and stops. The dancers mop their brows.*)

Stephen Vincent Benét, *The Devil and Daniel Webster* (1938)

- stage directions highlight the 'crowd' as one entity
- rhythmic speech
- generic term – no one person
- short lines mirroring each other

Task

1. a) Look at the overall way this short extract is constructed, focusing on the form. Read the lines aloud, so that you pick up any patterns or distinctive expression. Is there anything particular that you notice?

b) How has the writer conveyed the speech and action on the page? Look at the annotations as a starting point, and make notes about the following:

- Who speaks. What is unusual or different from most scenes in plays?
- How they speak. What is noteworthy about the length, sound or rhythm of the lines?
- Actions or gestures indicated by the writer. What are the actors doing?

WRITING ABOUT FORM

On the surface, how the writer has set out the speech and action – the length and style of the lines, and so on – may seem unimportant. However, such performative clues can reveal interesting ideas. Read what one student has said about these aspects here:

> By keeping the men and women generic and nameless, speaking together 'back and forth', the playwright conveys the idea of public opinion – and perhaps what the 'mob' or 'society' believes or doesn't believe. This is important in a play about reputation and morality.

— the formal features and evidence

— the effect of the writer's choices

Task

2. Look again at your notes. In what other ways is the idea of a community acting and thinking together almost as one body shown in this passage? Complete this paragraph:

The lines of speech between the men and women are distinctive because…

This creates a sense of…

This is particularly appropriate as they are taking part in a…

The overall effect is one of…

Form, then, has the ability to create dramatic effects, but also to convey a tone or mood that matches with a play's context or concerns.

Thinking more deeply: **language and form in modern drama**

Modern European and American dramatists, particularly from the 1940s onwards, began to experiment with representation of the ways people communicated, partly to reflect what they saw as 'real' speech, with all its hesitations, fragments and interruptions, and partly to reflect dislocation in the face of existential threats such as nuclear war. Benét comes before this time, but you can see how he is experimenting with dialogue too – in the sing-song rhythms of the crowd.

It is worth exploring the ways in which dramatists you study represented speech and dialogue on the page – and what its effects are.

Read the following opening to the play, *The Shape of Things* by Neil Labute. You have already read part of this in Unit 4.3.

A MUSEUM

silence. darkness.

a young woman stands near a stretch of velvet rope.

she has a can in one hand and stares up at an enormous human sculpture. after a moment, a young man (in uniform) steps across the barrier and approaches her.

ADAM

. . . you stepped over the line. miss? / umm, you stepped over . . .

EVELYN

i know. / it's '**ms**.'

ADAM

okay, sorry, ms., but, ahh . . .

EVELYN

i meant to. / step over . . .

ADAM

what? / yeah, i figured you did. i mean, the way you did it and all, kinda deliberate like. / you're not supposed to do that.

EVELYN

i know. / that's why i tried it . . .

Neil Labute, *The Shape of Things* (2001)

Glossary

Ms: pronounced 'miz', a form of address that does not distinguish between 'Miss' (an unmarried woman) and 'Mrs' (a married woman)

Task

3. The writer provides a note saying the / denotes 'an attempt at interruption or overlap by a given character'. Work with a partner to read the dialogue aloud together, trying to put in interruptions or overlaps where you can.
   - How easy was this to do?
   - In what way did it sound more or less like 'real' speech?
   - Were there any other effects you noticed?
4. Reread the dialogue on your own. Identify any examples where the writer has included:
   - verbal utterances that are not words (for example, 'err' to express uncertainty or as a filler to help the speaker pause)
   - informal expressions or abbreviations
   - punctuation to show how the speech continues or is broken up
   - repeated words or lines.

What is the point of all this? Is it simply to reflect how young people might speak in a real situation? That is certainly part of it, but it is more than that. Labute is still able to develop characterisation, for example.

Task

5. In what way does Adam's language differ from Evelyn's? Think about:
   - who speaks more
   - who has more hesitations and repetitions
   - who uses a polite, formal mode of address ('Miss')
   - who asks questions, and who states their position with certainty.
6. What does this suggest about the two characters?

But there is something else too: dramatists often talk of the fourth wall. This means that as well as the traditional three walls of stage – the sides and the back – there is an invisible fourth wall between where the audience sits and the stage. A lot of modern drama is about breaking through the fourth wall, so some productions feature characters who sit in the audience, or action that even directly involves the audience, speaking to them or bringing them up onto stage.

Task

7. In this scene, the fourth wall is partly being broken by the language because it is commonplace and everyday. However, in what way does the actual situation – the formal elements Labute has indicated relating to set and action – reflect this 'breaking-down of artistic barriers'? Think about:
   - what the barrier is between 'audience' (Evelyn) and the stage (the work of art)
   - how it is about to be broken down by Evelyn.
8. Think about the play or plays you are studying. Make notes on:
   - The modes of speech. To what extent do they reflect 'real' conversation or dialogue? To what extent could this be said to be 'naturalistic' language?
   - Whether there any other attempts to break through the 'fourth wall'. For example, this could be as simple as a character talking to the audience, or a more ambitious idea such as the way the set or stage design is described.

Key concepts: Naturalistic language Language which reflects more closely the real ways in which people speak emerged out of the Naturalistic Drama movement in the late 19th century (in the plays of European writers such as Strindberg and Ibsen). It sought to present ordinary people in plausible situations. Interestingly, in this example (*The Shape of Things*) you might ask how likely or artificial such a situation is, notwithstanding the naturalistic language.

EXPLORING STRUCTURE

It is possible, but unlikely, that the whole of *The Shape of Things* will take place in front of the statue in the museum with the same pace of speech and the same two characters. Dramatists want to engage and involve their audiences and this can be done structurally in a range of ways:
- withholding information either from the characters (often through **dramatic irony**) or from the audience
- foreshadowing: hinting at events to come through clues in speech or action
- juxtaposition: positioning events, scenes or ideas close to each other in the action so as to raise questions or create effects such as contrast
- shifts in focus or tone: switching from one set of characters, location or type of scene or action to another, for example from a fast-paced family argument to a quiet soliloquy – changes of scene or act can provide these shifts.

The lively passage taken from *The Devil and Daniel Webster* sets up some ideas about the play to come: Jabez and Mary are enjoying a happy wedding day, but 'gossip' is questioning where a poor farmer got his money from. At the moment, this is just a hint of trouble, which may or may not be significant.

Imagine you were the writer – in what possible directions could the story go now? We know that story structures (whether in plays or novels) often depend on conflict or problems (usually together). If things continued on a smooth, happy path, there would be no story.

Key term

dramatic irony: usually refers to situations where the audience knows something that the characters do not; irony occurs when the characters say or do something in ignorance of the truth

Task

9. Jot down three possible ways in which the play might develop. Think about:
   - how Jabez might have got the money
   - whether he has told Mary
   - whether there are any clues in the title of the play.

Now read the next scene from the play. This takes place *after* the wedding dance. As you read it, consider some of these structural questions:

- How does this scene differ in tone and style to the previous one?
- How does what you learned from the previous scene impact on the audience's response here?

JABEZ: Are you happy, Mary?

MARY: Yes. So happy, I'm afraid.

JABEZ: Afraid?

MARY: I suppose it happens to every girl – just for a minute. It's like spring turning into summer. But the spring was sweet. (*Dismissing the mood*) I'm sorry. Forgive me. It just came and went, like something cold. As if we'd been too lucky.

JABEZ: We can't be too lucky, Mary. Not you and me.

MARY (rather mischieviously): If you say so, Mr Stone. But you don't even know what sort of housekeeper I am. And Aunt Hepsy says –

JABEZ: Bother your Aunt Hepsy! There's just you and me and that's all that matters in the world.

MARY: And you know something else –

JABEZ: What's that?

MARY: How proud I am of you. Ever since I was a little girl. Ever since you carried my books. Oh, I'm sorry for women who can't be proud of their men. It must be a lonely feeling.

JABEZ (uncomfortably): A man can't always be proud of everything, Mary. There's some things a man does, or might do – when he has to make his way.

MARY (laughing): I know – terrible things – like being the best farmer in the county and the best State Senator –

JABEZ (quietly): And a few things, besides. But you remember one thing, Mary, whatever happens. It was all for you. And nothing's going to happen. Because he hasn't come yet – and he would have come if it was wrong.

MARY: But it's wonderful to have Mr Webster come to us.

JABEZ: I wasn't thinking about Mr Webster. (*He takes both her hands.*) Mary, I've got something to tell you. I should have told you before, but I couldn't seem to bear it. Only, now that it's all right, I can. Ten years ago –

A VOICE (from off stage): Dan'll. Dan'll Webster! (*Jabez drops Mary's hands and looks around.*)

Task

10. Reread the scene carefully and answer these questions.

a) Foreshadowing. What evidence is there that Jabez has done something he is ashamed of but which has not yet been revealed? Think about what he says and how he says it.

b) Dramatic irony. What evidence is there that Mary is unaware of any problem (unlike the audience, who are not in her shoes)? Think about what she says when Jabez comments about things he isn't proud of and when he mentions that '*he* hasn't come yet'.

c) What other evidence is there that, despite the wedding and apparent happiness, there are hints of darker moods or tones? Think about what Mary says about spring and summer.

WRITING ABOUT STRUCTURE

When you are dealing with a scene, you can work through it chronologically, tracing how ideas develop, or you can work through key ideas one at a time.

In the paragraph below, a student has chosen to write about the progress of the scene and how it builds on the previous one. This is in response to a question about how the writer has dramatised Mary and Jabez's relationship.

> This seemingly peaceful and intimate extract is juxtaposed with the wild social celebration of the opening scene. Yet, the opening two lines of the passage set up the idea that the idealised, romantic picture of young love is unsustainable. Mary says she is 'so happy' she is 'afraid' and this contrast suggests that things can only get worse from this moment on. It builds on the foreshadowing and hints at things not being all they seem, which the audience witnessed earlier in the dance. The effect is of something brooding, waiting to be released.

- reference to the overarching structure of the play
- reference to the structure of this scene in particular
- comment on the language
- structural phrases clarify the development of ideas
- summary sentence explains the overall effect

Task

11. Write about what Mary says next. Use structural vocabulary (such as the examples in the paragraph above) to clarify when and what is said, and what it might suggest about later events or actions. Begin:

The idea of a passing fear is developed when Mary talks about the feeling that…

Structurally, this…

SHIFTS IN TENSION AND TONE

In *The Devil and Daniel Webster*, the structure of the play serves to create moments of high tension and drama, contrasted with moments of relative calm and happiness. It turns out that Jabez made a deal with a character called 'Scratch' ten years previously when he was a poor farmer. In exchange for wealth and prosperity, he agreed to mortgage his soul to the 'devil' (in the form of 'Scratch'). Scratch appears at the wedding party and events take a terrifying turn.

Task

12. Where would the short set of lines on the right, which follow in a later scene, fit in a 'tension graph'? High or low – or somewhere in-between?

THE CROWD: Jabez Stone – Jabez Stone. Where did you get your money, Jabez Stone? (*SCRATCH grins and taps his collecting box. JABEZ cannot speak.*)

JABEZ: I – I – (*He stops.*)

THE CROWD: Jabez Stone – Jabez Stone. What was the price you paid for it, Jabez Stone?

JABEZ (looking around wildly): Help me, neighbors! Help me! (*This cracks the built-up tension and sends the CROWD over the edge into fanaticism.*)

A WOMAN'S VOICE (high and hysterical): He's sold his soul to the devil!

Task

13. Here is a summary of the events of the play, including the scenes you have looked at. Create your own 'tension time-line' in the form of a graph with the vertical Y-axis being 'Level of tension/drama' and the horizontal X-axis being 'Events of the play'. Plot the events along it.

a) The wedding and dances – the community together

b) Jabez and Mary speak – he tries to confess, but they are interrupted

c) Scratch appears carrying a tin box, snatches the fiddle and plays a discordant tune.

d) Someone grabs the tin-box. A moth is released but it speaks in the voice of a dead miser who also sold his soul to the devil.

e) The moth/voice says people should speak to Jabez. The crowd demand he confesses.

f) Jabez confesses, and Scratch plays the fiddle furiously creating hysteria in the crowd who flee.

g) Jabez tells Mary the whole story; Daniel Webster overhears and says he'll help them.

h) Daniel and Scratch put their cases to a jury of damned and dead souls.

i) The judge refuses all Daniel's arguments. Jabez is condemned to death and about to be taken away.

j) Daniel makes a final, passionate appeal to the jury, saying they were 'free' men once who had a choice, and they should give Jabez a choice.

k) The jury acquit Jabez and disappear into thin air.

l) Back in the 'real' world, Daniel makes Scratch swear never to bother Jabez again.

m) Scratch is chased out of town by the townspeople.

Wider reading

Structure and genre
There is a long tradition of poems, plays and stories in which mortals sell their souls to dark forces in return for prosperity. Most famous, perhaps, is *Dr Faustus* by Christopher Marlowe, in which a university professor makes a pact with the devil's servant Mephistopheles. There are also plays that have a similar setting to Benét's play. Richardson and Berney's *Dark of the Moon* reverses the situation: here a 'devil boy' falls in love with a local girl. If she remains faithful to him, then he will become mortal, but the local community have other ideas.

Final Task

Task

14. How does Benét create a sense of anticipation and growing tension across the three extracts in this unit? Write about:

a) how aspects of form emphasise the unity and power of the community

b) how the structure across the three scenes ratchets up the tension, for example in the way in which the playwright hints at, but holds back, information in the scene between Mary and Jabez, and the effect of that information coming to light in the third extract

c) how the differing forms of speech and dialogue in the scenes convey shifts in tone, mood and tension.

You could deal with each of these in turn, or write about the three scenes in order, tracing how ideas develop.

Checklist for success
Make sure you comment on the formal and structural aspects:
- ✓ Use clear structural terms (for example, 'build on', 'develop', 'echo', 'earlier', 'foreshadow').
- ✓ Refer to the way information is sequenced or presented.
- ✓ Refer to dramatic conventions, such as the names of characters or the stage directions.
- ✓ Refer to how performative aspects, such as stage action and modes of dialogue, contribute to effects.
- ✓ Explain the changes or contrasts in dialogue, tone and tension.

4.6 Exploring Shakespeare

Big question

• What should you be looking to explore in your study of Shakespeare?

WHAT IS SPECIAL ABOUT SHAKESPEARE?

So far in this chapter, you have looked at the way playwrights' decisions about form, structure, language, stage direction, plot and character can, when combined, create powerful dramatic impact.

Part of Shakespeare's impact on audiences comes from the way in which private and domestic concerns also have something to say about wider social, political or historical issues. Thus, while Macbeth may be an ordinary man grappling with ambition, the result of his *inner* conflict is the upheaval of the *outer* world – the kingdom of Scotland and even the upheaval of the divine order. Even when the state of a nation does not depend on a character's actions, the experiences they have seem to connect with our own. This is often referred to as Shakespeare's **universality**, although a lot of modern critical thinking has pointed to how rooted Shakespeare's characters and concerns are in their own time.

Key term

universality: the ability to appeal to people regardless of place and time

Task

1. Which of these quotations from Shakespeare have you heard before?
   • What do you think they mean?
   • Could you apply them to any situations in modern life or to events in the world?
   • Could you apply them to any of the other texts you are studying?

   a) 'All that glitters is not gold.'

   b) 'The course of true love never did run smooth.'

   c) 'The quality of mercy is not strained; / It droppeth as the gentle rain from heaven.'

   d) 'To be, or not to be: that is the question.'

   e) 'To thine own self be true.'

A student has written the following paragraph about Shakespeare's universality in *Macbeth*.

> Shakespeare's plots and characters endorse the class and political structures of his times. Order is generally restored at the end of his plays – in 'Macbeth', the warrior lord is killed and the rightful heir placed on the throne. It is also true that women are usually silenced or subjugated by marriage, and the nobility – whether kings, queens or lords and ladies – remain centre stage. Lady Macbeth, who dares to act like a man – albeit murderously – is killed off through suicide. Shakespeare is not 'of all time', as Ben Jonson stated, but very much of 'his time' only.

Task

2. Does the student have a point? Think about the Shakespeare play you are studying – or have studied: how universal are the ideas?
- Is there a cross-section of society?
- What happens at the end? Is order restored – and who has power?
- Can Shakespeare still be 'universal' even if he focuses on particular types of character and story?

SHAKESPEARE'S CHARACTERISATION

Whether or not you believe in Shakespeare's 'universality', it is generally accepted that many of his characters are **multifaceted**. This means that when you respond to his characters, you should look for the following:

- Motives. Simply saying someone is 'good' or 'bad' avoids looking into *why* a character acts in a virtuous or immoral way.
- Change or contrast. Characters often develop across a play; they might start as noble and well loved, but finish as despised and hated – or vice versa.
- Contradictions. It is possible for a character to be vain, ambitious, jealous, and so on, but for audiences to empathise with them regardless. You can enjoy a villain's cunning as much as their downfall.
- Issues and concerns. As stated earlier, what might seem domestic or personal can often reflect deeper or wider ideas or viewpoints.

Read the following passage from *The Tempest* (Act 1 Scene 2). The play begins on a small island inhabited by two people, an exiled Duke with magical powers and his daughter Miranda. The Duke, named Prospero, has the service of a spirit called Ariel and also a 'creature' called Caliban, who was already on the island when he arrived. In this passage, Prospero has ordered Caliban to appear.

> **Key term**
>
> **multifaceted:** having many sides, aspects or faces

CALIBAN: I must eat my dinner.   Caliban's feelings

This island's mine, by **Sycorax** my mother,   Caliban's background

Which thou takest from me. When thou camest first,

Thou **strokedst** me and **madest** much of me, wouldst give me

Water with berries in't, and teach me how

To name the bigger light, and how the less,

That burn by day and night: and then I loved thee

And show'd thee all the qualities o' the isle,

The fresh springs, brine-pits, barren place and fertile:

Cursed be I that did so! All the **charms**

Of Sycorax, toads, beetles, bats, light on you!

For I am all the subjects that you have,

Which first was mine own king: and here you sty me

In this hard rock, whiles you do keep from me

The rest o' the island.

PROSPERO: Thou most lying slave,

Whom **stripes** may move, not kindness! I have used thee,

Filth as thou art, with human care, and lodged thee

In mine own cell, till thou didst seek to violate

The honour of my child.

CALIBAN: O ho, O ho! **would't** had been done!

Thou didst prevent me; I had peopled else

This isle with Calibans.

MIRANDA: Abhorred slave,

Which any print of goodness wilt not take,

Being capable of all ill! I pitied thee,

Took pains to make thee speak, taught thee each hour

One thing or other: when thou didst not, savage,

Know thine own meaning, but wouldst gabble like

A thing most brutish, I **endow'd** thy purposes

With words that made them known. But thy vile race,

Though thou didst learn, had that in't which good natures

Could not abide to be with; therefore wast thou

Deservedly confined into this rock,

Who hadst deserved more than a prison.

CALIBAN: You taught me language; and my profit on't

Is, I know how to curse. The **red plague** rid you

For learning me your language!

PROSPERO: Hag-seed, hence!

Fetch us in fuel; and be quick…

William Shakespeare, *The Tempest* (1611)

Glossary

Sycorax: Caliban's mother, a witch

strokedst/madest: spellings of the verb forms 'stroke' and 'made'

charms: magic spells

stripes: lashes from a whip

would't: I wish that

endow'd: gifted/gave

red plague: disease producing red spots or sores

Task

3. What are your impressions of Caliban based on this passage?
Select words or lines he says or ones said about him by Prospero
or Miranda. Copy and complete the table below, adding points of
your own.

Quotation	Means	Impression?
'I must eat my dinner.'	He is hungry.	He feels his life is decided by Prospero.
'This island's mine,'	Clear statement that he 'owns' the island.	He feels Prospero stole it – that it was an act of invasion.
'Thou strokest and madest much of me,'	Prospero was gentle and caring to begin with.	
Taught him 'how / To name the bigger light, and how the less,'	Prospero was a teacher, showing him the names of the sun and the moon.	
'I loved thee / And show'd thee all the qualities o' the isle,'		

4. Based on the evidence you have gathered, which of the following
overview statements about Caliban do you find most convincing?
Give your reasons.

   a) Caliban is a violent, inhuman creature that cannot be tamed
   or civilised.

   b) Caliban is a victim who was abused after demonstrating love and
   kindness to Prospero.

   c) Caliban misused the education he was given because he resented
   Prospero and Miranda's arrival on the island.

   d) Caliban is childlike, simple and essentially harmless.

   e) Your own overview, which may be made up of a mixture of
   these statements.

From this, it is probably already clear that Shakespeare's characters can be
complex. Caliban does appear to have tried to do something awful, but
what might have been his motives? And whilst he behaves badly, he also
shows love.

Task

5. Write up an overview paragraph about Caliban that you might use as
part of an introduction to a longer essay about him.
   • Begin either with one of the statements above or your
     own wording.
   • Include at least one quotation from the passage.

Thinking more deeply: **exploring complex concerns through character**

It is tempting to address issues and concerns separately from character, but it is through character and action that Shakespeare explores particular ideas. Often, as you saw in Unit 4.3, such ideas are best described as questions, and in Shakespeare's work these questions are often complex and provocative.

Task

6. Which of the following questions do you think Shakespeare is exploring in the passage you have just read? Consider each idea carefully and find evidence to say whether these *are* ideas being discussed, in your opinion.
   - To what extent is **nature** more powerful than **nurture**?
   - What is the purpose of 'education'?
   - What does 'civilisation' mean and who decides?

7. The poet John Keats described Shakespeare's 'negative capability'. This was not a criticism but suggested the best writers allowed for uncertainties and a willingness for things to be mysterious.

   a) How can Caliban represent both the island's poetic beauty and brute savagery?

   b) What other **paradoxes** like this are there in the play, from what you have learned?

Key terms

nature: in Shakespeare, 'nature' has many meanings, from a more general one relating to the natural world, to here when it is used to mean 'human nature' – the instincts and traits we are born with

nurture: meaning, literally, to care for and help develop, but in contrast to 'nature', it refers to everything we are taught or learn after we are born, either from others or from the world around us

paradox: a situation or statement that involves two or more seemingly contradictory facts or qualities

Wider reading

Nature, character and Fate

In many of Shakespeare's plays, look out for the competing forces of nature, character and Fate. For example, in *Macbeth*, it is reasonable to ask: is Macbeth murderous/ambitious by *nature*? In other words, was he always destined to do terrible things? It might be more interesting in an essay response to consider how things might have turned out differently; in fact, Macbeth himself reflects upon this when, facing inevitable defeat, he says: 'that which should accompany old age, / As honour, love, obedience, troops of friends, / I must not look to have' (Act 5 Scene 3). These would have been the alternatives if he had chosen a different path.

Task

8. Write two or three 'big questions' you think Shakespeare is asking about life and the world in the play you are studying. Create a table like the one below and write these down in the left-hand column. Alongside, note down briefly what elements of the play – or any particular quotations – make you think this.

Shakespeare's big questions	Events or characterisation that suggest this is one of his concerns
1 2 3	

THE RICHNESS OF SHAKESPEARE'S LANGUAGE

The final element, perhaps, of the components that make Shakespeare's characters and concerns compelling is the language. You have already explored it in relation to the relationship between Caliban and Prospero, but it is important to consider how language at different points of the play extends or redraws our understanding of character. In other words, how it adds to the multifaceted characterisation.

Later in the play, Caliban links up with a pair of shipwrecked sailors in order to mount a revolt against Prospero. The sailors are frightened by strange goings-on on the island. Caliban calms them.

> **CALIBAN:** Be not **afeard**. The isle is full of noises,
> Sounds, and sweet airs that give delight and hurt not.
> Sometimes a thousand **twangling** instruments
> Will hum about mine ears, and sometime voices
> That, if I then had waked after long sleep,
> Will make me sleep again. And then, in dreaming,
> The clouds methought would open and show riches
> Ready to drop upon me, that when I waked
> I cried to dream again.

Final Task

Task

13. With close attention to language and tone, discuss Shakespeare's dramatic presentation of Caliban in both passages.

Plenary

Choose a main or reasonably important secondary character from the Shakespeare play you are studying. Using the 'mood board' below, add notes to demonstrate the ways in which you can explore the character to draw out their multilayered character.

How the character is presented when they first appear.	Things the character does that seem to suggest they are a particular sort of person.	Main issues, concerns or themes the character might represent through their story/language.
How the character is presented when they finally appear. Is there a change?	Things the character does that contradict or seem to suggest other facets to their character.	Any other issues, concerns or themes that could be linked to the character.

Task

9. What literary devices does Shakespeare use in this speech to describe the island? Identify:
   a) the use of alliteration
   b) the use of **onomatopoeia**
   c) the use of vivid imagery.
10. What is the overall impression given of the island?
11. How does the tone of the speech compare with the way Caliban spoke in the earlier passage?
12. In what way does this extend or develop your impression of Caliban?

Glossary
afeard: afraid
twangling: making a resonating, twanging sound

Key term
onomatopoeia: words or phrases that sound like the thing they describe, such as 'boom' or 'cluck'

Checklist for success
✓ Make at least three different points about the way Caliban is presented (aim to give a multifaceted response).
✓ Comment on what Caliban says about himself, others and the island/his situation on it.
✓ Comment on how you think Shakespeare wanted audiences to respond to Caliban.
✓ Include selective quotations to support the different points you make and comment on the impressions given by these language choices.

4.7 Approaching dramatic interpretation

Big question
- How can different interpretations help you to make sense of plays?

HOW IS INTERPRETATION IN DRAMA DIFFERENT FROM THAT IN OTHER GENRES?

Unit 1.10 introduced the range of ways you can interpret a text by putting different weight or significance on particular events or aspects of language. It also touched on different critical perspectives, which you can read more about in the 'Introduction to literary critical theory' at the end of this book.

All this is just as true of plays. However, when it comes to interpreting plays, one additional factor is the performative element, which you began to explore in Unit 4.5.

Read this simple extract from *The Tempest* (Act 4 Scene 1). Prospero has just been told that Caliban and the two foolish sailors are planning to kill him and take control of the island.

> **PROSPERO:** A devil, a born devil, on whose nature
> Nurture can never stick – on whom **my pains**
> Humanely taken, all, all lost, quite lost!
>
> William Shakespeare, *The Tempest* (1611)

Glossary
my pains: my efforts

Task

1. What are the different ways Prospero might say this? Try saying it:

   a) in a laughing, joking way – how ridiculous that he/they should try this!

   b) in an angry, fierce way – how dare he? I'm furious and they'll be punished!

   c) in a disappointed, sad way – I tried my best, and look at how I'm rewarded

   d) in any other way you can think of.

   Remember that any interpretation will need to be supported by the text itself.

2. Which of these ways (above) sounds most convincing, bearing in mind:
   - the earlier scene in Unit 4.6 (and any clues that might give us as to Prospero's general tone towards Caliban)?
   - any clues in the extract itself, such as the repeated words, the use of the exclamation mark, the meaning of the words chosen?

Wider reading

What happens to Caliban and the two shipwrecked sailors? Do they succeed in their plan? You can check out the rest of the play to find out!

POSTCOLONIAL INTERPRETATION

By imagining any given passage performed on stage, you can consider how far *your* interpretation can be carried by the weight of the lines. For example, you might think it highly unlikely that Prospero would say the lines above in a frightened, terrified way, but once you ask the questions – Is Prospero frightened? What might he be frightened of? – then this might open up other interesting areas for discussion.

One critical approach that is sometimes applied to *The Tempest* is a **postcolonial** one, and this can inform the performative interpretation too.

Broadly speaking, the term 'postcolonial' refers to the time *after* major empires of countries such as Britain, Spain, France and Belgium gave up the territories they had conquered, ruled and, in many cases, exploited for their raw materials, labour or geographical location. There is no set date, but for Britain it is usually taken to mean the time after the reign of Queen Victoria and World War I (1914–18) and coming to a head at the moment India regained its freedom in 1947. Many of the overseas territories run by such empires had also been slave colonies.

A postcolonial interpretation or perspective looks at how texts explore ideas about race, culture, questions of property and ownership, and also how the 'exotic' or '**other**' is viewed.

There are a number of ways in which *The Tempest* has been read as a postcolonial text. For example:

- The island is seen as exotic – a place of magic, difference and mystery.
- The island (or its people) is seen as a place to be exploited.
- Caliban is seen as 'other': foreign, dangerous and uncivilised (in Western definitions of the words).
- Caliban is treated as a slave.
- Prospero 'discovers' and conquers the island, putting it under his rule ('discovery' is a term disliked by many colonised nations who rightly say that it was already discovered by the original inhabitants!).

Key terms

postcolonial: refers to the time after major empires of countries such as Britain, Spain, France and Belgium gave up the territories they had conquered, ruled and, in many cases, exploited for their raw materials, labour or geographical location; postcolonial perspectives are often concerned with matters of colonisation, independence, migration and cultural identity

other: often used in criticism as a noun to express the way in which white imperial states viewed or constructed non-white societies, reducing them to inferior status as a result of perceived physical and social differences (not looking 'normal' for example)

Glossary

marketable: suitable for selling
pignuts: edible roots
marmoset: small monkey

Task

3. Read these selected quotations from the play. Link them to one or more of the ideas above:

   a) 'savage, […] wouldst gabble like / A thing most brutish' (about Caliban)

   b) 'Fetch us in fuel' (Prospero to Caliban)

   c) 'the isle is full of noises, / Sound and sweet airs, that give delight' (Caliban to the sailors he joins up with)

   d) 'This island's mine, by Sycorax my mother' (Caliban to Prospero)

   e) 'You taught me language' (Caliban to Prospero/Miranda)

   f) 'thou didst seek to violate / The honour of my child' (Prospero to Caliban)

   g) 'one of them / Is a plain fish, and, no doubt, **marketable**' (said about Caliban by a lord who is about to return to the mainland)

   h) 'he does make our fire, / Fetch in our wood, and serves in offices / That profit us' (Prospero about Caliban)

   i) 'I […] will dig thee **pignuts**, / Show thee a jay's nest and instruct thee how / To snare the nimble **marmoset**' (Caliban to the sailors)

Task

4. Look at these three representations of Caliban from productions of
The Tempest. What idea about him is conveyed in each case?

Left to right – Frank Benson, in a production from 1897; Alan Oke, in a production from
2012; Djimon Hunsou, in a film from 2010

5. How would a postcolonial approach change (or confirm) the way you
think about Prospero and Caliban?

   a) Is it fair to see Prospero as a coloniser – or does he in fact want
   the best for Caliban? (Sometimes patronage such as this was part
   of the process of colonisation.)

   b) Is it fair of Caliban to claim Prospero 'stole' the island from him?

APPLYING INTERPRETATIONS

You might be asked a question about the way Shakespeare presents a
particular issue or concern. This would be a chance to draw on some of
the interpretative approaches you have looked at. For example, you might
be asked:

> With close attention to language and tone, discuss the dramatisation
> of conflicting views in the extract from Act 1 Scene 2 in Unit 4.6.

For this, you could comment on:
- the performative aspects – how Prospero and Miranda behave and
  speak, and your interpretation of their tone or tones
- how elements of the postcolonial perspective might be incorporated.

Wider reading

It is worth exploring the
production history of *The Tempest*
(or indeed other plays) to see
how particular characters have
been represented. For example,
Caliban's 'otherness' has been
emphasised by the ethnicity or
accent of the actor chosen to
play him. Interestingly, this has
been interpreted in different ways
– as racist in itself or, conversely,
as highlighting racist attitudes.

Read the following extract from one student who is answering part of this question:

> The idea of conflict is introduced from Caliban's first, resentful words, 'I must eat my dinner.' This suggests that the division between Caliban and Prospero and Miranda, is one of evolution and physiology: he is a reduced to a creature who Prospero 'strokst'; they are rational human beings who taught him to love them, at least initially. In essence, he is presented as little more than a domesticated or trained beast. It is difficult to escape the view that Prospero exploits Caliban: he has freely shown him the 'qualities of the isle', yet Prospero colonises it for himself and his daughter, rather than sharing it equally with its native inhabitant. It is this that directly leads to the conflict about ownership, and later to the rebellion of Caliban and the two sailors – which could be seen as an uprising against an occupying force.

— initial clear observation showing how conflict is dramatised

— explains what the quotation seems to suggest

— expands on point by suggesting notion of 'domestication'

Task

6. After the first three sentences:

a) What new perspective does the student offer on Prospero's actions towards Caliban?

b) What evidence is quoted to support this?

c) What point related to a postcolonial perspective does the student make?

Final Task

Task

7. Write a further paragraph about how conflict is presented in this scene. You could comment on further evidence that suggests Prospero or Miranda act:

a) as authoritative outside powers

AND/OR

b) in a humane/inhumane way towards Caliban.

Plenary

Consider the play or plays you are studying. Select a short dialogue between two characters and try out 3–4 different ways of playing it. For example, change the status level of each character: first, read or play it so that character A is very low in power and status, and character B very high; then change it around. How far can you push the way a character speaks?

Checklist for success

✓ Begin with a topic sentence establishing a new view or point about how conflict is presented.

✓ Support that with relevant quotations from the extract in Unit 4.6.

✓ Comment on the tone of Miranda's speech (the performative interpretation).

✓ Continue with a point that includes terms or references that hint at a postcolonial view (for example, 'other', 'foreign', 'slave', 'power', 'conquering', 'exploit/exploited', 'danger', 'impose/imposition').

4.8 Writing a response to a scene from a play

Big question

- How do you plan a response to a passage-based drama question?

UNDERSTAND THE TASK (AS/A LEVEL)

When approaching a passage-based question at AS Level, it is important to consider:

- the writer's style and choice of language
- their choice of dramatic methods and structure
- how meaning is shaped by the writer's choices
- how the extract relates to the text as a whole
- how the extract might relate to wider concerns and issues.

You also need to understand the focus of the question so that your essay has a clear and purposeful structure.

Questions at AS Level can be worded in a number of ways. Consider the following AS Level-style, passage-based questions based on Winsome Pinnock's *A Hero's Welcome*.

> Discuss Pinnock's presentation of Len at this point in the play. You should make close reference to detail of both language and action in your response.

> With close reference to detail, discuss Pinnock's dramatic presentation of innocence and experience at this point in the play. You should make close reference to detail from the following passage.

> How might an audience react as the play reaches this turning point in Scene 7? You should make close reference to detail from the following passage.

Now, read the extract from *A Hero's Welcome* by Winsome Pinnock. (If you wish to refresh your understanding of the play, there are earlier extracts in Unit 4.2.) The play tells the story of a small Caribbean community in 1947. Len has arrived back from serving with the British forces in World War 2. Sis is a young woman; Minda is a slightly older friend of hers.

Scene 7

Lights up. In a clearing by a stream. The water reflects bright flickering light into LEN and SIS's faces. ——— creates a warm glow, a sense of softness

LEN: There it is. You see it?

SIS: No.

LEN: You're not looking. (*Takes her head in his hands and holds it steady*) There, can you see it now? ——— Len instructs or guides Sis

SIS: Yes. It's beautiful.

LEN: You like it?

SIS: Is it really a fish? It look like a tongue a fire, burning underwater. ——— Sis asking questions

LEN: Is a fish.

SIS: It's like magic.

LEN: It is magic Sis. All of it. All this.

SIS: Yes, I can see it. When you show me these things I see them like as if for the first time. ——— change of tone as Len refers to his past experiences

LEN: It's all new to me too Sis. I never saw any of it before. (*Slight pause*) Maybe everyone should fight a war. (*He moves slowly*) Have you ever seen a dead man?

SIS: No. (*Shudders*) Horrible.

LEN: Have you ever seen a man blown to pieces?

SIS: Stop it Len. I don't want to hear these things.

LEN: No. I don't suppose you do. I suppose you just want me to show you bright butterflies and flowers. You don't want to see dirt or ugliness. Life for you is love hearts and sugar sweeties. (*Pause*) Sometimes I just want to get away from all this… all the greed and everything. I just want to fly away sometimes, free as a bird. (*Pause. LEN has his back to SIS who approaches him from behind as if to touch him tenderly. MINDA enters and breaks mood.*)

MINDA: Sis

LEN: Hello, Min.

SIS: What do you want Minda?

MINDA: Your mother's looking for you.

SIS: What for?

MINDA: She says you'll know what for.

SIS: Tell her I'll come in a minute.

MINDA: She wants you now Sis. She said something about you not finishing what you was doing.

SIS: Give me one minute.

MINDA: She's mad as hell.

SIS: (*Hesitates the sighs. She's reluctant to leave.*) All right. See you Len.

LEN: Bye Sis.

SIS: Coming Min?

MINDA: In a minute.

SIS: (*Hesitates*) All right. (*She exits. Pause*)

MINDA: We ain't talked for a long time.

LEN: Wasn't so long I last see you.

MINDA: No I mean properly. We tease each other and joke around and things, but we never really talk.

LEN: What makes you think you can talk to me?

MINDA: Just a feeling.

LEN: Go ahead. (*Pause*)

MINDA: You look tired Len.

LEN: Yes.

MINDA: Thin too.

LEN: Uh-huh?

MINDA: You need looking after.

LEN: You think so?

MINDA: It's about time you was married.

LEN: So they keep telling me.

MINDA: Not to one of those wishy washy girls but a real tough woman.

LEN: You got someone in mind?

MINDA: (*She smiles*) I've always liked you Len.

Winsome Pinnock, *A Hero's Welcome* (1989)

Now read this example of a passage-based question.

Discuss Pinnock's presentation of Len at this point in the play. You should make close reference to detail of both language and action in your response.

Look at the highlighted parts of the question. You are being asked to:
- analyse in detail the writer's use of dramatic techniques: language, gesture, movement character interactions, stage directions
- directly link your analysis to the presentation of the character of Len
- focus on Len in this particular scene – for example, compared to how he might have been seen before it.

GATHER YOUR IDEAS AND EVIDENCE

Before you begin to write, you should collect the relevant points and evidence that you will need to complete a response. You can then include these in an outline plan.

This question asks you to focus closely on the writer's use of language and action. It is therefore important to consider general points about the language, structure and organisation of the extract.
- What is the situation? What is happening in the scene? Does this create any specific mood or tone that shapes how we view Len at the start?
- What does Len say to Sis? How does he speak and behave towards her?
- How does she react to him? What is the tone of their dialogue?
- What does the conversation between Sis and Minda suggest about Len?
- How does Minda speak and behave towards Len? How is the tone different?
- How does he speak and behave towards her?

Task

1. Read through the annotations that track the first part of the extract. Then add your own further notes based on the bullets above, either as a separate list or on a copy of the text.

PLAN YOUR RESPONSE

Now use your notes and annotations on the extract to create a structured plan.

You can approach this in a number of ways. One way is to *track* your way through the extract from the beginning to end, including relevant evidence and analysis as you go along. Another involves ordering your points according to the *methods* the writer uses to convey the character of Len, although that might lead you to make rather unconnected and disjointed points. A third way, would be to come up with three or four key ideas about Len and write about them in turn, supported by evidence in the extract.

In the *tracking* approach, you could use the notes above to help you organise your response.

In the *ideas*-based approach, you could organise your response as follows:

- The presentation of Len as an *older, wiser figure* in the extract, especially in relation to Sis – and how this might or might not link to his *earlier portrayal*.
- The *contrasting* way he is presented when *Minda arrives* – perhaps as *less worldly* and *wise* than he appears – and, again whether this is similar or different to his presentation elsewhere in the play. This might include reference to Len's *shift in status*.
- His *overall presentation* in the passage, and how this compares to elsewhere in the play, including *any other way* he is presented (for example, at the end when he reveals the truth about his war experiences). This might include the shifts in status between him and the women in the play as a whole: for example, how Nana seems to understand more of the world than him; how Sis moves towards independence in the final scene.

You can, of course, approach the question in another way. Whatever form of organisation you choose, you should:

- consider the effects of the dramatic methods used
- discuss the beginning and ending of the extract
- keep a tight focus throughout on how the techniques you have identified relate directly to the question
- comment on how the extract relates to the text as a whole.

To help you plan, read the following annotated student paragraph. Then read the comments below to help you structure your own response.

> At the opening of the passage, Pinnock constructs an almost magical space in which Len and Sis seem to exist in a sort of private communion with nature. Len is dramatised as a teacher or seer, with the 'bright, flickering light' creating a sense of Len shining rays of knowledge into Sis's naïve world. He elicits a response from her with these short utterances: 'There it is. You see it?', further developing this idea of him as the older man, guiding the eager learner.

sets context effectively

appropriate reference to stage direction/writer's method

explanation of point

further development of point, focusing on spoken language style

WRITE YOUR RESPONSE

Task

2. Now plan and write your response to the task below in **I hour**.

> Discuss Pinnock's presentation of Len at this point in the play. You should make close reference to detail of both language and action in your response.

You could begin by adding a further paragraph about how Len is presented as the wiser figure, but how, when it comes to his revelations about war, the tone changes from the opening section looking for the fish.

UNDERSTANDING YOUR TASK
(A LEVEL ONLY)

When approaching an A Level passage-based question, your response should follow *all* the guidelines given above for AS Level. However, there are some *additional* areas where you could develop your response:

- There should be greater coherence between commentary on the passage and reference the text as a whole in terms of the writer's overarching concerns and approaches.
- You should offer an enhanced personal response, incorporating different interpretations in your analysis.
- Try to evaluate the effectiveness of the writer's choices and presentation of ideas.

This means you may need to move beyond the passage more frequently and draw wider inferences about the topic or character. You may also need to offer further personal interpretation, considering different, and perhaps conflicting, sets of ideas.

Read this A Level-style question:

> Discuss the dramatic effects of the writing in the following extract, considering the way Pinnock shapes an audience's response to the characters and concerns of the play.

Look at the highlighted parts of the question. Here you are being asked to:

- analyse the dramatic effectiveness of the writer's choices – how they make an audience feel or respond
- make wider links to the presentation of Len, Minda and Sis across the whole play
- comment on issues and concerns that arise in this extract and are also relevant elsewhere in the play.

GATHER YOUR IDEAS AND EVIDENCE

You could use the *tracking* approach, working through the passage as it occurs:

- How do we/audience respond to Len and Sis at the start? What issues does this part of the extract raise? Can these be linked to earlier ideas? How does the characterisation of Len and Sis build on or develop what we already know of them?
- How does the entrance of Minda change the dynamic of the scene? How does the presentation of Minda build on what we already know of her? Does her arrival introduce any new issues? Does the relationship between Minda and Sis in the rest of the play have any bearing on the selected extract?
- What is the effect of the conversation between Len and Minda after Sis has left? Does this develop or confirm earlier characterisation and ideas?
- How does the whole extract fit with what has gone before and what happens later? What is the function of the scene, in that regard?

Alternatively, you could take an ideas-based response that moves between different parts of the extract, looking at the *dramatic effects*:

- the ways in which the audience *evaluates the different possible partners for Len* and what they offer – where our sympathies lie

- underlying *tensions or other feelings* aroused in the scene (for example, dramatic irony created by what we know of Minda's personal history)
- how *particular concerns* are developed in the scene: age/youth; innocence and experience; loyalty and love; war and peace
- how any of the characterisation, ideas or concerns relate to *their presentation elsewhere in the play* (for example, how Sis develops over the course of the play)
- how these same issues and concerns are introduced or developed elsewhere in the play.

PLAN YOUR RESPONSE

When thinking about other interpretations, it is useful to reflect upon:
- how *different performances* might modify the audience's judgements of the characters (for example, to what extent Minda might be played as a victim in this and other scenes, or how comfortable or uneasy we feel about the way Len/Sis's relationship could be portrayed)
- *how much weight* to give to particular issues or ideas (for example, whether the depiction of innocence and experience is more important than individual ambition or betrayal)
- how *wider contextual ideas* shape audience's responses (for example, about Britain's relation to countries still considered part of the Empire or the Commonwealth).

Read the sample paragraph from an A Level student's response below. This demonstrates ways in which these additional elements can be incorporated into an extract analysis.

Earlier in the play, Nana has referred to Sis as a 'lovesick dog' when talking to Len. There had been a clear sense of warning here – she is young and fragile, but Len seems to laugh the situation off, claiming he is more like a 'big brother' to her. This idea of him as someone Sis looks up to, and even idolises, is exemplified in the opening to the extract as Len acts as teacher, showing the child-like Sis where to see a fish. When the stage directions explain that he takes 'her head in his hands and holds it steady' we might respond in different ways: we might see this is as further evidence of Len's careful attention to a young person discovering the world, or as misguided and dangerous, playing with the emotions of an impressionable young woman.

(annotations:)
— reference back to earlier in the play

— focus on the specific detail of the extract

— offers two interpretations of Len's behaviour by looking at the dramatic action

WRITE YOUR RESPONSE

Task

3. Now using the support from the AS/A and A Level sections above, and with reference to the extract from Scene 7, plan and write your response to the passage-based task in **1 hour**.
Your teacher should be able to supply you with further extracts from the play and a summary of the action as a whole.

Discuss the dramatic effects of the writing in the extract, considering the way Pinnock shapes an audience's response to the characters and concerns of the play.

4.9 Evaluating responses to a scene from a play

Big question

- How do you evaluate your response to a passage-based drama question?

SAMPLE RESPONSES TO A SCENE FROM A PLAY TASK (AS/A LEVEL)

In this section, you will explore two responses to the first task in Unit 4.8. This will enable you to evaluate what makes a strong response and, using these responses and commentaries as a guide, help you to improve and develop your own responses to passage-based questions.

> ### Task
>
> Discuss Pinnock's presentation of Len at this point in the play. You should make close reference to detail of both language and action in your response.

1. Using the sample extract in Unit 4.8 as a model, read through your own response carefully, paragraph by paragraph, and complete an initial annotation (covering aspects such as assessment of overview, structure of response, analysis of language, form and structure, support from the text, reference to context where relevant, strength of conclusion).

2. Read the following response to the task below. As you read, think about:
   - what this student has done well
   - what they might need to do to improve the response.

Response 1

Len is presented at the start of the extract as someone who is kind and encouraging. His first words and actions show him helping Sis to see the fish in the water. He asks her if she 'sees it?' and when she is unable to, he 'takes her head in his hands and holds it steady'. Both the questions and his gesture are likely to make us think that Sis trusts and respects him, and is more than willing to do as he suggests.

— overview statement makes first point about Len

— references to the writer's methods

Once the fish is found, Sis's sense of wonder is like that of a child whose teacher has helped her discover or learn something new. Len's certainty – 'It is magic' and 'All of it'– expressed in short, definite lines develops this idea of him as teacher.

— develops idea of Len

However, the presentation of Len changes when he says 'I never saw any of it before' and refers back to his war experiences. He is saying that everyone needs to see terrible things to make them appreciate everyday events.

— clearly tracks structural change

As an audience, we might be reminded of the conventions of stories of damaged veterans returning from war. This is developed when his questions to Sis become darker and he asks if she's 'ever seen a dead man?'. This is followed by a long speech in which he seems to criticise the things he was showing Sis a few minutes earlier – like 'bright butterflies and flowers'!

passing reference to literary context/conventions

Towards the end of the speech, it seems as if it is Len who has become weaker and more fragile – especially when he says he wants to 'fly away', and become 'free as a bird'. Earlier in Scene 1 he has explained to Charlie what happened when a bomb dropped on his trenches and everyone was killed, so the audience might think this is what he wants to escape.

comment on Len but needs further interpretation

clear focus on use of language

When Minda arrives, the way Len changes is presented by the writer again. The connection between him and Sis is lost. Minda manages to persuade the reluctant Sis to leave and this allows her to have her chance with Len. In this dialogue, it is Minda who seems to take the lead. Her statements, such as 'You look tired Len' and 'You need looking after' develop the idea of Len suffering in his own way. The earlier picture of him as the all-knowing teacher seems to be less apparent now.

good knowledge but tends to recount story rather than comment

It is important, however, to remember that the audience know Minda is unreliable. She has already slept with a rich old man and is having an affair with her friend Ishbel's husband, Stanley. So, the audience is likely to feel increasing sympathy for Len. They probably think, oh she's got her claws in him now, and she is beginning to position herself as his wife-to-be. She seems to be telling Len that pursuing a dreamer like Sis is not good for him – she's 'one of those wishy-washy girls' rather than a 'real tough woman.'

good linkage to earlier parts of play

explains how this affects reaction to Len

attempt at personal response but too informal

So, Pinnock alters the way we see Len as the extract progresses. At first, he comes across as a wise, older, teacher-like figure, but by the end of the extract he seems vulnerable. Minda claims later in the scene that Len was the 'first person to ever break my heart' when she was even younger, but it is difficult to know if this is true. However, Len seems to swallow it.

useful summary statement

Clearly, Len has something magnetic about him. Both Charlie and Sis follow him around, and even if it is for her own purposes Minda wants to marry him. Nana might object to Len controlling her, but she has his best interests at heart. The audience will also find Len an attractive figure too.

important new point but not best to include in conclusion

COMMENTARY

This is a competent response with relevant knowledge and use of appropriate references and quotations. The response shows sound understanding, but reference to and analysis of what the writer does (rather than what the character does) could be developed further. Expression is clear and straightforward, though introducing new points in a conclusion should be avoided. There is a clear sense of the extract's relationship to the text as a whole, but the tracking approach, working through the extract section by section, rather limits wider interpretations and comment.

Task

3. Now read a second response to the same question. As you read, think about what this student has done that develops and improves upon the previous response.

Response 2

At the opening of the passage, Pinnock constructs an almost magical space in which Len and Sis seem to exist in a sort of private communion with nature. Len is dramatised as sort of teacher or seer with the 'bright, flickering light' creating a sense of Len shining rays of knowledge into Sis's naïve world. He elicits a response from her with these short utterances: 'There it is. You see it?' further developing this idea of him as the older man, guiding the eager learner.

— sets context effectively

— appropriate reference to stage direction/writer's method

— explanation of point

— further development of point, focusing on spoken language style

As the dialogue with Sis progresses, her own absolute trust in his version of events and her own poetic response to the fish, like a 'tongue a fire, burning underwater' indicates a strong personal connection between the two of them that is ultimately broken both by the writer's depiction of Len's own uncharacteristic morbidity and the appearance of Minda. The sudden, violent questions that Pinnock uses to express Len's changed tone to Sis – 'Have you ever seen a dead man?' and 'Have you ever seen a man blown to pieces?' – seem to be targeted deliberately at her, as if he wants to hurt her, to pierce her idealistic bubble. The ironic follow-up when he suggests she only wants to be shown 'bright butterflies and flowers' and 'love-hearts and sweeties' seems overly unpleasant and contemptuous. As an audience, it is likely that we would react by sympathising with Sis – it's not her fault she's innocent of the world – rather than condoning Len's words. Whilst Pinnock might want us to understand the traumatising effects of war, to foist them upon Sis seems misjudged.

— detailed analysis of language point

— excellent understanding of the tone of the language

— reference to political/historical context

The writer further explores Len's vulnerability, which has been hinted at in the speech he gives to Sis about the 'dirt and ugliness' of the real world, when Minda appears. Pinnock structures the scene so that Minda manages to get Sis off stage in order to have Len all to herself. Clearly, Pinnock wants to show that the women of the play find Len attractive; even Sis's younger brother idolises him and yearns to be a soldier when he gets older. But Minda's motives are unclear. What we do know is that she has lost her chance of financial security with the death of her rich, older lover, and that she is unlikely to prove a faithful wife given her affair with Ishbel's husband Stanley. Knowing this may make the audience revise their view of Len as a bitter veteran and give him the benefit of the doubt. Or Pinnock may intend us to view him as naïve and foolish.

— useful new point about Len

— good interpretative point

Len's dramatic status shifts suddenly when Minda appears. She drives the dialogue between them, commenting in simple assertions on Len's appearance: 'You look tired, Len.' and 'Thin, too'. The outcome seems inevitable. Minda warns Len off girls like Sis, 'wishy washy girls', in favour of a 'real tough woman' like herself. Pinnock shows that Len is blinded by her direct and effective pursuit of him.

very effective reference to drama methodology on status

Ultimately, the writer leaves us with a clear picture of Len's own innocence – his lack of awareness of the 'lovesick' Sis and the strategic Minda that we remember. Later, Minda betrays him, as she has done Ishbel, and runs off with Ishbel's husband. Len is presented as flawed and human, and Pinnock may wish us to forgive him his character's faults.

clearly expressed and argued conclusion

COMMENTARY

This is a highly perceptive response that sustains the argument about how the writer presents Len. Clear links are made to other points in the play both before and after this scene, and there is detailed and insightful analysis of language and action. Ideas are expressed extremely fluently and supported with relevant references, and there is evidence of interpretation, raising different approaches to Len's characterisation.

EXTRACTS FROM SAMPLE RESPONSES TO A PASSAGE-BASED TASK (A LEVEL)

Your response to an A Level task should include *all* the elements you have explored in the AS/A passage responses above, but *in addition* it should:

- analyse the effectiveness of the writer's choices – how successfully they make an audience feel or respond
- make wider links to the presentation of the Len, Minda and Sis across the play as a whole
- comment on issues and concerns that arise in this extract and are also relevant elsewhere in the play
- consider a range of possible interpretations.

Read this A Level exam-style question:

Discuss the dramatic effects of the writing in the following extract, considering the way Pinnock shapes an audience's response to the characters and concerns of the play.

Task

4. To help you evaluate the additional elements required, read through
   the extract from a sample A Level-style response below.
   As you read, think about:
   • what this student has done well
   • what they might need to do to improve the response.

Response 3

One of the key concerns of the play is the nature of heroism, and this
is something that is explored in the extract from the start. Pinnock
reminds us that there were black soldiers who fought on behalf of the
Commonwealth and, as this extract shows, were damaged by it. Sis,
however, has no interest in the geo-political. Her interest is purely
personal and she hangs on every word Len says, drawn to the vision he
paints of a world of 'magic' and beauty. This elicits from Sis her comment
that the fish is like a 'tongue a fire'. For her, Len is a symbol of bravery and
knowledge. But Len's position since he returned to the island from war is
not without complications. Having a young, innocent girl worshipping you
may be flattering, but idols come crashing down. War heroes are often
damaged in ways we don't expect.

However, the writer's presentation of Len is not straightforward. There
is a sense he is angry with himself. Perhaps the words are not intended
for Sis, but for him – to remind him that the island is not the paradise he
might paint it as, but evidence of him running away from the truth, which
we later find out is that he is not a war hero at all. So, when he says he
wants to 'fly away sometimes, free as a bird' we think it must be due to
war memories, the damaged veterans that we are used to from other
works such as Sherriff's 'Journey's End' or Cormier's 'Heroes'.

(annotations)
- clearly focuses on a key issue/concern
- reference to issues of empire and colonialism
- supporting reference begins to explore interpretation
- suggests alternative ways of seeing
- beginning to suggest a personal response, but a bit vague and unconnected to the text

COMMENTARY

This is a sound and relevant response with support from the text. There
is evidence of engagement with the text and some consideration of
personal interpretation, although underdeveloped. The reference to war
and empire as the backdrop to the play is touched on lightly but does
not bring a great deal to the overall analysis.

Task

5. Now read the extract from a second response to the same
   question. Think about what this student has done to develop and
   improve upon the first response.

Response 4

Pinnock's use of the literary trope of the damaged soldier either returning home or unable to deal with the consequences of being seen as a hero has been explored in many texts, including Rebecca West's 'The Return of the Soldier' and Robert Cormier's 'Heroes'. Here Pinnock gives it new life by featuring a West Indian man who has fought on the British Empire's side and has now returned to islands broadly untouched by war. From the start of this extract, the sense of the island's symbolic attachment to ancient myth and beauty is hinted at in the almost magical glittering of the 'flickering light' of the stream and Sis's comments that the fish is like a 'tongue a fire'. This sensual, almost erotic simile creates an expectancy, almost an electric charge to the exchange between the two. The island is presented as refuge, perhaps even as the embracing mother, welcoming the son home.

However, when Pinnock shifts attention from the immediate moment to the wider world, it is suggested that the island offers no real protection against the memories that have followed Len; war cannot be buried in a fishing expedition with an impressionable young girl. Of course, it is only at the end of the play that we learn about Len's false heroism – that he is not the idol Sis and the others have built him up to be. Perhaps the closing scenes create a new response in the audience, asking us to reconsider what we have felt about Len until this point: does it make us forgive or condemn even more strongly his bitter questions about whether Sis has seen a 'dead man' or 'a man blown to pieces'? In the earlier scene, Pinnock presented Len as perhaps cruel but truthful. However, when the writer reveals that Len never experienced these things, it also alters our final view of him on stage.

strong contextual reference linked to the text

perceptive analysis of the language and how it links to the issue initially explored

insightful personal interpretation

clear link made to later action

raising different interpretations about character

COMMENTARY

This is a confident and perceptive analysis with clear and thoughtful consideration of the extract's relationship to the play as a whole, and how Len can be seen according to which point in the play one observes him from. Excellent consideration of other interpretations, which are confidently explored and supported.

Final Task

Now that you have considered the sample response for either an AS/A or A Level exam-style question, reflect upon your own response.

Task

6. a) Use the guidance in the tables on the final page of this chapter (page 282) to assess whether you think your response could be classed as 'competent' or 'very good'.

b) What do you think were the strengths of your response? What could you do to improve upon and develop your own passage-based essays?

c) Using the examples above, write your own brief commentary at the end of your own essay with action points for development.

4.10 Writing a response to a whole play

Big question

- How do you plan a response to a discursive question on a play?

UNDERSTAND THE TASK (AS/A LEVEL)

When approaching a discursive question at AS Level, it is important to make your points across the play as a whole. In your study of your prose text, you will have explored the key dramatic elements of whole texts, covered in Units 2.1–2.7.

To approach the discursive question, therefore, you will need to draw upon your understanding of the following:
- the writer's choice of dramatic action and settings
- how far the text fits into existing genres or challenges them
- the structural features such as prologues, opening and closing scenes, dramatic climax and resolution
- how characters are created and how their thoughts and feelings are conveyed, for example through monologue, interactions and gesture.
- what is distinctive about the writer's style and use of language
- how meaning is shaped by the writer's choices
- the writer's wider concerns, ideas and issues.

You also then need to relate your understanding of the elements above to the focus of the discursive question.

Questions at AS Level can be worded in a number of ways. Consider the following exam-style discursive questions based on William Shakespeare's *The Tempest*:

A. In what ways, and with dramatic effects, does Shakespeare present the character of Caliban in the play?

B. Discuss the significance of the island setting in the play.

C. Ariel: 'What would my potent master?'
What does Prospero's use of magical power contribute to the play's meanings and effects?

D. Ariel tells Prospero at the start of the play: 'Remember I have done thee worthy service.'
In the light of this comment, discuss Shakespeare's presentation of Prospero and Ariel's relationship.

E. Caliban claims that he is 'subject to a tyrant'. In the light of this comment, discuss Shakespeare's presentation of ideas about government.

F. To what extent do you agree with Prospero's view of Caliban?

Look at the highlighted parts of questions **A–F**.
- This is a character-focused question, where you will need to explore the presentation and significance of the character in the whole text and the effect they have on the audience.
- These are issue/concern questions. You will need to trace the ways the idea is presented across the whole play.
- This setting-focused question is asking you to think about how this particular choice of setting is important in contributing to key issues, ideas, action or characterisation.

- These are relationship questions, which ask you to explore how two
  characters interact in response to a given prompt.

Now look in detail at the first exam-style discursive question:

> In what ways, and with dramatic effects, does Shakespeare present the character of Caliban in the play?

It is important to identify what this question is asking you to do. It is a
character-based question, but you should discuss:

- the *dramatic methods* (the 'ways') Shakespeare uses to present the
  character of Caliban
- the *effects* of these methods
- the *impression* created of his character
- Caliban's presentation *across the play as a whole*, not just in one or
  two scenes.

GATHER YOUR IDEAS AND EVIDENCE

You need to discuss how Shakespeare presents the character throughout
the play and how, at each point, the evidence supports or doesn't
support Prospero's statement.

Here are some sections of the play that you could focus on
(a summary of the play and these scenes are provided in the Teacher
Resource):

a) the explanation Prospero gives to Ariel about Caliban in Act 1
Scene 2

b) the angry dialogue between Prospero, Miranda and Caliban later in
the same scene

c) how other characters respond to Caliban (for example, Trinculo
and Stephano)

d) Caliban's speech at the start of Act 2 Scene 2 before he hides

e) what he tells Trinculo and Stephano about Prospero

f) his plan for usurping Prospero

g) Caliban's speech about the island in Act 3 Scene 2

h) the ending of the play – how he behaves and is treated.

Task

1. Match these quotations to the sections above:

i) 'A freckled whelp hag-born – not honour'd with
A human shape.'

ii) 'the isle is full of noises,
Sounds and sweet airs, that give delight, and
hurt not.'

iii) 'As I told thee before, I am subject to a tyrant,
a sorcerer, that by his cunning hath cheated me
of the island.'

iv) 'A most poor credulous monster!'

v) 'His spirits hear me,
And yet I needs must curse.'

vi) 'Thou most lying slave,'

vii) '…thou mayst brain him,
Having first seized his books – or with a log
Batter his skull,'

viii) 'I'll be wise hereafter,
And seek for grace. What a thrice-double ass
Was I, to take this drunkard for a god,
And worship this dull fool!'

When gathering ideas for this kind of task, you should identify other parts of the play that might be helpful. Your teacher may be able to supply you with a summary of the play and some additional extracts.

PLAN YOUR RESPONSE

Having selected relevant sections of the text, you can begin to formulate your argument. You can use the *tracking* approach, where you work through the text from beginning to end, or you could organise your response according to *a range of different points* related to the ideas in the task.

In the tracking approach, your points should come in order as they do in sections **a)** to **h)** outlined above. If you are organising your response according to different points, then you could use the following structure:

- Introducing Caliban via the overall *structure* of Caliban's story. What happens to him and why? What does this tell you? What had happened to him before Prospero arrived?
- His presentation as a servant/slave of Prospero – his actions, as reported by himself and others. What does he have to say about his treatment by Prospero? How might this link into ideas related to colonialism, slavery, and so on?
- His presentation in relation to ideas about education, nature and nurture, perhaps linked to the above.
- His presentation as a part of the conspiracy against Prospero – exploring the extent to which this might be taken seriously.
- His presentation as a creature of the island, in tune with its identity and 'qualities'.
- How we view him at the end of the play. What defining picture Shakespeare leaves of him as the play draws to a close.

Whatever approach you use you should remember to consider:
- the significance of the character to the text as a whole
- how the presentation of this character might reflect wider concerns and issues.

You can incorporate the two points above in your conclusion and/or introduction, but you could refer to these wider points throughout the essay where relevant.

For example, read through this sample student paragraph and annotations.

As an audience, Shakespeare shapes our attitude to Caliban in the words Prospero uses to link him to the devil from the start of the play. Before we even meet him, in Act 1 Scene 2, Prospero describes Caliban as a 'freckled whelp hag-born – not honour'd with human shape' which shapes our perspective of a creature compared to a young dog and born of a witch. Shakespeare's use of the word 'honour'd' implies that to be human is to be superior. This also touches on conventions of the time that associated virtue with beauty. The reference to his mother being a 'hag' also positions Caliban as otherworldly, alien and linked to the malignant spirit world.

clear point that immediately focuses on one of the ways Shakespeare constructs Caliban

supporting quotation and explanation links to idea of the 'devil/supernatural'

further exploration

begins to explore wide contextual ideas raised through the characterisation, but not developed or explained

Task

2. Write a final sentence for the paragraph that sums up how Shakespeare presents Caliban through Prospero's opening lines. You could also mention something about the effect these words have on an audience. You could begin:

These descriptions create a picture of Caliban as…

The effect is that the audience…

WRITE YOUR RESPONSE

Task

3. Now plan and write your response to the exam-style task below in **I hour**.

> In what ways, and with dramatic effects, does Shakespeare present the character of Caliban in the play?

UNDERSTANDING YOUR TASK (A LEVEL ONLY)

When you are approaching a whole-text question in the A Level paper, your response should follow *all* the guidelines given above. However, there is *one additional area* where you should develop your response:

• incorporate different interpretations in your analysis.

Now look at the highlighted parts of the following exam-style question.

> Caliban claims that he is 'subject to a tyrant'. In the light of this comment, discuss Shakespeare's presentation of ideas about government.

• This question makes direct reference to a particular quotation from the play which links to the key idea or issue.
• The question requires you to explore the idea with the quotation in mind.
• The question requires you to discuss the ways Shakespeare approaches the given issue – his dramatic methods and techniques.
• The word 'discuss' suggests you need to explore what these methods suggest – so different interpretations.
• In this question, the extent of the impact of an issue or concern is explored.

Therefore, when writing an answer to this question, you should:

• respond to the idea of Prospero as a 'tyrant' and Caliban as a 'subject'
• focus on the particular issue of government
• explore how the issue is presented dramatically at different points in the play
• consider opportunities to explore wider social, cultural and historical contexts
• consider different interpretations.

GATHER YOUR IDEAS AND EVIDENCE

As you collect your evidence for a whole-text A-Level response, you need to take these additional areas into account in your planning.

You could consider:

- ideas about kingship, government and exploration/conquering of new territories in the play (and, where relevant, drawn from contemporary views)
- how these are reflected by Shakespeare's choice of language and dramatic techniques
- how to incorporate other interpretations into your analysis.

PLAN YOUR RESPONSE

Whichever method of planning you choose, you will need to incorporate these additional features in a response at A Level.

When thinking about government you could consider the following scenes which are provided in the Teacher Resource:

a) Prospero as a failed ruler when Duke of Milan

b) Prospero's 'government' of Ariel, Miranda and Caliban – and the extent to which it could be considered a tyranny

c) the presentation of other leaders – Alonso, Sebastian, Antonio

d) Gonzalo's utopian version of a kingdom and how he would govern it

e) the 'shadow' government of Stephano, with his subjects – Caliban and Trinculo

f) the notion of government as colonisation

g) other sorts of 'government' – of the elements, of magic, of time/future.

When thinking about other interpretations, it is also useful to reflect upon:

- what constitutes 'good' government
- contemporary ideas about Italian city states
- your own response to the way the idea of 'government' is presented.

Task

4. Here are some quotations or references related to government. Match them to the points **a)–g)** above.

i) 'I, thus neglecting worldly ends, all dedicated
To closeness and the bettering of my mind'

ii) 'Flesh and blood,
You, brother mine, that entertain'd ambition,
Expell'd remorse and nature – who, with
Sebastian […]
Would here have kill'd your King'

iii) 'I have with such provision in mine Art
So safely ordered that there is no soul –
No, not so much perdition as an hair
Betid to any creature in the vessel'

iv) 'I' the commonwealth […] No occupation; all
men idle, all;
And women too, but innocent and pure;
No sovereignty; –'

v) 'This cell's my court: here have I few attendants,
And subjects none abroad'

vi) 'O King Stephano! O peer! O worthy Stephano!
Look what a wardrobe here is for thee!'

vii) 'I am subject to a tyrant – a sorcerer, that by his
cunning hath cheated me of the island.'

Now read the sample paragraph below from an A Level student's response. This demonstrates one way of incorporating these additional A Level features into a whole-text analysis.

Shakespeare places the issue of government at the heart of the play from the very first scene. The Boatswain questions whether the king and lords have the power to 'command' the waves, thus suggesting that in the face of natural elements, status means nothing. And yet we soon find out it is a man, Prospero, who has governed the waves with 'such provision of mine art' that no harm is done to the shipwrecked sailors. This is significant, as it suggests Shakespeare is raising complex questions: what sort of ruler has Prospero become? Is the man who can raise the storm the same as the one who was forced to leave Milan? Prospero uses magical power to command Ariel and the elements, and yet it was the very study of such 'art' that led to him losing his dukedom. At this point in the play, Shakespeare seems to be content to let the audience believe that 'government' can extend beyond the personal and political to the supernatural. Yet, by the end of the play, Shakespeare shows Prospero renouncing his magic when he chooses to return to Milan, even if it is difficult to see him surviving in the cut-throat world of Italian city-states.

- asserts the central role of 'government' in the play
- suggests a wide definition of government (not just the rule of people)
- opens up an interpretative debate about Prospero's abilities as a ruler
- reference to contextual idea – how the 16th century viewed Italian states

Task

5. Now using the support from the AS/A and A Level sections above, plan and write your response to the whole-play task in **1 hour**.

Caliban claims that he is 'subject to a tyrant'. In the light of this comment, discuss Shakespeare's presentation of ideas about government.

When you have completed your response, turn to Unit 4.11, Evaluating a response to a whole play.

4.11 Evaluating a response to a whole play

Big question

- How do you evaluate your response to a whole play?

SAMPLE RESPONSES TO A WHOLE-TEXT TASK (AS/A LEVEL)

In this section, you will explore two discursive, whole-play responses to the first task in Unit 4.10. This will enable you to evaluate what makes a strong response and, using these responses and commentaries as a guide, help you to improve and develop your own whole-text answers.

> ### Task
>
> Caliban claims that he is 'subject to a tyrant'. In the light of this comment, discuss Shakespeare's presentation of ideas about government.

1. Using the second sample paragraph in Unit 4.10 as a model, read through your own response carefully, and complete an initial annotation (covering aspects such as assessment of overview, structure of response, analysis of language, form and structure, support from text, links to other parts of the play, reference to context where relevant, strength of conclusion).
2. Read the following response. As you read, consider:
   - what this student has done well
   - what they might need to do to improve the response.

Wider reading

You may need to read the summary of the play with additional extracts; your teacher may be able to provide you with these.

Response 1

Government is an issue that comes up throughout 'The Tempest'. Shakespeare tells us the whole reason for Prospero and Miranda ending up on the island was that, as Duke of Milan, Prospero's rule was overthrown by his 'false brother' with Alonso's help. So, Prospero goes from government of an important Italian state to a 'poor cell' with just three subjects – Miranda, Ariel and Caliban. If nothing else, this shows how fragile power is. And the fact even Caliban describes him as a 'tyrant' suggests he can't rule through agreement.

What sort of ruler was Prospero when he was Duke of Milan? He admits he focused on the 'bettering' of his mind, 'neglecting worldly ends'. In other words, he spent too much time on his art and on learning, when he should have been paying attention to ruling. It was this taking his eye off the ball that meant his brother Antonio was able to overthrow him. The audience learn about this from the long dialogue in Act 1 Scene 2 in which he

— provides the overview for the essay

— evidence of ranging across whole play

— too informal expression

explains the past to Miranda, though there is lots of evidence she finds the story boring, with Prospero having to ask her, 'Dost thou hear?' on more than one occasion. This could be seen as evidence that Prospero has an egotistical obsession with himself. He's just not very good at dealing with people!

interesting idea about government, but could be linked more closely to Prospero's interest in magic and supernatural

The idea that Prospero does not find basic government easy is developed later in the same scene. First, he has to threaten Ariel with punishment in order to get him to carry out further tasks on his behalf. He even uses the same term – 'malignant' – meaning 'wicked' to describe Ariel as he later does to describe Caliban. It seems that only by threatening Ariel to 'rend an oak' and imprison him for 'twelve winters' does Ariel agree to be 'correspondent to command'. This mirrors the imprisonment of Ariel by Sycorax, which links Prospero less to the mortal world and more to the spirit world.

links to next point in play

suggested interpretation

Prospero's governance of Caliban is also one of fear, as the repeated reference to 'tyrant' shows. He uses Caliban to do 'offices that profit us', suggesting that the relationship of ruler to subject is one of tyranny and control. Caliban himself says later in the play, 'a plague upon the tyrant that I serve', which is his view of course but does seem to fit with the way Prospero rules. Perhaps Prospero has no choice: if it is true that Caliban tried to 'violate the honour' of Miranda, then maybe force is the only way to control him.

further inference drawn from language

Through the play, Shakespeare explores the idea of what makes good government. When Gonzalo talks about the 'commonwealth' in Act 2 Scene 1 – how he would rule the island if he were king – he says there would be: 'No occupation; all men idle, all – / And women too, but innocent and pure; No sovereignty –' The passive nature of these ideas – the negative 'no' and the adjective 'idle' – present a utopian vision of government. This at first seems to mirror the reality of the island: Miranda is 'innocent and pure' for example, but there is rule. And not everyone is 'idle' – both Ariel and Caliban are basically slaves serving Prospero's purposes.

detailed, thoughtful analysis of language, but 'utopian' context undeveloped

Rulers, generally, don't come out well from the play, as is shown in the final scene. It takes a life-changing event – the prospect of Alonso losing his son – to make him reflect on life, and finally return the dukedom of Milan to Prospero. He, at least, seems genuinely repentant: he asks Prospero to 'pardon me my wrongs'. Antonio and Sebastian, however, do not show this at all. In many ways, they are worse than Alonso, having planned to murder him and Gonzalo, but they are forgiven. What image of rule and government would this have given to a Shakespearean audience?

hints at contextual perspective but question needs to be answered

Shakespeare does not answer the question of what is good government, but he shows evidence of how not to rule. Prospero was a failed ruler when he was in Milan, and his brother did not present a moral alternative. Gonzalo's vision is idealised and unrealistic. The fact that the island is left to Caliban at the end of the play raises more questions than it answers.

useful summative sentence

COMMENTARY

This is a competent response, which follows the play sequentially in a clear way, supported with appropriate evidence from the text. There is some reference to context, but it is undeveloped, and expression is a little informal in places. There is relevant analysis of language choices, but greater interpretation could be demonstrated, exploring different readings or possible meanings as required at A Level. The organisation of the response covers the text as a whole. There needs to be far more reference to 'Shakespeare' and what he does as a writer.

Task

3. Now read a second response to the same question. As you read, think about what this student has done that develops and improves upon the previous response.

Response 2

Towards the end of the play, Shakespeare finally brings together rival rulers and a range of 'subjects'. Whether we are meant to view them as 'tyrants' or penitents who have learned humility is open to question. When Prospero welcomes Alonso to his 'court' at the end of the play, he tells him: 'Here have I few attendants, And subjects none abroad.' Lacking society, he chooses to break his magic staff and return to Milan, and take up his old position as Duke. It seems he is exchanging the government, or subjugation, of the alien, the other – of magic and the supernatural – for the government of the moral and worldly, and it is the dynamic relationship between the two that forms the backdrop for the play as a whole.

— excellent understanding of structure and places essay in context of the given quotation

The two worlds that Prospero was unable to reconcile in his earlier life are explored by Shakespeare in Prospero's explanation to Miranda in Act 1 Scene 2. On the one hand, we learn that he prioritised 'secret studies' of the dark arts, 'neglecting' the needs of his subjects. He failed to understand that to rule, one had to be visible. Antonio's strength is that he realises the need for 'outward royalty' – to be seen to govern. Prospero says Antonio was the 'ivy which hid my princely trunk'. Shakespeare uses this metaphor to develop this idea of Prospero the distant ruler, out of touch and without the political skills to promote the right people or to recognise the cunning strategy of his brother. We might argue that this blind pursuit of learning is impractical – and like others who seek to master the spirit world, such as Marlowe's Faustus, is doomed to failure.

— fluent expression embedding apt quotations

— light, but relevant touch on literary context

So, in a way, Shakespeare suggests the island is a gift to Prospero. Whether its magic and 'sweet airs' are created by him or already present on the island, it represents the chance of a new start: to govern using the powers he has acquired, with no real subjects – just a daughter and two strange creatures. But here he fails too, to an extent. Caliban claims that Prospero is a tyrant who 'cheated' him of the island through sorcery, but perhaps more accurately, Prospero simply does what all invading empires do – exerts power, colonises and exploits the land for their own needs. Like all colonising forces, he believes in his superior moral and intellectual worth, teaching Caliban his language, trying to civilise the 'brutish' native.

— uses contextual idea for original interpretation

And one could argue Shakespeare recognises this; by giving Caliban the poetic speech that sums up his own land's magical appeal, he suggests it is Caliban who is the true inheritor of the land. Prospero does not understand the land he governs, and in the end abandons it.

Shakespeare presents an alternative vision of government in Act 2 Scene 1 through the words of Gonzalo, but it is problematic. Whilst Shakespeare makes him the mouthpiece for a utopian vision of a 'commonwealth' in which 'Nature should bring forth / Of its own kind, all foison, all abundance, / To feed my innocent people..', the image of a Garden of Eden untouched by sin, bursting with life is positioned against the unreconstructed ambition of Antonio and Sebastian. Their ironic, cutting remarks questioning this vision would have no doubt struck a chord with contemporary audiences for whom land equalled property, and who knew government was won by force, not by thesis.

— expands field of reference to another idea

— detailed, perceptive language analysis

Good government, it seems that Shakespeare is saying, is self-government; to rule is to understand the limits of your power. At the opening of the play, the Boatswain ridicules the orders of his superiors saying that if they can 'command' the waves, then he won't stand in their way. Here, on a sinking boat, status and property mean nothing. Prospero's own power is confined to the magic he developed while neglecting 'worldly ends' and at the end of the play he realises it is not enough. Whilst he had been able to call 'forth the mutinous winds' – a rebellion he could handle – he found managing people and his subjects more difficult. Tyranny did not suffice. When he says, 'I'll drown my book', Shakespeare suggests Prospero is drowning an aspect of himself in service of a return to society, to community. A diminished ruler, but perhaps a better man.

— confident, personal interpretation

— circular conclusion links back to first paragraph

COMMENTARY

This is a highly perceptive and fluent response, which ranges confidently across the text as a whole. There is sustained analysis of Shakespeare's use of language, structure and form along with insightful exploration and multiple interpretation of key ideas, many linked to context.

Final Task

Now that you have considered the sample response for either an AS/A or A Level exam-style question based on a whole play, reflect upon your own response.

Task

4. **a)** Use the guidance in the tables on the final page of this chapter (page 282) to assess whether you think your response could be classed as 'competent' or 'very good'.

    b) What do you think were the strengths of your response? What could you do to improve upon and develop your own whole-text discursive essays?

    c) Using the examples above, write a brief commentary at the end of your own essay with action points for development.

DRAMA

What should you aim for in a competent response to the question?

Knowledge and understanding	You should show knowledge of the play and understanding of its concerns by making clear references to relevant scenes and events. Some use of quotations will make this more successful. Try to include some reference to context, making sure it's relevant to the points you make.
Analysis	Try to say something about the effects of the playwright's choices of language and imagery in dialogue, dramatic structure, and about the visual and aural effects of stage directions.
Personal response	You should offer something of your own interpretation. How does the dramatist's writing of the play, including dialogue and stage directions, help you understand the characters, plot events and its concerns?
Communicating effectively	Aim for a clear opening to your essay, showing you understand the question, and work towards a conclusion that returns to it. Make connections between your paragraphs and write clearly.
Literary criticism (A Level only)	You should show that you are aware that works of literature are not fixed and can be read in different ways. You might be able to quote a critic or a review, but you can also use phrases such as 'This could be read as…' or 'An audience might respond to this by…' Differing responses by audiences are a good way into this.

What should you aim for in a very good response to the question?

Knowledge and understanding	You need to show a detailed knowledge of the play and a subtle understanding of its concerns. Do this by making particular references to key scenes and episodes relevant to the question and by focusing your points with accurate quotations. Show some precise knowledge of context, made directly relevant to the particular point you are making.
Analysis	You should build your essay on exploration of how the dramatist expresses their ideas in dramatic form. Focus on the playwright and their presentation of concerns, scenes and characters. Refer to dialogue and stage directions. Think about how the play is structured to guide the audience's responses.
Personal response	You should communicate your own interpretation of the play, supported by clear evidence. Show how you read and respond to characters and events from the way that they are written. Try to 'see' a stage production in your mind.
Communicating effectively	Address the question consistently throughout the essay, so that every paragraph is clearly directed and relevant. Don't be afraid of having your own voice in your essays.
Literary criticism (A Level only)	You should show how your reading of the play has been influenced by different readings, whether these are from particular critics, reviews of productions, or just hypothetical different ways in which the play, or parts of it, might be read. Think about the implications of these differences. Think about how audiences might respond to the play in theatrical performance.

Chapter 5

Writing about unseen texts

Building on the topics and skills explored earlier in the Student's Book, this chapter suggests ways to respond with confidence to an unseen text. You will reflect upon some key considerations of responding to unseen texts, thinking about how to choose the right text and how to deal with tricky words and phrases. You will be guided through an effective process for responding to an unseen text, such as making notes on your initial impressions, establishing an insightful interpretation, and identifying and analysing literary methods.

The chapter will also emphasise the importance of carefully reading and answering the question. It will outline some effective ways of planning and structuring a response to an unseen text, as well as demonstrate how to write a sophisticated analytical paragraph.

You will therefore develop and extend your own writing skills, building towards full exam-style responses at the end of the chapter. You will have the chance to evaluate your progress against a range of sample responses.

5.1 Approaching a task on an unseen text

Big question

- How should you approach a task on an unseen text?

KEY CONSIDERATIONS OF THE UNSEEN TASK

Responding to unseen texts and extracts is not substantially different from responding to the texts you study elsewhere on your course. You will be provided with a focus in the question, and you should read the text carefully to ensure you develop a secure interpretation that relates to the question's focus. You will need to analyse how the writer has used form, structure and language to convey meanings and ideas. You should also apply your wider knowledge of the features of poetry, prose or drama to the unseen text.

Choosing the text

If you are given a choice of texts, make sure you read all the texts provided carefully and with an open mind. Do not rush this process. It is better to spend time making the right decision at the beginning rather than changing your mind halfway through.

Some tips on selecting the text:

- Do not choose a text just because it is the shortest one.
- Do not choose a text just because it is the first one you read – make sure you read all texts before making your decision.
- Choose the text you feel you might have the most to write about.
- Do not avoid a text just because it contains a single word or phrase you do not understand.
- Before you decide, make sure you understand the focus of each question.

Task

1. Read **Texts A**, **B** and **C** and the accompanying questions. Decide which text you would choose and explain the reasons for your choice.

Text A

Read 'My Father Would Not Show Us' by Ingrid de Kok (published in 1988). How does the speaker present her feelings about her father's death?

In your answer, you should consider language, imagery and verse form.

My Father Would Not Show Us

'Which way do we face to talk to the dead?'
Rainer Maria Rilke

My father's face
five days dead
is organised for me to see.

It's cold in here
and the borrowed coffin gleams unnaturally;
the pine one has not yet been delivered.

Half-expected this inverted face
but not the soft, for some reason
unfrozen collar of his striped pyjamas.

This is the last time I am allowed
to remember my childhood as it might have been:
a louder, braver place,
crowded, a house with a tin roof
being hailed upon, and voices rising,
my father's wry smile, his half-turned face.

My father would not show us how to die.
He hid, he hid away.
Behind the curtains where his life had been,
the florist's flowers curling into spring,
he lay inside, he lay.

He could recall the rag-and-bone man
passing his mother's gate in the morning light.
Now the tunnelling sound of the dogs next door;
everything he hears is white.

My father could not show us how to die.
He turned, he turned away.
Under the counterpane, without one call
or word or name,
face to the wall, he lay.

Ingrid de Kok (1988)

Text B

Read this extract from the opening of 'The Odour of Chrysanthemums', a short story written by D.H. Lawrence (published in 1911). The story is set in a coal-mining community in the Midlands, England. How does the writer present the setting and the characters?

In your answer, you should consider language, structure and narrative methods.

The small locomotive engine, Number 4, came clanking, stumbling down from Selston — with seven full waggons. It appeared round the corner with loud threats of speed, but the colt that it startled from among the gorse, which still flickered indistinctly in the raw afternoon, outdistanced it at a canter. A woman, walking up the railway line to Underwood, drew back into the hedge, held her basket aside, and watched the footplate of the engine advancing. The trucks thumped heavily past, one by one, with slow inevitable movement, as she stood insignificantly trapped between the jolting black waggons and the hedge; then they curved away towards the coppice where the withered oak leaves dropped noiselessly, while the birds, pulling at the scarlet hips beside the track, made off into the dusk that had already crept into the spinney. In the open, the smoke from the engine sank and cleaved to the rough grass. The fields were dreary and forsaken, and in the marshy strip that led to the whimsey, a reedy pit-pond, the fowls had already abandoned their run among the **alders**, to roost in the tarred fowl-house. The pit-bank loomed up beyond the pond, flames like red sores licking its ashy sides, in the afternoon's stagnant light. Just beyond rose the tapering chimneys and the clumsy black head-stocks of Brinsley Colliery. The two wheels were spinning fast up against the sky, and the winding-engine rapped out its little spasms. The miners were being turned up.

The engine whistled as it came into the wide bay of railway lines beside the colliery, where rows of trucks stood in harbour.

Miners, single, trailing and in groups, passed like shadows diverging home. At the edge of the ribbed level of sidings squat a low cottage, three steps down from the cinder track. A large bony vine clutched at the house, as if to claw down the tiled roof. Round the bricked yard grew a few wintry primroses. Beyond, the long garden sloped down to a bush-covered brook course. There were some twiggy apple trees, winter-crack trees, and ragged cabbages. Beside the path hung dishevelled pink chrysanthemums, like pink cloths hung on bushes. A woman came stooping out of the felt-covered fowl-house, halfway down the garden. She closed and padlocked the door, then drew herself erect, having brushed some bits from her white apron.

She was a tall woman of imperious mien, handsome, with definite black eyebrows. Her smooth black hair was parted exactly. For a few moments she stood steadily watching the miners as they passed along the railway: then she turned towards the brook course. Her face was calm and set, her mouth was closed with disillusionment. After a moment she called:

'John!' There was no answer. She waited, and then said distinctly:

'Where are you?'

'Here!' replied a child's sulky voice from among the bushes. The woman looked piercingly through the dusk.

'Are you at that brook?' she asked sternly.

For answer the child showed himself before the raspberry-canes that rose like whips. He was a small, sturdy boy of five. He stood quite still, defiantly.

'Oh!' said the mother, conciliated. 'I thought you were down at that wet brook — and you remember what I told you —'

The boy did not move or answer.

D.H. Lawrence, 'The Odour of Chrysanthemums' (1911)

Glossary

alder: a type of tree native to England

Text C

Read this extract from the play *Honour* by Joanna Murray-Smith (published in 1995) in which Sophie and Claudia are discussing Claudia's affair with George, Sophie's father. Claudia is six years older than Sophie. How does the playwright convey Sophie's and Claudia's different perspectives on George and Honor's marriage? In your answer you should consider characterisation, dialogue and the impact of Sophie's monologue.

CLAUDIA: What happens to Honor or George is not your problem. Is it? However much you want to feel things on their behalf, you never will. Because you don't really know who they are.

SOPHIE: I don't think I need a lecture about them, actually. I know them fairly well.

CLAUDIA: Well no. You don't. I know them better than you do.

SOPHIE: Oh, really.

CLAUDIA: I think I do.

SOPHIE: You've met my mother – ah – *once*?

CLAUDIA: Have you looked at the themes running through Honor's poetry?

SOPHIE: Well –

CLAUDIA: Have you ever even read it?

SOPHIE: I've – Yes – Of course I have.

CLAUDIA: Do we ever know our parents? Don't you look at those photographs of them in the sixties, when your mother had her hair long and looked so – so – ravishing – don't you look at them and think: My God. My God. She's Not Who She's Been Pretending to Be.

Silence.

Do you know what your father longs for or misses or regrets? Do you know about their loyalties to each other – Who needed less loving, who more?

SOPHIE: I know about my mother's loyalty.

CLAUDIA: Oh, come on. You're not – you're not that immature, really, are you? Not to know how many different kinds of loyalty there are and how two people seek love and how they deny it, the tiny shifts of power –

SOPHIE: No!

CLAUDIA: Do you even know how they came together? Who wooed who? And how they secretly despised –

SOPHIE: They didn't despise!

CLAUDIA: *All* lovers do! Some aspects of the other sending chills through them – that makes them wonder about other lives, lives not lived, lives not chosen that might have been – have been – *more* or *less* honourable.

SOPHIE: No!

CLAUDIA: You think I bewitched your father? (**Beat.**) He loves me.

Beat.

SOPHIE: Well, I suppose he might.

Beat.

You're so – you're so clear. You seem so clear about things. Whereas I'm – I'm so – I can never quite say what I'm – even to myself, I'm so inarticulate. (*Beat.*) Some nights I lie awake and I go over the things I've said. Confidently. The things I've said confidently and they – they fall to pieces. (*Beat.*) And where there were words there is now just – just this feeling of – of *impossibility*. That everything is – there's no way through it – (*Beat.*) I used to feel that way when I was very small. That same feeling. Not a childish feeling – well, maybe. As if I was choking on – as if life was coming down on me and I couldn't see my way through it. What does a child who has everything suffer from? Who could name it? I can't. I can't. (*Breaking.*) But it was a – a sort of – I used to see it in my head as a jungle. Around me. Surrounding me. Some darkness growing, something – organic, alive – and the only thing that kept me – kept me – *here* – was the picture of Honor and of George. Silly. (*Beat.*) Because I'm old now and I shouldn't remember that anymore. Lying in bed and feeling they were there: outside the room in all their – their warmth, their – a kind of charm to them. Maybe you're right and it was – not so simple as it looked, but they gave such a strong sense of – love for each other and inside that – I felt – I felt loved. And since I've gotten older I don't feel – (*Weeping.*) I feel as if all that – all the – everything that saved me has fallen from me and you know, I'm not a child anymore. No. I'm not a kid any more. But I still feel – I need – I need … (*Beat.*) I wish – I wish I was more – Like you. Like you.

Glossary

beat: a short pause in the dialogue

ESTABLISHING A RESPONSE

After you have chosen the text, you should underline key words in the question. Then read the text carefully again in order to establish and confirm your initial impressions and ideas. The questions in the following sections can be applied to *any* text in that form and can be used as prompts to help with your initial reading and annotations.

Poetry

a) What significance does the title have?

b) Is the poem based on a particular object, memory, person, experience, event(s) or place? If so, can you work out what it is / they are?

c) What ideas or concerns does the poem seem to engage with?

d) Is there anything distinctive about the overall form or shape of the poem?

e) How would you describe the tone of the poem?

f) Are you able to discern anything about the speaker of the poem?

g) Are there other important initial impressions in relation to the focus of the question?

> **Task**
>
> **2.** Read **Text A** again and answer the questions on the left.

Prose fiction

a) What happens in the extract? Can you work out a sequence of events?

b) What characters are you introduced to?

c) What do you learn about setting?

d) What is the overall mood/tone of the passage?

e) What do you think is the main idea or the main purpose of the extract?

f) Are there other important first impressions in relation to the focus of the question?

> **Task**
>
> **3.** Read **Text B** again and answer the questions on the left.

Drama

a) Which subject(s) does the dialogue address or explore?

b) What concerns or ideas does the passage explore?

c) What characters are you introduced to? Can they be distinguished in any way?

d) Can you work out the setting or situation? For example, is it a domestic setting? Professional? Classroom? Interior or exterior?

e) Are there any significant stage directions? Are you given any indications regarding how the piece could be performed? Who is on stage?

f) What is the overall mood/tone of the dialogue? Uncomfortable? Cooperative? Humorous?

g) What might the overall dramatic effects be on the audience?

h) Are there other important first impressions in relation to the focus of the question?

> **Task**
>
> **4.** Read **Text C** again and answer the questions on the left.

Dealing with unfamiliar words and phrases

As you read an unseen text, you may notice vocabulary or references you are not familiar with and which are not explained in a footnote. You might be able to work out what these words mean from the contexts of the sentence and the overall text.

If you are still unable to work out a word, phrase or reference in exam conditions, you should simply ignore it. Focus on the aspects of the text you are more confident with and use these to support your critical appreciation.

Task

5. Can you work out the meaning of the following words taken from **Text B**? The first has been completed for you:
   * colt – *This seems to be an animal; it is 'startled' by the train and runs with a canter* (Answer: A colt is a young male horse)
   * colliery
   * coppice
   * cinder track
6. Are there any other words you find unfamiliar in **Text B**? Can you work out what they might mean?

ESTABLISHING AN INTERPRETATION

After your initial response, read the text again in order to develop an overall interpretation that relates to the focus in the question. This involves reading the text carefully and identifying what its (often implied) meanings or perspectives are in relation to the focus in the question.

For example, in **Text A**, you may have identified that the poem describes the father's body and his previous illness. But this could be developed further: perhaps the poem implies a contrast between the stark, clinical presentation of the father's body with the considerate but uncommunicative way in which the father tried to hide his inevitable death from his family.

Task

7. Do you agree with the interpretation given above for **Text A**? Or do you think the poem suggests other feelings about the death of the speaker's father?
8. Read **Texts B** and **C** again. Write a sentence or two outlining what each text is suggesting about the focus in the question.

DEVELOPING A RESPONSE

In order to develop a more detailed response, you should read the text *for a third time* to focus on *how* the writer has used a range of methods to present meanings and perspectives in relation to the question. This will require detailed annotations.

At this point, you should also apply, in further detail, your knowledge of key, distinctive aspects of prose, drama and poetry. Some are listed in **bold** in Tasks **9–11** on the following pages as reminders of some of the methods you could consider. These are also explored in the previous chapters of this book.

You should certainly avoid mechanically applying these aspects as a simple 'checklist'; instead, be sensitive to the ideas and the distinctive qualities of the text. Meanings – especially those that relate to the focus of the question – should always be at the centre of your response.

Poetry

> ### Task
>
> **9.** Annotate **Text A** with your answers to the questions below. Each question encourages you to connect the method or technique with the focus of the question.
>
> **A. Structure and development of ideas**
>
>   **a)** How does the end of the poem connect to the beginning?
>
>   **b)** 'Face' is repeated a number of times in the poem. Why? How is the father's face presented differently at different points in the poem?
>
>   **c)** What are the effects of the patterning of 'He hid, he hid away' and 'He turned, he turned away'?
>
> **B. Vocabulary**
>
>   **d)** Which keys words describe the childhood home in the fourth stanza? What do they imply?
>
>   **e)** Which words suggest her father's reluctance to communicate?
>
> **C. Imagery and figurative devices**
>
>   **f)** How is the coffin described? How does it contrast with other images in the poem?
>
> **D. Poetic methods and aspects of form**
>
>   **g)** What are the effects of the very short lines in the first stanza?
>
>   **h)** 'away' and 'lay' are rhymed (twice). Why has the poet decided to rhyme these particular lines, do you think?
>
> You could also add to your annotations with any other methods or features you feel help the poet to present her feelings about her father's death.

Prose fiction

> ### Task
>
> **10.** Annotate **Text B** with your answers to the questions below. Each question encourages you to connect the method or technique with the focus of the question.
>
> **A. Narrative voice and perspective**
>
>   **a)** The writer uses a third-person omniscient narrator in this extract. What does this allow the writer to do with setting and characters?
>
> **B. Structure**
>
>   **b)** The writer sets the scene at the beginning of the passage. Where does the focus change to the mother? Where does it change again to her relationship with the boy? What are the effects of this overall structure?
>
> **C. Characterisation**
>
>   **c)** How is the mother – and her actions – described? What do these descriptions suggest about her character? What is suggested about the boy?
>
>   **d)** How do the different characters in this passage relate to and interact with their environment?
>
> **D. Dialogue**
>
>   **e)** What does the dialogue suggest about the relationship between the mother and her son?
>
> **E. Language and imagery**
>
>   **f)** How does the writer use language to suggest the train is a rather threatening presence? What could it symbolise?

g) How is the natural environment described? What impact does the coalmine appear to be having on the environment?

You could also add to your annotations with any other methods or features that you feel help the writer to present the mining town and the mother.

Drama

Task

11. Annotate **Text C** with your answers to the questions below. Each question encourages you to connect the method or technique with the focus of the question.

A. Characterisation and language

a) How does the playwright suggest Claudia is confident and Sophie less confident from the way they speak? Consider how fluent or how direct they are.

b) How does Sophie describe her mental state when she was a child in her long monologue? Find some techniques and comment on their effects.

B. Relationships: Who has power? Is there a struggle for control?

c) How does Sophie initially try to resist Claudia's assertions at the beginning of the passage?

d) How does the playwright suggest that Claudia largely dominates this exchange?

C. Structure and development in the passage

e) How does Claudia use questions to structure her ideas? How is her revelation 'He loves me' given greater significance by the playwright?

f) Despite Claudia's dominance, the passage concludes with Sophie's long monologue. What might the dramatic effects of this monologue be? How might the audience respond to Sophie at this point?

D. Stage directions and dramatic impact

g) Why has the playwright included a longer '*Silence*' after 'Pretending to Be'? What might the effects of this be in performance?

You could also add to your annotations with any other methods or features that you feel would help the playwright to present different perspectives on marriage.

Final Task

Task

12. Review your notes and annotations for each of the three texts you have explored in this unit. Write down what you consider to be the *four* most significant features of each text.

Plenary

Draw up a checklist of good advice to follow when approaching a task on an unseen text.

5.2 Structuring and writing a response to an unseen text

Big question

- How do you structure and write a response to a task on an unseen text?

READING THE QUESTION

> Task
>
> 1. Remind yourself of this question, on the right, on an unseen text from Unit 5.1. Copy and underline what you consider to be the key words.
> 2. What is an essay question beginning with the word 'How' encouraging you to do? In what ways does this relate to the word 'present'?

> Read 'My Father Would Not Show Us' by Ingrid de Kok (published in 1988). How does the speaker present her feelings about her father's death?
>
> In your answer, you should consider language, imagery and verse form.

STRUCTURING A RESPONSE

> Task
>
> 3. Reread the poem 'My Father Would Not Show Us' in Unit 5.1. Go on to remind yourself of your relevant notes and responses to the tasks you completed in Unit 5.1.

Once you have read the text a number of times and taken notes, you need to create a structured plan to the question. There are different ways of doing this:

- *track* your way through the text from the beginning to the end, including relevant quotations and analysis of methods as you go along
- *select key ideas* and analyse how each one is developed in the text, again including relevant quotations and analysis of methods.

For either method, you need to ensure that all the points you make relate clearly to the question.

> Task
>
> 4. The plan below uses the *tracking* method for a response to 'My Father Would Not Show Us'. Complete the plan by finishing the third point and adding two further points of your own.

First point:	Poem establishes speaker's feeling about her father with description of dead father's face; simple direct phrasing and short line lengths; uncaring and stark.
Second point:	Then describes the coffin; unusual depiction - 'borrowed' and the verb 'gleams'; structural contrast with the delicate softness of the pyjama collar to suggest speaker's complex feelings.
Third point:	Speaker's feelings change as she then remembers – possibly an alternative? – childhood with her father…
Fourth point:	
Fifth point:	

Task

5. The plan below uses the *ideas* method for a response to 'My Father Would Not Show Us'. Complete the plan by finishing the third point and adding two further points of your own.

First point:	The speaker seems emotionless over death of father; the 'cold' morgue/hospital and solemn, consecutively stressed syllables on line two (**spondee**); the speaker might not have felt particularly close to her father + suggests relationship is strained…
Second point:	Poem outlines and suggests how uncommunicative father was; repetition 'hid, hid away' modulating to more deliberate 'turned, turned away'; suggesting speaker's anger or frustration?
Third point:	The speaker's earlier childhood with her father is presented **ambiguously**…
Fourth point:	
Fifth point:	

Task

6. Which of the two forms of organisation outlined above – tracking and ideas – do you prefer for a response to this particular text and why?

You may find different approaches are more appropriate for different questions and texts. Of course, you can organise your response in other ways; however, you will always need to ensure that you explore the methods the writer uses to develop meanings and that all points relate to the focus in the question.

Writing an overview

Whichever method of organising your response you choose, always begin your response to an unseen text with an *interpretive overview*. This should contain:
- a very brief outline of the text
- the same or similar words to those used in the question focus
- an interpretation of the text, identifying what is *implied* and, therefore, establishing a central argument.

Task

7. Read this less developed example of an opening interpretive overview in a response to the question on 'My Father Would Not Show Us'. List three ways in which it could be improved.

Death affects us all and we respond to it in different ways. In this essay, I am going to look at the ways in which Ingrid de Kok presents feelings about her father's death. I will consider the different images in the poem, such as the description of the coffin, of her childhood home and her father's face, and de Kok's use of form including irregular stanzas and line length.

Key terms

spondee: in poetry, two consecutive stresses, as in this example from a song in a Ben Jonson play of 1600, where consecutive stressed syllables are shown in italics: '*Slow, slow, fresh fount, keep time with my salt tears*'

ambiguous: where a text is open to more than one possible meaning or interpretation

8. Read this second example of an opening interpretive overview in a response to the same question. Annotate the paragraph indicating where the following have been included:

a) a very brief outline of the poem

b) same or similar words to those used in the question

c) an interpretation of the poem, *identifying* what is implied about the speaker's feelings.

> 'My Father Would Not Show Us' describes, initially, the way the body of the speaker's father is displayed in a morgue or hospital. The speaker then remembers both her earlier childhood and how her dying father tried to cope with his illness. The speaker has a range of feelings about her father's death: his body is presented in a stark, emotionless way. However, the speaker then acknowledges, with sadness and perhaps even regret and frustration, how her father became increasingly uncommunicative as he chose to face death alone, away from his family.

WRITING AN ANALYTICAL PARAGRAPH ON AN UNSEEN TEXT

Following the interpretive overview, you should then stick closely to your plan, writing a clear sequence of analytical paragraphs.

Task

9. Read the sample paragraph below and annotate the following:
- link to the previous paragraph
- clear, focused **topic sentence**
- **embedded quotations**
- reference to the poet's methods with a clear link to the text's meanings
- appropriate use of terminology associated with the study of literature
- focused analysis of the quotations
- tentative phrasing to explore different interpretations, for example, 'This *could* be to…' or 'This *possibly* suggests…'

Key terms

topic sentence: a sentence at the start of a paragraph that indicates clearly what the focus of the paragraph is going to be

embedded quotations: wherever possible, quotations should be integrated into your own sentence: for example, 'the coffin is "borrowed" and "gleams unnaturally"'; it is often easier to do this with short quotations

> The speaker's coldness is not the only way the relationship between the speaker and the father seems fraught: the poem also outlines and suggests how uncommunicative the father was, especially as he approached his own death. He retreats symbolically 'Behind the curtains' to face his death alone. The poet repeats key phrases to suggest the father's reluctance to communicate. As his illness progressed, 'He hid, he hid away', suggesting perhaps his intense fear. This then modulates to the more deliberate 'He turned, he turned away' in the final stanza. This repetition perhaps indicates the speaker's developing frustration with her father's refusal to engage with his family.

10. Write a further paragraph, modelled on the one on the previous page, exploring the imagery in the poem, using the prompts below. Remember to use appropriate terms wherever possible and ensure they are always connected to the text's meanings.

> The father's refusal to communicate is also suggested and reinforced by the poet's use of imagery.
>
> The reference to the dying flowers 'curling into spring' behind the curtains suggests …
>
> As the poem progresses, further images are used, such as …
>
> This implies …

WRITE YOUR RESPONSE

Look again at the two plans (tracking and ideas) that you produced in tasks **4** and **5** in response to the question on page 292. Choose one plan and use it to write an essay. You may also want to use your notes and responses to the preceding tasks in this unit.

Final Task

Task

11. Plan and write a response to the question below in **1 hour**. The text can be found in Unit 5.1.

> Read this extract from the opening of 'The Odour of Chrysanthemums', a short story written by D.H. Lawrence (published in 1911). The story is set in a coal-mining community in the Midlands, England. How does the writer present the setting and the characters?
>
> In your answer, you should consider language, structure and narrative methods.

Checklist for success

Remember to apply the approaches to structuring and writing an essay covered in this unit:

✓ Organise your points carefully. Consider using one of the two forms of organisation explored here: *tracking* or *ideas*.

✓ Include a clear, interpretive overview at the beginning that establishes your own view in relation to the question.

✓ Link your paragraphs wherever possible and include a focused topic sentence in each one.

✓ In each paragraph, quote frequently and explore the writer's methods, especially how they convey meanings relating to the focus in the question.

Plenary

Review the responses you have written in this unit and answer the following questions:

- To what extent did the plan help you to write a more successful response?
- What did you find difficult when writing an interpretive overview?
- Of all the paragraphs you wrote, which one was the most successful and why?
- What do you now need to do in preparation for responding to an unseen text in an exam?

5.3 Evaluating responses to an unseen text

Big question
- How do you evaluate a response to an unseen text?

SAMPLE RESPONSES TO AN UNSEEN TEXT

In this section, you will explore two responses to an unseen text from Unit 5.1. This will help you to understand what constitutes a successful response to this kind of task. Also, using these essays and accompanying tasks as a guide will help you to improve your own response to an unseen text.

Task

1. Give yourself **1 hour** to respond to the following question on an unseen text. The text can be found in Unit 5.1.

> Read this extract from the play *Honour* by Joanna Murray-Smith (1995), in which Sophie and Claudia are discussing Claudia's affair with George, Sophie's father. Claudia is six years older than Sophie. How does the playwright convey Sophie's and Claudia's different perspectives on George and Honor's marriage? In your answer, you should consider characterisation, dialogue and the impact of Sophie's monologue.

2. Once you have completed the task, review your response. Write down three things you thought went well. Then write down two ways in which you feel your essay could be improved.
   You could consider:
   - the quality of your opening paragraph
   - your ability to communicate a detailed understanding of the text's meanings and ideas
   - the relevance of your quotations and how well they were embedded
   - your ability to accurately identify dramatic methods
   - the quality of your analysis of methods and quotations.
3. Read the following response and complete the accompanying tasks included in the annotations.

   Response 1

   > This extract is taken from a play called 'Honour' by Joanne Murray-Smith. In this extract, Sophie and Claudia are discussing Claudia's affair with George, Sophie's father. The passage begins with an exchange between Sophie and Claudia and ends with a long, emotional monologue from Sophie. Murray-Smith uses a range of dramatic techniques to present their different views on marriage. Claudia appears more confident and Sophie appears more innocent in her views.

   Why are these opening two sentences redundant?

   A straightforward summary of the different perspectives. How could this be improved? What specifically are Sophie and Claudia's different perspectives on George and Honor's marriage?

Initially, the audience may well be surprised by Claudia's strong ideas about marriage. She seems unapologetic over breaking up Sophie's parents' marriage. Claudia argues that George and Honor's marriage is completely separate from Sophie and, in any case, Sophie doesn't really know her parents, especially in the years before she was born. Claudia even claims that she knows them better than Sophie does.

In the dialogue, Sophie initially resists Claudia's assertions with a series of statements: 'I know them fairly well', 'Oh, really', 'You've met my mother – ah – once?' Perhaps understandably, Sophie is shocked that Claudia can claim she knows her parents better than their daughter. Her responses also establish the conflict between the two characters. Murray-Smith is perhaps suggesting that Sophie is less confident than Claudia and is establishing Claudia as by far the more dominant character.

Murray-Smith then proceeds to build upon this conflict between the two characters. Claudia asks questions that confirm her as a dominant character. She asks Sophie if she has 'looked at the themes running through Honour's poetry'. Sophie's response is an uncertain 'Well –'. Claudia seems to pick up on Sophie's reluctance by interrupting her with another question 'Have you ever even read it?' Sophie's response suggests that she hasn't read her mother's poetry and so cannot really know her very well. Claudia's questions enable her to control the topic of the situation and confirm her as a confident character.

The playwright uses stage directions sparingly in this extract. However, she does use a significant stage direction. Claudia says, 'Don't you look at them and think: My God, My God. She's Not Who She's Been Pretending to Be.' Then there is a 'Silence'. This is then followed by 'Do you know what your father longs for or misses or regrets?' Murray-Smith obviously considered it important that the silence occurs at this particular point. Claudia could be waiting for an answer to her question from Sophie, which is not forthcoming.

Despite Claudia's apparent authority through the majority of the extract, it is Sophie who concludes the passage with a long and emotional monologue. Her sentences are broken up: 'Whereas I'm – I'm so – I can never quite say what I'm – even to myself' and 'I feel as if all that – all the – everything that saved me'. Sophie also uses interesting words and images as she outlines how she felt as a child, such as 'as if life was coming down on me' and 'I used to see it in my head as jungle'. 'Darkness' is also given unusual qualities as being 'organic' and 'alive'. Despite its length, the monologue actually charts Sophie's emotional breakdown. This is confirmed in the two directions 'Breaking' growing to 'Weeping', clearly indicating to the actor that this monologue should be performed in a highly emotional way.

Secure understanding of some key ideas here, but what is missing in this paragraph?

These quotations are relevant and support the point being made, but are presented in a rather clumsy way. Improve this part of the paragraph by rewriting it to include embedded quotations.

Secure analysis, with appropriate use of tentative phrasing ('perhaps suggesting'), but could be developed further. Precisely *how* do these statements suggest Sophie's lack of confidence or control? Why has the playwright included the nonverbal vocalisation ' – ah – ', for example?

A reasonable explanation of the silence is offered, but there are some opportunities to explore alternative readings here. In what other ways can performance enhance this stage direction? What else could be suggested by this silence?

Some very well-chosen quotations here, but there is no identification of literary or dramatic methods; nor is there any analysis. Rewrite this section of the paragraph to include identification of techniques and specific analysis of the chosen quotations.

The analysis is secure and shows awareness of the dramatic form, but lacks development. *Why* would the playwright want to present this monologue in such an emotional way? What are the effects? What might Claudia's response be?

COMMENTARY

This is a competent, well-organised and effectively communicated response demonstrating a good overall understanding of the unseen text. Some very well-chosen quotations. There is analysis of some of the writer's choices, but it often lacks development, with little comment on specific details of the writing. Rather straightforward appreciation of literary and dramatic methods, and underdeveloped exploration of the different perspectives on marriage.

Task

4. Now read a second response to the same question. As you read, think about what has been done to develop and improve the previous response.

Response 2

The extract presents, through the dialogue and characterisation of Sophie and Claudia, two very distinctive views on George and Honor's marriage (and, by implication, all marriages). Claudia cynically argues that children never know their parents as well as they might think and that marriages are inevitably fraught battlegrounds. The playwright contrasts this with Sophie's rather more innocent view of her parents' marriage, concluding with a complex and emotional monologue in which Sophie admits she still has a childlike need to feel her parents' protective love.

— perceptive and concise interpretive overview

Initially, the audience may well be surprised by Claudia's strident ideas about marriage. She is shown to be unapologetic about breaking up Sophie's parents' marriage when she simply 'and directly' says to Sophie that it is 'not your problem' and 'you don't really know who they are'. Claudia's confidence is made clear from the very beginning of the passage as she argues, in 'a brutal, unembellished manner,' that George and Honor's marriage is completely separate from their daughter Sophie. She even claims that she knows them 'better' than Sophie does. She is, perhaps surprisingly, unapologetic over her affair with George.

— identification of literary and dramatic methods

Through the dramatic presentation of the two characters, Murray-Smith establishes a clear contrast between them. Despite ultimately admitting that she wishes she was like Claudia, Sophie initially tries to resist Claudia's assertions with a series of bitterly ironic statements: using litotes, she argues that she knows her parents 'fairly well' and seems to resist Claudia's argument with a dismissive 'Oh, really'. Perhaps understandably, Sophie is shocked that Claudia can claim she knows her parents better than she does. Such responses also help the playwright to establish the dramatic conflict between the two characters. However, in resorting to an almost childlike irony and underdeveloped responses, Murray-Smith is perhaps suggesting that Sophie is much less confident and articulate than Claudia; the writer confirms this in the concluding monologue. ⎤ ———— detailed analysis of method

Murray-Smith then proceeds to build upon this dramatic conflict between the two characters. Claudia asks a series of questions (ten in total) ⎤ that confirm her as a dominant character, on ———— patterns identified in the text
the attack. She asks Sophie if she has 'looked at the themes running through Honour's poetry'. Sophie's uncertain response is an incomplete utterance: 'Well –' . Claudia seems to pick up on Sophie's reluctance by interrupting her with yet another question, 'Have you ever even read it?' Sophie's response could be performed in such a way as to suggest ⎤ that she hasn't read her ———— secure awareness of the text in performance
mother's poetry. Claudia's questions enable her to control the topic of the situation as Sophie's resistance crumbles.

The playwright uses stage directions sparingly in this extract, leaving the delivery of the lines very much to the individual interpretation of the actors and director in performance. ⎤
However, there is a significant stage direction in the first half of the extract. After asking Sophie, with emphatic capitalisation, whether or not her mother is the person 'She's Been Pretending to Be', there is a longer '<u>Silence</u>' before Claudia continues with further questions. Murray-Smith obviously considered it important that the silence occurs at this particular point. Its full significance, however, will again depend upon how it is performed. Claudia could be waiting for an answer to her question from Sophie, which is not forthcoming. Sophie may well be trying to resist by refusing to answer the question; or, perhaps more interestingly, she is becoming persuaded by Claudia's opinions as she realises her mother has been repressing her authentic self throughout her marriage. ⎤ ———— a range of alternative interpretations offered and evaluated

Murray-Smith has structured the extract to accentuate the overall dramatic impact: despite Claudia's apparent authority through the majority of the extract, it is Sophie who concludes the passage with a long and emotional monologue. This contrasts with her earlier taciturnity. However, Sophie is a long way from Claudia's assured fluency. Murray-Smith fragments her sentences with dashes and they are frequently minor and incomplete, ⎤ as she appears to pick up ideas only to immediately ———— detailed identification of literary and dramatic methods
discard them: 'Whereas I'm – I'm so – I can never quite say what I'm – even to myself' and 'I feel as if all that – all the – everything that saved me'. This indeed confirms what Sophie is arguing in her monologue that, unlike Claudia, her confident words 'fall to pieces'.

Murray-Smith uses figurative imagery as Sophie outlines how she felt as a child. The similes 'as if life was coming down on me' and 'I used to see it in my head as jungle' confirm her feelings of chaos and loss of control. 'Darkness' is also presented metaphorically as it is given unusual, perhaps frightening, qualities as being 'organic' and 'alive' and therefore links semantically to the fearful 'jungle'. These combined images dramatically suggest an interesting, tragic insight into Sophie's character, as she admits to struggling with her mental health and acknowledges the importance of her parents. Despite the fact that Sophie's extended turn reclaims some control, the monologue actually movingly charts Sophie's emotional breakdown. This is confirmed in the two directions 'Breaking', growing to 'Weeping', clearly indicating to the actor that this monologue should be performed in a progressively emotional way. Despite Claudia's confidence and dramatically compelling argument, the audience's sympathy ultimately lies with Sophie in her desolate response to the breakdown of her parents' marriage.

Murray-Smith extends this sympathy to the final line of the extract. Sophie says to Claudia that she wishes she was more 'Like you. Like you.' This repetition confirms this as a surprising and complex conclusion to the passage: Sophie is despairing at the thought of her parents' separation and is the seemingly wronged daughter. However, ultimately, perhaps tragically, she wishes she had the confidence and assurance of her father's mistress.

- detailed identification of literary and dramatic methods

- frequent and concise analysis of methods and quotations

- sophisticated point on audience sympathy; secure awareness of form

- a powerful final sentence; a perceptive interpretation of the moral complexities of the extract

COMMENTARY

This is a fluent and perceptive response. Quotations are well chosen to support the points being made. Analysis is precise and insightful, showing detailed critical awareness of the possibilities of the text in performance. There is a sustained appreciation of literary and dramatic methods, with a confident application of terminology.

Task

5. Now that you have considered the two responses and completed the accompanying tasks, reflect upon your own response to the *Honour* extract.
   - Do you need to add or change your earlier annotations?
   - What do you need to do to improve your responses to an unseen text?

Final Task

Task

6. Complete the question below in **1 hour**. Apply what you have learned in this chapter as you read, plan and write your response.

> Read 'Sonnet V. To the South Downs' by Charlotte Smith. How does the speaker present her feelings about the landscape?
>
> In your answer, you should consider language, imagery and form.

Sonnet V. To the South Downs

Ah, hills beloved! – where once, a happy child,
Your beechen shades, 'your turf, your flowers, among,'
I wove your bluebells into garlands wild,
And woke your echoes with my artless song.
Ah! hills beloved! – your turf, your flowers, remain;
But can they peace to this sad breast restore,
For one poor moment soothe the sense of pain,
And teach a broken heart to throb no more?
And you, **Aruna**, in the vale below,
As to the sea your limpid waves you bear,
Can you one kind **Lethean** cup bestow,
To drink a long oblivion to my care?
Ah no! – when all, e'en hope's last ray is gone,
There 's no oblivion but in death alone!

Charlotte Smith (1784)

Checklist for success

✓ Read and annotate the question.
✓ Read the text to establish an initial response; consider the questions under the headings 'Establishing a response' / 'Poetry' in Unit 5.1 (page 288) to prompt your ideas.
✓ Read the text again to confirm a clear interpretation of the ideas and meanings in relation to the question.
✓ Read the text again and annotate with methods and analysis; for help with this, use the prompts given under the headings 'Developing a response' / 'Poetry' in Unit 5.1 (page 289).
✓ There may be some unfamiliar words or references. Try to work out what they mean from the context; if you can't, ignore the words and focus on other aspects of the text.
✓ Plan your response; consider using the tracking or ideas methods of organising your response and ensure you include an overview at the beginning of your essay.
✓ Write your response with a sequence of clear analytical paragraphs, plenty of quotations and analysis of methods and techniques.
✓ Leave enough time to proofread your essay.

Glossary

the South Downs: a range of hills in the south east of England
Aruna: a reference to the Arun, a river in Sussex, England
Lethean: relating to Lethe, a river of forgetfulness in the ancient Greek and Roman underworld that enabled souls to forget their previous existence

UNSEEN TEXTS

What should you aim for in a competent response to the question?

Knowledge and understanding	You should show knowledge of the form of your chosen text. Make specific references to aspects that are particular to prose, poetry or drama. Read and reread carefully so that you come to an understanding of the concerns, characters or events in the text. Use of quotations will make your points firmer.
Analysis	Try to say something about the effects of the form of the text. Think about aspects you have learned about in the Prose, Poetry and Drama chapters and focus on how these techniques are used in the text.
Personal response	You should offer something of your own interpretation. How does the writer help you understand the meaning and concerns of the text?
Communicating effectively	Aim for a clear opening to your essay, showing you understand the question, and return to it in your conclusion. Write clearly and make sure your paragraphs are connected.

What should you aim for in a very good response to the question?

Knowledge and understanding	You need to show a detailed knowledge of the form of the text, writing perceptively about its prose, poetry or drama features. Read and reread the text carefully to come to a confident conclusion about its concerns, characters or events. Make specific references to key parts of the development of the passage or poem, focusing your points with accurate quotations.
Analysis	You should build your essay on exploration of how the writer expresses their ideas, thinking about the features of the form. Using aspects you have learned about in the Prose, Poetry and Drama chapters, write about the writer's choices and focus on how they have used language and techniques to guide a reader's or audience's response.
Personal response	You should communicate your own interpretation of the text, supported with clear evidence from it. Show how you respond to the ways in which the writer has presented the text's meaning and concerns.
Communicating effectively	Address the question consistently throughout the essay, so that every paragraph is clearly directed and relevant. Don't be afraid of having your own voice in your essays.

Chapter 6

Key resources

6.1 Glossary of literary terms

alienation: when sympathy is removed or distance created

alliteration: repetition of sounds at the beginning of words

alluding: making a subtle reference or link

allusion: a word or phrase that makes reference to another place, person, story or event, thereby bringing to mind other, related ideas

ambiguity: the quality of being open to more than one meaning or interpretation

analogy: using your own imagery or comparison to explain characterisation

anapaest: a metrical foot consisting of unstressed, unstressed, stressed (a three-syllable group)

anaphora: a structured use of repetition where the same words or phrases appear at the beginning of lines

antithesis: the juxtaposition of contrasting ideas, phrases, or words so as to produce an effect of balance

assertion: a statement of belief that is not founded on facts or evidence

assonance: repetition of vowel sounds within words

ballad: poem, often with a refrain, retelling a true story or folk tale

bildungsroman: a novel that follows the development of a character from youth through to adulthood and maturity; a popular genre in the 19th century (for example, Charles Dickens's *David Copperfield*)

blank verse: a poem written in a regular metre (usually iambic pentameter) but without rhyme

caesura: punctuation used inside lines of poetry to create a pause

characterisation: the ways in which a writer creates or constructs a fictional character

chronological: ordering events according to the time at which they happened, with the earliest coming first, and the latest coming last

cinquain: a poem of five lines with the number of syllables rising from 2 to 4 to 6 and then 8 before returning to 2 for the final line

cipher: code for an idea rather than something to be taken at face value

circularity: the way in which the ending of a text reflects or revisits its opening

Classical literature: the literature of Ancient Greece and Rome (from around 1200 BCE to 455 CE)

climax: the part in a story where a crisis point is reached

commodified: turned into a commodity – something to be bought or sold

connotation: an idea or feeling that a word brings to mind in addition to its primary meaning (for example, 'dove' may connote 'peace')

consonance: the use of similar-sounding consonants in close proximity

context: the relationship between a text and its historical, social and cultural backgrounds

couplet: a pair of lines of verse, typically rhyming and of the same length

courtly love: a concept of love that originated in Medieval European literature, based around the noble and chivalric behaviour of knights towards ladies

dactyl: a metrical foot consisting of stressed, unstressed, unstressed (a three-syllable group)

dialect: language and grammar specific to a particular race, group or culture

direct address: when a speaker directs his words towards a specific reader (often using 'you')

dominant narrative perspective: where a story is told from the perspective of the dominant culture

dramatic form: what makes a play distinct from other types of writing such as novels and poetry, including how actions and speech are conveyed, and how time and settings are presented dramatically

dramatic irony: usually refers to situations where the audience knows something that the characters do not; irony occurs when the characters say or do something in ignorance of the truth

dramatic structure: the organisation of a dramatic text or passage, its shape or development over the course of the play, including aspects of time, order of events and plot devices

dual narration: where a writer uses two narrators in a prose work

dystopian: a genre where dysfunctional imaginary human societies are presented in the form of alternative futures or histories

elegy: a poem of serious reflection, often reflecting on, and lamenting, a death

embedded quotations: the skill of integrating quotations into your own sentence: for example, 'the coffin is "borrowed" and "gleams unnaturally"'; it is often easier to do this with short quotations

end-stopped: when a line of poetry ends with a punctuation mark

enjambment: when a line or stanza of poetry is not end-stopped, allowing the sentence to run straight on into the next line

epilogue: a concluding section or speech at the end of a literary work, often serving as a comment on what has happened

epiphany: in literature, this term describes a character's moment of discovery, revelation or realisation

epistolary: narratives told through letters

extended metaphor: a single metaphor that is introduced and then further developed throughout a text

feminist reading: literary criticism that challenges representations of women in texts and questions prevalent attitudes and assumptions about women and women writers

first-person narration: where the narrator tells their own story using the pronouns 'I' and 'me'

flashback: an interruption to the current events of a narrative, where a writer inserts past events in order to provide background or context

flat character: an uncomplicated character who doesn't develop or change over the course of a play, or exists only to advance the plot

focalised or limited-vision narration: where we see the events through a single character or from a restricted perspective

foreshadow: when a writer gives a sign or warning that prepares the reader for what is to follow later in the narrative

form: conventions of literary forms of prose, poetry and drama; can also refer to the way a text is ordered, presented or shaped on the page

fourth wall: the invisible wall that exists between the audience and the stage; while the audience can see through this 'wall', the actors act as if they cannot

free indirect discourse: a special type of third-person narration in which the narrator sometimes takes on the tone, lexicon and register of a character, thereby giving access to characters' thoughts and feelings

free verse: an open form of poetry that doesn't use a regular metre or rhyme scheme

genre: the characteristics of different text types (for example, tragedy, comedy and satire)

Gothic literature: a genre noted for its focus on horror, fear and death, with characters often facing terrible or supernatural events that test their mental state

haiku: a very short Japanese poem of 17 syllables and three lines

hexameter: six sets of metrical feet

historical context: important historical events and ideas in the real world outside the story

hyperbole: language exaggerated for effect

iambic: in metre, an unstressed beat followed by a stressed beat

imagery: a general term used to describe powerful language that draws vividly on the senses; it includes techniques such as simile and metaphor

in media res: Latin term meaning 'in the middle of things', used here to define stories that begin with the character already in the heart of the action (for example, 'She slammed the door and walked out…')

internal rhyme: rhyming of words within the text, not at the end of the lines

interpretation: evaluation and explanation of the different ideas within a text

interrogatives: questions

intertextuality: shaping a text's meaning by using another text; this can be a whole text (rewriting something from a different perspective), borrowing words or lines from another text, or making allusions and references to another text

intrusive narration: where the narrator occasionally comments directly on events in the story

irony: conveying your meaning by pointedly saying the opposite of what you actually intend to say

Jacobean: referring to the reign of King James I of England (1603-25)

juxtaposition: the act of placing two things side by side to create an effect through comparison or contrast

lexicon: the stock of words or vocabulary of an individual

lexis: the choice of vocabulary that builds an overall tone or picture in a literary work

limited-vision or **focalised narration:** where we see the events through a single character or from a restricted perspective

lyric poem: formal poetry, usually in the first person, that expresses strong personal feelings, often incorporating a repeated phrase

macro-level: across a large scale

Marxist reading: approach to literary criticism based on the economic and cultural theories of Karl Marx (1818–83) (see Unit 6.2)

metaphor: a figure of speech that directly refers to one thing by mentioning another for effect (for example, 'a cold white blanket covered the earth' referring to snow)

metre: the length and rhythm of a line of poetry

metrical foot: a group or set of syllables, such as an iamb

micro-level: at an individual or detailed level

modal verb: a verb that changes another by adding a sense of possibility or necessity, such as 'could', 'may', 'would'

modernism: term used to describe movement of 20th-century writers who broke away from older traditions and concerns, to experiment with new ideas, forms, structures and language

monologue: a long speech given by a single character

mood: the general feeling or atmosphere created by a writer's use of language – for example, gloomy, joyful, bitter, fearful, celebratory

Key resources

motif: an object, image or idea, used symbolically, that is repeated throughout a text

motive: in drama, the emotional goals or objectives of a character, such as the need to be loved or admired, or aims related more closely to the action, such as to become king or gain revenge on a rival

multifaceted: having many sides, aspects or faces

multiple narration: where a writer uses three or more narrators in a prose work

narrative order: the order in which events are related in a story, which may be different to the order in which they happened

narrative poem: a form of poetry that tells a story, often presenting the voices of a narrator as well as different characters

narrator: the person telling the story in a prose work

nature: in Shakespeare, either the natural world in general or 'human nature' – the instincts and traits we are born with

non-verbal: unspoken or not to do with words; for instance, an actor's physical performance rather than what they say

nuanced: having shades of meaning rather than one single clear idea

nurture: meaning, literally, to care for and help develop, but in contrast to 'nature', it refers to everything we are taught or learn after we are born, either from others or from the world around us

octave: an eight-line stanza or poem

ode: poem that praises a person, event or thing

omniscient narration: where events are recounted from an all-seeing perspective

onomatopoeia: words or phrases that sound like the thing they describe, such as 'boom' or 'cluck'

other: often used in criticism as a noun to express the way in which white imperial states viewed or constructed non-white societies, reducing them to inferior status as a result of perceived physical and social differences (not looking 'normal' for example)

oxymoron: a figure of speech in which opposite or contradictory ideas or terms are combined (for example, 'sweet sorrow')

paradox: a situation or statement that involves two or more seemingly contradictory facts or qualities

paraphrase: sum up in your own words

Parliament: place of government, but also those who are in government at the time

pastoral poetry: a tradition of poetry idealising rural life and landscape, often drawing a contrast between the innocence of a simple life and the corruption of urban or court life; typically, pastoral poems followed highly conventional forms

pathetic fallacy: the attribution of human feelings to inanimate objects, often used to reflect the action or mood of a text – for example, 'gloomy clouds' or 'clock's stern face'

pathos: a sense of pity or sadness

patriarchy: the organisation of society that gives power predominantly to men and excludes women

pentameter: five sets of metrical feet

performative: relating to the nature or essence of dramatic performance

person: the first person: '*I* left home'; second person: '*You* left home'; third person: '*He/she/Jo* left home'

personification: attributing human characteristics or a personal nature to something nonhuman

perspective: the point of view from which a story is told

Petrarchan sonnet: a sonnet form associated with the Italian poet Francesco Petrarch (1304–74), having an octave rhyming *abbaabba* and a sestet rhyming either *cdcdcd* or a *cdecde*

phonology: the way in which sounds are organised in language or text

plosive: a consonant produced by the release of a sharp burst of air when spoken (such as p, b or k)

plot: the plan or pattern of a series of events in a work of fiction, organised in a way that creates interest

poet laureate: a great poet, officially appointed by a government to compose poems for special occasions and events

poetic form: the type of poem and its rules regarding number and length of lines, rhyme scheme, and so on

polemic: a powerful attack on someone or some thing

postcolonial: refers to the time *after* major empires of countries such as Britain, Spain, France and Belgium gave up the territories they had conquered, ruled and, in many cases, exploited for their raw materials, labour or geographical location; postcolonial perspectives are often concerned with matters of colonisation, independence, migration and cultural identity

postmodernism: a late 20th-century style and concept that represents a departure from modernism, characterised by a distrust of theories, the self-conscious use of earlier styles as well as a mixing of different artistic styles and media

prologue: a separate, introductory section at the start of a literary or dramatic work

prosody: the patterns of rhythm and sound used in poetry, including stress and intonation

psychoanalytical criticism: approach to literary criticism that uses the theories of Sigmund Freud (1856–1939) and his followers (see Unit 6.2)

puns: words or phrases with more than one meaning; a play on words

pyrrhic: in metre, two unstressed beats

quatrain: a four-line stanza or poem

register: the level of formality or informality in language use

reliable narrator: one that can be trusted (because they have the whole picture and/or do not intend to mislead)

resolution: a solution or decision that occurs in a story in response to the crisis point

reversal of fortune: an obstacle or sudden problem a main character has to overcome; in longer texts, there may be several such reversals before the main character reaches the end of their journey, whether emotional or real

rhyme scheme: the way a poet chooses to rhyme lines – for example, the nursery rhyme 'Baa Baa black sheep have you any wool? / Yes sir, yes sir, three bags full' is an AA rhyme scheme – as 'wool' and 'full' are almost perfect rhymes at the end of the first two lines

Romantic movement: a Western artistic movement, from around 1800–1850, that focused on the truthful representation of emotions and nature

self-referentiality: when a writer refers to themselves or their own work in a text, or draws attention to their writing as something crafted and constructed (for example, by acknowledging the reader, admitting their view is unreliable or highlighting the limits of the form they are using)

sestet: a six-line stanza or poem

Shakespearean sonnet: a sonnet form associated with the William Shakespeare (1564–1616), using three quatrains and a couplet with an alternating rhyme scheme (*abab*, *cdcd*, *efef*, *gg*) and a volta at line 13

sibilance: repetition of sibilant sounds (s, sh, z)

sibilant: the characteristic soft or hissing sounds made by the consonants s, sh and z

simile: a figure of speech comparing one thing with another thing of a different kind (for example, 'cunning as a fox'); usually indicated by a word such as 'like' or 'as'

social context: important social events and ideas in the real world outside the story

soliloquy: a speech given by a character speaking their thoughts aloud, either alone or oblivious of any possible hearers

sonnet: a 14-line poem, usually written in iambic pentameter with a clear rhyme scheme and traditionally concerned with love

Spenserian sonnet: a sonnet form associated with the English poet Edmund Spenser (1552–99), using three quatrains and a couplet; recurring rhymes were used to link ideas through the sonnet (such as *abab*, *bcbc*, *cdcd*, ee) and a volta was added at line 9 to 'turn' the thought or argument

spondee: in poetic metre, two consecutive stresses, as in this example from a song in a Ben Jonson play of 1600, where the consecutive stressed syllables are in italics: '*Slow, slow, fresh fount, keep time* with my *salt tears*'

staging: information given about how the stage should look at various times in the play

stanza: group of lines in a poem, similar in meaning to 'verse'

status: the level of power of a particular character has, which can be external (for example, 'king' as opposed to 'servant'), or emotional or physical (stronger speech in an argument, for example); status can fluctuate in a play – a king may fall from power and then regain it; someone can be losing an argument and then win it

stream of consciousness: a narrative technique that presents the free flow of random thoughts, feelings and perceptions inside a character's mind

structure: the organisation or sequence of ideas, events or language in a text, including its shape and development; (when used in responses to questions) the construction of a relevant and supported argument appropriate to the question

style: the particular, distinctive approach or effect of a writer's use of language

subplot: a secondary plot in a story whose characters and events are connected in some way to the main plot

subversive: intended to weaken or destroy a particular aspect of society or to go against social or literary conventions

superlative adjective: the most something can be (such as 'best')

symbol: an object, image or action that takes on a meaning different from its literal sense

symbolism: device whereby an object, image or action takes on a meaning within a story that is different from its literal sense

tercet: a three-line stanza

tetrameter: four sets of metrical feet

tone: the mood or feeling created in a text

topic sentence: a sentence at the start of a paragraph that indicates clearly what the focus of the paragraph is going to be

tricolon: a rhetorical device that employs a series of three parallel words, phrases or clauses

trimeter: three sets of metrical feet

trochee: in metre, a stressed beat followed by an unstressed beat

trope: a recurrent literary device in which something has symbolic or metaphorical significance

universality: the ability to appeal to people regardless of place and time

unreliable narrator: one not to be trusted (because they do not have the whole picture and/or intend to mislead)

utterance: any single unit of speech, which might include sighs, cries, gasps, and so on

verse: a group of lines that form a unit in a poem or song; a stanza

Victorian period: the period of time in Britain when Queen Victoria reigned (1837–1901)

voice: the characteristic way in which a story is told

volta: Italian word for 'turn'; in a sonnet, the volta is the turn of thought or argument

word play: clever use of words, including puns – words with more than one meaning e.g. 'What did the cheese say when it looked in the mirror? Halloumi (Hallo me)'.

Type of work is indicated by colour: blue for prose works; green for poetry; purple for plays.

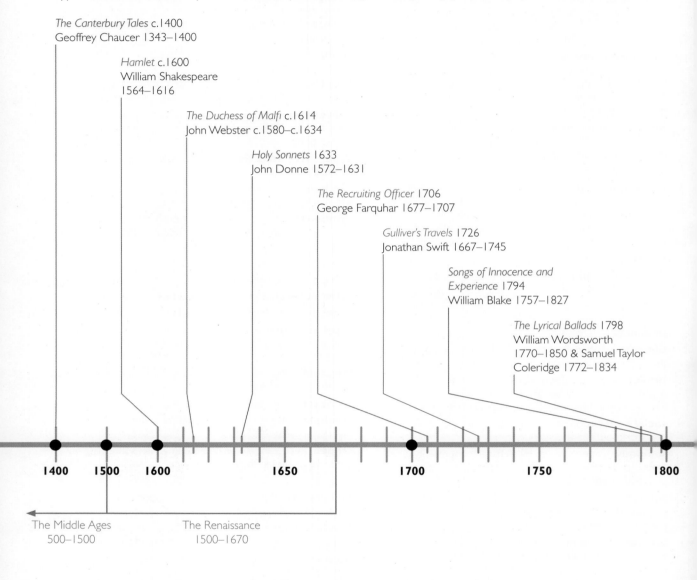

The Canterbury Tales c.1400
Geoffrey Chaucer 1343–1400

Hamlet c.1600
William Shakespeare
1564–1616

The Duchess of Malfi c.1614
John Webster c.1580–c.1634

Holy Sonnets 1633
John Donne 1572–1631

The Recruiting Officer 1706
George Farquhar 1677–1707

Gulliver's Travels 1726
Jonathan Swift 1667–1745

*Songs of Innocence and
Experience* 1794
William Blake 1757–1827

The Lyrical Ballads 1798
William Wordsworth
1770–1850 & Samuel Taylor
Coleridge 1772–1834

1400   1500   1600   1650   1700   1750   1800

The Middle Ages
500–1500

The Renaissance
1500–1670

| 1440 | 1517–1648 | 1760–1840 | 1789–1794 |
| Invention of printing press | The Reformation | Industrial Revolution | French Revolution |

| | The Restoration 1660–1710 | 1775–1783 American War of Independence | |

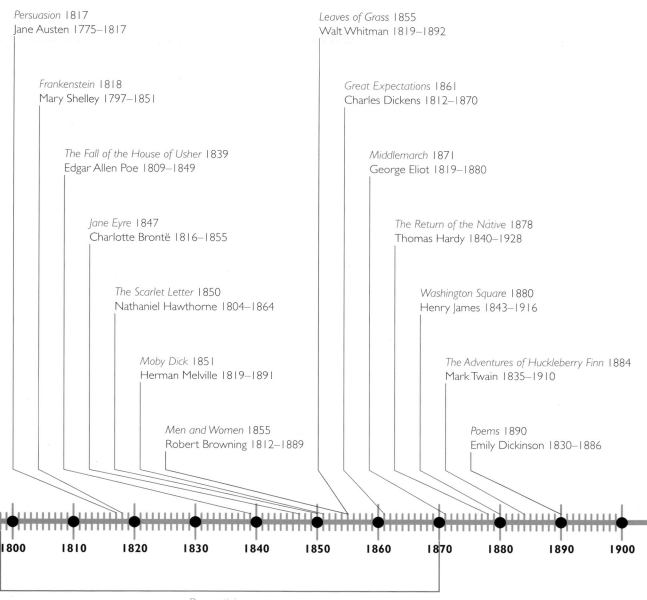

Persuasion 1817
Jane Austen 1775–1817

Leaves of Grass 1855
Walt Whitman 1819–1892

Frankenstein 1818
Mary Shelley 1797–1851

Great Expectations 1861
Charles Dickens 1812–1870

The Fall of the House of Usher 1839
Edgar Allen Poe 1809–1849

Middlemarch 1871
George Eliot 1819–1880

Jane Eyre 1847
Charlotte Brontë 1816–1855

The Return of the Native 1878
Thomas Hardy 1840–1928

The Scarlet Letter 1850
Nathaniel Hawthorne 1804–1864

Washington Square 1880
Henry James 1843–1916

Moby Dick 1851
Herman Melville 1819–1891

The Adventures of Huckleberry Finn 1884
Mark Twain 1835–1910

Men and Women 1855
Robert Browning 1812–1889

Poems 1890
Emily Dickinson 1830–1886

| 1800 | 1810 | 1820 | 1830 | 1840 | 1850 | 1860 | 1870 | 1880 | 1890 | 1900 |

Romanticism
1798–1870

| 1803–1815
Napoleonic Wars | 1840
Treaty of Waitangi | 1861–1865
American Civil War | 1884–1885
Scramble for Africa:
Berlin Conference |

1848
Year of Revolution in
Europe

Key resources

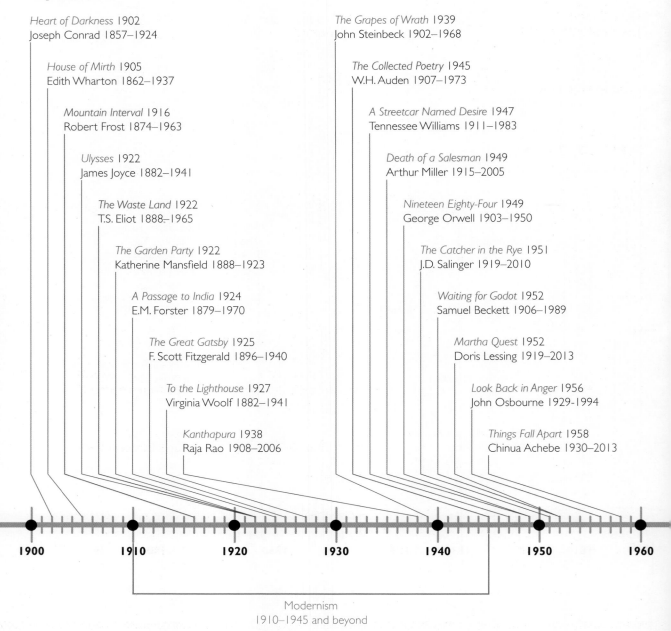

Heart of Darkness 1902
Joseph Conrad 1857–1924

House of Mirth 1905
Edith Wharton 1862–1937

Mountain Interval 1916
Robert Frost 1874–1963

Ulysses 1922
James Joyce 1882–1941

The Waste Land 1922
T.S. Eliot 1888–1965

The Garden Party 1922
Katherine Mansfield 1888–1923

A Passage to India 1924
E.M. Forster 1879–1970

The Great Gatsby 1925
F. Scott Fitzgerald 1896–1940

To the Lighthouse 1927
Virginia Woolf 1882–1941

Kanthapura 1938
Raja Rao 1908–2006

The Grapes of Wrath 1939
John Steinbeck 1902–1968

The Collected Poetry 1945
W.H. Auden 1907–1973

A Streetcar Named Desire 1947
Tennessee Williams 1911–1983

Death of a Salesman 1949
Arthur Miller 1915–2005

Nineteen Eighty-Four 1949
George Orwell 1903–1950

The Catcher in the Rye 1951
J.D. Salinger 1919–2010

Waiting for Godot 1952
Samuel Beckett 1906–1989

Martha Quest 1952
Doris Lessing 1919–2013

Look Back in Anger 1956
John Osbourne 1929-1994

Things Fall Apart 1958
Chinua Achebe 1930–2013

1900 1910 1920 1930 1940 1950 1960

Modernism
1910–1945 and beyond

| 1914–1918 First World War | 1939–1945 Second World War | 1947 Indian Independence and Partition |

1917
Russian Revolution

310

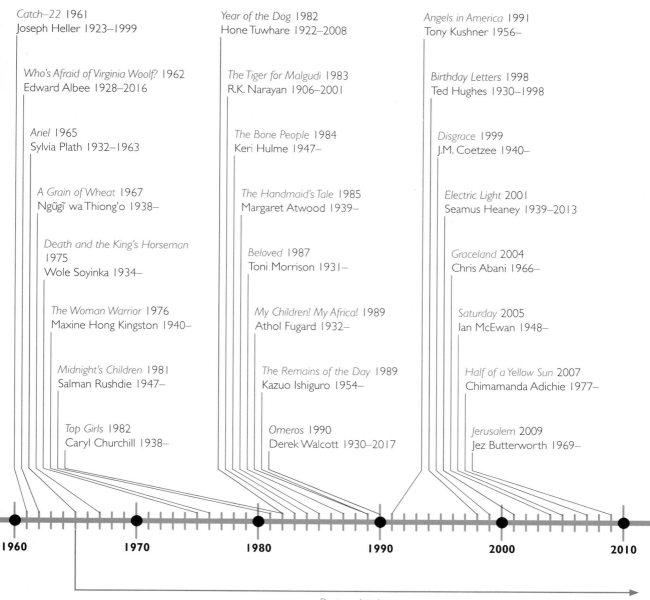

Catch–22 1961
Joseph Heller 1923–1999

Who's Afraid of Virginia Woolf? 1962
Edward Albee 1928–2016

Ariel 1965
Sylvia Plath 1932–1963

A Grain of Wheat 1967
Ngũgĩ wa Thiong'o 1938–

Death and the King's Horseman 1975
Wole Soyinka 1934–

The Woman Warrior 1976
Maxine Hong Kingston 1940–

Midnight's Children 1981
Salman Rushdie 1947–

Top Girls 1982
Caryl Churchill 1938–

Year of the Dog 1982
Hone Tuwhare 1922–2008

The Tiger for Malgudi 1983
R.K. Narayan 1906–2001

The Bone People 1984
Keri Hulme 1947–

The Handmaid's Tale 1985
Margaret Atwood 1939–

Beloved 1987
Toni Morrison 1931–

My Children! My Africa! 1989
Athol Fugard 1932–

The Remains of the Day 1989
Kazuo Ishiguro 1954–

Omeros 1990
Derek Walcott 1930–2017

Angels in America 1991
Tony Kushner 1956–

Birthday Letters 1998
Ted Hughes 1930–1998

Disgrace 1999
J.M. Coetzee 1940–

Electric Light 2001
Seamus Heaney 1939–2013

Graceland 2004
Chris Abani 1966–

Saturday 2005
Ian McEwan 1948–

Half of a Yellow Sun 2007
Chimamanda Adichie 1977–

Jerusalem 2009
Jez Butterworth 1969–

1960 **1970** **1980** **1990** **2000** **2010**

Postmodernism
1965–today

1960–1964 Main period of African countries' independence	1990 Establishment of the world wide web	2001 Attack on the World Trade Centre (9/11)	2008 Election of Barack Obama as first African-American President of USA
	1990–1991 Dissolution of the Soviet Union	2004 eBook readers become commercially available	2010 'Arab Spring'
	1994 Democratic government in South Africa, marking the end of Apartheid		2016 Election of Donald Trump as President of USA

6.3 Introduction to literary critical theory

Critical theories have developed to discuss the various ways in which people read literary texts. They offer different insights into texts and lead to different readings or interpretations.

Among the most important theories are **feminist**, **historical**, **Marxist** and **psychoanalytical** theories, while many international texts can be considered to be **postcolonial** literature. What follows will give you a useful general guide to these different approaches to literary texts.

FEMINIST CRITICISM

Feminist critics highlight, within literary texts, ways in which women are hindered from developing as independent and creative by male characters or by a male-dominated society. At the same time, feminists also celebrate powerful, independent female characters. By these means, they seek to challenge **patriarchy** – the organisation of society that gives power predominantly to men.

This extends to literature written by women, as there has also been an interest in challenging ways in which women writers have been read, edited or overlooked in the past. Feminist critics argue that many of the perceived differences in gender are based on cultural assumptions and prejudices. Charlotte Brontë's *Jane Eyre*, for example, can be said to both conform to and challenge patriarchy, depending on ways its two key female characters, Jane and Bertha, are read.

HISTORICAL CRITICISM

A historical approach to literature places literary works firmly within their historical and cultural context in order to understand them more fully. By making links between the texts and the time in which they were written, including historical events, social circumstances and facts about the author's life, historical critics seek to find insights into the texts.

Critics have found, for example, that an understanding of the circumstances in which Shakespeare wrote his plays and the way in which they were originally performed opens up new interpretations of his work. The rapidly changing social conditions brought about by the Industrial Revolution became the focus of a number of 19th-century novels, including *Hard Times* by Charles Dickens, while more recently, Kate Grenville has described her novel *The Secret River* as 'my act of acknowledgement' of Australia's settler history.

MARXIST CRITICISM

Marxist literary criticism is founded on the economic and cultural theories of Karl Marx (1818–83). Marx argued that society's economic organisation determines the economic, political and social power of different groups within society. Marxist critics, therefore, are often concerned with the economic and power structures within literary texts and in particular, the treatment of the less powerful by the powerful.

A good example of this is Ngũgĩ wa Thiong'o's novel *A Grain of Wheat*,

Key term

patriarchy: the organisation of society that gives power predominantly to men and excludes women

Wider reading

Two central books discussing feminist theory are Sandra Gilbert and Susan Gubar's *The Madwoman in the Attic*, (which bases its title on Bertha from *Jane Eyre*) and Elaine Showalter's *A Literature of Their Own*.

Wider reading

Stephen Greenblatt's *Will in the World* is an account of Shakespeare's life, examining how his experiences shaped his plays. Another key work on Shakespeare is a collection of essays titled *Political Shakespeare*, edited by Jonathan Dollimore and Alan Sinfield.

Wider reading

One of the most influential Marxist critics is Terry Eagleton. He has written a very good guide to various literary theories, *Literary Theory*, and also specifically Marxist works, such as *Marxism and Literary Criticism*.

which focuses closely on the difficulties for rural and poor characters in Kenya's struggle for independence. Quite different is David Lodge's novel *Nice Work*, which puts together a university English lecturer and a factory owner to take a playful look at literary theory, particularly Marxist theory.

PSYCHOANALYTICAL CRITICISM

This approach to literature uses the theories of Sigmund Freud (1856–1939) and his followers. Freud argued that people respond to societal and moral constraints by suppressing their fundamental urges in their subconscious, and that these suppressed desires would sometimes manifest themselves in unconscious actions, such as dreams, instinctive reactions and slips of the tongue.

Freud's ideas about the unconscious mind can be used to explore characters' motivations, actions and speeches. It is a particularly helpful approach to **Gothic literature**. The gothic short stories of Edgar Allen Poe are compact horror stories; 'The Tell-Tale Heart' and 'The Masque of the Red Death' are good examples. Shakespeare's play *Hamlet* explores the state of mind of its hero as he grapples with the possibilities of revenge for his father's murder, and offers productive psychoanalytical readings.

POSTCOLONIAL LITERATURE

Postcolonial literature is usually written by authors from previously colonised countries, either living in those countries or having migrated from them. It is often concerned with matters of colonisation, independence, migration and cultural identity, and critical approaches to it often combine the theories described here. The narrative point of view, chronology and language of the text are often of key interest.

TRYING THE DIFFERENT APPROACHES

This passage is from *North and South* by Elizabeth Gaskell, published in 1855. In the passage, Margaret, from southern England, has come to live in a northern English city and is visiting Mr Thornton, at a time of unrest.

Read it through, and then consider some different ways in which it might be read using critical theories.

> **Key term**
>
> **Gothic literature:** a genre noted for its focus on horror, fear and death, with characters often facing terrible or supernatural events that test their mental state

> **Wider reading**
>
> Freud's *The Interpretation of Dreams* is the starting point for psychoanalytical theory, while Maud Ellmann's *Psychoanalytic Literary Criticism* is a useful selection of essays exploring the development of the theory.

> **Wider reading**
>
> For a thorough exploration of approaches to postcolonial literature, read *The Empire Writes Back* by Bill Ashcroft, Gareth Griffiths and Helen Tiffin.

She saw their gesture – she knew its meaning, – she read their aim. Another moment, and Mr Thornton might be smitten down, – he whom she had urged and goaded to come to this perilous place. She only thought how she could save him. She threw her arms around him; she made her body into a shield from the fierce people beyond. Still, with his arms folded, he shook her off.

'Go away,' said he, in his deep voice. 'This is no place for you.'

'It is!' said she. 'You did not see what I saw.' If she thought her sex would be a protection, – if, with shrinking eyes she had turned away from the terrible anger of these men, in any hope that ere she looked again they would have paused and reflected, and slunk away, and vanished, – she was wrong. Their reckless passion had carried them too far to stop – at least had carried some of them too far; for it is always the savage lads, with their love of cruel excitement, who head the riot – reckless to what bloodshed it may lead. A clog whizzed through the air. Margaret's fascinated eyes watched its progress; it missed its aim, and she turned sick with affright, but changed not her position, only hid her face on Mr Thornton's arm. Then she turned and spoke again:

'For God's sake! do not damage your cause by this violence. You do not know what you are doing.' She strove to make her words distinct.

A sharp pebble flew by her, grazing forehead and cheek, and drawing a blinding sheet of light before her eyes. She lay like one dead on Mr Thornton's shoulder. Then he unfolded his arms, and held her encircled in one for an instant:

> 'You do well!' said he. 'You come to oust the innocent stranger. You fall – you hundreds – on one man; and when a woman comes before you, to ask you for your own sakes to be reasonable creatures, your cowardly wrath falls upon her! You do well!' They were silent while he spoke. They were watching, open-eyed and open-mouthed, the thread of dark-red blood which wakened them up from their trance of passion. Those nearest the gate stole out ashamed; there was a movement through all the crowd – a retreating movement. Only one voice cried out:
>
> 'Th' stone were meant for thee; but thou wert sheltered behind a woman!'
>
> Mr Thornton quivered with rage. The blood-flowing had made Margaret conscious – dimly, vaguely conscious. He placed her gently on the doorstep, her head leaning against the frame.
>
> 'Can you rest there?' he asked. But without waiting for her answer, he went slowly down the steps right into the middle of the crowd. 'Now kill me, if it is your brutal will. There is no woman to shield me here.' You may beat me to death – you will never move me from what I have determined upon – not you!' He stood amongst them, with his arms folded, in precisely the same attitude as he had been in on the steps.
>
> Elizabeth Gaskell, *North and South* (1855)

FEMINIST APPROACHES

According to a feminist approach, Margaret could be seen as a victim of male violence and Mr Thornton takes a different traditional male role in trying to protect her. Note he has a 'deep voice' while he tries to send her indoors, using his male authority. Once she is struck by the stone, he points out to the crowd that it is a woman they have harmed, and Gaskell tells us they are 'ashamed'. Protectively, he 'held her encircled'.

All that is quite traditional and conforms to 19th-century patriarchal views. You can also see, though, how Gaskell challenges those views. It is Margaret who first notices the nature of the hostility of the crowd and in fact tries to protect Mr Thornton – 'she threw her arms around him' first and speaks to him in imperatives. While Mr Thornton is angered by the suggestion that he has 'sheltered behind a woman' and re-establishes his masculinity by walking into the crowd, a careful reading recognises how Elizabeth Gaskell is testing gender archetypes and promoting a strong, independent female character who can stand up not only for herself, but also for a man.

MARXIST APPROACH

Mr Thornton is a factory owner and the men causing the unrest are his workers. The third-person narrative takes Margaret's perspective on events. Margaret and Mr Thornton are representatives of the powerful middle class and are the only characters named, so they have the authority in the passage. The workers are anonymous; they are described as 'fierce people' with 'terrible anger' and Mr Thornton calls them 'cowardly'. In this passage, the narrative position, therefore, sides with the economically powerful and suggests that the economically dependent are irresponsible and dangerous, people who need the order and guidance of their superiors.

Elizabeth Gaskell's novel as a whole, however, takes a much more sympathetic view of the workers and highlights many injustices. Even within this passage, you can see that Gaskell is careful to suggest that this behaviour is not natural for the workers. They are 'victims of reckless passion' led on by a few 'savage lads' and Gaskell makes very clear their remorse when Margaret is hit, as they are 'open-eyed and open-mouthed' with shame.

HISTORICAL APPROACH

The time in which this novel was written is very important, as are some circumstances of Gaskell's life. She, like Margaret, was forced by changes of circumstance to move from southern England to the north. This was the middle of the 19th century, the height of the Industrial Revolution, which transformed northern English cities with the establishment of factories and mills, particularly for the weaving of cotton. Working people often had to abandon their lives in villages and move to the growing cities for work. Working conditions in the factories were poor, often dangerous, and workers were badly paid. That meant that their living conditions too were very poor, with inadequate sanitation and ill health. The workers in the passage are protesting about their working conditions and about the fact that Mr Thornton has brought in workers from Ireland who will work for lower wages, putting them out of work. This historical context allows you to understand the grievance between the employer and his employees much more fully.

PSYCHOANALYTICAL APPROACH

A scene of so much action might not initially seem appropriate for psychoanalytical analysis, but thinking of it in psychoanalytical terms raises some different ideas. As discussed above, at two points in the passage the central characters consciously try to protect each other – Margaret 'threw her arms around him' and Mr Thornton 'held her encircled'. Throwing your arms around someone, though, is often an act of affection and, subconsciously, Margaret and Mr Thornton could be demonstrating their feelings for each other, even though they do not consciously recognise those feelings.

There are further suggestions of this in the writing too. Gaskell includes the word 'passion' twice, and although this refers to anger in the passage, it is therefore an episode of heightened emotion, at the climax of which Margaret is struck and bleeds, with the clear reference to 'the thread of dark-red blood'. It is possible to read this as a metaphor for passion and for sexuality, augmenting the reader's understanding of Margaret's and Thornton's unconscious feelings.

POSTCOLONIAL APPROACH

North and South, of course, is not a postcolonial text, but we can still look at aspects of it from a postcolonial perspective. A key aspect of the historical understanding is that the mills of northern England processed cotton imported form the USA, where it was grown on large plantations worked by slaves originating from West Africa. An understanding of this helps us realise that Thornton's wealth is not only based on his own employees, who protest at their ill treatment, but on the forced labour of slaves who were treated far worse. It is interesting to note that while Elizabeth Gaskell demonstrates her concern for the welfare of Lancashire mill workers, guided by her Christian principles, her novel never considers the plight of the slaves growing the cotton.

PULLING IT ALL TOGETHER

While each of these approaches illuminates different aspects of the passage, none of them presents the 'right' way to read it, and there are other approaches that are not discussed here. Importantly, though, you can see that you do not have to use any one approach exclusively. In this case, a combination of approaches leads to a rich interpretation of this excerpt from the novel.

Here is a student, who is studying the text, responding to this passage. Look how the different approaches are helpful to her illumination of the text:

This passage is a crucial episode in the novel, revealing key aspects of Gaskell's characterisation of Margaret and Thornton. Their actions hint at their later union but the catalyst defines what separates them. That catalyst is the mob of protesting workers, angered at their poor working conditions and in whom Margaret, like Gaskell herself, has a keen and sympathetic interest. Indeed, the novel and its heroine were written to bring the difficulties of factory cotton weavers to the attention of those who wore their fine cotton. While Thornton tells Margaret 'This is no place for you', he makes a misjudgement, dismissing her as the weak and frail woman of patriarchal construction, and failing to realise both that she has an informed interest in the workers and will also, in due course, have a romantic place by his side. These attitudes and Gaskells' proleptic hints occur throughout the passage, as Margaret 'threw her arms around him' – a very forward gesture for a woman to make, protecting a man – and Thornton later 'held her encircled'. Both these gestures in the text refer to protection, but as in a different context they could refer to loving embrace. Gaskell perhaps hints at unconscious desires which come to fruition later in the novel.

The awareness of working conditions opens up possibilities of a Marxist response.

A historical appraoch shows the understanding of the author's writing.

The changing judgements of women are a key feature of Feminist criticism.

An awareness of how the text suggests the unconscious mind, following Freudian ideas.

IMAGE ACKNOWLEDGMENTS

The publishers wish to thank the following for permission to reproduce photographs. Every effort has been made to trace copyright holders and obtain permission for the use of copyright materials. The publishers will gladly receive any information enabling them to rectify any error or omission at the first opportunity.

Key (t= top, c = centre, b = bottom, l = left, r = right).

p.7 Brian A Jackson/Shutterstock; p.8 pixelparticle/Shutterstock; p.11 phiseksit/Shutterstock; p.12 Photo Coalesce/Shutterstock; p.13 Mike Mareen/Shutterstock; p.16 AF archive/Alamy Stock Photo; p.17 The Granger Collection/Alamy Stock Photo; p.18 AF archive/Alamy Stock Photo; p.20t Sinan Niyazi KUTSAL/Shutterstock; p.20b Chiyacat/ Shutterstock; p.23 Charles Edmund Brock/British Library/Bridgeman Images; p.24 Celli07/Alamy Stock Photo; p.25 Ondrej Prosicky/ Shutterstock; p.29 Alma-Tadema, Lawrence/Private Collection/ Bridgeman Images; p.30 FRITZ GORO/The LIFE Picture Collection/ Getty; p.32 Paul Aniszewski/Shutterstock; p.33 vesilvio/Shutterstock; p.36 dbimages/Alamy Stock Photo; p.41 Tommy Trenchard/Alamy Stock Photo; p.44 Africa Media Online/Alamy Stock Photo; p.47 927 Creation/ Shutterstock; p.51t Chronicle/Alamy Stock Photo; p.51b Chronicle/ Alamy Stock Photo; p.57 medeia/Shutterstock; p.58tl Geraint Lewis/ Alamy Stock Photo; p.58tr Everett Collection Inc/Alamy Stock Photo; p.58b AF archive/Alamy Stock Photo; p.60 Bernd Göttlicher/Alamy Stock Photo; p.61 Teri Virbickis/Shutterstock; p.62 DEA PICTURE LIBRARY/Getty; p.63 ClassicStock/Alamy Stock Photo; p.65 AF archive/ Alamy Stock Photo; p.67 canadastock/Shutterstock; p.68 Joseph Finnemore/Private Collection/© Look and Learn/Bridgeman Images; p.70 Chronicle/Alamy Stock Photo; p.71 Pictorial Press Ltd/Alamy Stock Photo; p.73 HikoPhotography/Shutterstock; p.76tr Ryan DeBerardinis/ Shutterstock; p.76tl Helen Hotson/Shutterstock; p.76br George Burba/ Shutterstock; p.76bl Tithi Luadthong/Shutterstock; p.77t KGPA Ltd/ Alamy Stock Photo; p.77b pxl.store/Shutterstock; p.79 thislife pictures/ Alamy Stock Photo; p.80 Chronicle/Alamy Stock Photo; p.81 Chronicle/ Alamy Stock Photo; p.82 ImagesofIndia/Shutterstock; p.83 Marmaduke St. John/Alamy Stock Photo; p.89 Homer Sykes/Alamy Stock Photo; p.91 Andrej Safaric/Shutterstock; p.92 Douglas McGrath/Bridgeman Images; p.93 STILLFX/Shutterstock; p.94 Alinari Archives/CORBIS/Corbis via Getty Images; p.96 Matej Hudovernik/Shutterstock; p.99 Granger Historical Picture Archive/Alamy Stock Photo; p.103 Val Wilmer/Getty Images; p.105 CBS Photo Archive/Getty Images; p.106 Niday Picture Library/Alamy Stock Photo; p.109 Mary Evans Picture Library; p.111 Andre govia Holdings/Shutterstock; p.114 American Photograph, (19th century)/Private Collection/Peter Newark American Pictures/Bridgeman Images; p.124 Dermot Blackburn/Alamy Stock Photo; p.137 UyUy/ Shutterstock; p.138 reddees/shutterstock; p.142 Visun Khankasem/ Shutterstock; p.145 Yermolov/Shutterstock; p.151 PRISMA ARCHIVO / Alamy Stock Photo; p.152 Georgios Kollidas/Shutterstock; p.154 Steve Oehlenschlager/Shutterstock; p.156 Heritage Image Partnership Ltd/ Alamy Stock Photo; p.157 Andreas Zerndl/Shutterstock; p.159 Design Pics Inc/Alamy Stock Photo; p.162 GobyOneKenobi/Shutterstock; p.164 Guenter Albers/Shutterstock; p.165 vyasphoto/Shutterstock; p.167 North Wind Picture Archives/Alamy Stock Photo; p.169 Historical

TEXT ACKNOWLEDGMENTS

The publishers wish to thank the following for permission to reproduce copyright material. Every effort has been made to trace copyright holders and obtain permission and reproduce material in this title. The publishers will gladly receive any information enabling them to rectify any error or omission at the first opportunity.

Extracts on pp.17, 39 from 'The Man Who Saw Himself Drown' by Anita Desai from *Diamond Dust and Other Stories* by Anita Desai, Houghton Mifflin Harcourt, 2000, copyright © Anita Desai. Reproduced by permission of the author c/o Rogers, Coleridge & White Ltd., 20 Powis Mews, London W11 1JN; An extract on p.24 from *Saint Joan* by George Bernard Shaw, Penguin. Reproduced by permission of The Society of Authors, on behalf of the Bernard Shaw Estate; The poem on p.41, 'I am my own mother now' by Stella P. Chipasula from *The Heinemann Book of African Women's Poetry,* edited by Stella and Frank Chipasula, 1995, p.133, Heinemann. Reproduced by kind permission of the author; Extracts on pp.60, 111 from *Rebecca* by Daphne Du Maurier, copyright © The Chichester Partnership, 1938. Reproduced with permission of Curtis Brown Group Ltd on behalf of The Chichester Partnership; An extract on p.63 from *Nervous Conditions* by Tsitsi Dangarembga copyright © Ayebia. Reproduced with permission from Ayebia Clarke Publishing Limited at www.ayebia.co.uk; An extract on p.66 from *A Room with a View* by E.M. Forster. Reproduced by permission of The Provost and Scholars of King's College, Cambridge and The Society of Authors as the E.M. Forster Estate; An extract on p.73 from *A Family Supper* by Kazuo Ishiguro, Penguin, 1983, copyright © Kazuo Ishiguro. Reproduced by permission of the author c/o Rogers, Coleridge & White Ltd., 20 Powis Mews, London W11 1JN; An extract on p.77 from *Saturday: A Novel* by Ian McEwan, Jonathan Cape, copyright © Ian McEwan, 2005. Reproduced by permission of The Random House Group Ltd; Nan A. Talese, an imprint of the Knopf Doubleday Publishing Group, a division of Penguin Random House LLC; and Vintage Canada/Alfred A. Knopf Canada, a division of Penguin Random House Canada Limited. All rights reserved; An extract on p.82 from *A Passage to India* by E.M. Forster. Reproduced by permission of The Provost and Scholars of King's College, Cambridge and The Society of Authors as the E.M. Forster Estate; Extracts on pp.83, 103 from "The Arrangers of Marriage" by Chimamanda Ngozi Adichie, from *The Thing Around Your Neck*, pp.167-186, copyright © Chimamanda Ngozi Adichie, 2009. Reprinted by permission of HarperCollins*Publishers* Ltd; The Wylie Agency (UK) Limited; and Vintage Canada/Alfred A. Knopf Canada, a division of Penguin Random House Canada Limited; An extract on p.96 from "Marriage is a Private affair" by Chinua Achebe, from *Girls at War: and Other Stories*, copyright © Chinua Achebe, 1972, 1973. Used by permission of The Wylie Agency (UK) Limited; and Doubleday, an imprint of the Knopf Doubleday Publishing Group, a division of Penguin Random House LLC. All rights reserved; An extract on p.104 from *Nineteen Eighty-Four* by George Orwell, Martin Secker & Warburg 1949, Penguin Books 1954, 1989, 2000. Copyright © George Orwell, Eric Blair, 1949. Copyright © Houghton Mifflin Harcourt Publishing Company, 1949 and renewed by Sonia Brownell Orwell, 1977. This edition copyright © the Estate of the late Sonia Brownell Orwell, 1987. Introduction © copyright Ben Pimlott, 1989. Notes on the Text © copyright Peter Davison, 1989. Reprinted by